"We may have all come on different ships, but we're in the same boat now."
—Martin Luther King Jr.

Responses to *Crossing the Line*

When reading Michael's book, I literally ran out of superlatives to describe each chapter. Early on, I predicted that it would easily be the best book ever written on culture and race from both biblical and practical perspectives, and I ventured to say that I thought it would probably end up as the best ever written on the subject, period. It is simply mind-blowing to me, and I'm not a person who passes out compliments easily. I believe it will immeasurably help those who desire to follow God's design for his family, regardless of skin color or culture. God bless you, Michael!

Gordon Ferguson, teacher, Dallas Church of Christ, Dallas Texas

As a black man who has been a disciple for thirty-five years and served seventeen years in the full-time ministry, I just wanted to read the entire book without stopping. Everything I read addressed a concern I had but did not know how to express. I no longer have to be the voice of reason on race. Michael's book does it for me with far more palatable language and exponentially more spirituality. I'm a changed man just from reading it. This book should be required reading for any disciple. I have never seen anything on race even remotely close to it. It will be the family relationships Bible in the body for years to come.

Tony Chukes, Denver, Colorado

I knew that Michael Burns' *Crossing the Line: Culture, Race, and Kingdom* would be a compelling read. His interesting personal story as it relates to this subject, his biblically informed worldview, his love for the lesser-known backstory behind events that people take for granted, and his authenticity come out when he speaks and teaches. As I jumped in, I found myself learning things that I should have learned in my youth. There are many choice morsels that Michael brings to a discussion that is both timely and necessary. I believe that *Crossing the Line* will provide insights that give us pause for self-reflection and conversation starters for meaningful dialogue.

Steve Staten, Bridging International,
organizational health consultant, Chicago, Illinois

CROSSING THE LINE
CULTURE, RACE, AND KINGDOM

MICHAEL BURNS

Crossing the Line: Culture, Race, and Kingdom

© 2017 by Michael Burns

ISBN: 978-1-946800-22-0. Printed in the United States.

Illumination Publishers cares deeply about the environment and uses recycled paper whenever possible.

All Scripture quotations, unless indicated, are taken from the *Holy Bible, New International Version,* (NIV), Copyright © 2011 by Biblica, Inc. Used by permission. All rights reserved worldwide.

Interior design: Toney C. Mulhollan. Cover design: Roy Applesalmy

Illumination Publishers titles may be purchased in bulk for classroom instruction, business, fund-raising, or sales promotional use. For information please email paul.ipibooks@me.com.

About the author: Michael Burns is a teacher in the Minneapolis-St. Paul Church of Christ. He is a graduate of Wesley Seminary of Indiana Wesleyan University (MA). He taught high school history in the central city of Milwaukee for nearly ten years. He is a national and international biblical teacher at churches and workshops. He is the founder and director of the Ministry Development and Training Academies centered in Minneapolis, Minnesota, and serves as an instructor in the Ministry Training Academies in Africa. He is the author of the C.O.R.E. series of books. He married his wife, MyCresha, in 1997. They have two sons and reside in Roseville, Minnesota.

ILLUMINATION
PUBLISHERS

CONTENTS

Foreword 7

Introduction 9

Section 1: Where We Are At

1   Losing Race 22

2   Two Sides of a Coin 36

3   The Chaos Creature 56

4   Dual Wisdom 65

5   Jesus and Phinehas 76

Section 2: Another Way

6   The Beautiful Revolution 96

7   The Promised Family 113

8   More Disciple than White 124

Section 3: Race and Culture in the New Testament Church

9   Troubled Waters 139

10   Choose from Among You: Validation 153

11   I Opposed Him to His Face: Confrontation ... 165

12   For the Glory of God: Sacrifice 182

13   Accept One Another: True Diversity 196

14   The Way of the Cross: Self-Sacrifice 214

Section 4: The Power of Culture

15   Culture Clash 228

16   Pliable Culture 242

17   Forging Ahead 263

Appendix A: Bible Study—God's Promised Family 281

Appendix B: Poem 283

Notes 284

To my incredible wife,
MyCresha; I couldn't do it without you.
I am unspeakably grateful for the
courage and strength my sons show every day,
and to my parents for teaching us to
love and respect every
human being for who they are.

And to Uncle Charles and Aunt Sue;
thanks for blazing the trail.

Foreword

I grew up in the southern part of the United States of America, born the same day that Martin Luther King Jr. was murdered. I share this because, as an African American male, it sets the backdrop of an extensive involvement with racial and cultural experiences. I was a black man attempting to thrive in a world where many nonblacks felt I should not even exist. Until God transformed my life I was on the hostile side of those experiences, carefully watching for any sign of prejudice so that I could strongly oppose it. Before I learned about Jesus breaking down the wall of hostility between people of different races, cultures, and socioeconomic backgrounds, I was against prejudice for the simple fact that it was against me and my people. Now, because of my love for Christ, I can serve as the lead evangelist of the Columbia Church of Christ in Columbia, South Carolina, a diverse congregation dedicated to following in the footsteps of Christ, whose goal was to bring all men to him. Because of God's grace, I serve as the chair of a team dedicated to promoting international diversity inside the church. If you knew me in the past, you might consider this the transformation of a modern-day Saul turned Paul.

This book is a wonderful reminder that the dialogue about race must happen and continue to happen in God's church. Michael's commitment to bringing understanding to all sides is amazing and inspiring. His strong character, wealth of experiences, life and professional education, and most of all his love for God have allowed him to create this masterpiece. His devotion to God and his humility in facing the challenges that exist in the daunting racially charged climate that divides our country encourages me. He, like me, believes that the answer to the problem is God's kingdom—the obedience of his people to bring up the issues, face them, and resolve them. In his book, Michael does a fantastic job educating, challenging, and motivating those wounded by their encounters with racism to be the light of the world through devotion to Christ and love for one another. He does this using parables, historical facts, and his own personal stories and those of his family.

I could not put this book down! It was engaging and stimulating, reminding me that my true identity is in Christ first, moving me to examine my own concepts of race, and encouraging me to do my part in creating unity among people despite their differences. Before reading this book, the task of keeping the conversation going in the churches seemed, at times, overwhelming and maybe even a little useless. After all, bringing up the subject of race can be such an emotional undertaking, and the emotion most often dredged up is anger. That is a fire that, once ignited, is a hard one to put out in the church. Michael explains with brilliance that the conversation *has* to happen. Through Jesus, God brings unity to all who obey him. And Michael uses the Scriptures to clearly show God's intent and purpose for unity for his creation. This moved me to look for even greater ways to keep the conversation going in God's church.

Our unity is at the heart of Jesus' sacrifice on the cross; it was his prayer (John 17:20–21). We are all equals at the foot of the cross, where Jesus willingly hung as the sacrificial lamb for the sins of the world.

Michael and I serve together on the diversity team. For years, I have admired his work in churches on the continent of Africa and in the United States, and it is an honor to serve with him. He was appointed a teacher in the Churches of Christ in 2007 and currently serves as the congregational teacher for the Minneapolis Church of Christ.

This book is a must-read for every man and woman who wants unity among people. I encourage you to keep your mind open as you go on this journey, to look for ways to understand and keep the conversation going. My prayer is that this book will help you to continue to grow in your knowledge about race and culture for God's glory.

Scott Kirkpatrick, evangelist,
Columbia Church of Christ

Introduction

C.S. Lewis, in his preface to *The Screwtape Letters,* wisely floated the idea that "there are two equal and opposite errors into which our race can fall about the devils. One is to disbelieve in their existence. The other is to believe, and to feel an excessive and unhealthy interest in them. They themselves are equally pleased by both errors." Since he is always up to his same old tricks, I believe the great deceiver would be quite happy with people who don't believe that racism is an issue in our society and in the church, as well as those who see it in everything that happens in the world.

When my older son was fifteen years old, he came home upset from one of the first days of his freshman year of high school. Even though we had lived in the medium-sized Wisconsin town of Appleton for nearly two years, he was still adjusting to a very different culture and environment from the one in which he had grown up in Milwaukee. On his face was a mixture of anger and hurt as he tried to reconcile that he didn't care and yet cared deeply what another student had said to him that day.

"Hey, what's the difference between a bench and a black man?" My son's classmate had run up to him with this little riddle, perhaps assuming it was funny. My son is African American; the other student was white. "What?" my son responded, more with incredulity and annoyance than any desire to know what the answer was going to be. "A bench can support a family," the other boy blurted out before bursting into uproarious laughter and being joined by a handful of students standing around them.

In that moment, my son, who had been raised his whole life to love his enemies and never resort to violence, wanted nothing more than to drill his balled-up fist as deeply into this boy's face as he could. He was wounded, furious, and numb all at the same time. He didn't know how to process it. We had told him his whole life that he would one day have to face prejudice and bigotry. We told him that he would have to deal with racism in this world. It's just a fact of life for most people of color who live in the United States. (Throughout this book, I will use the term "people of color" to denote all nonwhite Americans and not exclusively black Americans. It is the same, and often worse, in other places around the world, but in this book we will focus almost exclusively on the United States.)

I am what our society calls white. My wife, MyCresha, is black. We met in 1994 when she was three months pregnant, and we were engaged to be married by the time our son was born. We married in 1997 when he was about two and a half years old, and we moved to Milwaukee, Wisconsin.

Within a month of living there we were invited out to church five or six times in various places around the city. The last time someone reached out to us, we went home and dug up the other invitation cards we had been given, only to discover that all the invitations were to the same church. We decided that maybe God was trying to get our attention, so we went for a visit. At the time, we were little interested in church and had never been particularly impressed with any that we had visited. The biggest factor in our disinterest was that we just didn't like that the churches we had visited were almost exclusively white or all black. That just didn't seem right to us.

The moment we walked into the Milwaukee Church of Christ our view was drastically changed forever. Just walking into the building, before the preaching had even started, we experienced our first "gospel sermon." The church was incredibly diverse. There was a mind-blowing mixture of ethnicities, skin colors, socioeconomic statuses, and cultures. The worship styles were varied and inviting to both my wife and me; and I can assure you, our preferences were unalike. Many of you may have had a similar experience, and I'll admit that sometimes I forget just how amazing that first moment of discovery was for us. We had never known there could be anything like that.

We studied the Bible for longer than I'd care to admit, mostly because of my pride, but eventually both my wife and I were baptized, well before our son's fourth birthday. As disciples of Jesus, we learned much about living out God's kingdom, marriage and parenting, and many more areas. And so the kingdom of God and our family of churches became our son's reality. We spent nearly every day with disciples. They were our primary family, and all our boy knew was diversity, unity, and the harmony of the kingdom.

When he was in the seventh grade, we moved from Milwaukee to the Appleton area. We had been leading the campus ministry full time for a couple of years, and I had become a teacher in the church by then. We went to Appleton to lead the small church there that had been planted a few years prior. We prayed, sought a lot of advice, and eventually decided to move there and help in any way we could.

We knew that it would be an adjustment. We were moving from a large city to a town you could drive through from end to end in less than fifteen minutes. We also knew that the area was ninety-six percent white at the time, so continuing to build diversity in the church would take some doing. Even under those circumstances, the church in Appleton was already diverse. They were also a small, loving family that embraced us, supported us, and loved our children. By the time we moved there, we had a four-year-old son, Elijah, as well. So our boys continued to be surrounded by love, diversity, and unity. As much as we tried to tell them what the world could be like, they had not experienced some of the more difficult aspects of it.

Until, that is, our oldest came home and told us the "joke" about the bench and the black man. Not long after that, he went to sit by a friend at lunch in the cafeteria and was told by another boy that he had entered the "whites only" part of the lunchroom and needed to take his "nigger" self somewhere else. How could this kid, you might wonder, get away with that? Because it was a school of nearly 1,500 with fewer than ten black students. We went to talk to the principal, who told us that we had, unbeknownst to us, moved into a "white flight" district, where people had moved from larger cities in Wisconsin to escape the "minority creep" into their communities. The principal seemed to think that there was not much he could do, especially because our son didn't want the individual students punished, not wanting to deal with the potential backlash. The principal then suggested that our son could join the LGBT club there, because that was where they recommended that "minorities" go for support, and this was the only "minority" club in the school. We politely told him "Thanks, but no thanks," and walked out.

In the end, nothing much happened and our son had an extremely difficult time in that community. That's a major understatement, but the rest is his story to tell, not mine. As much as we loved the church there, we finally felt that we had to change location and did so just before his senior year in high school, when we moved to the Twin Cities in Minnesota, where we now reside.

What always struck me about those difficult years was the sharp contrast between our lives in the International Churches of Christ and what we saw in the world around us. The racial, ethnic, and cultural diversity was the first thing we fell in love with about the church and continues to be near and dear to our hearts. We have always been proud of the fact that inclusion of people groups was part of the DNA of our movement from the very beginning. We were building diverse churches in places like South Africa before apartheid was toppled. We were multicultural long before it became popular and trendy.

Along the way, we learned that this beautiful diversity has its challenges. The more varied and diverse a people are, the more difficult it will be to create and maintain unity. That's a fact. And while we heard of and experienced little dustups or complaints over the years, for the most part what we saw and felt was this amazing and manifold kingdom of God that consisted of people of every tribe, language, and nation, so to speak.

But as we experienced through our son the division and ugly hatred that can slink around the world like a giant, invisible snake, God put it on my heart to deal with the issues of culture and race in our family of churches. Over the years, it seemed like we had learned to take diversity for granted in many places. And like in anything else that is taken for granted, cracks appeared. Not on the surface, of course. You can come any Sunday morning and see the same amazing mix of cultures. But in the day-to-day life of the community, tensions seemed to be rising. There was growing unease for some at what they felt was the lack of nonwhite leadership in our movement. Little pockets of culture clusters popped up within the body of Christ as people gravitated more and more toward those with whom they felt more naturally comfortable and with whom they had more in common.

When we moved to Minnesota in 2012, what had been a burning ember in my heart was fanned into flame by the Holy Spirit. I felt compelled to take up the issue of culture and race in our family of churches. I didn't want to. I hesitated greatly. I was worried that it wasn't necessary; that it was making a mountain out of a molehill. I was worried that I wasn't the right person to do it. I still have many of those fears. But I felt compelled, and so I began a journey of research and discovery.

I had spent eight years in Milwaukee teaching high school history before going into the ministry, and as a historian, one of my specialty areas had been early America up to the Civil War. I studied through American history again, focusing on race and culture issues. I also set out to talk to every disciple I could about this matter to get a feel for where things were at. As a teacher in our family of churches, I have the privilege of traveling often and visiting other churches around the country and the globe, so I had many opportunities to talk to disciples from all over the world.

What I found in hundreds of conversations was that there is still much good and much to be proud of when it comes to our cultural and ethnic diversity. Most disciples love their church and they love the kingdom of God. They love the ideal of being God's one family of all nations, and they love their brothers and sisters.

But I also found that many brothers and sisters of color were grieved and a part inside of them was in mourning; not all, but a definite majority. What I heard primarily was fear. Fear that the prejudices and inequities of the world had crept into our beloved church. They were bothered by the pattern of silence in the face of incidents of racial injustice that were playing out in the media. They were concerned at the perception of a mounting lack of representation of people of color in all levels of church leadership.

As I continued to listen, I heard a growing pattern of dissatisfaction in many churches about the cultural environment. People of color, particularly African American brothers and sisters, often felt that there was a dominant white culture in the church and that their voice and culture were either allowed only token input or not heard at all (although there are a few cases where the opposite is true). I recognized that frustration, because it is one that I have heard from my own family and close friends who are disciples.

I heard tales from single sisters who complained that they had been told many times by several brothers that they would consider dating them or even marrying them if they weren't black. Since interracial relationships are so common in our movement, I must admit that this one surprised me, but as I asked around further of both men and women, I found it was not an isolated phenomenon.

When I asked brothers and sisters if they had ever experienced prejudice or racism, or felt condescended to in the church on the grounds of their race, the most common response was laughter. Of course they had. Was I kidding?

Of all the conversations that I have had, though, the response that I heard over and over again is still the most concerning and least surprising to me of all. And I must admit, it saddens me that it didn't surprise me. In fact, I heard variations of this response so often that it almost seemed like it was scripted somewhere: "I love my church and my brothers and sisters, but most of the time I feel very comfortable and accepted here as long as I act white." Wow! Take a minute and let the weight of that sink in. What that means is that many brothers and sisters in our family of churches don't feel that they can truly express themselves according to the culture in which they were raised and feel most naturally comfortable. They play act, in some ways, at church and can only be themselves elsewhere.

Although that certainly is not the experience of every disciple of color, I was hearing that it was the experience of many. My wife can tell you that she has felt that way many times. The challenging part is that most disciples who are white are completely unaware of this. We tend to not even be aware that the church family has a prevailing culture, let alone that it is a white one. The problematic part is when the predominant culture is made aware and they either reject the notion outright or fail to do anything meaningful about it. And while it is most often the case that the predominant culture in our individual churches tends to be white, it is true that there are a few cases where black culture has become predominant and black members have ignored or been unaware of the needs of others. Thus, it can go both ways (and both are bad), although it is heavily weighted toward what I am describing.

Our world is embroiled in ethnic division and strife. It seems that the more the world proclaims harmony, love, and unity, the more deep divisions and problems surface. There have been great strides in the United States and around the world in equity between people groups, especially legally. But the last few years have shown that the issues of racism and inequity are original sins in the United States and many other countries, and will simply not go away. For every two steps forward, it feels like there are one and seven-eighths steps back.

It is simply outside the scope of this book or my ability as a writer to address the racial, ethnic, and cultural divisions and problems in our country and in our world. I'm not convinced there even is a solution to be found in the world. It's a little like trying to dry off with a towel while standing at the bottom of the ocean.

I will consistently attempt to avoid the urge to offer solutions to the problems that the world faces. My attempts at analysis and responses will be limited in scope. In Section 1 of this book I will primarily consider the white-black relationship in the United States. I understand that there are many other racial and ethnic issues, but right now in this country this is the one that is center stage. In dealing with this relationship, I hope to provide scriptural themes in Section 2, principles in Section 3, and analysis of cultures in Section 4 that will be applicable and useful for ethnic situations and countries beyond my primary focus.

The main purpose of this book is to push open further the doorway into dialogue and discussion among disciples, individual churches, and our entire church family. There is often discomfort and reluctance to honestly and openly converse about these topics that can be so personal and emotional. But perhaps an example will help bring a better perspective on this need.

Follow along with me as I relate a little parable that will explain why I think it is important for us to engage in the topics of culture, race, and kingdom. Imagine that my wife comes to me one day while I'm out working in the yard, and says, "When you're done with that, can you come into the kitchen so that we can talk about something." You may have noticed that there is no question mark at the end of that sentence even though it warrants one. That's because every husband reading knows that this is not a question. It is a statement of what had better take place in the next few minutes.

I have no idea what she wants to talk about, but I am already feeling irritated because I was focused on the lawn and don't want to deal with any issues right now. Plus, everything is good, so why ruin it with a talk? As I walk into the room, she blurts out, "You know I love you, but…" Allow me to stop right here. You know this is not going to be good, right? Any sentence that starts with "You know I love you," is about to drive off a cliff real fast. It's in the same league of this-is-not-going-to-be-pleasant with "I don't mean to be rude, but…," "Just hear me out first…," "What had happened was…," and "You know we've been friends for a long time, right?" None of those conversations is likely going to end well.

"You know I love you, but," she says, "we really need to have a talk about our marriage."

My immediate thought is, "Oh, Lord, take me now! Either you come back or just take me to you, but I do not want to have this conversation." You must understand; I was in the middle of something. This is a busy day. And besides, these talks are of no value anyway. Our marriage is great. Oh, we have little things, like anyone, but mostly I am nearly perfect and she's acceptable too, and so it works. You know what messes things up? These talks. They get her all lathered up with mostly imaginary things that aren't even problems. We don't have enough time together, or I did this or didn't do that, or she doesn't feel close to me right now. And those are just the starter complaints. They can get much more appallingly imaginary.

And most of the discussions she wants to have are simply divisive. She takes a great marriage and creates problems with her infernal "we need to talk" discord. Well, not today, sister. This tyranny and playing the "talk" card ends here and now.

So I tell her, "No, we're not going to talk about this." She looks a bit taken aback, but before she can respond, I continue. "We have a great marriage; things are good. Why are you trying to mess that up?"

"Think of this biblically," I go on. "The Bible makes it clear that we were once two separate people but when we came together in marriage, we became one flesh. That's all there is to it," I proudly state. "Why dredge up things from the past?"

She listens to me and then calmly says, "I want to talk about something from this morning."

"Ahh," I quickly blurt, "that's the past!"

"Right now we are unified," I continue, "because we are one. It's great to be one. I love that we are one. That's biblical truth. Nope, no argument there. No conversations needed. I think we're good and we should just move along and enjoy our goodness."

Now, I'd like to give you, my friends, a moment to ponder what you think my wife's response might have been. Did she meekly turn around while thinking to herself, "He's right; he's always right—we *are* unified. I don't know why I wanted to cause problems"? Or do you suppose that her soft and gentle look of understanding quickly turned to a steely gaze of annoyance and determination, and she firmly stated in a controlled staccato, "We need to talk now, and we are going to talk about this"?

Before any of you start to search the Internet to find out who disciples me, I will remind you that at the beginning of this little parable I asked you to "imagine." It never happened. But imagine if it did. How would she respond? How would *you* respond?

There is no question about what the Bible teaches here. Both testaments bear witness that when a man and woman come together in marriage, the two become one flesh (Genesis 2:24; Matthew 19:5; Ephesians 5:31). Husbands and wives should submit to one another (Ephesians 5:21), with wives focusing on submitting to their husbands as the church submits to Christ (v. 22), and husbands focusing on the call to love their wives as Christ loved the church (v. 25).

I would love to say that that hot day nearly twenty years ago was the end of the story of us becoming one. I would love to tell you that at that point we became perfectly united and there has never been any selfishness, discord, or conflict between us since. I would be thrilled to relay to you that we have experienced nothing but goodness. But we all know that simply has not been the case. It has been hard work. We brought with us all our baggage, sin, hurts, and mistrusts that had been collected during our lives up to that point. We have even added a few of each since we tied the knot. The process of becoming one has been challenging but incredibly fruitful and of inestimable worth. I wouldn't change the struggle for the world. Our marriage has been amazing, but it has been an undertaking.

I can't deny that there have been many times over the years when my wife has grown upset with something that I have done or failed to do. I have not communicated well. I have been thoughtless. I have not understood or listened to her perspective. I have made assumptions and often been incorrect. Each one of those instances has had the potential to become a threat to our unity and oneness. Nearly every incident of conflict becomes an opportunity to either divide us or to communicate, exercise humility, and learn about one another, growing closer and closer to the oneness that we aim for.

My wife is an incredibly gracious and patient woman, but I do manage to come near her limits at times. And the fact that we come from contrasting social and cultural backgrounds only adds to the room for misunderstanding, miscommunication, or just general trouble.

When she has been hurt or feels neglected, marginalized, or misheard, the way I respond is everything. How well would it go over if I threw some theological truths at her about the two becoming one? Beautiful truths can be used destructively and obscure the real issue. What was once a goal—unity—has been turned into an obstacle that shuts down conversation, ends communication, and widens the gap between us.

The simple reason for that is that when a man and woman join in marriage to become one flesh that is the start of the journey, not the destination. You don't get married, become one, and now the work is over and all that's left is to preserve the perfect unity and oneness that you have achieved.

In the same way, imagine if a black brother or sister wanted to talk to me about what they have experienced in the church, why they feel culturally marginalized at times, or the hurt they feel from what is happening in our country. What if I responded in that conversation the way I described speaking to my wife? What if I said, "Brother, why are you trying to cause division? There is just one race, the human race. The Bible is very clear on that. The only answer to racism is not to complain or see it as a boogeyman behind every bush. We are all one in Christ, so you need to repent of this divisiveness. God has already joined us together and there is no black or white."

And imagine that, when my friend asks if it's a conversation that we could have as a church and maybe even do some teaching on it, I respond by telling him that such conversations are pointless because they're just going to dig up conflicting feelings and perspectives and divide our fellowship.

These sentiments about being one in Christ are not just made up. I have heard those statements and ones like them expressed often in the fellowship. There is no question that there is great truth behind these ideas, but if we leave it there, such beloved truths of God's kingdom can quickly become empty platitudes.

The truth contained in those statements is that we *are* all one in Christ. That's an undeniable biblical reality for those that have been immersed into his life. There *is* only the one, human race, say the Scriptures. But as in a marriage, this is the starting point. When God's people seek to obey the Scriptures by being comprised of all nations and people groups, a difficult process has begun. What comes next is a lot of hard work. These little slogans that we toss out, like "There is just one race, the human race," and "We should all be colorblind" often serve as conversation enders, not starters. If I responded to my wife with the idea that she shouldn't bring up issues or try to work on our marriage because we are one, that would be flippant. It would twist a truth into an agent of stagnation. The same is true if we toss out platitudes when it comes to the topics of racism, race, and culture.

Here's the rub: statements like "We are one" are true, but they only remain true if a lot of effort, honest conversation, and difficult changes are constant. The minute that environment fades away is the moment that those statements cease to be true. Bringing up concerns and wanting to talk about them in an open and real way is not disruptive; it is the foundation for true unity and continued growth.

When people look at me I want them to see me for who I am. I want them to notice, for example, that I am male. As part of God's plan, I am also white. I don't want to receive any advantage for those things, but I do not want to be treated as though I am not a male and am not white, or that I am just like everyone else. To tell me that you don't see me as male would be a little hurtful, to be honest. To tell a person of color that you are colorblind is to deny part of who they are so that *you* feel more comfortable. We don't intend that, but that is the result.

These topics will not always be easy to talk about. Race and culture can be among the most sensitive themes imaginable. We will be tempted to run away from the hard work of pursuing racial unity and maintaining true cultural diversity in the body of Christ. We will be tempted to throw out platitudes so that we don't have to hear perspectives and experiences that make us uncomfortable.

The church is in danger. There is always the danger that we will bring in worldly ways of thinking and believing into the body. Various political arguments and special-interest groups can pull at us, and we can align our thinking with elements of our culture much more than with the Bible and more than we are aware of. But it is these simple statements, which contain kernels of biblical truth that can suppress true growth rather than foster it, that endanger us just as much, if not more, than worldly thinking. It is incredibly perilous to think we are fine and don't need to talk when that is exactly what we need.

There is no question that issues of racism, race, and culture have once again taken center stage in our society. These are issues that bring out deep passion and potential conflict in the world; and because disciples live in this world, they affect us, our mission, and our unity.

If we're not careful and don't address these topics biblically and with great love, patience, and grace, they could wind up ripping us apart. Every potential problem like this, though, can be a pitfall or a platform. It can be our undoing or an amazing opportunity to put the power and wisdom of the true gospel on display. It is encouraging that these conversations are now taking place in some locations. I am under no illusion that this book is the beginning of something. It is a continuation and it is a call for learning, understanding, and, most of all, open and honest discussion.

My assertion in this book, however, may sound a bit odd at the beginning. It is my contention that race is not the real problem in our world today. Of course, we can always say that sin is the real problem, and that is true, although not always helpful when addressing complex situations. Race is an invention of society. It is something that divides and that is real enough, but it is a social construct meant to keep people groups identified and separate. Because it is a much-used and understood concept, however, I will continue to use the term throughout this book, though at the same time I will seek to show it for what it is.

The real problems that threaten division within the body of Christ are related to race but do not directly flow from it. I don't believe that there are any disciples out there who believe that one group of people is inferior to another because of their skin tone. No, what continues to cause problems are history, culture, perspective, and the solutions that are typically offered by the world.

We will examine all those agents of division before delving into the true answers that we can find in God's word. The good news is that perhaps the biggest cause of internal strife and division in the early church was the issue of ethnicity and culture. That means that the New Testament Scriptures are full of principles and teaching that will propel us forward in our search to be the unified people of God that he has called us to be.

This book is not just about race and ethnic issues. I will certainly attempt to deal with those things, but at the heart of it all, I intend to write about how the gospel and the kingdom of God impact our individual cultures and bring us together to operate as one family. The concepts and ideas, then, will go beyond racial issues and get to the heart of the matter of culture. I think this is fitting, because race is simply one aspect of culture. It is there, in our cultural differences, that we find potential for conflict that goes far beyond one issue or identity marker. So that will occupy the lion's share of our attention. But it is also in our cultural differences that, when we come together as one people, God is brought the most glory.

One final note before we proceed. Not everyone is a reader. Some might typically start a book this size and never finish it. Others wouldn't normally make it past this point, or maybe you're only here because some-one you know that is a reader asked you to read this paragraph. Some will get bored in the early chapters as we examine some important history. Others will like the history but find the chapters that carefully examine the first-century church and the Scriptures for direction through these difficult issues to be a bit tedious. Some will not care for my style of writing. Others are simply not interested in this topic and don't find reading about it a valuable way to spend their precious time. Of all of you who fit into one of these categories, I am going to make a special plea: read this book for others, if not for yourself. These are important issues for many of your brothers and sisters in Christ, and the topics discussed here are a vital aspect of us moving together in a healthy and unified fashion. I always remind my biblical students that they should have the attitude of learning for the person behind them. I ask you to do the same. Push your way through this book, if need be, for others. If you are willing to do that, I thank you.

CROSSING THE LINE

Section One
Where We Are At

Chapter 1

Losing Race

My wife and I had been disciples for about a year by the time the new millennium rolled around. We had already developed many deep friendships that continue to this day. One evening we invited a married couple over for dinner. They were quickly becoming good friends and still have a dear and wonderful relationship with us. This was the first time they had ever been to the apartment that we lived in at the time. It is somewhat important to this story to know that they are both black.

As they walked into our apartment, the smell of the delightful meal that my wife had cooked was wafting through the air. They stopped briefly in the front hallway to look at a row of pictures that had been carefully framed and hung on the wall. Since it was the first thing that you saw when you walked in, it had become pretty normal for us to stand there for a moment or two while people quickly looked over the pictures. Sometimes they would comment politely about how much our son had grown or make some other small talk, and other times they would just nod without remark and then move into the apartment.

This time was different, though. As they were looking at the pictures, the wife, without turning toward me, pointed to a picture of my parents. With a quizzical tone to her voice she said, "Who are these old white people?" I looked to see which picture she was pointing to and then responded, "Oh, those are my parents." Her head snapped around somewhat violently and she stared at me with piercing eyes. Then she cocked her head to one side and her face contorted as she blurted out rather loudly and forcefully, "Are you white?"

I must admit that made me laugh. I had never been asked that question before. Through the laughter I think I was able to muster up the confirmation, "All my life." That brought a look of shock and confusion to her face and she stood there motionless for a moment. She then came back to reality, shook her head and replied, "I always just thought you were a light-skinned brother."

Looking back on that, it's still amusing to me. I have very fair skin, and while I try to be as inclusive culturally as I can, I've always thought that by society's standards I tend to speak and act "white" (whatever that means). I certainly had never been mistaken for anything other than a white guy before. But her confusion brings up a good point. What *is* race? What does it even mean to be black, white, red, yellow, or brown? Where does the idea of race come from? Is it a biblical idea? Is it scientific?

The Origins of Race

Since shortly after the Garden of Eden, human beings have found ways to divide and segregate themselves from other groups. We'll look at that phenomenon in more detail in Chapter 5. One of the newer ways to do that, though, is race. Race is the supposed separation of humans into distinct and separate subspecies based, primarily, on skin color. Racism takes place when one group of people form a separate identity based on ethnicity, skin color, or some other reason for collectivity and subsequently dominate, exclude, oppress, or take efforts to eliminate another group based on an arbitrary set of differences that they believe are hereditary and cannot be changed. There is no clear evidence for the concept of race or the practice of racism before the period known as the Middle Ages.

It is during the Middle Ages that the systemic classification of Jews as the people of the devil appears as the first concrete case of blatant racism. This seems to be the opening verse of the song of racism and a racial worldview that has continued to dominate into the twenty-first century. There had always been hate between various groups, but this was the first time that people of a specific nationality or ethnicity were categorized into a group that was based on heredity and so was unalterable.

During the thirteenth through fifteenth centuries, Europeans explored and traveled around the world, which greatly increased their contact with and awareness of people groups with much darker skin coloring than theirs, in the regions of Asia, Africa, and the New World. Because they felt that expansion and conquest was their destiny and right, as they came into contact with these people groups of color, they enslaved and, in some cases, exterminated them.

The initial explanation and justification for the deplorable treatment of people with darker pigmentation was that they were unsaved pagans and savages, but that quickly transformed into arguments focused on the color of their skin. As it became easier and more economically beneficial to enslave darker-skinned people, primarily Africans, justifications came to be based on the characteristics of the "black race." Up to that time, it was understood that the darker-skinned people of Africa are a vast potpourri of shades, nations, and tribes, from various geographical locations, and with varying connections. Now, all the people that populated a continent of 326.9 trillion square feet were lumped together as one group: black. The justification for enslaving Africans gradually shifted from a religious to a racial one. They were one race, and plainly an inferior one at that.

In the early days of racial theory, it was purported that Ham had sinned against his father, Noah, and been cursed as a result. The punishment was dark skin and a promise that his descendants would be kept in bondage.

As that thought took hold, the whole of humanity was divided up into races. Attempts to identify separate ones have usually settled on three to five. The most commonly identified separate races are the black or Negroid race; the yellow or Mongoloid race; and the white or Caucasian race. Other classifications sometimes included have been the red or Indian race, the Australoid race, and the Samoid race.

As the period of Enlightenment came to prominence, the subject of race moved from the twisting of Scripture to place its foundation on scientific arguments. In the eighteenth century it was generally accepted theory that the races were mere subdivisions of one human species. By the late nineteenth century, however, after the widespread acceptance of Darwin's theory of evolution, it was argued that the races were entirely separate species.

Because the notion of race was basically invented by Europeans, they naturally built into it the idea that the white race was the favored or superior group. The anecdote about my friends, though, illustrates that the idea of race is very fluid and somewhat undefinable. History demonstrates that even the idea of what qualifies an individual to be considered white has changed over time.

The idea of separate races is not something found in the Bible and is not scientifically sound. It could be argued that the idea of whiteness is a concept that has been manipulated over time to preserve prestige and power for a specific group of people. Just reading that might make some of us feel defensive, but it shouldn't. If it's the truth, then as disciples we should seek to understand it so that we can transform our thinking and keep moving toward God's vision for humanity.

In the seventeenth century in Virginia, nearly a thousand poor blacks and whites rebelled against the ruling elite of the colony, including Governor William Berkeley. It eventually took troops from England to quell the uprising, but similar rebellions would take place in other colonies, such as

Maryland. The response of the rich and powerful was swift and led to a systemic effort to break the bond between white indentured servants and blacks, both free and slave. Before the rebellion in Virginia, now known as Bacon's Rebellion, poor blacks and whites were bonded together as one group based on their economic conditions and subservient status. They were treated similarly and saw themselves as virtually the same. The Virginian landowners enacted the harsh Virginia Slave Codes, which served the purpose of creating a racial caste system. They saw how dangerous it would be for their position of power if poor blacks and whites continued to identify as a group based on wealth. They made efforts to distinguish between the "lower" black race and white people. Rich Southern whites now emphasized solidarity with poor whites based on race; better this than to allow blacks and whites to identify based on class. They convinced poor whites that simply because they were white they were not in the lowest class. They might be poor, but at least they weren't black. Once that was accepted, it was an easy sell to convince them that blacks were the enemy because if they got ahead at all, it would be at the poor whites' expense and take away the little power they had as whites.

To further reinforce the racial barrier, white indentured servants were given a status that they had not previously enjoyed, were allowed to own property and guns, and were often given the task of policing the plantations to keep order. The classes were now comfortably divided along racial lines, and the power of the rich white elites was safe for the time being.

Other Southern states soon borrowed from Virginia's Slave Codes[1] and cemented the idea of white and black as distinctly separate groups, all the while selling the mantra to poor whites that blacks were their enemies. Almost overnight, the divide between rich and poor had changed to a divide between white and black. White was good and normal, and blacks were lesser and something to be feared and had to be kept at bay.

As the United States transitioned from British colonies to a full-fledged nation, the idea that whiteness was right and the norm became established as part of the country's DNA. The Declaration of Independence stated that "all men are created equal," but a quick survey of the treatment toward members of the First Nations, Mexicans, blacks, and other groups of color clearly demonstrates that by "men," they meant "white men." From the inception of the United States, white was the embodiment of what it meant to be a human being. Other groups were considered lesser levels of humanity.

Moving forward through the nineteenth and twentieth centuries, the definition of "white" vacillated to meet the needs of those in power. There were times during this period that Jews, Germans, Irish, Italians, and various Slavic and Eastern European groups were not considered white. They were often subjugated, oppressed, and compared to people of color. When it became inconvenient or dangerous to continue the oppression of certain groups, they were granted the status of white and came to be considered part of the white race. This may seem odd, but to be white wasn't a status automatically granted just because a group had lighter skin. As America expanded West and more immigrants came in larger numbers, the concept of whiteness expanded to bring them into the fold.

The Scientific Blunder

I briefly mentioned Darwin's theory of evolution above, and it's important to return to it, because it helped to shape and bolster much of what became the conception of race in the late nineteenth through the twentieth century, a conception that continues in many respects to this day. A biological basis for race was occasionally propounded before Darwin's world-changing *On the Origin of Species by Means of Natural Selection,* but that became the standard view after his work was published. It is often overlooked that the full title of Darwin's book was *On the Origin of Species by Means of Natural Selection, or the Preservation of Favoured Races in the Struggle for Life.* Darwin argued that all life, including humans, had evolved from a common ancestor. His theory quickly became the standard scientific view, and it removed, in the minds of many, any role of a Creator that set humanity apart as a special part of creation. It eventually became the typical belief among scientists that the existence of races was a scientific fact and that various species of humans had broken off from one another long ago and evolved separately. Of course, the standard belief was that the white race was the most evolved and that darker races were more closely related to apelike ancestors. In fact, the common debate of the late nineteenth and early twentieth centuries was whether black people were more closely related to apes or to white humans. People of color had consistently been likened to beasts before the acceptance of evolution, but now there was a scientific underpinning and an air of legitimacy to these charges.

As a result, it was not uncommon in the late nineteenth and early twentieth centuries for zoos in the Western world to display human beings of color, particularly Africans. The argument was that blacks that had been born and encultured in the Western world had been somewhat civilized, not unlike a domestic animal. But those from Africa were still in their wild state and had similar rights, or lack thereof, as any beast. Men and women of dignity and inestimable worth in the eyes of God were thus kept in cages and put on display for people to come observe them.

In 1906, a young Congolese man named Ota Benga was put on display in the monkey house of the Bronx Zoo in New York. He was put in a cage with an orangutan and a parrot and touted as an example of a living "apeman." How could such a monstrous action be tolerated? An article of the time in *Scientific American* asserted that:

> Even today, ape-like negroes are found in the gloomy forests, who are doubtless direct descendants of these early types of man, who probably closely resembled their simian ancestors.[2]

Complaints rang out, largely from the black Christian community, who argued against the display based both on Ota's humanity and on the idea of what they viewed as the unbiblical evolutionary theory being hyped. The New York Times responded with an editorial piece which argued that based on science and the existence of race, Benga was probably enjoying himself and it wasn't that big a deal.

> We do not quite understand all the emotion which others are expressing in the matter... It is absurd to make moan over the imagined humiliation and degradation he is suffering... Ota Benga, according to our information is a normal specimen of his race or tribe, with a brain as much developed as are those of its other members... Pygmies...are very low in the human scale, and the suggestion that Benga should be in a school instead of a cage ignores the high probability that school would be a place...from which he could draw no advantage whatever. The idea that men are all much alike except as they have had or lacked opportunities for getting an education out of books is now far out of date.[3]

Having experienced the savage brutality of Belgium's King Leopold's conquest through the Congo and his own interactions in New York, Benga eventually became despondent when he realized that he would likely never be able to return to Africa. Tragically, he took his own life in 1916.

While it was likely not Darwin's intent, his theory of evolution led to a notable increase in racist thinking. The accepted thinking became that the nonwhite races did not have the genetic capability to be elevated to the status of fully civilized human beings. This served as the justification for all kinds of past, present, and future mistreatment of people of color around the world. Darwin himself would cite his shock at the wide difference "between savage and civilised man," arguing that the gap was greater than that "between a wild and domesticated animal." He would go on to say that "viewing such men, one can hardly make one's self believe that they are fellow-creatures, and inhabitants of the same world." He even compared people of color to "lower animals."[4]

The point of all this is for us to understand the common thinking that came to be accepted in the scientific community and eventually became the basis of the curriculum taught in schools around the country. This acceptance of the concept of a scale of evolution among the races of humans eventually led to the growing movement of eugenics in the early half of the twentieth century, which was based on the belief that, since some races were less evolved than the white race, based on the fact of survival of the fittest, they would eventually die out anyway. Eugenics was the program that would help that along and keep the white race from being pulled back down the evolutionary scale through interbreeding. It promoted the idea, among others, of sterilizing people of color to bring about their eventual disappearance from the genetic pool of humanity.

The acceptance of the fairytale of more than one race and of the theory of survival of the fittest greatly fueled the colonization policies of many European countries and was used to justify the brutal treatment meted out to people of color. During a massive famine in the latter portion of the nineteenth century, British ships sat in Indian ports stocked full of food that was gleaned from the fields of their Indian colony while countless numbers of Indians starved to death. The British justification was that they should be thanked by humanity for simply helping along the survival of the fittest and the removal of lower races. Estimates now pin the Indian death toll at the hands of this type of racial thinking by the British and others to over thirty million.

Rather than causing any of us to feel shame or guilt or to get defensive, this should remind us of how far off the rails humanity can go when we substitute our own wisdom for God's.

This racialist worldview came to a head under the Nazi regime. That's when the curtain was pulled back on how destructive and ugly the theories of man can be when they are divorced from biblical truth. But the Nazis weren't vehemently opposed around the world at first; this was not so much because the world was unaware of their intentions or what was going on—although most of the world did not know the extent to which the Nazis had gone in their genocidal rampage—but because the Nazis were, in many ways, espousing the accepted scientific theories of the day. Race was considered the primary determinant of people's character, intelligence, and worth, and the white race was widely accepted as the pinnacle of racial evolution.

A Dangerous Myth

In 1942, however, a British-born anthropologist, Ashley Montagu, released a book entitled *Man's Most Dangerous Myth: The Fallacy of Race.* During the summer between my sophomore and junior years in college, I was perusing the shelves of my town's library looking for something to read during long, boring nights of sitting at the front desk waiting for customers to come into the furniture warehouse store where I worked. I stumbled upon this book and it looked intriguing, so I checked it out. As I began to read, my mind was blown. Montagu was an avowed evolutionist and trained scientist arguing eloquently that the idea of race was a social construct that had no scientific footing. There are distinctions and differences in the various ethnicities of humanity, he argued, but those are no more significant than hair or eye color. Montagu turned a critical eye toward the invention of race as largely a justification of slavery and went on to demonstrate that the idea of racial superiority of one group over another was absurd and unfounded.

There were two things that caused my strong reaction to the book. The first is that it was written in 1942. Montagu had published this revolutionary work in the middle of WWII, nearly fifty years before I first read it. And yet we were still being taught in my high school and college classes that race was a scientific fact. We were taught the distinct characteristics of each race, and while it was stated that no one race was superior to another, the mere acceptance of the idea of various human races had to lead almost inevitably to an assertion of superiority by one group over the rest.

The other thing that blew my mind was that I already knew all the things that Montagu was asserting. His theories are now accepted as the standard for science, as modern science agrees that there is no such thing as varying races among humans. There are ethnic differences in appearance, skin tone, skeletal structure, and so on, but these are all small variations. Scientists now agree that all humans have descended from one common ancestor, a woman that they usually trace to somewhere in Africa or the Middle East.

Guess Who Was Right

But I knew all this. Before you think I'm coming off as a know-it-all, I'm not claiming to have more scientific knowledge than this esteemed anthropologist who was ahead of his time. The reason I knew all that he was asserting, that humans were one race with minor variations and diversity that had all come from one ancestor, was that growing up my parents taught me the Bible. I'm forever grateful. As much as our modern scientific culture likes to mock the Bible and cast aspersions on this so-called backward, antiquated religious book of myths, the facts are incontrovertible: the Bible told a different story about humanity than did the scientific community and the accepted knowledge base of the world from at least the Middle Ages through the middle of the twentieth century. The Bible, correctly interpreted, had it right all along.

"From one man," declared Paul in Luke's work of covenant history, the Acts of the Apostles, "he made all the nations, that they should inhabit the whole earth" (Acts 17:26). The Athenian audience that Paul addressed that day held to the belief that they had sprung from the soil of the surrounding area separately from the rest of humanity. The idea of all humanity coming from one man and one woman was largely unique when compared to the origin stories from around the world.

Although this idea was mocked for centuries, mainstream science now confirms this aspect of the biblical account. The discovery of DNA and the mapping of the human genome have only further confirmed the concept of one race. Geneticists have settled that there is no statistical difference between the so-called races. What that means is that using skin color and physical features as markers to separate and distinguish between human groups is arbitrary.

Imagine a world where all the people with blue eyes kept to themselves and only interbred with one another. If someone was occasionally born with a different eye color, they would be marginalized and pushed out of the society. Imagine that at the same time those with green eyes created their own society and those with brown eyes did the same. Life would be difficult for those with blue-green eyes because they would never be accepted by any group. Now imagine that these communities began to truly see themselves as independent segments of humanity and even put forth theories that their race of humanity, say the brown-eyed people, was superior to the others, eventually developing apart from the others and evolving their own distinct culture. It wouldn't be long before wars would break out between these separate "races" of people.

We could offer the same example with hair color or some other physical feature. Here is the important point: skin color as a reason to separate and distinguish humanity is just as subjective as eye color or hair color. We only have separate pockets of people based on skin color because human beings elected to do that.

It hasn't always been that way. Humans have always separated for various reasons, of course, but it hasn't always been based on skin color. For instance, it is notoriously difficult for Egyptologists to determine what "race" the ancient Egyptians were because they rarely, if ever, mentioned skin color. They seemed to mix rather indiscriminately with people of other national origins. A certain shade of skin might be common to a particular nation, but it was never seen as a reason to discriminate. They knew that Hittites might be lighter skinned than Cushites, but for them, it was education and national loyalty that mattered, not skin color.

Scientists now confirm that all human beings are simply varying shades of the same color. How much melanin we have in our skin cells determines whether we are very light brown, medium brown, or very dark brown. We must, then, get it firmly in our minds that the very concept of race is a myth. It is an arbitrary and rather ridiculous means of categorizing human beings by one physical characteristic.

Genesis 1 and 2 tell us that God created human beings in his image. They also tell us that all beings descended from Adam and Eve. From there the Bible chronicles the descent of humankind into various families that eventually became tribes and clans and then nations. But it never wavers on this: every nation can trace itself back to Adam and Eve. Some will occasionally argue that we can all trace our origins back to Noah, but that's likely not accurate. Noah, his wife and three sons, and their three wives all survived the flood, but nowhere does the text indicate that the wives of Noah's sons were also their sisters. That would most likely mean that they did not descend from Noah. If we do the math, that means all their children had half of their DNA from a source other than Noah. So it is only Adam and Eve that we can confidently identify as our original ancestors.

Why is this important? An incredible amount of sin and carnage have come because of a mistaken notion. Worldly wisdom brought us the idea of races, created largely on inherited skin color. But if that very notion is wrongheaded, then as the people of God, we must understand this at a very deep level so that we can embrace and display the truth. It will not be as easy as we might like to think. Once ideas are accepted into the common worldview, they are about as easy to uproot as it would be to yank a forty-foot oak tree from the earth with your bare hands.

The societies of our world were formed with the threads of the conception of human races woven into their very fabric. Our institutions, our cultures, our families, our identities, and so much more have the idea of race built into them. Most people find it acceptable at one level or another to distinguish between humans based on their skin color. We instinctively see others with particular skin tones and physical features and categorize them into corresponding racial groups. If we can't easily identify which race someone belongs to, it's probably because they are "mixed." Even that term shows how deeply rooted the concept of race is and how easily we validate it.

The Biblical Account of Humanity

So how did we get the so-called races? In Genesis 11 we are told that humanity banded together so that it could set itself up against God and his rule. We will return to this idea in detail in Chapter 5, but for now I will simply note that God brought division to the peoples of earth due to their sin and rebellion against him. This was not part of his final plan for humanity, but he did allow it for a time. We are taught in the very next chapter of Genesis that God set about to solve the problem of human division when he came to a Chaldean man named Abram and asked him to leave his people. We'll pick up that story in Chapter 8.

Genesis 10 chronicles the division of humanity according to clans, languages, territories, and nations. The incident at the Tower of Babel found in chapter 11 seems to be the cause of the division described in chapter 10. As the descendants of Noah's sons spread out across the planet and inhabited it once again, they divided, not just into human groups, but by geography and distance. The act of spreading out across the globe caused the process of genetic isolation. What that means is that one small group might have certain predominant features, including skin, eye, and hair color, along with a certain bone structure and distinct facial characteristics. If human groups had remained near one another, all these genetic variances would not have come about, as family lines would have been constantly mixed together. Before the flood it is unlikely that there would have been any identifiable groups or "races" based on things like skin color, because there was this constant genetic mixing. But after the flood, genetic isolation occurred and eventually resulted in the so-called races.

Think of it like one of those sampler cheesecake packages that you can buy at warehouse clubs like Sam's Club or Costco. They typically have fourteen slices with two pieces each of seven unique flavors. As each people group wandered farther away from the rest, they took their unique flavor, or genetic characteristics, with them. Once they got as far away as modern Russia, China, Africa, and beyond, these groups were no longer able to mix together again. The differences in physical features were locked in place, so to speak. And it remained that way for many hundreds of years. There were always some pockets of interaction, overlap, and mixing, but large population groups of human beings were cut off from each other, each with just a slice of the genetic cake.

If we were to go back to the post-flood time around the Tower of Babel and mix things up differently, sending off different combinations of groups, the same effect would happen but likely with changed results. There are certain physical features and characteristics that are often associated with one shade of skin, but if we were to start over, we could easily wind up with entirely new combinations of characteristic physical features with skin colors. The truth is, all these "racial" features are just part of the larger genetic pool that humanity draws upon.

The great irony of recent history is that when gene pools are not isolated from each other, the norm for human skin tone seems to be medium to darker brown rather than very light or "white."

To recap, the Bible teaches that humans were made in God's image and all descended from one set of human parents. The descendants of those parents eventually grew isolated from one another and settled into various tribes and nations, with the differences in physical characteristics between those groups being increasingly emphasized as this isolation developed and remained.

For hundreds of years, mainstream science rejected that notion. It argued, instead, that humans were divided into subspecies known as races, distinguished by their unique physical characteristics. It contended that the races either developed completely separately from different apelike ancestors or they shared a common ancestor and then branched off from one another long ago and developed through evolution into distinctly different groups. It was further posited that, given time, they would continue to grow apart and many of the less-developed races would eventually cease to exist.

Only recently has science done an about-face and turned to theories that are much more closely aligned to what the Bible has declared all along. All humans come from one set of human parents and there simply is no such thing as race. This is not a book about scientific theories, nor do I intend to bash science. I simply offer up the truth that for a long time, scientific theories were wrong, while the Bible has been proven gloriously correct. That's important for us to know.

Should We Dump Race?

So, does this mean that because there is just one race after all, that's all there is to it? We could just stop here and that would be the end of the book. In a word, no. While there is no such distinction as race, genetically speaking, history is much more complicated than that, isn't it? If, while driving, I swerve off the road to miss something hurtling at me, only to realize that it was my imagination and there was nothing there in the first place, that doesn't mean that I will not suffer the consequences of driving off the road. While race is an invented concept scientifically, the impact and effects of it are all too real, and we will need to deal with them.

Should we then abandon the term "race" and the language that emanates from that concept? In a perfect world, yes. But we don't live in a perfect world. We do live in a world of division. We live in a world where there are large groups of people who find their identity based on the tone of their skin and their "race." I am under no illusion that this book is going to change all that. Even though the term "race" is notoriously problematic and imprecise, it is a well-understood term in the common vernacular and so has some value when discussing these matters. For reasons of effectiveness and ease of communication, then, I will continue, at times, to use the term "race," but I urge the reader to keep in mind the history and mythological nature of this concept.

Ultimately, I believe that the way forward for God's people is to deeply understand the reality that race is a socially constructed concept meant to divide humans. My contention in this book is that the only way to combat that is through the solutions brought to bear by the kingdom of God.

Before we move into the next chapter, we need to define a few terms. What is race? What about racism, prejudice, and bigotry? Each one of these words has complexities to its meanings, and we could quibble for a long time about the specifics of each one. For now, though, I will simply supply the reader with the definitions that are growing in their acceptance today and will be what I mean when I use these terms.

- **Race** – A group of persons related by common descent or heredity; the traditional divisions of humanity, the most common and broad being the Caucasian, Mongoloid, and Negroid groups, categorized by alleged distinctive physical characteristics.

- **Racism** – A system of domination or oppression of one ethnic group or racial collective over another based on differences that are believed to be hereditary and unchangeable. For racism to exist, a group must have the power to enforce their dominance through either overt or implied means.

- **Racialism** – Treating others or acting in such a manner that emphasizes or embraces the legitimacy of the concept of race and/ or the differences between the so-called races. In short, it is to act like race is a real thing and that it matters, whether that action is positive or negative.

- **Prejudice** – A negative or unfavorable opinion or feeling formed about another and based on preconceived notions rather than fact, thought, or reason.

- **Bigotry** – The intolerance of a group, creed, opinion, belief, lifestyle, or worldview other than one's own. Whereas prejudice is a feeling, bigotry is putting those feelings into action.

Questions for Discussion

1. Why is it important to know that the idea of separate races and much of racism developed as a justification for slavery rather than being a cause of it?

2. What do you feel are the differences today between "races" of humanity?

3. Do you think it is important for all Christians to know the origins of the concept of race and the biblical teachings on it that are presented in this chapter? Why or why not?

4. Can you share a time when your race had a negative impact on your life?

5. Do you struggle with prejudice, bigotry, or stereotyping of others? Have you ever struggled with those things at any point in your life?

*Note: For all the discussion questions in this book, it is best to have a mature disciple lead the discussions in order to guide the group and shepherd it away from strong negative emotional expressions, derailing the conversation from the primary topic, and tendencies to drift into nonproductive areas of dialogue. You want honest and open discussions, but they must be guided toward a spirit of love, grace, and forgiveness. Do not allow the discussion to turn into a criticizing or slandering exercise, but rather keep it to constructive and honest feedback that will help move the conversation forward and edify the body of Christ.

Chapter 2

Two Sides of a Coin

In early 2015, social media sites across the Internet exploded over arguments about a dress. Almost instantly, it seemed, everyone was obsessed with the color of a dress in a picture. It wasn't a famous dress, mind you, or particularly important in any way. It was just a dress. Some people saw the picture of the blue and black dress and could not fathom what all the fuss was about. Why would people spend any time arguing about a picture of a run-of-the-mill blue and black dress?

Other people were looking at the picture and were also wondering what was causing all the commotion, because, after all, it was just some silly white and gold dress. Why were they seeing it on their newsfeed almost constantly?

And just like that, the world was split into two groups. Now, it was not two different pictures. It was the same picture. Some people's eyes interpreted the picture and told them it was blue and black, while others looked at it and their eyes interpreted the picture as white and gold. It is a fascinating phenomenon, but it's true. They would look at the exact same picture and come away with two completely different interpretations of what they just saw.

Some people argued to the hilt that the way they perceived the picture was the only correct way to really see it. Some scientists even stepped in to get to the bottom of it and explained what colors the dress itself really was. But that wasn't the point. What the controversy over the dress illustrated and exposed is that some things are subject to interpretation and that we can come away with unlike interpretations of the same set of facts. It can make it really difficult for people to get along when they construe things very differently. That's especially true as the importance of the facts under discussion increases.

When we moved from Wisconsin to Minnesota, my sons came away with widely divergent interpretations. My older son faced a lot of prejudice and bigotry in Wisconsin. It was intense and affected him so deeply that, he has since told us, it caused him to seriously consider taking his own life. His impressions of the state are for him almost completely colored by his personal experiences. He still loves many individuals from his home state, but for him, Wisconsin as a whole is a bad memory and that's just how he views it. He sees it in a negative light as a negative place.

My younger son had an entirely different experience. He did not encounter many personal instances of prejudice. He was unaware of any bigotry or racialist attitudes, unless he heard about it from his brother. Now that we live in another state, he longs to go back to Wisconsin one day. He sees the state through positive memories as a positive place.

Not too long ago, I walked into the kitchen to find them arguing about whether it was a good place or a bad place to live. They were each adamant about their position. But what I found most interesting was that they were equally certain that the other was just plain wrong. In their minds, there was no room for any other interpretation, no room for a different experience-based perception and reality.

I grew up in Wisconsin. I love the state. I love the city I grew up in. I love the landscape and the people. I love the sports teams. I have often joked that I am Badger born, Badger bred, and when I die I'm Badger dead. That was my truth; my reality. But then I saw what my older son went through and I had a choice to make. I could deny his experience based on my own, or I could accept that he had a totally different but equally valid reality. He had gone through things that I largely had not seen or was unaware even took place. I had seen small signs of the prejudice and bigotry in the state while growing up, but they never really affected me, so I was able to dismiss them as minor anomalies from the whole. My other option was to listen to my son and validate his experiences. When I put together his truth with mine, I come up with a richer, fuller picture of what is real. Wisconsin can be a wonderful place. But it also has some very dark things happening there. Neither should be dismissed. And when I encounter someone who doesn't have a nothing-but-love impression of it, based on their experiences, I cannot simply sweep their truth aside and argue that it is wrong because of my own. I can even understand why my son decided that he was no longer a Green Bay Packers fan and is now a Minnesota Vikings fan because he likes Minnesota better (although that was a tough one for me).

The truth is that often, those with a negative view are aware of the good side but it is outweighed by the bad they have experienced. I can understand that. I can comprehend why, at this point in his life, my son sees the state of Wisconsin the way he does. But I also have to be aware that when I tout the good side of things, it can easily come off as though I am dismissing his experiences and dismissing him. I do not want him to feel that way. So I listen. I learn. I validate what he went through. And I allow it to give me a more holistic view of the situation.

I spent a little time developing this concept here because I think it is a vitally important one for the people of God. The body of Christ is diverse racially and otherwise. That means the disciples have dissimilar experiences and backgrounds, and we tend to view the world in quite different ways. The more diverse we are as a group of people, the more difficulties this presents, because we have a larger assortment of perspectives and interpretations while working together in a tight space. This was equally true for the church of the first century. They had Hellenistic Jews, Hebraic Jews, Samaritans, and Gentiles of all sorts living together as family. They brought varied worldviews with them into the body, and it was tough. We will get to all of that in later chapters, but in the first section of the book, we are working through some of our own situations so that we can try to locate where we are at. This way, we will be prepared by the time we get to the situations in the early church to understand their solutions and how they can best be applied today.

Two Very Different Stories

In 2016, the United States had an incredibly contentious election. Some saw it coming. Many others did not. Most people knew that the country was divided, but they had little perception of how deeply divided it really was. It all came to a head when Hillary Clinton became the nominee for the Democratic Party and Donald Trump became the nominee for the Republican Party. I will not get political here; that's not the point. But the election exposed groups of people with opposing interpretations of the world based on contrasting experiences, that's for certain. Each side became increasingly convinced that the other side was wrong, ignorant, dangerous, and would ruin the country if they gained power.

That's one thing. I'm not going to address that situation directly. But it was another thing when those same attitudes of enmity and varying worldviews suddenly clashed in our family of churches. You could look on Facebook on any given day and find disciples of Jesus arguing over history, politics, and power. The country, and some brothers and sisters, was dividing into two broad interpretations of history. Let's call them story 1 and story 2.

Story 1 in America starts with the arrival of the brave Pilgrims. They landed on a continent sparse in population because it had been ravaged in the previous century as members of the First Nations contracted diseases that were unwittingly brought across the ocean by explorers and traders. Those first arriving colonists made friendly contact with the people of the First Nations and received a great deal of help from them. They worked together and both groups survived. Before long, and as more settlers arrived, conflict ensued, as it usually does when groups of people come into contact with one another. The next 150 years are a mixed bag. Some land was taken by settlers, but much of it was purchased. There were many sad instances of conflict and war, but the more important part of the story is that progress marched on, and out of a virtual wilderness a new society was built.

By the mid-1770s the country had grown into thirteen established colonies. They eventually grew so strong that they declared their independence from Great Britain and forged their own nation. This nation was special. It was built on principles taken largely from the Bible and invested trust and freedom in the individual in a way never before seen in the world. The country was imperfect, but the founding documents were brilliant. They held out the promise of rights given to each person by their Creator, rights that cannot be denied or taken away. They offered the hope of progress that would one day be applied to all people. Many were uncomfortable with the subjugation of others, and while unable to bring that to an end in their day, they laid the foundation for it to one day be done away with.

Story 2 starts with the arrival of Columbus and other explorers in the late fifteenth century. They discovered nothing other than lands that were already populated by human beings. They unleashed a century of genocide and disease, albeit the disease was not intentional, on the people of this "new world" and had devastating impact upon it. As the hordes of European settlers came, they pushed hard against the First Nations living here. Sometimes they bought the land, but it was often taken through threat, force, or swindle. Treaties made were consistently broken. It wasn't a battle between groups of equal size or force. It was an invasion, and while both sides committed violence and even atrocity, the Europeans were far more powerful and eventually overwhelmed the First Nations.

As the country transitioned from colonies to a nation, they had to come to terms with the fact that the enslaving of other human beings was not only tolerated, but various states, and arguably the country as a whole, thrived economically on the backs of these enslaved people. There was a smattering of slaves from other races early on, but very quickly it was limited to Africans, and America joined in the brutal practice of the transatlantic slave trade with gusto.

Anything else that happened during this time, no matter how great and how successful the nation became, must, according to this story, be viewed in light of the fact that the First Nations were seen as savages and largely exterminated. Hitler cited America's treatment of these native peoples as one of his inspirations for his Final Solution. It must also be viewed in the light of slavery. Yes, they built a powerful nation, but it was at the expense of black men and women. Families were torn apart; people were dehumanized and raped regularly. In some instances, they were forced to breed, sometimes with members of their own family. Forensic anthropologists argue that they were worked so hard that it literally killed many slaves. When the country was founded upon the proposition that "all men are created equal," it included a compromise that would count slaves as only 3/5 of a human being for legislative representation and taxing purposes (though such a stance really stripped them of any equal recognition of humanity at all), with no right to vote or have a say in what would happen to them. The founders might have viewed all men as being created equal, but they evidently saw only those of one skin color qualifying as human beings.

Now, those are two very different stories, aren't they? Which one is true? Your answer will reveal a great deal about how you view the world. But here is the prickly reality: our churches are composed of people who sincerely believe that story 1 is the accurate version. They are also made up of people who sincerely believe that story 2 is the accurate version. I have no intention of trying to choose sides. That is not what is important for the body of Christ. I have to stop here and say again that right now we are only determining where we are at. We will save solutions and the biblical prescription for later. The reality is that both stories are true. They are two different interpretations and perspectives of the same, complex history.

We could pick sides and argue until the cows come home about which story is more accurate, but where would that get us in light of the kingdom of God? The point is not to get bogged down with the issue of who is right or wrong, but to recognize that these are the different world-shaping ways that brothers and sisters understand the history of our people. And we bring these stories and ways of viewing the world into the church. Rather than arguing and trying to prove the other side wrong, what if we tried to come together and see both views as true? Additionally, since none of this history is based on scriptural truth, it should not be the hill we choose to die on.

When it comes to my sons' views of their home state, both perspectives are true and based on experience. They have simply interpreted things differently and have chosen to emphasize some things more than others. Surely, we can understand that.

A New Side to the Story

Jesus entered a world that was deeply divided politically between those who supported the Roman occupation of Israel and those who wanted nothing more than to rid the land of them. In the final week of his life, Jesus walked into that minefield of conflicting opinions one day in the temple court. The Pharisees tried to trap him into taking one side or the other. Should Jews pay Rome's taxes? If he said "yes," the anti-Roman Jews would have a fit. If he said "no," the politically powerful Jews and Rome itself would have justification to take him down. There was no way out.

Or wasn't there? Rather than taking sides or getting involved in the world's squabbles, Jesus built on the grand biblical teaching about image. Human beings were made in God's image but had corrupted the ability to reflect this image when they embraced sin and did their own will rather than God's. Humanity had rejected the very purpose for which God made them and spiraled down into their own petty affairs and conflicts. "Whose image is this?" Jesus asked as he pointed to a coin with Caesar's own likeness imprinted on it (Matthew 22:20). If Caesar wants to think that gathering up money and exalting himself at the same time is the biggest concern, let him do it. It's not a controversy worth starting. But as for those in the crowd, as for us, give to God what is God's. What is God's? Is it the right interpretation of history and current events? Is it taking the right side historically or politically? Jesus' point was that Caesar had imprinted coins with his image; that's what was dear to him. But God had imprinted human beings with his image and he wants us back. He wants to restore his image in us. That should be the center of our attention. That's what matters.

We come into the church with widely different views of the world. That's to be expected. We may never convince one another that our perspective is the right one, that our story is the accurate interpretation of events. The way forward, I think, is for us to remain focused on what is important to God, namely the unity of his people. He wants to restore us to his image. When we get bogged down in matters of politics and history we can easily lose sight of that.

A Dark Time or a Shining Moment?

We will continue the two stories, then, not to try to convince one group or another that they have the right or wrong story, but simply to help us understand where each of us is coming from. The point is to understand why some current events hit some people hard and barely register on the scale of others. It is to understand the baggage that some visitors bring with them as they enter our community life. It is made in the hope that we can stop arguing and stop calling the others wrong, stupid, or worse. It is made so that we can understand the viewpoints of others and perhaps put them together with our own and come out with a deeper, fuller perspective. The lesson in the two stories is to strive to embrace the ethos that when one part suffers, the entire body of Christ suffers (1 Corinthians 12:26a). It is to help prepare us to accept one another (Romans 15:7) so that we can focus on what is truly vital for the world: for the people of God to reflect his image (2 Corinthians 3:18) to a world that is in darkness and desperately in need of some light.

Back to story 1. The time between the founding of the country and the Civil War was an incredible one. The nation was still finding its legs, but the genius of the founding documents was beginning to shine through. For the first time in history, government was of the people, for the people, and by the people rather than being for the rulers. The leaders belonged to the people rather than the people belonging to the leaders. The British were repelled from the country once and for all, and the nation expanded rapidly. Vast tracts of land were purchased from the French and secured from the native peoples, and the economy boomed, especially in the North where slavery was outlawed and manufacturing took hold. There was trouble on the horizon, though. The South continued to allow slavery and build their economy on it. This led to an overemphasis on states' rights and would eventually lead to war. Progress was made during this time, though, as the slave trade was outlawed and there were a growing number of free black men and women in the North.

Story 2 finds entirely different points of emphasis. The country grew, but often at the expense of the First Nations. Treaties were broken, atrocities committed, and the treatment of these people was increasingly brutal. Slavery intensified, and while the slave trade was ended, fugitive slave laws were passed, forcing runaway slaves to be returned to brutal conditions in the South. Manufacturing exploded in the North, but it was built largely on the cotton economy of the South, which was dependent upon slavery. Abolitionists increased in number and power, but they rarely argued for the equal treatment of black people as human beings; they mostly just wanted slavery eliminated. Some churches spoke out against slavery and inhumane treatment of other races, but most either stayed silent or endorsed these beliefs and practices.

As we return to story 1, the Civil War begins. It was a glorious example of the greatness of the United States. Hundreds of thousands of white people were willing to put their lives on the line for the elimination of slavery. It is a shining demonstration of the progress of our nation. It is never perfect, but the founding documents always leave room for more people to come fully under their protection and freedom. As society develops and evolves, the truths in the documents are realized more each day. Abraham Lincoln kept the country united, led the North to victory over the South, and ended slavery.

In story 2, the Civil War is the outcome of a country built on the original sin of enslaving, brutalizing, and mistreating people of color. The South fought an entire war to preserve their right to own other human beings. The North began the war as a means to keep the South in the Union, and only later turned to arguments of ending slavery when it became politically expedient. Lincoln may have wanted to end slavery, but the average Northerner didn't care all that much one way or the other.

Story 1 finds the period after the Civil War to be a celebration. Millions of people were freed at a great cost to the nation—but they were now free. They could enjoy the freedoms and opportunities that America provides. They could go anywhere and be anything they wanted. The country gradually transitioned from an agrarian nation to a nation of industry and manufacturing. The economy grew. Our power and influence increased around the world. The nation expanded West, and although the period of Reconstruction after the Civil War was largely a sad mess, the country made it through and began to thrive and allow its people to thrive too.

Story 2 gives importance to completely different elements. After the war, black Americans were given their freedom and the right to vote and enjoyed a brief period of respite. They were originally promised that the land of large plantation owners would be divided among them and each former slave would receive forty acres of land and a mule to work it. That promise was quickly dropped due to political pressure, and the moment of freedom was closed. A harsh program of terrorism ensued for blacks, primarily in the South. The KKK became one of the most powerful groups in American history. Most black people were denied the vote through a series of racist Jim Crow laws, and these became the order of the day as a deeply unfair system of segregation and inequity was set up.

Huge tracts of land were given away in the West, but almost exclusively to whites. The opportunity to obtain advanced education and college degrees was greatly expanded, but only for whites. The economy continued to expand, but the opportunities were nearly all limited to whites. The freedom that came after the Civil War quickly proved to be a sham. Blacks across the nation were discriminated against and lost more and more rights. In 1896, the Supreme Court, in Plessy v. Ferguson, upheld the doctrine of segregation to be legal and just.

The theory of evolution had come onto the scene shortly before the war ended and was used to justify a separate evolution of races. Centuries of bigotry and dehumanizing behavior now had the force of scientific argument behind them. Blacks, it was taught, were lower on the evolutionary scale. Debates took place in the scientific community as to whether people of color were closer to apes on the scale or to white human beings.

Slavery was over, but not the subjugation. Whites had full access to the opportunities provided by the growing economy, but blacks did not. They were largely stuck in the South with no political power, no opportunity to own property, little access to decent education, and little chance to participate in the so-called American dream. All the while, the growing perception in white society was that blacks were less capable, lazy, and of lesser intellect, so their continuing poverty was either their own fault or just a natural result of their lower genetic capability. As a result, the racialist attitudes of inferiority and criminality that developed to justify slavery have proven to be more long-lasting, insidious, and damaging than slavery itself.

The Turn of a New Century

By the turn of the century, says story 1, the country was really beginning to come into its own. Between 1900 and the 1950s the country encountered incredible turmoil. We made it through World War 1, the Roaring Twenties, and the Great Depression. The time of the Depression was a brutal challenge, but America survived, largely because of the fortitude of her citizens and the freedoms of the founding documents that enabled them to adapt to and ride out huge storms like this one.

As Hitler took power in Germany and threatened to take over the world with his allies, the United States tried to stay out of the war, but the attack on Pearl Harbor by Japan changed all of that. America could no longer stay on the sidelines. With the power of the US armed forces applied around the world, Nazism was defeated and the world was saved from a menacing attack.

Segregation was still a sad anomaly, but progress was made there too as Jackie Robinson broke the color line in professional baseball; and in 1954, the Supreme Court ruled, in Brown v. The Board of Education, that the system of segregation was inherently inequitable and had to go. Despite its challenges, the country continued to progress and strive toward the dream of all people being equal.

Story 2, of course, sees it differently. The system of oppression was arguably even worse than in the previous century. At least in the nineteenth century you could see it; although less obvious in the twentieth, the power of segregation continued to wreak havoc in access to home ownership, generational wealth, quality education, and personal liberty.

World War II was a mixed bag. Great good seemed to come from it for the world, but in the United States, Japanese people were imprisoned into camps based solely on their Japanese heritage, and black GIs suffered through segregated armed forces only to return to a homeland where they were still not afforded the full rights of a citizen. Education grants given to soldiers after the war were only partially effective, as most black soldiers, if they received grants, had to go primarily to underfunded black colleges, while their white counterparts thrived in the best universities and beyond.

Economic and social policies continued to punish black Americans. Home loans were systematically denied to people in lower income neighborhoods that were deemed "unsafe"; and red lines were drawn around these entire areas on industry maps to indicate zones that would not receive funds for home improvements or purchase of a home. The inner cities in major Northern metro areas were swelling with black Americans who were fleeing the blatant terrorism of the South. These economic policies put a virtual fence around the inner cities and kept African Americans locked into a cycle of poverty that had its roots in the time before the end of the Civil War. Whites moved out of the big cities in droves to the suburbs, and they took a massive amount of wealth and jobs with them. This meant further economic decline and lack of opportunity for a people who were denied the practical right to vote in large areas of the country.

The overall state of affairs for blacks and other ethnic groups continued to decline during the first half of the twentieth century. In the South, violence and lynchings became a horrific, but normal, way of life. Black people were cemented into a second-class citizenship around the country and could not use the same public facilities as whites, culminating in things like public places having restrooms for men, women, and coloreds.

Throughout history, the dominant group has always created a definition of oppression and racism that excludes their behavior and absolves them from any perceived wrongdoing. This time period was no different. In May 1946, nearly seven out of ten white Americans believed that "Negroes in the United States are being treated fairly."[5] Each generation likes to believe that progress is being made and that there is no real racial problem in the present, but we can look back and see that this was definitely inaccurate.

The Civil Rights Era and Beyond

Story 1 continues the march toward progress. The Civil Rights Movement led by Dr. Martin Luther King Jr. was inspiring, peaceful, and full of hope. It showed the greatness that can come as a result of the liberties afforded the citizens of the United States. We may, unfortunately, have to fight for them sometimes, but they will come if we persevere. In America people are judged, to paraphrase Dr. King, by the content of their character rather than the color of their skin.

While opportunities are always available for Americans to succeed no matter their race, this period is checkered with dark spots. Many ethnic groups have not grabbed hold of the American dream, discouraged in large part by destructive governmental policies that have allowed millions of babies to be aborted, have discouraged the strength of the family unit, and have not been hard enough on crime in areas besieged by it. America has had her flaws, no question, but this country is still the best country in the world. It is the most prosperous nation in all history. It is still the best place for anyone of any race to come and succeed. If you work hard enough, you can be whatever you want to be. Overall, America is a shining success story, and if people can't see that, they are just victims who don't want to earn their place and work hard for what is available.

But this ignores much, says story 2. Segregation and the Jim Crow legal system simply morphed into more subtle forms of racism and oppression in the latter half of the twentieth century. Many hold up Dr. King as a paragon of liberty and virtue today, but ignore the detail that he was considered vile vermin by most whites in the 1960s. He was denounced far and wide and fought against every step of the way, and not just by those in the Deep South. He eventually achieved progress but at great personal expense to him and his followers.

It took nearly one hundred years for black Americans to see the passage of the Civil Rights Act of 1964 and finally achieve legal equality in areas like voting and labor. But a new force was beginning to run roughshod through the black communities around the country.

These areas that were already the victims of poverty, poor and unequal education, and lack of opportunity also had drug problems. Statistically, drug use in the inner cities was about the same as in any other part of the country, with numerous studies confirming that blacks and whites used drugs at about the same rate. Yet there was a new emphasis on getting tough on crime and drugs, and this war on drugs went straight to the inner cities. It did not, curiously, go to white-dominated college campuses that had higher drug-use rates. Rather, it ripped through the central cities, skyrocketing imprisonment rates for black Americans and almost always making the communities worse off in many ways.

Since 1964, very little progress has been made, if any, in diminishing the gaps between blacks and whites in education rates, income rates, and incarceration rates. The effects of 250 years of slavery and another 100-plus years of racist realities such as Jim Crow, segregation, and individual bigotry have led to a huge gap in our society. The high school graduation rate for black males is 47 percent nationally, which is nearly 28 percentage points lower than for white males.[6] In Wisconsin, my home state, the gap between black and white graduation rates soars to 51%. According to a recent study by the Pew Research Center, the median household income for white families is $71,300, but it is $43,300 for black families. There is almost the same gap for households headed by black and white college graduates.[7] That same study shows that the wealth of the average white family is over $144,200, but it is just $11,200 for black families. Home ownership is 28 times higher among white families than black families, says the study. Racism may not be the only cause of this state of affairs, but it certainly must be one of the major factors.

Individual black Americans may have achieved certain levels of fame or success, but they are the exceptions; those things are not realistic goals for most. The country has its positive elements, but it is a country whose very foundations were the genocide and forced labor of people of color. These aren't events that happened 150 years ago and should now be forgotten. People never tell Jews they should forget the holocaust and move on, so why should they tell that to black people? The systems of racism continue to have negative ramifications for people of color, and those who refuse to recognize that are foolish and ignorant.

There is a further complication that I will only briefly mention. I have been speaking in very general terms of two ideologies, but there can be complexities within the two. After reading the section above, a couple of friends of mine, one white and one black, pointed out that there are multiple stories within both the typical black and white perspectives. Some black Americans embrace both stories to a degree and desire to get past the racial divide, integrating within the larger society as best they can, which is often very well. Others do not embrace the mold of white society and do not make much of an attempt to fit into it. They are often more confrontational and unafraid to make others feel uncomfortable with their thoughts and ideas. Still others are largely unaware of story 1 themselves or are unwilling to rock the boat, so they go to great lengths to keep their "blackness" hidden away, so to speak, in order not to make whites feel uncomfortable. There is also a spectrum of white Americans that range from just wanting to get past all the racial stuff and not deal with it, all the way to those that struggle with guilt for abuses of the past. So, while I do think the analogy of the two stories helps us in seeing the perspectives of one another, we must keep in mind that there are varying spectrums within the larger framework.

The Monopoly Game

To return to the two-stories concept, which story is accurate? Granted, they are gross oversimplifications, but they do capture the essence of what many people hold to be true. Some of my readers will gravitate to story 1 and think that it is obviously the closest to truth. Others will embrace story 2. But what if they are both largely true? What if instead of arguing about who is right and who is wrong, we listened to each other and respected the experiences and viewpoints of others as understandable given their experiences? What if we put these two realities together and came up with a new and fuller truth that gave respect to the experiences of both groups? As a Christian family, it is vital that we are able to do this.

The events that happened in history continue to have an impact today. They just do. Let me give an example that might help us understand the impact of the history of our country on our fellow citizens who are black, regardless of which story you have embraced as more true.

Imagine a scenario in which four people were set up to play a game of Monopoly for the first time in their lives. They sat in chairs numbered one through four. What they didn't know was that the game had been rigged. The person in the first chair began the game with all their money taken and distributed among the other three players. That means that the people in chairs 2, 3, and 4 would each start with $2,000 rather than the normal starting amount of $ 1,500. All players were then told that there would be one significant rule change. Each time a player passed Go they would receive the standard $200 only if they had a net worth of more than $1,800. With that in place the game began.

How do you think the game would go? Chances are good that the person in chair #1 would struggle. Not only would they not have any money to purchase property or pay bills, they would find it incredibly difficult to amass enough wealth to start receiving the benefits of passing

Go. If the same scenario were replayed a hundred times, there would likely be two or three times where a person in chair #1 broke through the stacked deck and managed to do well, but most times that would not be the case.

Now imagine that in the middle of the game, each player was replaced by a new player who would sit in their chair and take over for them. The new players would know the rule about passing Go but would be unaware that the starting money was taken from the player in chair #1. What would be their reaction? If you took over for chair #2 on four or five separate occasions, what would you think? Wouldn't you start to wonder what was wrong with the people who sat in chair #1? Why were they always so bad at this? Why were they so frustrated? You might even point out to the poor soul in chair #1 that you are all playing by the same rules, so they just need to work a little harder or get better at the game. And while from one perspective all the players are playing by the same rules, they really are not, are they?

There are several places in the New Testament where men who wish to proclaim the gospel begin with a history lesson of some kind. They want the audience to understand what has gone on in the past in the world in which they live so that they can properly understand how to absorb and apply the good news of the kingdom of God. Stephen does this when confronted by the Sanhedrin in Acts 7. Paul gives a quick synopsis of history and philosophy while standing before the people of the Areopagus in Acts 17, and Peter does something similar when addressing the crowds at Pentecost in Acts 2. This is something of what I have attempted to do here. If we understand our history, we can understand how we got to where we are today, how it continues to affect us, and how we can effectively move forward.

For some of our brothers and sisters, the history of our country, as well as the history of the church and of the world at large, is an often painful one. It has damaged their ancestors and left them feeling the effects of generations of sin and harm. That is true and undeniable. For others, they have never experienced that part of the world. It has been a pretty good place for their ancestors and for them. Hard work has always equaled success, and the sky is the limit. The problem comes in when either person denies the reality of the other. The first person is not weak, a complainer, or trying to be critical and divisive. But the second person is not a monster either. They might each be ignorant of the other's experiences and perspective. That's okay. What is not okay is to remain ignorant. It's not okay to deny the truth of the other and to call them names or proclaim that they are wrong and just plain idiots for thinking the way they do.

When we do open our ears and listen to one another while giving the benefit of the doubt to the other person's experiences and truth, we often find that it changes us. It's like sitting in a room with a temperature of 90 degrees. Meanwhile the room next to us is 50 degrees. Neither room is very comfortable, but if we open the door and let the air mix together we get a comfortable 70 degrees.

Our culture seems to be growing in its divisions and chasms. Everyone that agrees with me is right and the other side is not just wrong, they are crazy. They are lunatics. They are dangerous. They are bamboozled idiots who don't know what they are talking about. There is a growing intolerance for other points of view.

This two-story narrative tends to divide into two general categories of responsive strategies. One can be grouped together under the heading of personal responsibility. Both the causes and the solutions, according to this view, lie primarily in the realm of cultural factors. The struggles of a particular race or group of people have to do with their own responses to the conditions they have experienced, and they have the ability to pull themselves out of that situation. The other category can be summed up with the phrase "structural solutions." Those without power cannot change the structure without a meaningful response by the white community to remove the obstacles. These two sides then duke it out and accuse the other of being completely out of touch with reality. There is a great divide here, but what if there is merit to both arguments? What if we moved toward the position expressed by author Shelby Steele: "Blacks can have no real power without taking responsibility for their own educational and economic development. Whites can have no racial innocence without earning it by eradicating discrimination and helping the disadvantaged to develop."[8] When we listen to one another and put truths together, the result is much stronger.

Talking Past One Another

One of the major problems in our world right now is that often when people who are considered white and those who are considered people of color do talk to one another, not only do they have opposite perspectives, they also are using different meanings for the same language. The effect is that they wind up talking right past one another. Much talking takes place with little communication.

What I mean is this: When it comes to the topic of racism, most white people tend to use the word "racist" when they are actually thinking of prejudice and bigotry. They do not feel that they are prejudiced. They don't act in bigotry. They accept all people for who they are. So when they hear so much talk of racism in the world or in the country, they look around. They don't see anyone they know acting bigoted. Then what's all the fuss about? Maybe there are a few rogue people out there hanging onto their backward prejudice, but when it comes to the vast majority of people, that's just not true, right? We could debate, of course, about whether that is the case or not. It would help to remember, if you are white, that it's very possible that prejudice and bigotry happen a lot but you wouldn't see it because you're not the recipient of it or the perpetrator of it. But that doesn't change the fact that when the idea of racism is brought up, most whites think of these limited cases of prejudice and bigotry. Racism is largely a thing of the past in the minds of many. For them, people only continue to bring it up because they have a victim mentality and want special privileges for being the target of something that rarely happens anymore.

It's different for most black Americans. When the concept of racism is raised, they generally think in terms of the system of oppression and power that has been in place for hundreds of years. They think of the Monopoly game. They think about how the color of their skin matters every day for them, in little ways and in big ways. They think of hundreds of years of subjugation and denial of rights to those that have come before them. They think of how this stacked deck continues to affect most of them day in and day out. The ongoing effects of generational inequities in access to land ownership, gainful employment, education, and political clout, continue on and on, not to mention the continuing subtle effects of centuries of propaganda concerning the inferiority of races of color in relation to those of the white race. When they hear a white brother or sister say that there really is no racism today or that it's so limited that it shouldn't affect anyone, it really hurts. They think, "Are you out of your mind?" The idea that racism is not a major force in the world today is absolutely absurd in light of their experiences.

So both people are talking past one another. Although they are using the same language, they are talking about different things. If not corrected, this can lead the white person, who is rooted in their experiences and understanding, to dismiss the claims of the black person. They dig their feet in. "I just don't know anyone racist and I don't think it's a big problem. It's a media invention." The black person then digs their feet in. "Of course, there is racism. I feel it every day. Are you insane?" Before long the white person might begin to think that their brother or sister in the church is a whiner who is trying to create problems that aren't there, or has bought into the agenda of certain political groups or the media. The black person might begin to think that their white brother or sister is unloving, ignorant, reading the wrong websites and watching the wrong news channel, and maybe even a low-key bigot themselves.

If we keep in mind the imagery of the Monopoly game, though, some very important truths can come to the surface for both sides. The player who is seated in chair #1 is the person who had their money taken at the beginning of the game and has been dealing with the rules that restrict the receipt of money for passing Go to those with a certain level of wealth. For the other three, it's a very different game, but they haven't set up the rules. They didn't defraud anyone. It's even possible that if they never inquire about the other person's experience in passing Go, they might never know of the disparity that these "equal for everyone" rules have wrought. They are not personally cheating or harming anyone. That's their truth and that's all they know.

When player 1 complains or protests that the game is unfair, the other players could easily scoff and say that they are wrong, or are making it up, or are making excuses. But player 1 is feeling the effects of the oppression of the system of the game on every play, aren't they? While the others prosper under the rules that are "the same for everyone," they struggle. When they assert that they are mistreated and being cheated, the other players look at what is going on and think they are playing the victim. Yet these players are simply unaware of the truth of the other. And player 1 can also be unaware of the true experiences of the other three. Those three can be genuinely unaware of what has taken place or even that such a thing could take place. That puts the responsibility on players 2, 3, and 4 to put in the work to listen to player 1 and learn of their reality, and vice versa.

If players 2, 3, and 4 never do anything, the game is never going to change. They can never cheat once, and the game will still be rigged. This is the importance of genuine communication in which we respect one another's experiential truth and then remain open to learning about it and letting it influence our own. It demands that we ensure that we are speaking the same language and meaning the same things, and are not talking past one another.

Here is a truth that we must all consider and understand: if every single ounce of prejudice and bigotry were gone from the world, it would not mean that racism would be gone. When we are not personally prejudiced and think that is enough, it is like the players in the Monopoly game thinking that as long as they don't cheat, the game, which was slanted from the start, will then be fair. Because bigotry is an individual phenomenon, it can be dealt with and repented of quickly. But true racism is a long-standing, entrenched ideology that is unseen and not spoken of. You will never know it's there unless you experience it or intentionally go looking for it. And here is the kicker: because our culture tends to come into the church with us, racism can be entrenched in a church that doesn't have a shred of prejudice or bigotry in it. The effects of unequal schooling, of limited opportunity, of wealth disparities, of presumed leadership capacity, and of what is deemed "proper" cultural behavior, can worm their way into the body of Christ, with most disciples being completely unaware.

Until we all open our minds to one another's perceptions, we will be prone to believing a one-sided truth. Just because someone is unaware of racism, that does not make them a bigot. Just because someone protests the racism that they experience, that doesn't make them a crybaby, a troublemaker, or a race baiter. We must listen and learn, and when we do, we must let the truth of their experiences mingle with the truth of our experience to create a newer and more complete perception of reality.

It Doesn't Just Disappear

The effects of sin continue for generations; that's biblical truth (Exodus 20:5, 34:7). We can escape such things through the power of the gospel, but it is not an automatic process. The effects of racism wreak havoc in the lives of Americans, black, white, and other, every day. And for many African American families, memories and fears of the past don't fade quickly.

Memories of injury live on in families for ages. The book of Esther details Haman's ongoing plot to destroy the Jewish remnant during the reign of King Xerxes. In Esther 3:1, we are told that he was an Agagite. This seems to indicate that he was somehow a descendant of King Agag, who had been killed along with most of his people, as recorded in 1 Samuel 15, for their unrepentant rebellion against God. Approximately 500 years later, Haman had not forgotten and was still nursing his lust for revenge against Israel. The effects of sin continue for many generations.

The impact of mistreatment and oppression doesn't simply go away because those in power decide that everything is fine now. It takes much more than that. If, after three hours, those in the Monopoly game decided to do away with the restrictions on passing Go, that wouldn't address the considerable effects that would continue to be felt from the first three hours of play.

These things that stay in the memory banks of families often have a hand in how they interact with others, how much they trust people in authority, and their level of fear that conditions could one day go back to the worst of times.

In my wife's family, there is a strong memory of her great-uncle's fate when the family still lived in Mississippi. He left the house one day and never came back. He was later found cut into small pieces and had to be collected by the family and placed in a garbage bag; he was a victim of the Ku Klux Klan. Of course, no one saw anything, the local sheriff was apparently disinterested in finding the culprits, and justice was never served. That incident was seared into the family consciousness. My wife's great-grandfather was also murdered by members of the Klan. And although she comes from a gracious family that has intentionally attempted not to retain bitterness for this and many other incidents, the scars remain.

We must understand that things like this shape where our brothers and sisters are coming from, and it's easy to see and even understandable why they are so aware of and fearful of racism or prejudice becoming predominant in the church they love. Maybe we can even begin to understand why some communities have a hard time trusting authority figures like policemen. When it has been passed down from generation to generation that they are not a group that can be trusted, and there are some strong historical reasons to bolster that belief, we can at least begin to see why things are the way they are. That is not to justify sinful responses or violent behavior of any kind, or to take sides, but we can at least begin to see the perspective of others in an empathetic way.

This is where not demonizing one another, but rather listening to each other, getting on the same page, and putting our experiences together will benefit us all. Our black brothers and sisters, and other people of color as well, may very well have experienced the effects of racism in their life as a result of sin in the world. White brothers and sisters may very well be unaware of or unaffected by it. But these white brothers and sisters are often on the leading edge of dealing with feelings of prejudice and bigotry, in themselves and others, when they do become aware of them, even if they are largely ignorant of the silent but deadly racism that still exists in our society, and sometimes in our churches. Rather than mistrusting one another and creating enmity where it need not be, imagine the power of a united family of churches across the globe that didn't just worship together but dug deeply into difficult conversations with no preconceived notions about one another; a community of faith that didn't just enjoy a lack of bigotry but worked together to eradicate the virulent effects of sin and racism that affect so many of our brothers and sisters.

Let me be clear about what I'm not trying to accomplish. I have very definite views on the things above. I do believe there are truths in both worldviews presented. I do believe there are two broad sides, each of which marginalizes the accurate points of the other view. Historically speaking, I do feel that the second story has often been glossed over and forgotten far more than the truths of the first story. My personal belief is that racism and prejudice do exist and harm many people. Spending two decades being married to a black woman and raising black sons has made it incontrovertibly evident to me that I can do things in our society that they cannot. I get the benefit of the doubt more often than not, based largely on the color of my skin and my culture, while they typically do not. But I am not trying to convince you of that if you don't buy it. I'm not trying to move a disciple from one belief to the other. I'm not trying to move you from one political party to another (I will have more thoughts on politics in Chapter 8).

Some disciples are passionately on one side of the spectrum of beliefs when it comes to the topics of race and racism, while others are passionately on the other side. I do believe we need to listen to one another, but not just so that we can convince the other person that we are right and they are wrong. That is a rebuke. There may be times and places for that. But that's not the thrust of what I'm trying to do here. I don't believe this is a realistic strategy, and it's not the one that Paul employs, as we will see when we get to Section 3.

Questions for Discussion

1. Which of the two versions of US history is the one that you grew up understanding and embracing?

2. What did you learn about the different perspective of others from considering both versions of the story?

3. What are some of the ways that events in history continue to have an impact on your life today?

4. What did you learn from the analogy of the Monopoly game? Does that help change your perspective on people different from yourself?

5. Do you agree with the assertion that white people and black people typically tend to mean different things when speaking of racial issues? If so, what impact do those differences have?

Chapter 3

The Chaos Creature

Through the years, I have had the opportunity to give a few courses on the techniques and science behind teaching and preaching. One thing that I always highlight in those classes is the idea that any lesson or sermon should be able to be summarized in one sentence. If you can't do that, then the lesson is probably not very good, or at least it tries to cover too much. So I like to have students practice writing one sentence that encapsulates the whole. It certainly helps to keep the lessons focused and centered on the most important thing. But it serves another purpose. It allows the speaker to see the finished product. They know where they are going with their speech, and that means that everything they say throughout their oratory will work toward that end goal. For each sermon or lesson, it's like giving the audience the picture on the puzzle box as they put the puzzle together. It makes everything they are doing a whole lot easier.

This principle is true in most walks of life. Do you want children who grow up to be sacrificial, loving, and serving disciples? Then keep your eye on that goal every minute while you're raising them. Richard Williams, father of Venus and Sabrina, knew from the time that they were born that his endgame was to make them tennis champions. He pushed them—hard. Everything he did during their formative years was aimed at that target, and they reached it. His daughters are now two of the greatest tennis players of all time. We can't protect and shelter our kids, shielding them constantly from hurts, hardship, and sacrifice, and then stand surprised when they balk at sacrificial discipleship as they move into their teen years. The future must determine the present.

God's Plan and the Serpent

The New Testament reveals that God's endgame all along was to reveal himself to the world through Jesus Christ. He would one day have a Christ-shaped family. Everything in history, every part of it, was working toward God having a people that entered into the life of the Messiah, his

Son. To put it into one sentence would look like this: "For those God fore-knew he also predestined to be conformed to the image of his Son, that he might be the firstborn among many brothers and sisters." If that sentence looks familiar, I didn't write it. It's Romans 8:29.

God had a plan for humanity. He didn't just create them to see where his experiment would wind up. He had an objective in mind. In this chap-ter, we will consider the endgame and the problems that humanity has caused that work in opposition to it, but we will not yet start to dig into the solutions that God has in store; that will come later.

The early chapters of Genesis are all about God bringing order and design out of chaos, creating a temple in which he can dwell with his peo-ple. He creates a human being and puts him in the center of that creation as his steward and ambassador. This man is the creature that will bear the vocation of representing God's will and purposes into the rest of creation.

But the man needs something more. In the middle of his account of God's good creation, the author cites one thing that is not good: man is alone. We tend to claim that all an individual needs is their relationship with God, but the text says something else. God is a community in and of himself, and he wanted the man to see that he needed community too. He needed a woman with whom he could create community.

Into the bliss of that community comes a creature of chaos, the ser-pent. We aren't told where he came from or how he got there, but he gets right to the work of chaos by sowing division. He starts with planting the seed of disunion between God and his human creations.

By chapter 4, the chaos and division has spread. One son kills another. Once humanity threw off God's will and rule and replaced it with their own, the result was and has continued to be separation and disunity. The next seven chapters tell that sad story.

Even a worldwide flood of cleansing and new beginning doesn't rid humanity of the disease of disunity. We must not miss that this tendency toward division is not part of God's intent for humanity. It is one of the insidious results of sin. Humans exalt their own will over that of God's and put their own interests first. We become addicted to this. We put ourselves and our group over and against others, and division happens.

After the flood, a scene is described in Genesis 11 in which humans try to unite against God's will once again. In the chaos of the fallen world, the only thing worse than division is when humans try to unite on their own, because they will inevitably disunite and rebel against God. The whole world, we are told, had "one language and a common speech," but when humans have rejected God's will and lordship, the inevitable end is division. And in this case, their attempts at unity erupt into full-blown division against God.

In response, God temporarily works against his ultimate plan for humanity by confusing their speech and shattering humanity into an untold number of languages which eventually would result in numerous tribes and cultures.

God's Puzzle Box

What is God's puzzle box, his final goal for his creation? Throughout the pages of the Bible we see hints, glimpses, and snapshots of it, but it all comes together in one vivid image in Revelation:

> *After this I looked, and there before me was a great multitude that no one could count, from every nation, tribe, people and language, standing before the throne and before the Lamb. They were wearing white robes and were holding palm branches in their hands.* Revelation 7:9

The mirror that was shattered into a thousand pieces has been put back together in a glorious celebration before the Lamb. God's people are composed of humanity that comprises every nation, every tribe, every people group, every language. To fully cover today what was being communicated then, we might add the concepts of every race, every ethnicity, and every culture.

I was running along the cliffs of Hermanus, South Africa one morning with a good friend. As we made our way down the winding path that overlooked the Atlantic Ocean, we were watching for whales. It was a bit tricky because our attention constantly had to dart back and forth between the uneven path before us and the majestic view of the ocean to our right. But our persistence was rewarded. Every so often a whale would break the surface of the water and we would get to see one of the most amazing parts of creation. Throughout our time on that path, the whales continued to crash through the glassy surface and into our vision.

Just as those whales made regular appearances, followed by a period of silence, so the idea of all the nations coming to worship God as part of his people is a theme that continues to resurface throughout the Old Testament and into the New.

After the separation into the nations described in Genesis 11, God comes to Abraham and his descendants throughout the rest of Genesis and promises that all the nations will be blessed through Abraham. Since the problem of the nations is their sin and the resulting division, we can only assume that the ultimate blessing will deal with those twin problems. All the nations will be blessed because of this promise that God gave to Abraham and renewed with his descendants (Genesis 12:1–3, 18:18, 22:15–18, 26:4–5, 28:14). Near the close of Genesis, while Abraham's grandson passes along a blessing to his son, Judah, he says that the scepter will not depart from Judah "until he to whom it belongs shall come and the obedience of the nations shall be his" (Genesis 49:10).

During the time of the sojourn in Egypt and the ensuing Exodus, God's purposes became a bit obscured, but even then, he wanted Pharaoh reminded by his ambassador Moses that he had raised up Egypt's leader so that God might show Pharaoh his power and that his "name might be proclaimed in all the earth" (Exodus 9:16). When Israel sunk into disobedience during their time in the wilderness and God threatened to Moses that he would dispossess them, Moses pleaded with the Almighty, making the case that "if You slay this people…, then the nations who have heard of Your fame will say, 'Because [Yahweh] could not bring this people into the land which He promised them by oath, therefore He slaughtered them in the wilderness'" (Numbers 14:15–16 NASB). God relents and affirms that indeed, the whole earth will one day be filled with the glory of the Lord (Numbers 14:21).

Under the reign of David, God's plan to bless the nations resurfaces once again clearly and brilliantly. It is not just for Israel that God acted, but to bring blessing and declare his glory among all the nations (Psalm 9:11, 22:27–28, 86:9; 1 Chronicles 16:8, 22–33). At the dedication of the temple, David's son Solomon reiterated God's goal that one day "all the peoples of the earth" would know God (1 Kings 8:41–43).

The Psalms, many of which came from the time of David, championed the goal of the salvation of the nations; for example, Psalms 22:27, 45:17, 67:1–4, 72:11–17, 86:9, 96:2–10, and 105:1.

The prophets continued to trumpet the theme of God restoring the nations to himself. "In the last days," says Isaiah, and goes on to foretell of a time when God's kingdom would be established as "chief among the mountains." He goes on to say that "all nations will stream to it," and then describes those nations transforming their weapons of war and division into instruments of peace and cooperation (Isaiah 2:2–4 NIV 1984). Isaiah later cites the vocation of God's servant people to be "a light to the nations" (Isaiah 42:6–7 NASB). It is God's goal, says Isaiah, that all the nations will turn to him and be saved and come before him with every knee bowed and every tongue acknowledging him (Isaiah 45:22–24). His obedient servant will, says God through Isaiah, "be a light for the Gentiles" to bring his salvation "to the ends of the earth" (Isaiah 49:6; see also Isaiah 52:10, 14–15, 56:6–7).

The prophet Daniel had a vision in which he saw one like a son of man "coming with the clouds of heaven." He is given the authority, glory and power of the Ancient of Days, to reign over "all nations and peoples of every language" (Daniel 7:13–14) in the everlasting kingdom (Daniel 7:27).

The book of Jonah highlights God's desire that his rule and salvation would spread to all nations, not just Israel. Through his Messiah, says Micah, the greatness of God will "reach to the ends of the earth." (Micah 5:4–5). Habakkuk declares that the earth will be filled with the knowledge of the glory of the Lord (Habakkuk 2:14), and Zechariah speaks of a time when many nations will be joined to the Lord and become his people (Zechariah 2:11), and the Lord will be the king over the whole earth (Zechariah 14:9, 16). Malachi says that God's name will "be great among the nations, from where the sun rises to where it sets" (Malachi 1:11).

God loved the nation of Israel and set her apart for a special purpose, but he never lost sight of the fact that he was working toward reconciliation with all the nations. He was unrelentingly passionate about piecing back together what was shattered at Babel. God made humanity to be a unified one, and sin had insidiously divided us. But God has never given up. Throughout history he has been intentional in bringing about a family of all peoples.

That's the challenge when it comes to being a unified family of all nations, cultures, races, and peoples. It's not easy. It takes a great deal of effort, because time, history, and a lot of research have shown that if left to our own devices, humans will tend to congregate with those with whom they have the most in common with and feel the most comfortable.

All Nations, Undivided

I was at a weeklong teen camp with my son recently, serving as a counselor. It was an incredibly well-run camp that filled the kids up with spiritual teaching and fun memories that will no doubt last a lifetime. Most of these kids have grown up in our family of churches, so being around a diverse group of disciples is normal for them. Even still, as the week went on and they got more comfortable and a little bit crazy, their personalities and their cultural comfort zones started to appear. What appeared was subtle at first and then became increasingly obvious with each mealtime. The students were sectioning off by race. It wasn't a conscious decision, and it certainly wasn't malicious. It just happened as they began to express themselves musically, do one another's hair, and engage their sense of humor. Groups formed.

To the credit of the camp directors and counselors, they quickly saw what was happening and quietly addressed it with some of the students, who took lightning-quick measures to remedy the situation. It turns out that they were unaware of it and were eager to ensure that things like that didn't happen in the future.

Situations such as that are not rare, even in a church that finds its identity in being multicultural and integrated racially. In our world of division, being a family of all nations and people groups is to swim upstream. It will be an arduous journey that can never be taken for granted. The minute we do that is the minute we will start to lose what God has fought so hard to give us.

Jesus never lost sight of God's dream to have a family of all nations. "But wait," you might ask, "didn't Jesus himself say that he was sent only to the lost sheep of Israel?" It's true, he did (Matthew 15:24). When he sent out the twelve on their inaugural mission journey, he even told them to only go to the lost sheep of Israel (Matthew 10:5–6). When Jesus used language like this, he was not rejecting God's plan for the world, he was beginning it. Israel was God's lost sheep (Jeremiah 50:6) and he was the Messiah Shepherd who would gather the wayward lambs (Ezekiel 34:11–12; Micah 5:4–5). When Jesus spoke of being the shepherd to the lost sheep, he was fulfilling messianic prophecy. Israel's role was to be a light to the nations to draw them to the Lord. Jesus had to fix the light before it could shine, so his first mission was to gather faithful disciples who would, in him, be restored to the vocation of the true Israel. Once gathered, it would be their job to be a light to the Gentiles and bring them into the family.

Only it took them awhile to grasp that fully. Right before Jesus would publicly and spectacularly ascend to the throne in heaven, he gathered his disciples around him and gave them a clear directive.

> *Then Jesus came to them and said, "All authority in heaven and on earth has been given to me. Therefore go and make disciples of all nations, baptizing them in the name of the Father and of the Son and of the Holy Spirit, and teaching them to obey everything I have commanded you. And surely I am with you always, to the very end of the age."* Matthew 28:18–20

When Jesus spoke of bringing all nations into a state of discipleship, he wasn't thinking of "nations" in terms of the sociopolitical entities that we have today, as though our job is to get the gospel to the 196 nations currently identified in the world at present and then we're done. The phrase that Jesus used referred to more what we would call people groups or ethnicities. If we gravitate to an idea like people groups, then experts estimate that there are somewhere in the range of 13,000 to 24,000 around the world. Look at your own church and then your surrounding community. Even if you're in a church that is ethnically diverse, it is unlikely that you have yet brought the gospel to every people group in your own community. We still have a job to do to live up to Jesus' vision for his people.

Jesus was resolute: his community of disciples must include people of every nation. This is at the center of the gospel. As we have seen, this was always the plan and Jesus knew it well. The divisions of the present age due to sin had to be done away with. A church that is not constantly and passionately striving for diversity and to bring people of every tribe, language, people, and nation into their community is not a church that is reflecting and embodying the full gospel.

Although it was made plain that God's family that was being created around his Messiah would be of all people groups, I'm sure you've noticed that the disciples didn't seem so quick to carry out those orders. It took them years, apparently, before they took Jesus' commission seriously and start preaching the gospel to the nations, right? Were they slow to understand? That wouldn't be entirely out of character. Were they rebellious? That doesn't seem to match the evidence. Were they unmotivated? Again, that doesn't seem to be the case.

For the first disciples, Jesus' call to preach the good news to all the nations didn't come out of nowhere. They were well aware of the above promises that somehow God's people would one day include and be a blessing for people to the ends of the earth. The key likely comes at what has come to be known as the Day of Pentecost. There in Jerusalem were "God-fearing Jews from every nation under heaven" (Acts 2:5), writes Luke, who then goes on to list a sample of nations from all across the vast Roman Empire and the known world. Surely, they must have been blown away by how faithful God was to his promises. Here were Jews from many nations. This is how God would fulfill his promises. Surely this is how Jesus would see his dream fulfilled to make disciples of all nations.

They weren't rebellious or unmotivated; they just weren't thinking broadly enough. They were looking at things from a human point of view and not God's. They understood that Jesus' people were to be one people, one family. So it made sense that they would consist only of Jews. In fact, they probably marveled at how God had spread Jews around the world just so his word could be fulfilled. God's revolution had begun.

But God had much bigger plans, as Acts goes on to carefully document. In Acts 2 the gospel is preached to Jews of all nations, but that is just the start, not the fulfillment of God's plan. The next several chapters document how God's family spreads to include all peoples. In chapter 8, the word of God is preached to the Samaritans. That would have been a hard pill to swallow for Jewish Christians who despised the Samaritans. So just as the Spirit had come upon the people in a special and miraculous way to show that God was finally creating his family and fulfilling his promises, the Spirit came on the Samaritans. The Holy Spirit made it visibly apparent that, yes, the Samaritans, who were ethnically only half Jewish, were part of God's plan too. The Spirit had uniquely been poured out at Pentecost to open the doors to the family, and now he uniquely poured out his visible blessing outside of the Jewish people. The revolution was gaining momentum.

In Acts 10 and 11 God goes even further. Can salvation come to the household of Cornelius, a Gentile? This is a bridge too far. Even the Jewish Christians who may have had to begrudgingly accept the Samaritan Christians would not be able to fathom welcoming the unclean Gentiles into God's family. So the Spirit does something radical and supremely unique. Just as he would occasionally come upon unrighteous people in the Old Testament, he comes upon these Gentiles and gives the visible verification that God's Spirit was accepting them into the family of Christ. The timing was impeccable. Just as Peter was vaguely mentioning that the prophets testified to everything that was going on (Acts 10:43), the Spirit poured out on them. What had just happened was not lost on the circumcised believers. This was exactly as the prophet Joel had predicted (Joel 2:28). The Gentiles were in. This left no room for argument. It didn't mean that they were saved at that precise moment; it meant that the door had been opened to them just as it had been to the Jews and Samaritans. God had spoken and there was nothing left to do except baptize them into Christ. The revolution was in full swing. It is important to note that this miraculous and limited coming "on" of the Spirit is different from the universal act of the Spirit coming "within" God's people at baptism (Acts 2:38).

God's promises to restore all the nations and bring them into his kingdom had begun. It's not a nice side dish to have a diverse church in the body of Christ. It is a central part of the good news. God has reversed the division and devastation of the Garden rebellion and the Babel debacle. In Christ, we are one people, one family, one kingdom. But the story doesn't end there. That was just the beginning of the hard work and struggle for this church family that was now unlimited in its boundaries and borders.

Challenging the Chaos Creature

In the same way, creating churches that are diverse, consisting of peoples from a variety of nations, ethnicities, cultures, and economic backgrounds, will be just the beginning. Starting a diverse community is, as the early church found out, the easy part. Keeping that unity in a fallen world was their biggest challenge, and it will be ours as well. Fighting the chaos creature has never been easy.

I do believe that we need to have productive and very deep conversations on the topics of race, history, and our wide-ranging perspectives, but with the goal to understand one another, not to try to convince each other. I'm not sure we could even do that. I think the idea that we can educate the other side and all come to the same way of viewing things one day is a monolithic dream that is rooted in worldly philosophy. We have different experiences as a result of division in the world, so our perspectives will differ. The way forward is to embrace an entirely new and unexpected solution to the problem of division: God's solution.

Before we really begin to delve into God's solution for the division that the chaos creature has caused, in the next chapter we will look at the solutions that the world has to offer.

Questions for Discussion

1. Why is it important for God's people to always keep before us that we are to be a family of every tribe, language, and nation?

2. In what ways do you see the sin of division active in the world today?

3. Do you see racial divisions present in big or little ways in your church right now or in the past?

4. Do you live in an area that is predominantly one race or work somewhere that is somewhat racially segregated in practice, or do you live and work in areas that are primarily multiethnic? How does this affect you and your outlook on life?

5. Keeping unity in a fallen world can be our biggest challenge as God's people. What do you think are the biggest threats to unity in your church right now?

Chapter 4

Dual Wisdom

"What is the primary goal of any institution of higher learning?" His question was a good one and sent a roomful of eighth graders into a tizzy of murmuring and squirming in their chairs to come up with the right answer so that they could be the first to raise their hand and give the correct response. I was wondering myself what the answer might be and thought I had a pretty good notion. I was sitting next to my son as one of the chaperones on his school's field trip to the biggest university in the state of Minnesota. My son gave our answer, "To create opportunities for their students," but it was wrong, at least according to the recruiter and host for the day. After several more wrong answers, it became apparent that no one was going to offer up what he was looking for, so he laid it on us. "The goal of any university," he declared, "is to teach their students to solve problems." I was impressed with the answer. You could make a case for others, but it's a pretty good response.

Then he gave them a handout about solving problems. Just below the title was this little piece of wisdom: "Trust your instincts. Trust what you feel. Trust your heart. It will never betray you." I was with him until I saw that. "Really?" I muttered under my breath. "That sounds more like a recipe for disaster."

Although that may sound like good advice to some, I would take issue with it for the most part. There is a time, I suppose, to trust your instincts and go with what you feel, but that can get you into a whole lot of trouble. Thinking like this tends to cause more problems than it's worth. Apply that logic to selecting someone to marry. Carry that nugget of wisdom with you into your marriage, and it holds until your heart is drawn to another person. Ponder the depth of its insight as you struggle with forgiving someone who is not deserving of being forgiven. It's worldly wisdom. A heart apart from the Holy Spirit is selfish, whimsical, untrustworthy, deceitful, and yes, wicked (Jeremiah 17:9; Genesis 6:5). The plain and simple fact is that the wisdom of the world doesn't fix many situations at all. It might mitigate or manage a problem, but rarely does it truly fix anything.

Two Paths

Studies estimate that the number of Americans who experience occasional to frequent stress and anxiety tops the eighty percent mark. One of the most common responses to typical anxiety is alcohol. When the grip of anxiety tightens, many people have a drink or two to loosen the hold. They think that it will dull their stress and relax them, but instead it makes it worse as it reduces the mind's ability to cope with the stress. Others turn to coffee and think that helps, but coffee deepens the feelings of stress and can worsen panic attacks. Still others that suffer with hyperventilation try to breathe in slowly and deeply, but that also makes the situation worse, it has been discovered. Experts in the field, however, say that people's most common response to anxiety and depression is to "mope," that is, to go and be alone so that they can sit and think and work through it. Rather than sitting it out, the experts recommend being around friends, engaging in activity and exercise, and trying new things. What this all means is that quite often what we feel like doing not only doesn't work, it makes the situation worse.

Even more extreme and effective methods like therapy and medication can sometimes work, but often they just mask the problem. There are plenty of difficulties that human ingenuity and knowledge can solve or improve. We have made unbelievable progress in many areas of life through the course of human history. But when it comes to the big things, things that have to do with human desires, decisions, and morality, we just can't seem to get a handle on those. Oh sure, we think we have the answers. Our world is more than ready to offer up its wisdom in all kinds of areas, but it never seems to be effective. The way the world solves problems tends to resemble someone squeezing a partially inflated balloon. When you squeeze the air out of one area of the balloon it just bulges into another part. You will never get rid of the air by squeezing; you just wind up shifting the air from one side of the balloon to the other.

This is not to get into an argument and say that there aren't times when professional therapists or doctors are necessary because the Bible has all the answers. Sometimes we do need trained professionals to help implement biblical thinking, but wisdom that is not rooted in biblical truth or that sets itself up against biblical truth is likely to fail in the long run.

When we talk of topics like anxiety and worry, consider the wisdom of Jesus as it pertains to the everyday stresses of life (this is different from areas of mental illness that go by similar names, such as clinical depression or anxiety orders). Jesus doesn't offer stress-reducing activities or breathing techniques. Those might help manage symptoms, but they don't deal with the problem.

From a worldly perspective, Jesus' solution seems quite foolish. He simply says don't worry about your life; don't worry about your daily provisions like clothes and food. But before we begin to think that it's not all that helpful to just tell someone not to worry, we realize that Jesus is showing them the result, not the solution. They don't have to worry about those things—it is possible to get there. How? By recognizing who your father is. He says the pagans have to worry about the gods punishing them and being angry, or not providing for them. It was believed that the gods were capricious and moody and one never knew whether they would provide. In reality, there are no other gods and the people were just fending for themselves and rightfully worrying about it. But knowing God as Father is to know him as the provider. He promises that he will provide our basic needs if we submit to his rule in our lives and keep that as our highest priority. That's it. Put our minds on the Father and not our so-called problems, and trust him. The degree to which we do that is the degree to which our anxiety and worry will dissipate.

Who would have seen that coming? We overcome the worries of life by simply looking at the character and promises of God through Jesus Christ and knowing that he will provide exactly what we need—not want, but need. That's it? And yet, that is by far the most effective solution for worry and anxiety that could be found anywhere. It's worked for me. I'm sure it has for many of you.

I'm not saying that there is no worthwhile knowledge, wisdom, or truth in the world. There are nuggets here and there. But when it comes to the big problems in society, the world seems at an absolute loss to offer up lasting solutions.

Poverty has been around as long as human society. Some countries have found ways to be relatively wealthy while others remain mired in impoverished conditions. But even in the wealthiest societies, there are always many who are poor. It's not always true, either, that nations have tried to do away with poverty. Some have accepted it as a way of life or assumed that the people stuck in it are there because of nature or through some fault of their own. They are poor because they are somehow lesser or less deserving. Other nations have tried to eliminate poverty within their borders. They have all failed. Some have reduced it or helped alleviate the situation, but not one society has eliminated poverty, ever.

Worldly Wisdom Applied

In 1964, the President of the United States, Lyndon B. Johnson, declared a war on poverty. The richest nation in the history of the world was going to take head-on the problem of lack within its boundaries and drastically reduce, if not outright eliminate, poverty. That sounded good, and many Americans were behind it. There seemed to be no reason that the most prosperous country in the world could not figure out a solution to this crisis once it put its collective mind to it.

Since Johnson's plan was rolled out, America has spent $22 trillion on the war on poverty. When adjusted for inflation, economists argue that this is more money than the United States has spent on the combined cost of all its military conflicts and wars since the American Revolution. With that much money spent, there is little doubt that poverty would be dealt a death blow, right? I'm sure that if we could travel back to 1964 and ask someone what they think will happen to poverty if $22 trillion is spent to eliminate it, they would be certain that it would be banished from the country.

Sadly, that's not the case. Virtually the same number of Americans are listed as poor today as in 1964. By practically every metric, the war on poverty has not worked. It was a good effort, but it has been a dismal failure at achieving results. Some may argue that it has kept things from getting worse, and that may be true, but that's hardly an effective result. Others will argue that other methods would have achieved better results, but that remains untested.

In 1971, President Richard Nixon declared a war on drugs. Since that time, the United Nations decided to join in and declare a worldwide offensive against drug proliferation. Once again, we would have to assume that the richest and most powerful country in the world would be able to make a huge dent in that terrible problem, especially when most of the other nations have vowed to join in their efforts.

But again, where we would expect to find success, we find only abject failure. Drugs are actually cheaper now than twenty years ago and are of higher quality.[9] Drug activity, drug cartels, and drug usage are all bigger problems now than they were when the war on drugs began. It seemed like the answer, but it has proven to be another dismal failure. Now many are beginning to question whether governments should even make drugs illegal and continue to fight against their import and infiltration.

Some countries may have been able to regulate drug use and limit trafficking, but no country has been able to figure out how to keep people from using harmful and destructive substances. In some places drug use is viewed as criminal behavior and fiercely opposed. In other places drugs are seen as a health issue and dealt with as such. Those places statistically seem to have better success overall, but they too have been unable to wipe out substance abuse.

Violence is another great example of the ineffectiveness of worldly wisdom. No country, society, or government in the world has been able to eradicate violence among their people. It just has never happened. Some societies are more violent than others or have higher crime rates; some have done a better job than others in curbing crime and violence; but the world simply does not have the answer. According the United Nations, nearly 500,000 people are victims of violent homicide each year, and that does not include deaths caused by wars between nations.

That's stunning, when we take a minute to dwell on it. Nearly half a million people die each year at the hands of another human being. While the numbers have changed over time as a result of growing populations around the world, the incidence of murder has likely been fairly steady throughout human history. The first tangible and recorded act of murder goes back to not long after the power of sin was first released into the world (Genesis 4:8).

It almost doesn't matter what major societal problem we look at, the kingdoms and systems of the world do not seem to have an answer, whether it is poverty, substance abuse, violence, or any other large issue. This is especially true when it comes to the problem of division among humans. Look into any epoch of history and any corner of the globe, and you will find no answers to the division caused by sin. Once Adam and Eve were separated from God, division burst into the human experience and has been with us ever since, despite humanity's best efforts to solve it. It has taken many forms, including division among individuals, tribes, nations, ethnicities, and most recently race. And although in this book we have focused on the racial issues between blacks and whites, there have been conflicts between countless other races and ethnicities. Every person, every tribe, every nation, every ethnic group, and every race is marred by sin. It is sin that is the problem; and the world simply cannot find an answer to sin.

These problems of poverty, substance abuse, crime, violence, and the like are universal to the human experience, but they manifest themselves in unique ways in each society, time, and place. When it comes to our country, the issues are enormous, and many of them seem to be getting worse. It is not my purpose here to examine what has caused these specific problems in our nation. We'll let the experts argue about that. Nor is it my purpose to find solutions to these issues outside of the kingdom of God. In fact, that's the whole point. I am convinced that worldly wisdom simply will not suffice. As stated previously, once the problem is pushed down in one area, it simply bulges up again in another. A solution is proposed and implemented but often creates equal or worse problems somewhere else. One political party gains power and puts their solutions into place that may have some effect on the problems they are focusing on, but they create a new set of problems. Then the other party comes into power and they go after fixing what the previous group did, but create a whole new series of failings. It's a never-ending cycle.

I'm not saying that Christians should not be aware of these issues and even active in dealing with them; but it does, I believe, become a real problem when we lose sight of the fact that the world is not going to solve these things. They never have been able to, so why would we think that will change?

Let's go back to the issue of race as one of the leading causes of division in our world today. It has an ugly and complex history and causes deep societal problems that threaten the stability of our country. Whether we agree on the causes or not, there are huge gaps between blacks and whites in the United States and in many other countries when it comes to economic stability, education level, incarceration rates, and numerous other areas. Those differences are real. The tension and animosity that sometimes occur between collective racial groups is also real, although there are many exceptions. Race is a major issue in our world, no matter how we slice it.

When I was in grade school, a big movement began around the idea of diversity. We were going to celebrate our differences and bring all the people groups together. To do so, we would learn of each other's history and culture and grow to appreciate others in new and exciting ways. We were told that this would end racism and separation in our lifetimes. So, did it work? I have yet to find a poll or any statistic that shows any marked improvement in these areas. The great movement of celebrating diversity seemed like a wonderful idea. It seemed like a no-brainer that would surely have positive effects. Yet it did not and will not, because it does not get to the root of the problem. Since we are still dealing with laying the foundation of understanding where we are at in our world and society today, and are not yet at the point where we start to look at answers from the Bible, we will avoid the temptation to move toward specific biblical perspectives and direction. Rather, we will spend the remainder of this chapter considering the folly of trusting in worldly wisdom and solutions and the effectiveness of embracing godly wisdom.

The Differences Between Two Wisdoms

When confronted with the clash between cultures, ethnicities, and races, we are posed a challenge, because Christians want solutions to these issues just like everyone else. We all seek wisdom to deal with these monumental difficulties. And the Bible seems to confirm that impulse. "Blessed are those," say the Scriptures, "who find wisdom, those who gain understanding" (Proverbs 3:13). The verses that follow (3:14–18) go on to describe wisdom as being more profitable than silver, a better investment than gold, more precious than rubies, more desirable than anything else in the world, leading her pupils to pleasant and peaceful places, and bringing blessing to all who take hold of her. Likewise, Ephesians 5:15–17 says to "be very careful, then, how you live—not as unwise but as wise, making the most of every opportunity, because the days are evil."

"Therefore," continues Paul, "do not be foolish, but understand what the Lord's will is." So, shouldn't we seek after wisdom and try to solve the deep and dividing issues of the world? We find a very important directive in the book of James that helps us to answer that question:

> *Who is wise and understanding among you? Let them show it by their good life, by deeds done in the humility that comes from wisdom. But if you harbor bitter envy and selfish ambition in your hearts, do not boast about it or deny the truth. Such "wisdom" does not come down from heaven but is earthly, unspiritual, demonic. For where you have envy and selfish ambition, there you find disorder and every evil practice.*
>
> *But the wisdom that comes from heaven is first of all pure; then peace-loving, considerate, submissive, full of mercy and good fruit, impartial and sincere.* James 3:13–17

This confirms for us that there is more than one kind of wisdom. Not all wisdom is cut from the same cloth. There are at least five important differences between godly wisdom and worldly wisdom.

First, they have a sharp contrast in their source. Earthly wisdom comes from man. Human knowledge is its origin and also its limitation. It seems good by the world's standards, but by God's standards it is absolute foolishness (1 Corinthians 1:20). Worldly wisdom typically appeals to our senses in that it feels right, but that hardly makes it right. Earthly wisdom often finds its source in satanic thinking (1 Timothy 4:1) even though it often seems good, logical, and helpful (see 2 Corinthians 11:14). Heavenly wisdom, on the other hand, comes from God (James 1:17), so it can always be trusted. When it is diligently applied, it will bear fruit.

Second, they have contrasting impact. Worldly wisdom fails to solve the real problems, or it creates more. This is on display in the life of Abraham. God had promised him an heir, but Abraham did not see how that could be since he and his wife were very old. So he and Sarah hatched a plan for him to impregnate her servant girl. It seemed like it made sense, but it caused more problems for them and future generations than we can ever quantify. God's wisdom, though, always bears the kind of fruit that lasts and that matters.

Third, they have contrasting compositions. Since godly wisdom comes from God, it is unique in that we will never find contrasting opinions or wisdom sources with heavenly wisdom, because God is one. One of the main complications of earthly wisdom, however, is that it comes in many shapes and sizes because it comes from more sources than we could count. Thus, one person accepts one source of worldly wisdom and becomes convinced that all others are wrong, stupid, ignorant, and misinformed, while at the same time, someone else embraces a different source and becomes equally convinced that the problem is the other people and their ignorant beliefs. Because there are many sources of worldly wisdom, by its very nature it divides humanity.

Fourth, they have contrasting natures. At the heart of worldly wisdom are envy and selfishness. Humans almost can't help it. We are mired in activities that help ourselves or one group but often hurt others, whether by intention or accident. This unspiritual knowledge and wisdom often revolve around power, position, prestige, and privilege. Heavenly wisdom is focused on God's will and brings counterintuitive and unexpected solutions. It will usually seek to bring true peace (Romans 12:18). It is gentle (2 Timothy 2:24–25). It is willing to accept the beliefs of others in matters of opinion (Romans 14:1) and personal liberty (Romans 14:19–21). It is quick to forgive and to show mercy (James 2:13). It shows no unfair favoritism or partiality (James 2:1–13). Godly wisdom is free of hypocrisy and will call its adherents to no longer live for themselves (2 Corinthians 5:15) but to be willing to sacrifice and lay down their lives for others (Philippians 2:1–5).

Lastly, they have contrasting fruit. James says that earthly wisdom causes disorder and encourages evil practices. Remember, that evil doesn't always *look* evil in the eyes of humanity. Processed sugar is one of the sweetest, most enjoyable, most addicting substances known to man, but from the body's perspective, it is pretty close to pure evil. The world's wisdom often seems good and looks like it is doing good, but if it is not rooted in God's word, it very likely will end up harming more than helping. One example will suffice here. Shortly after World War II, most of the world's nations got together and agreed to carve out some land in the historic area of Palestine to give as a homeland for Jews who had been horrifically persecuted during the war. I am not taking sides on this issue here, but simply pointing out that many thought this was a good and helpful solution at the time. Yet it has done nothing but cause conflict ever since. Heavenly wisdom produces purity, peace, and consideration. It is submissive to God's will, full of mercy, impartial, and sincere.

You might argue that while worldly solutions often fail and have their limitations, so does godly wisdom. The church is imperfect; Christians fall short all the time. Although this is true, there is a big difference in the reasons for failure. Worldly wisdom will always fall short, even when applied perfectly. The failures with godly wisdom occur when it is not fully adhered to or implemented. When it is, it will succeed every time.

The Unexpected

We need to keep in mind that God's solutions are not only better; they are usually unexpected and unusual. Who would have thought of a family to solve the problem of sin? Who would have expected a worldwide flood? Who would have ever seen a human like Jesus coming? In 1 Corinthians 2:7–10, Paul illuminates the truth that if the powers of darkness had understood what God was doing through Jesus, they would never have sent him to the cross. God's wisdom was unforeseen and unexpected.

You want to talk about unexpected? In Revelation 19, John describes a vision of a great battle where the beast and all the kings of the earth are amassed against the armies of heaven led by a figure that we know to be Jesus. He is wearing many crowns, and his robe is dipped in blood. Over the years there has been a tremendous amount of ink spilled on this passage and this great and final war between Jesus and the armies of the earth. Many commentators and readers miss the intentionally symbolic nature of the book of Revelation. Because of this, they often spectacularly miss the significance of this vision. The armies amass against the King of kings, but there is never a physical battle. He is a lion, but he is also the Lamb that was slain. The blood is his own, not that of his enemies. And how does he defeat the army that is bearing down on him? With the sharp sword of God's word that comes from his mouth. He defeats his enemies with his own self-sacrificial blood and the word of God. Who would have seen that coming? Who would have anticipated that as a solution? Self-sacrifice and God's word to win an epic battle? God's wisdom is truly amazing.

Here is the conclusion of the matter: When worldly wisdom is applied, it very often produces conflict somewhere else or creates new problems. When God's wisdom is applied, it may come into conflict with the evil of earthly wisdom, but if followed, it will produce peace and righteousness.

Here is what this means for us when it comes to topics like culture and race: We are the people of God. We cannot be swayed by worldly wisdom. We cannot become so convinced of one ideology or political mindset that we can no longer distinguish between earthly and heavenly wisdom.

This is a constant temptation. I have fallen prey to it at times myself. Worldly wisdom often seeps into our thinking and then without realizing it, we marry it to biblical thinking and come up with a hybrid that is no longer valid. Haggai learned through direct revelation about this. When something that is earthly and defiled comes into contact and is mixed with consecrated or holy things, the holy thing is defiled rather than the defiled thing becoming holy. As the gravity of that lesson sunk in for Haggai, the Lord told him, "So it is with...people" (Haggai 2:14).

Worldly wisdom is not consistent. It comes in many types and flavors, so by its very existence, it creates sides and divisions. As we will examine in sections 2 and 3 of this book, the kingdom gospel is transcendent. Its wisdom is unique; there can only be one. There is room for variety within that oneness, but it can never divide. Heavenly wisdom is the only thing that can call us out of the present human condition and truly make real and lasting changes in the world.

I will not even take the time here to examine some of the popular ideologies and prescriptions in our world today. In the end, I believe they will fail. They will come to nothing. As I have said repeatedly, even if they somehow solve one problem, they will create another. Quite frankly, when it comes to the big problems in life, I am uninterested in political solutions, community activism, and the like. If the solutions don't emanate from God's rule and his kingdom, they are doomed to failure. I wholeheartedly believe that. My hope is that you do too. Before we begin to move into what I see as God's vision, his wisdom, and his solution for his people and the world, I believe we need to look at the role of race and ethnicity throughout the Bible. This will help orient us correctly as we move forward in this discussion.

Questions for Discussion

1. Have you ever fallen prey to trusting in worldly wisdom of a specific type?

2. Give an example of worldly wisdom that you have heard applied to problems of race and ethnicity in America.

3. Have you or any of your relatives been effected negatively by worldly solutions to the problems discussed in this chapter, such as poverty, substance abuse, or crime?

4. Can you think of any examples where you have seen worldly wisdom and biblical wisdom fused together and accepted by Christians as true and wise?

5. What are some steps we can take to ensure that we are keeping a proper perspective on worldly wisdom and trusting in godly wisdom?

Chapter 5

Jesus and Phinehas

Do me a favor. Read the next sentence and do what it says after you have read it. Close your eyes and while they are closed, get a mental picture of Jesus in your mind.

Okay, you can open your eyes. Perhaps I should have encouraged you to read the next two sentences instead of just one. Hopefully you opened your eyes and are back to reading this. What did you picture? What did Jesus look like to you?

Does it matter what Jesus actually looked like? Yes and no. Scripture never gives a detailed physical description of him. Those who knew him seem largely uninterested in such things. The closest the writers of the gospels ever come is when they describe the transfiguration, and even then, the focus is on his heavenly transformation rather than what he looked like bodily. There is a physical description of sorts in Revelation (1:14–16), but Revelation is a deeply symbolic book, so any portrayal found there probably needs to be examined for its symbolic meaning more than for an historical one. Isaiah prophesies about the Messiah to come, saying that "he had no beauty or majesty to attract us to him, nothing in his appearance that we should desire him" (Isaiah 53:2). Some have pointed to this passage to assert that Jesus was homely. But the point here is probably more that he wasn't special or majestic in any way. Nonetheless, it doesn't get into any specific physical descriptions. In the end, Isaiah's point is likely that he just looked like a normal person. Plus, standards of physical beauty change dramatically over time, so it wouldn't mean all that much to us today if Isaiah was trying to communicate that he was ugly.

If Scripture seems unconcerned with Jesus' physical appearance, should we care? No, in the sense that Jesus is transcendent and came for all people. Anyone who is willing to enter the life of Christ is welcomed into his body and his family (Galatians 3:26–29). Jesus obviously was a Hebrew, but exactly what he looked like and what color his skin was shouldn't matter.

Did You See a White Jesus?

But things are not that simple, are they? Because of what human beings have done in the two thousand years between Jesus' life on earth and where we stand today, what he looked like does have to matter. Here's why: When I asked above what Jesus looked like, what did you picture? Let me be more direct and to the point. Was he white, with blond or light brown hair, tall and thin? Chances are good that he was.

The church I grew up attending had several pictures of Jesus hanging throughout the building. In one picture, a warm and jovial Jesus sat as children piled onto his lap, mesmerized by his words. In another, Jesus braved the rugged landscape of the wilderness carrying a lost sheep that he had found. Perhaps the pièce de résistance was a reprint of the famous painting, the Head of Christ, created by artist Warner Sallman in 1940. Since its creation, this painting has become the iconic image of Jesus in modern times. The one thing that the pictures all had in common was that Jesus was decidedly white. He had long hair, thin features, and very fair skin; and based on those pictures and every movie I had ever seen about Jesus, he was also stunningly handsome. This was par for the course. In addition to pictures and movies, every Christmas card, every picture of Jesus in Bibles, virtually everywhere I looked, I saw a white Jesus. This was pervasive in the Western world in which I grew up. So much so that once, in my early twenties, I walked into someone's house who had a picture of Jesus depicted as more of what appeared to be a black man, and I was deeply offended and irritated that they would change the race of Jesus just to make him seem more like them. Of course, I knew even then that Jesus was Hebraic, but somehow it never clicked with me that first-century Jewish people were hardly what we would call white. It never occurred to me that *my* image of Jesus was created to look more like me!

I don't believe that, in the case of my experiences, those around me were intentionally foisting a whitewashing of the gospel to deliberately prop up a white supremacist version of the Christian story, but it was very "caucasianized" just the same, mostly by inaction than by anything else. Every Bible story book I read depicted almost exclusively white characters. Noah was a kind, elderly white gentleman with a long beard. David was a handsome white lad. Jesus and the apostles were always white. That was my perception growing up. To this day, when I visualize a scene from Jesus' life in my mind, something very much like Sallman's Jesus pops into my head for a second, and I have to be very intentional about seeing something else, something more accurate.

He Definitely Wasn't White

Forensic anthropologists, archaeologists, and historians all agree that as a Middle Eastern Jew of the first century, Jesus almost assuredly had medium to dark brown skin. And given all the walking around and work that he did outside, he was probably quite suntanned as well. The earliest depictions of Jesus in art show this historical truth, as they display a more classically styled Asiatic man of dark brown complexion. That was consistent until the sixth century, when Byzantine artists first depicted Jesus as a man with white skin, a long beard, and hair parted down the middle. While it was erroneous at this point, it wasn't harmful, at least not yet. But over time, this light-skinned Jesus replaced the more historically accurate version and became the standard for depictions of the Messiah. People tend to naturally depict others as looking more like themselves, but it was inaccurate and they surely must have known that this was not what a first-century Jewish man would have looked like.

If we fast-forward a thousand years or more, we find Western Europe in the throes of colonialism and expansion. A close second to the economic motivations for colonialism was the missionary zeal that often followed, to call the darker-skinned "heathens" around the world into submission to Christ (I do not mean to imply that missionaries haven't also done countless good things around the world). Everywhere they took this variety of Christianity mixed with colonial dominance, they sold a version of the white Jesus. Christianity was often misused to prop up slavery and justify its horrors and the abuses of colonial conquest; and the purveyors of this syncretized version of Christianity and power seemed to go out of their way to make sure that everyone understood that Jesus was white.

Seventeenth-century America was one exception. In these early days of America, white Jesus wasn't a major factor. The Puritans rejected the practice of having any physical depictions of Jesus. They even rejected the "Publius Lentulus letter" which had grown quite popular by the seventeenth century. This letter was a well-known forgery created sometime in the fourteenth century as an attempt to look like a first-century description of Christ. It described him as having hair the color of a "ripe hazel-nut," parted in the middle and flowing and wavy once it got past his shoulders. It is a description that any supermodel would be proud of. It goes on to describe Jesus with smooth white skin of a slightly ruddy complexion, and a well-manicured beard. For hundreds of years the letter was known to be a fake, but over time it was accepted as authentic, most likely because it reinforced popular stereotypes.[10]

White Jesus as a Weapon

As the Puritan influence in the country waned, the image of white Jesus took hold powerfully. It helped slave owners justify their cruel treatment of others as they carefully explained that Jesus was a white man and that other races were the result of a curse. The doctrine of the curse of Ham was the standard biblical teaching in the West for hundreds of years. In short, this teaching asserts that Ham was the son of Noah who violated his trust and sinned against his father, who then struck back at him by cursing him and his descendants forever with dark skin, the sign of the curse, along with the status of being slaves to the descendants of Ham's other brothers. This was not some goofy aberration that could be found only in the Deep South. It was accepted as biblical fact in most of Christianity for centuries. Blacks were slaves because they were the descendants of Ham. They should, they were told, accept that and be grateful that whites were sharing the gospel with them at all and giving them the chance to be forgiven and accepted as Christians.

White Jesus helped to make this lie possible and assisted many people to accept it without reservation. The reality of the Genesis 9 account of Noah and Ham is quite different, however. Noah did not curse Ham; he cursed Ham's son Canaan. The text never makes it clear why, but one possibility is that the way Ham's actions are described was a euphemism for sexual sin (compare the original Hebraic phrasing of Genesis 9:23 to Leviticus 18:7 and 20:11). The curse against Canaan, then, would not be a case of him being punished for Ham's sin. Rather it seems to be a prophetic curse against Ham's descendants who will be like him in his sexual sin. Whatever was going on here, it seems certain that it was referring to the Canaanites and has nothing to do with black Africa. There is no indication that the curse is dark skin, and in fact, this narrative has nothing to do with race in any way. Simply put, the curse-of-Ham ideology is absurd textually, but it did its damage for hundreds of years.

The white Jesus myth was often intentionally used to justify treatment of nonwhite people and convince them that they were a lesser grade of human being. The mythology of white superiority was built up and strengthened immeasurably by the intentionally false depictions of Jesus.

As a Jew, Jesus was an ethnic minority in the Roman Empire. Jews were marginalized by Romans, Greeks, and other non-Jewish groups in many imperial cities. As an infant, Jesus was a target of ruler-sanctioned infanticide, fled to Egypt as a refugee, and faced Roman tax collectors' exploitation. Throughout his life, he knew the pain of being a member of an ethnic group whose culture, religion, and experiences were marginalized by those in power.[11]

In other words, the real Jesus was everything that this white Jesus being peddled across the globe was not. Jesus did not have power; he did not subjugate others. He was part of an oppressed ethnic minority. He knew what it meant to be cast off into the margins by the powerful elite.

Just imagine how differently history might have gone if the lie of the white Jesus wasn't accepted or spread. How much more difficult would it have been to justify slavery and colonialism if Jesus had been honestly depicted to darker-skinned people as he really was, a dark-skinned man? Perhaps it would have been impossible.

We can never know for certain the specifics of what Jesus looked like, but based on the genetics, culture, and lifestyle in first-century Palestine, we can be fairly certain that Jesus was a bit on the shorter side, stocky and perhaps a bit muscular, with dark brown skin and hair. From this perspective, then, what Jesus looks like does count. Because so much abuse and oppression happened using white Jesus as a weapon and tool, it matters.

It is odd that last year when a new *Star Wars* movie came out with a black man in one of the starring roles, there was a great deal of outcry, debate, and controversy surrounding it. Imagine the storm that would hit if a new Hollywood blockbuster came out about George Washington and starring Don Cheadle as Washington. Yet most Christians don't even stop to think twice about white Jesus. Because of sin and abuse, it does matter that we strive for and demand authentic depictions of Jesus.

Jesus' color doesn't have a bearing on our salvation, but it does have to do with the mission. Think of a biblical topic like the name of God. Does it matter what name we choose to use when addressing God, whether it be Father, God, Jehovah, or Yahweh? No, not normally. But what if we are studying the Bible with someone who has spent the last six months studying with Jehovah's Witnesses? That topic has almost certainly been misused to beat them down and hurt them spiritually. They will have been told that their worship and prayers are invalid and offensive to God unless they address him by his proper name, which they are told is "Jehovah." But Jehovah was never the covenant name of God. That name is derived through faulty translating work. The true covenant name for God as recorded in the Hebrew Bible is YHWH. But does it matter? It does, because the concept has been misconstrued to hurt someone. We need to correct a wrong, and so it does matter that we not concretize this false teaching and use the term "Jehovah" in this case where doing so could hurt or confuse someone.

Is a Perception Change Important?

As we will see in Chapter 7, God calls us to be a cross-cultural family of all nations. There should be no such divisions as race in the world, but there are for now. We cannot fully change that in the present age. But we can recognize that a false version of Jesus was created and used to subjugate people for hundreds of years. It was misused to prop up a myth that one race was superior to the others. The image of Jesus became a weapon. If you were honestly unaware of all that (and you may well have been), you are no longer.

Are we willing to see the image of white Jesus as something that has been used as a destructive tool and has hurt many people? Are we willing to return to the transcendent Jesus by returning to a more faithful image? That might sound counterintuitive, but because the image of white Jesus has been so seared into our collective consciousness, it is naïve and ineffective to simply say that it doesn't matter or that we just won't use an image of white Jesus anymore. To counteract the damage done to God's message of salvation for all people, we must, I believe, deconstruct the white Jesus image. We need to actively teach about this abuse and show people what the real Jesus would probably have looked like. We should never, of course, worship images of Jesus, and in that respect, what he looked like is irrelevant. But it is important that we teach truth and correct the mistakes of the past, which makes it important for us to affirm and embrace a dark-skinned Jesus.

The problem with religion, and specifically large numbers of Christian groups, using or misusing the concept of race is not just something of the distant past. Within the last year, I was on a two-hour plane ride from Lusaka, Zambia to Johannesburg, South Africa. I was traveling with my wife and a couple that has become some of our very best friends. The three of them are all African American. Due to a small hiccup with our tickets, I wound up sitting two rows back from my wife, and one row back and across the aisle from our friends. Not only that, but I received the dreaded middle seat of three, a position I normally avoid like the plague. In the window seat was a rather large man in his early fifties that I could tell immediately was Afrikaner.[12] I happened to be reading a book about the history of race and culture in the United States. I didn't know it, but he was also reading my book. After a few pages, he turned to me and asked if I knew what the Bible had to say about this.

This was right up my alley, so I was all ears. He then proceeded to tell me that all the major characters in the Bible, including Adam, Abraham, Moses, David, Jesus, and Paul, were white, and that the idea that they were people of color is nothing more than propaganda. He then explained to me that the biggest sin in the Bible, one that spans from Genesis to Revelation, is the sin of mixing the races. He spent nearly thirty minutes explaining to me the details of his doctrines. I listened, spellbound by the inaccuracy and yet complexity of his ideas. I wish that I could say that I have never heard theology like this before, but sadly I have, both in Africa and the United States. After patiently listening to his theories, I respectfully went through the Bible with him from cover to cover and tried to show him where he was wrong. I made my points and then easily refuted his objections. Eventually we got to several points that he had no answer for. After staring blankly for several seconds, I think he realized that he had gotten more than perhaps he bargained for when he started the conversation. He turned back to me and said, "I'm in construction." That was the end of our biblical conversation.

While this man's theology is not entirely unheard of, those of his ilk are far outnumbered by those who don't spend much time thinking about the race of people in the Bible. While I understand the instinct that some people will have to see this as a nonissue, I believe that because there has been such a misconception and resultant abuse about the presence or importance of people of color in the past, there is great value in understanding what the Bible does teach.

The Bible in Color

Did black Africans, for instance, play a role in the Bible at all? It might surprise you to know that there are over fifty references in the Hebrew text of the Old Testament to Cush or Cushite. "Cushite" was the term used in the ancient world to refer to black Africans. The sheer number of references is an indicator that the Cushites played a significant role in the biblical narrative.

The popular perception given today is that whites played a major part in biblical history while black Africans played little to none. In addition, little consideration is given to other ethnicities and people of color. Moses is portrayed in a movie by Charlton Heston, Noah by Russel Crowe, Jesus by Jim Caviezel, and very few see a problem with that. But because these things have been used to reinforce often negative racial stereotypes, they do matter.

While the ethnic world of the Old Testament was somewhat fluid, and hard lines of demarcation were not made the way they often are today, we can make some general statements about the primary groups described in the pages of the Law, the Prophets, and the Writings.

The Israelites, Canaanites, and other people groups from the era were likely a complex mixture of ethnicities that saw the differences between people groups more along the lines of language and religion than skin color. But the fact is that they would tend to share the skin color and characteristics of modern Arabs. Biblical scholar J. Daniel Hays writes that "it is important to attempt a description of the average Old Testament Israelite. For Anglo-European Christian readers, it is critical to come to grips with the fact that these people were not blue-eyed, blond-haired Caucasians."[13]

There is a bit of confusion when studying the Cushites of biblical times because there were different terms used by different groups to describe the same culture of black Africans who lived primarily south of Egypt in what is now Sudan. These include "Cushite," "Nubian," and "Ethiopian" (which is not related to modern-day Ethiopians). The Hebrew Bible primarily uses "Cush," but English translations occasionally substitute "Ethiopian." The NIV renders references to the people and place as Cushite and Cush, respectively, except it inexplicably uses "Ethiopian" in Jeremiah 13:23, and until the 2011 version it used "Nubians" in Daniel 11:43.

The ethnic makeup of ancient Egyptians is a topic of hot debate in the world, but the most likely scenario is that they were primarily a fluid mix between Asiatic and black African peoples, leaving them with a range between medium and dark brown skin. Hays writes that "although the details are uncertain, it does appear that the Egyptians emerged out of an indigenous group that contained both African and Asiatic elements, and benefited from the unique environmental situation of the Nile Valley."[14]

The last major people group that we find regularly playing a role in the Old Testament narratives are the Indo-European groups such as Philistines and Hittites. Concerning this group, Hays writes:

> Thus, if today's readers of the Bible want to find people of 'Caucasian' appearance in the Old Testament, the Indo-European Philistines and Hittites are probably the closest. However, even the individuals from these ancient Indo-European groups probably resembled the people of modern Greece or Turkey more than they may have resembled the people of modern England or midwestern America.[15]

It is important that today's Christians, particularly those that happen to be of white descent, recognize, celebrate, and emphasize the multiracial and ethnic background and diversity of the Old Testament. "White North American Christianity," Hays contends, "has a strong historical tendency to be ethnocentric, and part of this distortion is to project Caucasian people back into all aspects of the biblical story. Coming to grips with the multi-ethnic, non-Caucasian cultural context of the Old Testament is a critical foundational step in developing a truly biblical theology of race."[16]

When we delve into the biblical narrative, we do not find any mention of divisions like ethnicity and race before Genesis 10. This is likely due to there being a constant environment of intermixing, and therefore no racial distinctiveness had yet developed. Modern genetics strongly indicate that in tracing characteristics back to this time, it is genetically implausible that Adam and Eve and the others of this pre-flood world had anything other than medium to darker brown skin. From the starting point of darker skin, genetics can account for all of the racial mutations and variations, but if we start from white skin, then it would be virtually impossible to produce the dark brown and black skin tones.[17]

Some have argued that Genesis 10 splits the world into three distinct racial groups with the Semites descending from Shem, black Africans from Ham, and the remaining groups descending from Japheth. This is based on shaky theology. The reality is that Genesis 10 does not have racial identity in view, but rather is describing the geopolitical divisions and separation that would later lead to ethnic isolation and uniqueness.

The Theological People of God

When we fast-forward to the account of Moses and the Exodus, some interesting details begin to emerge. As the descendants of Abraham were leaving Egypt, the author of Exodus tells us that "many other people" (Exodus 12:38) went with them. An analysis of this term indicates that it carries ethnic connotations, and further examination of the Egyptian histories from the time indicates that it is quite probable that a large portion of these "many other people" were Cushites.[18] The significance of this is that a good portion of Israel became Israelites because of their obedience to God rather than strictly by ethnic means. Entrance into Israel was theological more than biological.

Adding credence to this view is the reality that Moses married a Cushite woman. Numbers 12 is unclear as to where Moses' other wife Zipporah was by this time, but it may have been in between the time that Moses sent her away and before Jethro brought her back. But as Moses marries a black African woman, Miriam and Aaron protest. It is easy for us to read our preconceptions into passages like these and assume that they were upset because she was a lowly black woman. It is far more likely to be the case that it was just the opposite. Apparently, Aaron and Miriam had not yet fully wrestled with the addition of so "many other people," including a good number of Africans. But the Cushites were respected in the ancient world and well known as noble warriors. The Hebrews were the slaves. This woman may have been enslaved as well, but if there was a racial bias it would have been much more likely that they thought Moses was marrying "up" rather than "down." The stronger possibility is that Miriam was expecting Moses to follow the Egyptian conventions of the day and to marry her, making her his "queen," but this marriage derailed that and enraged Miriam and her brother.

There are biblical passages such as Deuteronomy 7:1–4 which forbid intermarrying, but this is usually in reference to Canaanites, and is always theological rather than biological.

The facts that "many other people" left Egypt with Israel and that Moses married an African woman were likely to be seen by the author as partial fulfillments of God's promise to Abraham to be a blessing to all peoples of the earth (Genesis 12:3). God punishing Miriam with leprosy is a clear indicator that he approved of Moses' marriage and strongly suggests that he approves of interracial marriages that are theologically united.[19]

It appears that Moses was not the only member of his family to take part in an interracial marriage with the new black Israelites. Moses' brother Aaron had a grandson named Phinehas. His name is an Egyptian one and literally means "the Cushite" or "the Nubian." If we were putting that in today's vernacular, his name would mean "the Negro," or "the black African." This was a name used in this Egyptian era which referred to Africans and not just a vague indication of darker or slightly darker skin.[20] It would have been a common cultural phenomenon for other members of Moses' family to marry other members of the family of his Cushite wife. It is very possible that Phinehas' mother was Cushite. While that specific part of the picture is speculation, what is not speculative is that Phinehas was most likely a black man of Cushite descent.

This man is held up as one of the most righteous in Israel. He is the one with whom God made an eternal covenant (Numbers 25:11–12). Imagine if the translators of the KJV had understood this and rightly translated Numbers 25:11–12 to read that God was making an everlasting covenant of peace with "the Negro." That would have sunk a lot of proslavery Scripture twisting right there.

So the Israel that emerged from the Exodus generation was a melting pot of skin colors and ethnicities. It is important to understand that this wonderful mixture of people and ethnicity was Israel, the people of God. At all levels, Israel was an ethnic mixture of people groups, with the one exception seeming to be Caucasian. This is not said to minimize or demean people of Caucasian descent, but to help explain the reality of the biblical world and the true place of all people in that world.

Some Bible readers over the years have noticed that both Esau and David are described in the Bible as being white with ruddy complexions and red hair. That is incorrect. The term used to describe them both comes from the Hebrew word 'admoniy, which finds its roots in the word 'adom. Both of these terms mean "red." It is then assumed that this must refer to faces that blush or turn red; an indication, it is said, that they were white. This is certainly what my Afrikaner friend on the plane asserted. But that's not what "red" meant in Hebrew. The term can describe a "red" horse (Zechariah 1:8) or a "red" heifer (Numbers 19:2). The way that we would describe that color animal today is dark brownish-red. So the terms for Esau and David indicate not that they were white people who occasionally blushed and turned "red," but that they had noticeably brownish skin, possibly indicating that they were a bit darker than their siblings.[21]

We won't go into it here other than just to mention it in passing, but a good case can be made for the idea that the Queen of Sheba, who famously came to visit King Solomon, was a Cushite.

The Time of the Prophets

There are many other periods of Cushite influence in the biblical narrative, including the one during the reign of King Hezekiah when Egypt was ruled by Cushite Pharaohs. But we will skip ahead to the time of the prophets of Israel. Isaiah points to a time when the people of all nations, including Cush, will finally submit to God's rule (Isaiah 45:14) and say that "in the Lord alone are deliverance and strength" Isaiah 45:24). Isaiah speaks frequently about the people of all nations coming to salvation at the time of the Messiah, and the people of Cush are specifically mentioned as being among them.

Amos picks up a similar theme. He writes, "Are not you Israelites the same to me as the Cushites?" (Amos 9:7). Most commentators of the twentieth century showed their bias by assuming that this passage was meant to humiliate Israel by showing them that God thought no more of them than to compare them to a "far-distant, uncivilized, and despised black race."[22] Another commentator unfoundedly claims that the only thing that could be said of the Cushites is that they "were a distant, different folk whom the Israelites knew mostly as slaves."[23] Hays counters this, correctly noting that "there is absolutely no evidence anywhere in the Ancient Near East that the Cushites' reputation was associated with slavery."[24]

What this passage actually seems to be saying is that God cares for the Cushites as much as he does for Israel. Amos 9:12 refers to "all the nations that bear my name." Surely those nations include the Cushites, since one of the psalmists fondly declares that one day Cush will acknowledge the Lord and submit herself to him (Psalms 68:31, 87:4).

The Cushites were particularly active in the Near East, including in Israel in the eighth century BC. It makes sense, then, that the prophet Zephaniah is said to be the son of Cushi (Zephaniah 1:1). This was not an uncommon name during this time, and strongly indicates a very specific connection with Cush, quite possibly that Zephaniah's father was Cushite, although that cannot be concluded definitively.[25] Zephaniah confirms that when the peoples of the earth begin to "call on the name of the Lord," the people from Cush and beyond will be among those worshippers (Zephaniah 3:9–10).

In the book of Jeremiah, the Cushite Ebed-Melech, who was quite possibly a high-ranking military officer living in and representing Egypt,[26] plays a major role in showing solidarity with Jeremiah and faith in Yahweh as he confronts the king and saves the prophet's life. While the nation of Israel abandoned and persecuted Jeremiah, special attention is given to the Cushite who saved him.

The New Testament in Color

By the time we move into the world of the New Testament, Alexander the Great and his world conquest had changed much. The ethnic world in and around Israel had become even more diverse. Added to the mix are those that we describe as Greco-Roman. One difficulty in analyzing this group, though, is that they are not really a single ethnic group. Being Greco-Roman had more to do with education and culture than birth. Differences in skin color were noticed but not emphasized in the first-century world. The Greco-Romans split the world into two broad categories: the Greeks and the barbarians, with barbarian referring to anyone who did not speak Greek or Latin and who did not embrace the Greco-Roman culture.

Ethnic mixing was widespread in Greco-Roman society. Trade routes flourished under the Roman Empire, which greatly increased interaction among ethnic groups. In addition, Roman soldiers commonly received their citizenship after twenty-five years of service and were encouraged to retire in the land where they served, which was generally outside of their native region. This contributed to an increased mixing of people groups. The Roman Empire was also bustling with slaves, most of whom were

Gauls and Celts who came from the Western European areas of modern-day Germany and Britain. These slaves were not isolated but were absorbed into the ethnic mix that was the Roman Empire.

By the time of Jesus, Jews were spread around the empire, with estimates that two-thirds of the Jews in the New Testament world lived outside of Israel and that perhaps as much as seven percent of the city of Rome's population was Jewish.[27]

Cushites continued to have a major presence in the Roman Empire, as did an influx of Northern Africans, including the people groups that the Egyptians referred to as the Libyans, but who are called Berbers today.

Although the ethnic situation in the Roman world of the first century was complex and mixed, it is during this time that those who would be considered Caucasian or white truly enter into the biblical narrative for the first time, primarily as Romans, although even to say that is a bit tenuous because of the true melting pot of the Roman Empire.

Ethnically speaking, Jesus and most of his disciples were Hebraic and would have been rather dark-skinned men and women.

Africans of note in the New Testament would include Simon of Cyrene, who helped Jesus to carry the cross. His ethnicity is unknown, as Cyrene is located in modern-day Libya in Northern Africa, but there was a Jewish settlement there as well, so he may very well have had an ethnically diverse background which included black African.

Acts 8 highlights the account of Philip meeting an Ethiopian official while he was traveling back to Africa and helping this man to become a baptized disciple. It is almost certain that he was a Cushite and not from the region of modern-day Ethiopia. His conversion takes place before the significant outpouring of the mission to the Gentiles that was symbolized and embodied by Cornelius' conversion in Acts 10. His radical conversion shows that the gospel really would be for all people and to the ends of the earth. In Acts 8 we find a thrilling start of the fulfillment of God's prophecies that the Cushites would be among the people who would one day submit to God and his Messiah and join his kingdom.

In Antioch, among the central leaders and teachers in the church were Lucius, who was from the North African city of Cyrene and Simeon who was called Niger, a moniker that very likely indicates that he was a black African.[28]

Contemporary Issues

This all has importance because of the previous abuses and omissions. It counts because it shows that God's people have always been diverse. It matters because there is a disturbing but growing perception today, especially among people of color in America, that Christianity is a "white man's" religion. This is demonstrably false; it is for all people of all nations. Ethnically speaking, whites were among the last to the table. Christianity spread quickly in Africa long before slavery began to ravage the continent and was widespread in Asia and the modern-day Middle East.

There are groups today, such as Muslims and proponents of African ancestor worship, who have begun to make inroads into the black community with claims that Christianity is not for black people. It is, they claim, the religion of slavery and whites. This could not be further from the truth.

It is true that Christianity was misused to justify slavery and segregation. Slaves were taught only certain tenets of Christianity. Passages about slaves submitting to masters were taken out of context. Blacks were never taught from books like Philemon, where Paul makes clear that within the Christian community, slavery was irrelevant and all men would be treated like brothers. There was, for all intents and purposes, no slavery within the Christian community. Paul never called for the eradication of slavery, I believe because he would have had no power to make a difference in the Roman world in which he lived, but also because he did not want Christianity to become an issue-oriented religion. He wanted it to become the embodiment of Jesus' vision of establishing the kingdom of God. We will examine the impact of the kingdom and what it means for this topic in the next section.

American slaves were taught that the great hope for them in Christianity was that if they were docile, submissive, and obedient, and worked very hard, they could escape their rightful heritage of slavery as descendants of Ham and recipients of his curse, and they could go to heaven one day. They were told that only in heaven could they escape the curse of Ham and their dark skin, the sign of the curse.

Preachers like the famed Puritan minister Cotton Mather told blacks that they should be comfortable in their slavery and not try to alter it, because God had ordained them to be slaves. He told one black man just before being hung for trying to escape to freedom that it was pride that tempts the black man to think that he should be free when God has divined for him to be of a lesser status. He confidently told the man that pride goes before destruction and then ordered him hanged.

This submission to inferiority in this life was even included in baptismal vows, as this one from the eighteenth century demonstrates:

> You declare in the presence of God and before this con-
> gregation that you do not ask for the holy baptism out of any
> design to free yourself from the Duty and Obedience that you
> owe to your Master while you live, but merely for the good of
> Your soul and to partake of the Graces and Blessings prom-
> ised to the Members of the Church of Jesus Christ.[29]

So, yes, Christianity was misused and the Scriptures were abused and often became a weapon against people of color. But the response to that is fairly simple: the men and women who perpetrated this were not truly Christians. They were not declaring the whole gospel. They were much more akin to those in Matthew 7 that Jesus describes as being on the broad road to destruction because they hear the Word but don't obey Jesus as Lord.

After the Civil War, most blacks were systematically and consistent-ly disallowed in white churches or they were segregated from the rest of the body with no say, no power, and no positions of authority within the church. This caused an explosion of black churches in response to the pol-icies of the white-dominated churches. It was the opposite of the gospel.

There is no doubt that the Abolitionist Movement against slavery was often a result of the sincere Christian beliefs of many, but the much louder voice in American Christianity was always in favor of slave trade, slav-ery, and segregation. And many of the Christian abolitionists were solidly against slavery but still held views of white superiority and black submis-sion to white rule once the slaves were freed.

We must admit that the sad chapter of segregation in American histo-ry has an important role even within our own church history and ancestry. Most Protestant denominations split in one fashion or another during the time leading up to the Civil War. I grew up in the Wesleyan Church, which had split from the Methodist denomination in 1843 over objections about slavery from those that would form the Wesleyan Church.

The fellowship of the churches of Christ has always claimed that their brotherhood never split along racial lines and has remained diverse since its founding. But author Wes Crawford, the preaching minister at the Glenwood Church of Christ in Tyler, Texas and adjunct faculty member at Lubbock Christian and Abilene Christian Universities, says that's just not accurate. In his book, *Shattering the Illusion: How African American Churches of Christ Moved from Segregation to Independence*,[30] Crawford carefully chronicles the fact that there have always been two separate groups within the one, a white Church of Christ and a black Church of Christ. They worked very hard at keeping up the illusion of one movement, he says, but most of the interaction between the two involved the white branch behaving paternalistically and condescendingly toward their black brothers and sisters. There was some level of interaction between the two groups during the 1940s and 1950s, thanks in large part to the work of black preacher Marshall Keeble; but his death in 1968 and a lawsuit against one of the universities of the churches of Christ, David Lipscomb, which claimed that it was a hostile environment for black students, firmly established the divide between the two wings of the Church. Since that time, the white churches of Christ and the black churches of Christ operate functionally as two separate groups with little significant interaction, although they claim to still be one body. Crawford makes the case that, despite all the good aspects of the churches of Christ, they have always reflected the racial divide of the South, while perpetuating an illusion of unity.

In an open letter to the churches of Christ that appeared in *The Christian Chronicle*[31] the authors challenge the members of the fellowship with a choice: "We can allow the racism that abounds in America's popular culture to set the agenda for the church. Or we can allow the biblical vision of the kingdom of God to determine what we believe, how we feel, and how we act." They go on to cite the systematic ambivalence, if not outright hostility, from the white churches of Christ toward the Civil Rights Movement of the 1960s and toward the overall plight of African Americans. They conclude with the belief that they have come a long way, but "we can—and must—do better."

Our family of churches finds its origins in the churches of Christ; specifically, most trace it to the Crossroads Movement, with it finally establishing its independence completely in 1991, although 1979 is usually the year cited as when the split really took place. From its inception, our brotherhood has been doggedly committed to racial diversity and unity, not just in name but in practice and in the life of every congregation. We find our origins in the campus ministry, and these ministries that would eventually form the churches of the International Churches of Christ set their roots in diversity. There was not an intentionally stated plan from the beginning to be diverse, but with evangelism efforts that were concentrated primarily on campuses and in large metropolitan areas, diversity seemed built into our growth from the start.

Eventually that was understood as a central piece of our identity and part of what God was doing through us. This growing commitment to racial diversity came to a high point, perhaps, in the 1995 International Conference in Johannesburg. We had planted a racially diverse church in Johannesburg while apartheid was still the law of the land, and that conference, taking place just one year after the fall of apartheid, was a celebration of the uniqueness of what God had done in crafting us as a family of all nations. So from the very beginnings of our family of churches, we have been built on racial unity.

That does not come without significant challenges. On consecutive days in September and October, 2016 near Philadelphia, Pennsylvania, a meeting of elders, evangelists, and teachers from our family of churches met to discuss the issue of racial diversity in our fellowship, specifically in the United States. The meeting was facilitated by Walter Evans and Darren Gauthier. The committee formulated and answered four primary questions to help identify the current situation and ongoing needs within our fellowship of churches, although it was not just a clinical meeting. It was emotional and cathartic for many present. They prayed, laughed, and cried together as they formulated several probing questions aimed at the present and future for our diverse family of churches. The questions are as follows:

1. Are there problems of diversity insensitivities in our movement?
2. Is the racial strife in our society affecting some of the disciples in our churches?
3. Apart from the world around us, do we need to increase our awareness of diversity in our local churches?
4. Are we being reactionary regarding racial issues in the church and the world around us?

The committee answered the first three questions in the affirmative, and added an answer in the negative for the final question. Below is a brief synopsis of the explanation to each of their answers.

Are there problems of diversity insensitivities in our movement? Yes. Those present did not feel that the insensitivity that had occurred at times was a result of intentional acts of unrighteousness, but did indicate a need to increase sensitivity, training, and awareness of others, including their culture and historical experiences and perspectives. It was affirmed that we are one in Christ, but there is still a need to grow in our acknowledgement and understanding of what various parts of our local congregations experience in the world.

As a response, the committee recommended "some form of diversity training and the need to identify and work with segments of our congregations that feel disconnected with the leadership because of cultural or racial differences."

Is the racial strife in our society affecting some of the disciples in our churches? Yes. While it was acknowledged that the intensity of this experience varies with the composition and location of each church, the growing tension and conflict in our society has had an impact in our movement. Particular attention was given to the fact that black brothers and sisters are negatively affected and tempted with hurt and critical feelings when there is no public awareness in the body of Christ regarding the racial and cultural unrest in our country. The silence and lack of teaching on the topic has led to a steady drift toward "civilian affairs," worldly solutions, and alignment with secular personalities rather than the kingdom solution and the cause of Christ. We are called, the group in Philadelphia noted, to "weep with those who weep," and we should minister to any segment of the church that is hurting.

As a response, the committee responded that "Although we would not recommend dedicating a whole Sunday worship service to [immediate] social issues, public statements of understanding and prayers regarding racial issues are encouraged. We would recommend congregational involvement in community-based service programs to help increase awareness, understanding, and healthy communication regarding cultural diversity."

Apart from the world around us, do we need to increase our awareness of diversity in our local churches? Yes. Our family of churches needs to grow in the proactive involvement and instruction in what disciples will face in the world. The more we engage on that front, the less we will be tossed back and forth by societal trends and opinions. This also helps safeguard against reactive discussions. It was also identified that there need to be regular opportunities for various unsettled groups in the body to express their perspectives and frustrations in a constructive and godly way with the leadership of their local church, or the appropriate body given the situation.

In response to this issue, the committee "would recommend identifying capable advisors to hold prayer devotionals and town-hall type discussions with as many of the church leadership present as possible. We would also recommend that periodic workshops be held with the congregation to help navigate difficult topics like communication, sensitivity, and social media. We also suggest that church leaders contact other congregations that have had success with these events [such as Columbia, SC; Denver, CO; Philadelphia, PA; Chicago, IL; Minneapolis, MN; and St. Louis, MO]."

Are we being reactionary regarding racial issues in the church and the world around us? No. the church, it was noted, should be a haven for all to leave the divisions and cares of the world, but that doesn't mean that we can become insensitive to our brothers and sisters who are troubled or feel unsafe when they are not in the immediate environment of the body. These issues of the world can distract us from the mission and the message if they come to dominate a church or worldly solutions are embraced. Thus, a balance must be struck. This will likely be an ongoing process and mistakes will be made, but there is a need to develop cultural sensitivities so that we can embody and proclaim the message of the gospel.

The committee recommends "that church leaders act sooner, rather than later, on these issues by seeking help and advice. We hope to have a gathering in 2017 for US church leaders to learn more about these issues as well as other topics that will help us all shepherd our congregation to unity and better understanding of one another."

Conclusion

This Philadelphia meeting was not a one-time event. There is currently an ongoing group called the Diversity Team which consists of over a dozen men and women of varying ethnicities from across the United States. They meet regularly to pray together, discuss situations, and strategize how to best educate, address issues, and be an ongoing resource for all disciples and churches. The impact of this committee will, in my opinion, continue to grow and become more visible in the coming years.

Questions for Discussion

1. Do you agree with the suggestion that our understanding and presentation of Jesus' ethnicity is important because of the history behind the subject? Does it make you feel at all uncomfortable to think of a distinctly nonwhite Jesus?

2. Do you have any hesitation, discomfort, concern, or questions about interracial marriages?

3. Why do you think some ground has been gained in the last several decades for the concept that Christianity is the "white man's" religion? What can we do to combat that line of thinking?

4. Do you think it hurts or helps Christianity to be candid about the sin and failings of those who claimed Christianity in past centuries?

5. How would you characterize race relations in our family of churches? How about in your local congregation?

CROSSING THE LINE

Section Two
Another Way

Chapter 6

The Beautiful Revolution

Our world seems to have a relatively new obsession. No, it's not money, fame, sex, or power. Those have been around seemingly forever. Now it seems that you can't watch a movie, take in a new TV show on the Internet, or pick up a book without being besieged by the apocalyptic theme. Whether it is nuclear holocaust, economic collapse, a deadly pathogen, or a dreaded zombie apocalypse, we are infatuated with the aftermath of the downfall of society. It probably has something to do with the fact that the American culture has reached a zenith of wealth and comfort, and our biggest collective fear is to lose all of that. So stories about what we would do if that happened fire our imaginations and spark a latent panic inside, because they connect with our greatest anxiety.

I think most folks are simply entertained by these scenarios and like to imagine what they would do and how they would respond. I don't have many practical, useful skills for a world suddenly thrown back into the Dark Ages, so I suspect I would be among the first to die.

There are some, though, that take this sort of thing very seriously. They don't just believe it could happen; they anticipate that it will. These folks are commonly called preppers. I have never seen it, but I'm told there is a television show that chronicles the life of those preparing for the postapocalyptic world. They expect that in the very near future the reality of the world is going to change drastically, and so they prepare constantly for it. In fact, for many of them, it becomes a consuming and important part of their lives. Why wouldn't it, if you really believed that this was what the future held and that it was coming sooner rather than later?

Imagine if someone came to you and told you they had scientific proof that some global cataclysm was going to instantly change the atmosphere of the world to become almost identical to the moon's. I urge the science enthusiasts not to get too caught up in the particulars here. But say you were told that this would happen precisely one year from now, were presented with evidence, and you believed it. So, now what? What would you do in the next year? Would you go on and live life as normally as possible? Would you change anything? My suspicion is that your life would change radically. You would begin to prepare just as those preppers do. You would start to organize your environment and everything in it so that it would survive the radical changes. You might fix your furniture to the floors and stabilize the things in your house. You would prepare your bathrooms and plumbing so that they would work. You would get all the supplies and tools that you would need in this new world. And you would probably start to tell everyone who would listen to prepare themselves.

The long and short of it is that you would begin to anticipate the future and live in many ways as though it had already arrived.

In this section of the book, I will examine three main areas that I believe are foundational to how we approach and understand the topics of race, culture, and kingdom. Having a solid familiarity with the topics of the kingdom of God, the family of God, and our identity in Christ will prepare us to understand how the first-century church dealt with these difficult issues and how we can as well.

We begin this section, then, with this chapter briefly considering the kingdom of God.

The King

In a narrative that is dripping with the buildup and tension of a modern-day blockbuster, after being accused of high blasphemy, Jesus is arrested in the middle of the night. After a sleepless night of interrogation and abuse, he is exhausted. Rather than his horror being over, though, it has just begun. The Jewish leaders are little more than paper tigers in the face of the superpower Roman Empire, so they drag Jesus before the highest ranking official in Israel, Pontius Pilate.

The Jews had long been waiting for the kingdom of God. Prophets like Isaiah and Daniel spoke of it coming in a new and powerful way one day when God would send his own Spirit and his Messiah to overthrow the pagan powers of the world and bring the entire earth under the benevolent rule of the Almighty God. Most Jews were waiting for the future to finally arrive, and they were growing impatient.

Was Jesus the one? Would he be the Messiah who would end Roman rule and bring Israel to her rightful state as the people of God who would do his will and enjoy his presence once again? Would this finally be the time when the resurrection of the righteous would take place and the age to come begin—the time when evil was done away with as were God's enemies, and he would rule his people as their king for the rest of eternity?

Would this be the end of the present age, or to use modern vernacular, the end of time? There was much to make some think that Jesus was that one. But there was even more to make others think that he wasn't.

So when Pilate asks him point blank, "Are you the king of the Jews?" (John 18:33), we the readers should be on the edge of our seats. John has left clues throughout his gospel, after all. He began his gospel account with strong echoes of Genesis 1 (John 1:1–2), signifying that what he was about to record was so monumental that the only language that could contain this story is that of the creation. This is another creation event, indicates John. "In him was life," he says, signaling to his first-century readers that the man about whom he was writing was the very embodiment of the life of the age to come. It would be like saying heaven was a man who came to the earth in the flesh. This Word, the very wisdom of God, "became flesh" and, according to John, "tabernacled" (a distinct reference to something that only God alone would and could do) among his people.

This was it. The answer was finally here. Was he the Messiah? Was the kingdom about to come? A simple "yes" would be all that anyone needed. But Jesus rarely gave an expected answer. "My kingdom," he stated matter-of-factly, "is not of this world. If it were, my servants would fight to prevent my arrest by the Jewish leaders. But now my kingdom is from another place" (John 18:36). Pilate thought that he could slot Jesus into one of the comfortable categories into which everyone else he had ever met in his life would fit. Jesus, he assumed, was just another revolutionary, trying to establish a new kingdom based on ethnicity, geography, political power, nationalism, or all of the above. But Jesus could not be confined to any of those bases of kingdoms. He was bringing the kingdom of God, but it was not like anything the world had ever seen or could even imagine. The future was indeed breaking into the present, but it was different than anyone had envisioned, and they had trouble wrapping their minds around it. And so do we today.

Throughout John's gospel, he uses the phrase *zoe aionios*, which is often translated "eternal life" in English. Modern readers tend to think that this simply refers to the eternity that awaits us after we die, but that would be to reduce its meaning. It does mean that, of course, but much more. *Aionios* means "the everlasting age" or "the age to come." When the early Christians used that phrase, they were referring to God's future age that they believed the Messiah would usher in one day. It was that time when God's enemies would be vanquished, sin would be eradicated, and God's people would dwell with him forever in this resurrection age of restoration (see Matthew 19:28 and Acts 3:21 for this idea).

The explosive idea in John for his Jewish readers was that the arrival of the age to come wasn't an end-of-the-world event. In Christ, it had happened in the middle of time, not at the "end of time" in the way that the Jews all thought. They were sure that the resurrection and the age to come would happen at the end of all things. "I know," said Martha, "he will rise again in the resurrection at the last day" (John 11:24). Jesus replied, "I am the resurrection and the life" (John 11:25). All that the Jews had been waiting for was embodied in him. Jesus was the resurrection and the life of the age to come, and he came to give it to his people now, in the present age. To put it succinctly, the age to come crashed right into the middle of the present age. When we enter into the life of Christ at our baptism, we are entering into the age to come. We don't have to wait. We can start to anticipate and live the life of the coming age right now. Of course, that doesn't mean that the resurrection has fully come, but that we start to live this very different life with totally different values while still in the present age. This is the kingdom of God.

The Good News of the Kingdom

We can often make the kingdom of God a rather complicated subject, and while it is incredibly deep and complex, the basics of it are simple. Any time anyone in the ancient world spoke of a kingdom, it meant one thing: it was the reign or dominion of a king. The kingdom of God, then, is the reign of God in the lives of his people. That's what Jesus meant when he spoke to Pilate. Surely, Pilate was confused. He had never heard of such a thing. The throne room of this kingdom could not be found in some geographic location. God's realm, heaven, is where this kingdom originated. It was a real kingdom, as real as any on earth, but it was also radically different.

Jesus summed it up perfectly as he taught his disciples to pray. "Your kingdom come," he prayed, "your will be done, on earth as it is in heaven" (Matthew 6:10). This is an example of Hebraic parallelism, in which a statement is made and then restated in a different manner to expound upon the meaning of the first statement. What does it mean for the kingdom to come? How does that happen? It's simple, explains Jesus: when God's people do his will in the present age as though they were standing in God's very throne room, that's the kingdom. Imagine the light and life of the body of Christ if everything we did, we did with the same zeal and obedience as though we were standing directly in the presence of the watching eye of the Almighty King. The kick in the gut is that we *are* in his presence. I wonder why we so often fail to realize that?

If I can be blunt here, so much of modern Christianity seems to be ineffective because it has the wrong emphasis. In Romans 1:16, Paul says that he is not ashamed of the gospel because it is "the power of God that brings salvation to everyone who believes." "There you have it," says much of Western Christianity in the modern era. "The gospel is about a loving God making a way for you to be saved. He wants to become your personal savior and Lord." With that as a starting point, most of the rest of the Christian life then emanates from this personal relationship between individuals and God. Being part of a church is nice, but it pales in comparison to the importance of your own walk with God. And on that storyline goes.

But if we go back and read the New Testament without the assumption that this personal salvation angle is the focus of the gospel, that is hardly the impression we walk away with. Jesus didn't begin his ministry by proclaiming the good news about personal salvation. He proclaimed the kingdom of God (Mark 1:14–15). In the world in which the gospels are set, and certainly in the gospels themselves, "the gospel" always meant a proclamation about the rule of a new king. It was the "good news," which is what "gospel" means. It meant everything was about to change because there was a new king whose new kingdom would bring all sorts of benefits (and responsibilities) to his subjects.

Paul speaks of this in Romans 1. The good news is that there is a new King in the world. Paul lays out the gospel in verses 1–4. In verse 16 he says that the effect or power of that gospel is to save the people who subject themselves to this new King. Yes, Jesus died on a Roman cross, and it doesn't seem like what God had promised; but Paul declares that he is unashamed of this message because it really is God's good news, his kingly announcement, and it will save everything. He's not just limiting the power of the gospel to going to heaven when you die. This King wants to rule and bring the saving power of his kingdom to every aspect of life now.

A relationship with God is important, but to reduce the announcement that Jesus is the king of all creation to only that would be like claiming that the sum total benefit of being a citizen of the United States is that you can have a friendship with the President. Obviously, there are some differences between our relationship with God and the President, but hopefully you get the point.

In Isaiah 52 we find a passage written to the people of Israel who had been sent off into exile. They were defeated and wondering where God even was. Were they still his people? Isaiah foresees a messenger coming with good news to proclaim their freedom and salvation. The message? "Your God reigns!" (Isaiah 52:7). In other words, God will rule one day, and when that day comes it will be good news. This immediately precedes the famous passage about the suffering Messiah who will defeat death and free his people from everything that oppresses them.

All Authority

The kingdom of God is the gospel. It is the best news we could ever have. There is a new King, and he has authority over everything that brings fear and destroys God's creation. In Matthew 5–7, Jesus takes his disciples to the side of a mountain and, like Moses, tells them what it will look like to live under God's rule. He lays out an entirely different reality that is more of a radical shift from life under the earthly powers than if the atmosphere were to change to become like the moon's. Those in this kingdom will value total reliance on God; they will not seek their own benefit; they will even sacrifice for the sake of their enemies. This is otherworldly stuff. No one had ever heard of a kingdom like this. Who could just declare this whole new way of living? That is precisely why, at the end of the Sermon on the Mount, Matthew highlights that the crowds were amazed at Jesus' teaching, but even more so at his authority (Matthew 7:28–29).

Matthew's gospel then goes on to show the level of authority that Jesus had, and it was truly mind-boggling. He immediately heals a man of the most feared disease of the day. He had authority over infirmities—that was a kingdom announcement if ever there was one. There would be no disease in the age to come, and Jesus was giving out samples of that. Yes, Jesus had been going around announcing the kingdom of God, but he had also been doing more than that. The Roman centurion is the first one to get it. He asks Jesus to heal his servant and even refers to him as his "Lord." He recognizes Jesus' authority. We don't know how, but he does. The centurion knows that Jesus doesn't even have to come in person. Kings can just say the word and it is done, and that's what he sees. Jesus wasn't just announcing the arrival of God's kingdom in the present age, he is the King.

The whole creation, Paul tells us in Romans 8, has been suffering since the time of humanity's rebellion against God as king. Every part of life suffers. Why do we have hate in the world? Because God is not king. Why do we have division? Because God is not king. Why do we have violence? Because God is not king. Why do we have racism and prejudice? Because God is not king.

The message of Jesus' life was the good news that God was finally becoming king through Jesus. But how? Not through power, prestige, or any of the other worldly methods that we might have expected. Neither were the people of Jesus' day expecting that. Where was his army? When would he start to talk about overthrowing the Romans? It was shocking that Jesus believed that God's kingdom would come through sacrifice; that God would become king through a sacrificial act for the benefit of his enemies. That's what Jesus did on the cross, and that's why the gospel writers present the crucifixion as an act of royal installment and enthronement.

Matthew goes on to show that Jesus had authority over all kinds of illness, including the demonic powers (Matthew 8:14–17, 28–34). He exercised authority over even the wind and waves (Matthew 8:23–27), something only Yahweh could do, according to the Old Testament. But it went even further than one could imagine. In Matthew 9:1–8, Jesus shows that he had authority over sin. He could forgive sin! What kind of king could do that?

Matthew has much more to teach us about this King, but it all comes to a head at the end of his gospel. "All authority," says Jesus, had been given to him, and he goes on to tell them, "Therefore go and make disciples of all nations" (Matthew 28:18–19). This wasn't a case of Jesus simply exercising his power. "I'm the boss, so go do what I say." The content of the message, the good news itself, is that Jesus has all authority. We no longer have to be tyrannized by the world's power and authority. It no longer has control over us. Jesus the King has complete supremacy. What could be better news? Now, go, he says, and tell everyone. Tell them how to escape the hate, fear, evil, and sin of the world. You no longer have to be a hapless victim. There is a new king and his kingdom is open to all. His resurrection was the defeat of death and the demonstration that he really is the King.

Wow! Take a moment to let the full gravity of that sink in. This changes everything. Personal salvation? That's amazing, but this is much bigger than just that. Jesus was creating a whole new world. He was creating a society where we are not victims of the authority of a fallen world. He wanted a kingdom. We will live under his reign and authority, and that will save us in every way. This is why, in Romans 10, Paul says that if we confess that "Jesus is Lord" we will be saved. He's not talking about the finer points of salvation doctrine there. He is saying that when we accept Jesus as King, we will come under his protection and deliverance in every way. We will start to live by the values and reality of the future right now. When we love our enemies, for example, we are declaring that Jesus is really our King, because when the age to come fully arrives, there will be no enemies. That means we can't have any now. We do his will on earth as though we were in heaven.

But how do we bring this reign to bear? The same way Jesus became enthroned: through self-sacrifice for the benefit of others. That is perhaps the foundational ethic of this kingdom.

The kingdom is built on three aspects of this same virtue of self-sacrifice. The first aspect is that to enter the kingdom requires that we die to ourselves (Luke 14:27). Jesus left no room for doubt about this. If we want to enter his life and enjoy his authority, then we must give up our lives, our authority, our way of doing things. We cannot love the things of the world and the kingdom, because they are on the opposite ends of the spectrum.

The second aspect is just another way of saying the first, that we must give up everything. The kingdom is like "treasure hidden in a field," said Jesus, and when a man found it he was full of joy "and sold all he had" so that he could buy the field (Matthew 13:44). The kingdom is like a merchant searching for the very best pearls. When he finally found one, "he went away and sold everything he had and bought it." If you "do not give up everything you have," proclaimed Jesus, you "cannot be my disciples" (Luke 14:33). If the kingdom authority of Jesus extends to every part of our life, then it must be matched by our giving up everything about our lives and the world. We are to give up our will, our solutions, our opinions, our identity, and everything else.

The third aspect is that at the very heart of the kingdom is to suffer and sacrifice for the benefit of others. We don't seek justice for ourselves. We don't seek fairness. We seek the benefit of all involved. That's what Matthew 5:38–48 is all about.

This becomes clear if we keep in mind that this is all about the kingdom of God and what it will look like on earth. We are in a strange time when the kingdom authority has come and is available in Christ, but we are still in the present age. That's what was so shocking for the first disciples. It was not so surprising that the kingdom had finally come. What baffled them was that the present age had not come to a thunderous conclusion. They were not expecting the overlap. And it is that overlap that causes tension. It would be easy to live under the King's authority if we were fully in the age to come and in the immediate presence of the Lord each day. How much easier would it be to live a kingdom life if all evil were gone? But that is not yet the case. We have to constantly live in the tension of being kingdom people surrounded by the rebellion of the present age.

A Very Different Kingdom

It is here that we must understand some basic tenets of the kingdom of God and how it differs immensely from the kingdoms of the world. In essence, the kingdom is the authority of Jesus applied in the lives of his people. That means that the kingdom of God is a collection of people that behave like Jesus. In his work, *The Myth of a Christian Nation,* author Greg Boyd outlines five distinct differences between the kingdom of God and the kingdoms of the world.[32] I will utilize these five contrasts while supplying my own analysis of their importance. They will, I believe, help us to set our course as kingdom people and illustrate what this has to do with the problems of race and ethnicity that we see in the world today.

A Contrast of Trusts. The kingdoms of the world trust power and coercion. Whether it be the sword, political power, or beating down opposing positions and opinions, the world trusts power over others. This comes in many different forms, but they can all be traced back to the power over others to compel them, in one way or another, toward what is wanted from them. This is not the case in the kingdom of God. The kingdom of God advances not by power over but by power under. Jesus demonstrated this for his disciples by washing their feet and calling them to go and do likewise. The greatest will be the last and the servant of all (Mark 9:35). Power under does not try to impose its rule on the rest of the world. It proclaims its authority, shines as a light, and invites others to come enjoy the liberation afforded in the kingdom of God.

A Contrast of Aims. The kingdoms of the world seek to control behavior. That is the whole point of laws, authorities, borders, and the like, in the world. The kingdom of God is about true transformation to God's will and his way of living. This is why Paul, when describing the fruit of the Spirit in a kingdom-drenched life says, "Against such things there is no law" (Galatians 5:23). You cannot legislate the life of the kingdom. It must be chosen and can only come through the transformative power of the Holy Spirit. When Paul gave instructions on kingdom living, he was careful to point out that his influence extended only to those who have chosen the kingdom and should not be mandated of those outside it (1 Corinthians 5:10). We cannot and should not try to control their behavior. That would be to try to establish the kingdom through means of the world, and it simply won't work. After you have dealt with your own sin, taught Jesus, go and help your brother with his; but "do not give dogs what is sacred; do not throw your pearls to pigs" (Matthew 7:6). Be a city on the hill, but if someone hasn't chosen the life of the kingdom yet, don't force it on them or expect it out of them. Don't go disciple someone about their lack of kingdom behavior if they are not a kingdom citizen.

A Contrast of Scopes. The kingdoms of the world are tribal in nature. This takes many forms, but they are rooted in division and "my group" versus "your group." That instinct comes from the values of the world, as does the need to invest in defending one's own group. Worldly kingdoms are always either defending or trying to advance their own nation, ethnicity, religion, ideology, or political beliefs. Because there are many different groups, conflict is the natural result. The kingdom of God, though, is universal in nature and scope. It focuses on loving all people as God loves them. It seeks to reflect the love of Christ to all people without condition. There are no enemies for those in God's kingdom, as far as it depends on us. The kingdom transcends all those divisive and world-shrinking tribes. That is why Christians cannot allow these small tribal-type divisions to carry any weight over and above the kingdom and divide us in matters that simply hold no weight in a life inside God's reign.

A Contrast of Responses. The weapons that we have at our disposal are not the weapons of the world (2 Corinthians 10:4). The kingdoms of the world, says Boyd, are intrinsically tit for tat in their response. It is an eye-for-an-eye world. That simply perpetuates the violence, the problem, or the argument. Whatever the conflict is, the response of the world will only keep it going and give more credence to the "power over" values of the world. The kingdom is different. We do not carry the sword, figuratively or literally. We carry the cross. We don't return evil for evil, hate for hate, violence for violence. The message of the cross is that we take the suffering upon ourselves for the benefit of the other. We don't cower to the power or fight it; we take the negative impact of it upon ourselves to demonstrate the good news of a new authority. If someone slaps you, don't be weak and let them; don't fight back; look them in the eye and show them the strength of the kingdom by which you will allow them to do it and not respond in the ways the world does. Jesus returned evil with good. He prayed for his enemies. He loved those that hated him. Rather than retaliation, we seek the good of those who think they are our enemy.

A Contrast of Battles. For the kingdoms of the world, everything seems to be a battle. When your core values revolve around power over others, seeking your own self-interests, tribalism and division, and responding in kind to those that oppose you, the only possible result is a battle. But as we have said before, it is not the nature of the kingdom of God to have earthly enemies. If it did, it would not be the kingdom. When those who say they are Christians talk about winning the culture war or engage in political battles, it is not the kingdom authority that they are living under or displaying. The warfare of the kingdom is not against enemies of flesh and blood, it is "against the rulers, against the authorities, against the powers of this dark world and against the spiritual forces of evil in the heavenly realms" (Ephesians 6:12). If anything has "flesh and blood," it is not our enemy; and our only valid weapon is the love of the kingdom. The moment we forget or reject that is the moment we have walked outside of the authority and boundaries of the reign of Jesus the King.

Heavenly Citizenship

We cannot become Christians and disciples without becoming part of the kingdom of God. Admittedly, this is in such contrast with the individual salvation message that has permeated much of Christian culture in modern times, that it can be a challenge for us to realize the full implications of the differences. Our primary mission is not to "help people get saved." Our primary mission is to teach them to become disciples in God's kingdom. This is precisely what Paul meant when he urged the Philippians to recognize that their "citizenship is in heaven" (Philippians 3:20). We can easily see the necessary progression that Paul describes in that passage:

1. Recognize that worldly accomplishments and ways are meaningless (Philippians 3:7–9).

2. Become like Jesus in his self-sacrifice for the benefit of others (Philippians 3:10–11).

3. Constantly strive, strain toward, and grow in this kingdom life (Philippians 3:12–14).

4. Live out the citizenship that we've already been given in Christ (Philippians 3:15–20).

Paul wrote to a community of believers that was quite familiar with the concept of citizenship. Philippi was founded by retired Roman soldiers who had been given their citizenship, and like many others, encouraged to settle away from Rome with the goal of showing those in the far reaches of the empire what it looked like to be a citizen of Rome. They were to model the Roman culture to those around them. Paul knew that there were sharp differences between Rome's power and the power of the kingdom, but the disciples back then could learn something from that picture of Roman citizenship, and so can we. We are citizens of heaven. Paul's point is not for us to just hold on and help as many as we can to be saved, waiting for our evacuation. He is calling us to live out the life of the kingdom that is based on the model of Christ that he had so vividly described in Philippians 2:5b–11 and called them to embody in Philippians 2:1–5a.

This takes total commitment. That's why following Jesus is so simple and at the same time so challenging. If we "seek first his kingdom and his righteousness" (Matthew 6:33), Jesus said in no uncertain terms, we will find God's provision in all things. If we reduce this to mean "seek church attendance above all else," or "seek to be really moral above all else," we drastically reduce the holistic nature of the kingdom and create a parody that is often grotesque in its incompleteness. What Jesus desires for the subjects of his kingdom is total loyalty and commitment to his reign. My love for my family, my country, my political agenda, my ethnicity, or anything else cannot ever take precedence over the kingdom of God. In fact, I will find that many of those things must be laid down before entering, and those that I can bring in with me, like love for my family, must take their rightful place in submission to the King.

We are to live in the present age as though Jesus had already come again. Our environment will be the world, but our actions should be rooted in otherworldly values. People should look at the kingdom communities and see an entirely different reality lived out. Hate? No, we strive for sacrificial love for all. Racism? No, everyone is invited into and is equal in this kingdom. Poverty? Not here; we provide for the needs of one another. Politics? They divide; the kingdom message is superior and different if we will put down our politics and listen.

Theo-politics

In one sense, of course, the good news of the kingdom is deeply political, or to use a term that I prefer, theo-political. To say that "Jesus is Lord," as the early Christians typically declared at their baptism, is to acknowledge that Caesar is not. One of the favorite Psalms of the early Christians was Psalm 2. It is quoted or alluded to in the New Testament dozens of times and referred to often by the Christians of the later first century and the second and third centuries. In that psalm, we see a striking attitude toward the politics and power structures of the world once the Messiah comes. To summarize, the Psalmist lays out the following ideas:

> **Psalm 2:1–3** Why do the nations insist on rebelling and anointing their own kings?
> **Psalm 2:4–6** God is bemused and angered by this, as he has already chosen his King to rule his creation.
> **Psalm 2:7–9** The One promised will one day be enthroned as the king and his realm will somehow cover all the nations.
> **Psalm 2:10–12** Be wise and exercise earthly authority with the recognition that it is a secondary authority to the real King.

Israel was obviously a political nation-state. Even though God always called her to be separate from the other nations and trust him as their King, they eventually rejected that and chose a human king. This action kept them embroiled in worldly politics throughout the rest of their history. But the kingdom of God is different. It is a real kingdom that demands the sole loyalty of its subjects, but it does not participate in the same power structure that the kingdoms of the world do. For this reason, Christianity has never truly prospered when it has become embroiled in politics or gained the power of a nation-state. It is not designed that way. The kingdom is intended to be a sample of heaven. When someone finds an outpost of God's people living under his kingdom rule, they should be able to look and say, "Oh, that's a little bit of what it will look like to live in the age to come under God's reign. I see love and not hate. I see all nations and not division. I see sufficiency for all rather than lack and surplus. Now I get it."

By its very nature, the kingdom cannot engage in politics in the way that the world does. As we discussed above, the world operates mostly through power over, coercion, and control. Those are foreign concepts to the kingdom. God's rule must be chosen. We don't have the space here to get into a full discussion of the role of politics and the kingdom of God, but I will touch on it briefly.

If Christians choose to become involved in politics personally, that is their decision. If they choose to vote, and whom they decide to vote for, should be decisions dictated by their kingdom convictions. But as a whole, it is my contention that the kingdom of God does not and cannot play a part in the political ideologies and political structures of the world, and I would urge disciples to have a strong biblical basis to yoke themselves to an ideology or candidate. We simply don't find any direction under the new covenant to engage in worldly politics or to try to change the power structures of the world. Instead, the kingdom is an invitation to come create an entirely new society that lives outside of the mainstream and shows a different way. It is a city on a hill.

In Romans 13, for example, Paul urges the Christian community to respect the governing authorities. But his purpose is for the exact opposite reason than to become involved in their affairs. He wants the saints to stay out of political power, whether it be rebelling against the state or supporting it. For kingdom citizens, they may have been living within the geographic borders of the Roman Empire, but they were aliens and foreigners, with loyalties in conflict with the empire and a completely separate agenda.

This is one of the reasons that Paul never called for a ban on slavery in the Roman Empire. To do so would have risked turning the church into a political movement that would have had to play the power games of the world to succeed. Instead, he told slaves to be the best light they could be. He called masters to treat their slaves with sacrificial love. Within the Christian community, he urged them to treat one another as the brothers they were, and in his letter to Philemon, he hinted that the natural way to do that was to free their brothers that were slaves. The principles laid out by Paul destroyed slavery as an institution of power and control within the community of the kingdom, but at the same time it protected the believers from becoming ensnared in worldly politics. He wasn't being political, but he was being theo-political.

Jesus seemed to avoid political entanglements at every turn. When the people wanted to make him king, he refused. Perhaps the incident in Jesus' life that most demonstrates his aversion to worldly politics and power comes in the wilderness during his forty-day fast. The devil comes to him with various temptations meant to derail his role as Messiah. We must assume that Satan offered things that he could deliver or they wouldn't truly be temptations. He takes Jesus to a high mountain and lays out his offer. If Jesus will bow down and submit himself to the devil, then he will make Jesus the ruler over all the kingdoms of the world.

Would you have wanted Jesus to take that deal? Just think of it. He would have been the King over all the kingdoms on the globe. Think of all the good that he could have done. Surely, he could have ended war, put a stop to hunger, put everyone to work, taken care of the poor, and much more. His list of accomplishments would have been almost limitless. He could have created a utopia, right? Yet Jesus thought that acknowledging the authority of Satan and his politics of power would not be worth it. The kingdom of God is more valuable than all the political solutions added together. Jesus could have been the greatest political leader of all time, but he chose the kingdom instead.

True, the New Testament never forbids the kingdom from worldly politics, but it never directs us toward them either; in fact, it seems to firmly lead us away from them at every turn. Some have argued that the apostolic church didn't engage in Roman politics because they would not have had the opportunity. But the church of the second and third centuries did have the opportunity, and they roundly rejected it because they asserted that politics and power were not compatible with the kingdom of God. Writing in AD 195, early church leader Tertullian said, "In us, all ardor in the pursuit of glory and honor is dead. So we have no pressing inducement to take part in your [politics]. Nor is there anything more entirely foreign to us than affairs of state."[33]

In Chapter 2, I described the conflict between Jesus and the Pharisees over whether Jews should pay Roman taxes or not. It was a hot-button political clash of his day, and no matter what Jesus answered, he would be taking a side and angering people. So, what would he do? He chose not to play in these power games at all.

The real issue was not whether or not taxes were to be paid. Look at those coins with Caesar's image on them. If he valued them so much and wanted them so badly, let him have them. But as we have seen, humans were designed with God's image on them (Genesis 1:26–27). That's what Jesus cared about. The image of God has been corrupted by humans doing their own will rather than God's, but in the kingdom it can be restored to a reflection of him (2 Corinthians 3:18) through the Messiah who is his image (Colossians 1:15). That's what God cared about and that's what the people of God should care about. Jesus' answer was theo-political, meaning he refused the political structure and games of the world, while taking them head-on at the same time. What we can be sure of is that he was not calling for dual loyalty to the kingdom of God and a kingdom of the world.

For the first three centuries of Jesus' kingdom, disciples rejected any role in the Roman Empire. They stood in such opposition to the ways of the world that they were violently persecuted for two centuries. That continued into the third century but slowed down in the latter half, with a few sharp exceptions, as Christianity expanded and became difficult to persecute. In the early fourth century, that all changed. The Roman Emperor Constantine converted to Christianity. There is an interesting contrast here. In the third century, a Roman emperor, Philip the Arab, wanted to join his Christian wife at an Easter vigil. The church leaders, unimpressed with his power, would not let him until he publicly confessed and repented. It is said that he readily did. Constantine, on the other hand, faced no such challenge to denounce his role if he was going to be a disciple. It is impossible to know whether this conversion was sincere or politically motivated, but he was never confronted to become a full disciple and to repent and lay down his worldly power. Instead, he co-opted Christianity and within just a few years there were Roman armies fighting wars in the name of Christ, something that would have been unthinkable to the Christians of the first three centuries.

This compromising with the world led one blogger to brilliantly create an imaginary scenario where Luke Skywalker takes Darth Vader's hand and rules together with the Empire rather than leaping into the unknown abyss. He uses this to illustrate his assertion that the church of the fourth century took the hand of the Roman Empire by melding together church and state. The Roman Empire fell soon after this coming together of Christianity and Rome, and Christianity has reattached itself to a catalog of other empires since.[34] But the kingdom of God cannot be married to a kingdom of the world, no matter how good it might seem.

I am not arguing that politics are evil or completely worthless. They have some value in keeping order and organizing life, but they cannot solve the big problems that face humanity. I think of them like the musicians on the deck of the Titanic. They brought a little bit of comfort in the midst of a terrible situation, but they could do nothing about the rapidly sinking ship. Our treasure and trust should be in the kingdom. Since our treasure is not in politics, then, neither should our heart be. Politics can be helpful in regulating certain aspects of society, and one approach may be more effective than another in the unemployment rate or the revitalization of a neighborhood. Those things are not insignificant. But politics cannot deal with the underlying ills that cause the true problems in our world and result in division. Only the gospel can do that.

Disciples who are committed to one side of the political spectrum or the other often cause hard feelings and sentiments of division in the body just as much as do race and ethnicity issues, although since the two areas are complexly intertwined, separating race issues from politics is tricky. Disciples who consider themselves conservative politically will become exasperated at the idea of Christians who think of themselves as liberal politically, and wonder how they could support politicians who work in favor of things like abortion and other social issues that stand opposed to the word of God. Meanwhile, those who have affixed themselves to a liberal worldview look at their conservative brothers and sisters and can't believe that they would support political parties that endorse constant wars and positions that they feel perpetuate or protect racism, mistreatment of the poor, and many other moral issues. The problem is that both groups of disciples act as though these political philosophies are part of their true identity. They are convinced that anyone on the other "side" is wrong and cannot possibly be a Christian while supporting the politicians, political ideologies, or political parties that they do. What if they are both right? What if a kingdom worldview and mindset are so countercultural, unique, and otherworldly that being a seek-the-kingdom-first person is entirely incompatible with the solutions of the world and its politics? What if this is part of what Paul was referring to when he said that the weapons we fight with are not of this world? (2 Corinthians 10:4–5).

There will be times when political stances of one party or the other overlap with the kingdom agenda, but more often they both will have platforms that blatantly oppose kingdom values. Do we want to be yoked with any worldly agenda to that degree? If kingdom responses, positions, and solutions mirror one political party or the other, then what is the point of the kingdom? How is it still good news when it looks just like the world?

The kingdom of God must be our highest priority and the sole recipient of our loyalty. It is an entirely new way of living. When Jesus declared, in various ways, that the kingdom of God was finally breaking into the present age in a tangible and accessible manner, he was inaugurating a beautiful revolution. He was calling us to a different reality with different trusts, different aims, different scopes, different responses, and different battles. "Don't you know," queried James, "that friendship with the world means enmity against God? Therefore, anyone who chooses to be a friend of the world becomes an enemy of God" (James 4:4).

I believe firmly that, as disciples, if we do not have a solid grasp on what it means to be part of God's kingdom, we will always be in danger of getting sucked back into the world's arguments and political squabbles. We will be prone to seeing things as the world sees them and taking a side rather than being the alternative, offering the world a picture of what it looks like to have God as King of every aspect of life. This is as true of the issues of race and culture as in any other facet of life. Before we start to get into specifics, though, there are two more foundational aspects that we must consider: the family of God and our identity in Christ.

Questions for Discussion

1. How would you explain the kingdom of God to someone who had never heard of it?

2. What keeps you from doing God's will on earth as it is done in heaven?

3. Which of the five contrasts between the kingdom of God and the kingdoms of the world stands out to you as having the most impact on the issue of racial division?

4. What do you think of the early church's stance on politics? Do you think their positions had anything to do with their ability to impact the world so powerfully with the message of the kingdom?

5. Do you think disciples in our fellowship of churches are too involved or passionate about politics, not enough, or it's just about right? What about your local congregation?

Chapter 7

The Promised Family

In the summer of 1992, I was back in my hometown of Janesville, Wisconsin during the summer break from where I was attending college in Oklahoma. That summer put Janesville on the national map, if ever so briefly. A former police informant and allegedly shady used car salesman spent the early part of the summer trying to organize a national meeting of leaders of the Ku Klux Klan. He wanted to increase their notoriety and membership in the area. There was an immediate backlash in the community against the Klan activity he was stirring up. Janesville had never had a reputation as a very integrated or progressive community, but most people certainly did not want the KKK running around the vicinity.

The meeting was set for August but then was cancelled due to the overwhelmingly negative reaction of the community. The day that it was scheduled, hundreds of people, as I remember, showed up at the county courthouse to rally and protest the Klan. Unbeknownst to them, though, most of the Klan leaders had come to the local organizer's house despite the public announcements that the meeting had been called off. Everything seemed to be fairly calm until Geraldo Rivera pulled into town.

He and his producers informed the crowds at the courthouse that the Klan leaders were at the house on the south side of town. The crowd, including Rivera, quickly made their way there. As you can imagine, chaos ensued, and the handful of police officers that were on the scene could barely keep the two groups apart. Rivera got into an argument with one of the Klansmen, who called him some racial epithets and then kicked him in the leg. Rivera responded by unloading a fist square into the man's jaw. It was at that point that pandemonium broke loose. In the end, the two sides were separated without much damage or injury, and everyone went home. That would be the last time, that I know of, that the Klan would attempt to meet in our town or anywhere nearby. But, for the next five years or so, any time I told someone the name of my hometown, they would stop and look quizzically as if they had heard the name but couldn't quite place where they had heard it. I would then mention Geraldo, and they would blurt back, "Of course, the Klan fight." I would have to sheepishly respond, "Yeah, that's us."

It was no surprise that Rivera and the Klansmen fought. They were on opposite ends of the spectrum in ideology, philosophy, beliefs, and just about everything else. But what if it wasn't Geraldo? What if it had been a fellow Klansmen that rolled up to the house that afternoon. What if they seemingly held to the same beliefs? What would it have taken for the other Klansmen to want to kill this new comrade within just a few minutes?

Those Are Fightin' Words

John records a scene in his gospel where Jesus caused that very re-action. A group of Jewish people were following his teachings and even believing what he was saying (John 8:30–31). It was good stuff. They were on board. But then in what was apparently just minutes, they were ready to kill him. What could Jesus have possibly said that was so offensive to them that it would turn them from supporters to a violent mob in an instant? Take a moment to read John 8:31–58 and see if you can figure it out.

Assuming you have read the passage, do you see what Jesus said that was so offensive? For many people, the quickest way to get them angry is to insult their family. Jesus doesn't quite do that in the typical way, but the issue here between him and the Jews has everything to do with family.

The first indication that this exchange is not going to end well comes when Jesus implies that they must be set free. That comes with a parallel implication that they are slaves somehow. Given the history of the Jewish people in Egypt and their current situation as a vassal state of Rome, they were particularly sensitive to the charge of being slaves. Despite the earthly subordination, they, as the family of Abraham, didn't view themselves as slaves of any man. So the insinuation that they needed to be set free was deeply offensive.

Jesus then lays out his central point in verses 34–38: that they are slaves to sin. And as such, they are not members of "the family." He is the Son, and he has a permanent place in the family, but they have no such status. Then in one fell swoop, Jesus asserts that they are going to try to kill him and implies strongly that Satan, the father of lies, is their true father.

The Jewish response to all this? "Abraham is our father." When I picture the scene in my mind, I can almost hear them yelling at this point. But why would this be their response? Jesus has just accused these Jews of being enslaved to sin and outside of "the family." To what family was he referring? And why would they respond with affirmation that they were

Abraham's descendants? And maybe even more puzzling, what does all this have to do with us today?

The Great Promise

The first eleven chapters of Genesis paint a bleak picture for God's creation. Humanity has rebelled against God's will and brought division and rebellion to every corner of the earth. God sends a worldwide flood, but even that doesn't seem to hold off the problem for very long, and by chapter 11 the world is right back into the depths of sin and rebellion.

Then suddenly the Lord comes to a random man living in ancient Mesopotamia. This conversation and a later one between him and God are recorded in Genesis 12 and 17. God calls Abram to leave his family, and promises him three important things:

1. God will make Abram into a great nation/family (Genesis 12:2).[35]

2. Those descendants would be the source of blessing for all people on earth (Genesis 12:3).

3. Abram would be the father of many nations.

This would be God's solution to sin? A family? There was a hint of this in Genesis 3:15 when God declared that one day the offspring of a woman would crush the head of the deceiver, but there were no further clues to such a plan until the time of Abram, who would later become Abraham. If we peek ahead to Galatians 3 we see that this is exactly what Paul believed. When he's reminding the Gentile Galatian believers who they are in Christ, he tells them that they are the fulfillment of these promises. As Paul sees it, God's promise to Abraham was not that one day many different people groups would be able to trace their lineage and religion back to Abraham. No, that's not it. Paul argues that God "announced the gospel in advance to Abraham" (Galatians 3:8). His point there is that what God told Abraham was that he would one day have a family that consisted of all nations. And the Galatians were part of that family.

This promise to Abraham, that his family would be the source of blessing for all people of the world, was central to the identity of Israel. In their collective understanding, that is who they were and what their purpose was. They were this promised family. The only thing they didn't understand fully was how their family could consist of all nations and how exactly God would bless all the peoples of the world through them; but they never doubted God's promises. The prevailing thought, early in the first century, was that when the Messiah returned and the age to come began, he would judge the pagan nations and rule Israel. Israel, in turn, would justly and faithfully rule over the repentant nations, bringing them blessing and reconciling them with God in that age to come.

The trustworthiness of God's promises was a central part of his righteousness in the eyes of the ancient Jews. Their belief was that "the Lord is trustworthy in all he promises and faithful in all he does" (Psalm 145:13). "You have found [Abraham's] heart faithful to you, and you made a covenant with him... You have kept your promise because you are righteous" (Nehemiah 9:8). In the language of the Jews, for God to be righteous meant specifically that he was faithful to his covenant promises. If he ever failed to be faithful to a promise, then he failed to be God. So any teaching that implied that God was not faithful to his promises could automatically be understood as a false teaching. The teaching was wrong, not God. As Paul wrote in his letter to the Romans, "What if some were unfaithful? Will their unfaithfulness nullify God's faithfulness? Not at all! Let God be true, and every human being a liar" (Romans 3:3–4).

The promise given to Abraham appears frequently and in many forms throughout the Old Testament, and is a central feature of the hope that Israel had in God. We see these same themes evident in Isaiah's prophecy concerning the time of the coming of the Messiah. Isaiah uses the symbol of a mountain to speak of the coming of God's kingdom in 2:2–4. He says that many peoples will come to follow the ways of God and become one people. Those people of the nations, who were previously at war with one another, will beat their instruments of war into instruments of peace with God as their ruler.

By the time of the first century, then, the big questions for the Jewish people were, how could God possibly fulfill all the facets of his promises to Israel, and when was he going to do it? How was he going to bring blessing to all the nations through them as Abraham's descendants?

When Paul and the other apostles began to preach that Jesus was the Messiah and that in order to be part of God's family, individuals had to die to themselves and their own identities and enter the life of Christ, that was a major stumbling block for the Jews. The reason? God's promises. They already were the family of God. How could these Christians claim that they had to do something else in order to be part of God's family? Those questions only intensified as Gentiles were brought into the fold. If they had to be baptized into Christ to be saved, then this "gospel" was making God out to be unfaithful to his promises to Israel. It was claiming that the blessing came through Jesus and not Abraham's descendants.

That's precisely the reason that Paul begins his letter to the Romans by saying that he was "not ashamed of the gospel, because it is the power of God that brings salvation to everyone who believes" (Romans 1:16). He goes on in verse 17 to state that in the gospel the righteousness of God is revealed. Paul's point? That God is shown to be faithful to his promises through the good news of Jesus. In fact, it is only in the gospel, Paul will argue throughout his letters, that God's promises to Abraham are fulfilled. That is why he argues in Galatians 3:8 that God announced the gospel in advance to Abraham. This is where it was going all along, says Paul.

As we covered in Chapter 3, the promise that God would eventually extend his blessing to all nations is a central theme of the Old Testament. But it was one that the early disciples were slow to pick up on. My speculation is that the events surrounding Pentecost had something to do with that. When the Spirit was poured out that day and 3,000 were baptized into Christ, the book of Acts tells us that among that group were Jews from every nation. Surely, they must have rejoiced that they were seeing God truly fulfill his word. This is how "all the nations" would be blessed. Jews had been scattered to all the nations and now they were being brought into Christ. Promise given, promise kept.

But, of course, the rest of Acts chronicles how that was not the case. We'll cover in Chapter 9 how the Spirit would make it plain that the gospel would go to the Samaritans (Acts 8), the Cushites (Acts 8), and the larger Gentile world (Acts 10); with Peter finally having the lights go on as he was preaching to Cornelius' household: "I now realize how true it is that God does not show favoritism but accepts from every nation the one who fears him and does what is right" (Acts 10:34–35).

But the argument of a first-century Jew would still have been that the Christian gospel made God out to be a liar because the promises were that salvation would come through Abraham's family, not Jesus and his little band of Jews and a growing number of Gentiles. Paul should be ashamed of the gospel, they would argue, because it makes God out to be unfaithful.

It is to that charge that Paul offered one of the most important defenses of the gospel in the entire New Testament. It is found in Romans 9:6–13. "It is not as though God's word had failed," he starts off. He then goes on to show how, yes, God gave Abraham the promise, but Abraham had two sons, and that promise was passed to Isaac alone. It is only Isaac, the younger son, who was God's child of the promise. Isaac then had two sons himself. Again, it was not the older son who received the promise and inheritance as expected. It was Jacob. He was given the promise and not Esau, who was moved to the side just as Ishmael had been. The pattern, implies Paul, was there all along. The older brother did not receive the promise but the younger did. Not all of Abraham's descendants received the promise, but some did, so God was faithful.

In the same way, Israel was God's firstborn son (Exodus 4:22) but, like Isaac, Jesus was the unique son of the promise (John 3:16). He was a descendant of Abraham. Thus, blessing is found in him for all nations who enter Christ and become part of God's family. "So in Christ Jesus you are all children of God through faith, for all of you who were baptized into Christ have clothed yourselves with Christ. There is neither Jew nor Gentile, neither slave nor free, nor is there male and female, for you are all one in Christ Jesus. If you belong to Christ, then you are Abraham's seed, and heirs according to the promise" (Galatians 3:26–29).

"For no matter how many promises God has made, they are 'Yes' in Christ" (2 Corinthians 1:20). Every single one of God's promises was fulfilled in Christ.

A Family Fight

That brings us back to John 8 and the confrontation between Jesus and the Pharisees. Now we can begin to fully understand the argument there. They were Abraham's seed. They were the promised family, or so they thought. But they were wrong, says Jesus in no uncertain terms. That's why in a moment they went from nominally believing him to being ready to kill him. He had just told them that they were not part of God's promised family. Their identity was shattered if what he was saying was true.

Throughout Jesus' ministry he sent clear signals that he had come to gather up and become God's promised family. His people would be the true descendants of Abraham. That's important for us to understand. Jesus did not come to create a new religion, in the way that we often think of that word. He came to create a family.

In one of the shocking moments in Jesus' life, he was teaching a crowd when someone burst into the group and announced that his mother and brothers had arrived. Social convention of his day would dictate that he stop and go out to them, showing honor to his mother especially. But Jesus floored everyone there. "'Who are my mother and my brothers?' he asked. Then he looked at those seated in a circle around him and said, 'Here are my mother and my brothers! Whoever does God's will is my brother and sister and mother" (Mark 3:33–35). In three sentences, Jesus just redefined centuries of Jewish practice and belief. Family was the highest priority in the Jewish culture, and he had just radically redefined it. Who brings you security, comfort, and identity, and defines your status as God's people? It's not based on birth, biology, or blood. It is whether or not you are a disciple of Jesus. That is how Jesus defines family.

In another instance, a woman called out to Jesus, "Blessed is the mother who gave you birth and nursed you" (Luke 11:27). She was offering him a blessing that implied shared family honor and identity. He was doing great things, so the honor would be shared with his mother and other family members. Once again, though, Jesus turns that on its head: "Blessed rather are those who hear the word of God and obey it" (Luke 11:28).

We don't have the space here to look at any other examples in depth, but it is evident that Jesus was forming a family built around him. Time and again throughout his ministry he called people to the pattern of Abraham, the call to leave one's household and be part of God's new family and promise. This doesn't mean that the early Christians abandoned or disowned their physical families, but they also understood quite well that this family was their new priority and identity.

For them, the family language used throughout the New Testament wasn't just symbolic. It was real. They had been born "again" into this new family (John 3:3–5). They understood that for those who believed in the life of Christ "he gave the right to become children of God—children born not of natural descent, nor of human decision or a husband's will, but born of God" (John 1:12–13). They were siblings who were given the same calling (Hebrews 3:1). They should do good to everyone, but especially to the "family of believers" (Galatians 6:10). They were once separate from Christ, and "excluded from citizenship in Israel and foreigners to the covenants of the promise, without hope and without God in the world" (Ephesians 2:12). But through the blood of Christ (Ephesians 2:13) a new humanity had been created out of the two (Jew and Gentile) and they could rest assured that they were "no longer foreigners and strangers, but fellow citizens with God's people and members of his household" (Ephesians 2:15, 19).

The trouble for us is that we like to think we understand the whole family thing, even if we did not see all the specifics in the Scriptures. We call each other brother and sister, right? God is our Father, isn't he? But if we're honest, we tend to use that language more as a metaphor than to express a new reality. When you entered Christ and the body of believers at your baptism (1 Corinthians 12:13–14), did you realize that you were switching family allegiances like a bride leaving her parents and joining to her husband, her new family?

A New Race

Writing near the close of the second century, early church leader Clement of Alexandria wrote that "God brought our race into communion by first imparting what was His own, when He gave His own Word, common to all, and made all things for all. All things therefore are common, and not for the rich to appropriate an undue share."[36]

This is where it really starts to get interesting for us. For the ancients, the concepts of family, race, and nation were all intertwined. Thus, they believed that when they died to themselves and entered the life of Christ, they not only entered a new family, they were also part of a new nation. But even more than that, God had formed an entirely new race. "His purpose," explained Paul, "was to create in himself one new humanity out of the two, thus making peace." In so doing, he made the racial distinctions of the past irrelevant; they had been wiped away. "Here there is no Gentile or Jew, circumcised or uncircumcised, barbarian, Scythian, slave or free, but Christ is all, and is in all" (Colossians 3:11).

This does not mean that there will not be challenges or that we will not have colliding cultures that need to be respected and melded together. We will get to all that in Section 4. But it does mean that when it comes to who we are in Christ, we are members of an entirely new race of humanity. We are Christian. And this is where so many of us go wrong and miss the enormity of what God has done. In Christ, there is no American or Syrian. There is no black, white, Asian, or Hispanic. There is no Democrat or Republican. We are one family. We are one nation. We are one race. As for me? My heritage is Scottish and a mix of other Celtic ethnicities, but my race is Christian.

Many of us still struggle with this, if we are being sincere. Yes, we see ourselves as Christian, but when push comes to shove, we often exalt our American identity or our racial identity or even our familial identity above our citizenship in the kingdom of God and our status as children in his family.

There is a growing divide in our family of churches over issues of race and politics. Yes, we must have these conversations. Yes, we must listen to and learn from one another. Yes, we must be open to the perspectives of one another. But the starting point is to realize that we are one race, one nationality, and one family. Justin Martyr, an early Christian in the mid–second century, declared that "we who hated and destroyed one another, and on account of their different manners would not live with men of a different tribe, now, since the coming of Christ, live familiarly with them."[37]

As disciples who live in America, do we view global politics primarily through the lens of a people with brothers and sisters of our own family scattered in nations around the world, or do we view things from an American perspective? Do we view these events through the eyes of our Father and with loyalty to the household of God? When a tragic incident happens between a young black man and a white police officer, do the loyalties of our previous races kick in? Do we start to feel tension with our brothers and sisters in the family because they "just don't get it"?

Are We Really Family?

In 1 Corinthians 6, Paul chides the believers for taking one another to court. Apparently, there were some conflicts that had broken out between brothers and sisters and they were suing each other. Paul's response is biting: "The very fact that you have lawsuits among you means you have been completely defeated already" (1 Corinthians 6:7a). In the culture of the first century, family was the most important bond, whether Jew or Gentile. The sibling relationship was considered to be the closest and the most worthy of loyalty (even more than the spousal relationship). That is why Proverbs 18:24 says that "there is a friend who sticks closer than a brother." On the one hand, Paul understood this intimately. On the other hand, he also understood that in the culture of his day, lawsuits were normal. People would not let themselves get cheated or wronged, with one exception: it was considered a cultural no-no to take one's family members to court. In those cases, it was better to be wronged.

And that is precisely Paul's point in this passage: "Why not rather be wronged? Why not rather be cheated?" (1 Corinthians 6:7b). When they took each other to court, they were sending a palpable message to the world that they were not really family after all; they were not the new race; they were not the kingdom of God. Since being the family of God was the whole point and the fulfillment of God's promises, to send the signal that they weren't family members was to have lost before they even got started. It didn't matter how they resolved it in the end; the message had been sent loud and clear.

What messages about family have we been sending the world? Is it the amazing message that God has fulfilled his promises and has brought together "persons from every tribe and language and people and nation" as one kingdom and one new race? (Revelation 5:9).

That a central aspect of the gospel is that God's people will be the promised family of all nations must be declared and demonstrated at all times. It is a reversal of the division of Babel, a fulfillment of the ancient promise to Abraham. It is the embodiment of Jesus' ministry and teaching. It is the first taste of the gospel that many who come into the fellowship for a visit will get. This is why the potential split between Jew and Gentile believers that we will detail in the next section of this book was so alarming to Paul. They could not have a Jewish Christian community and a Gentile Christian community. To do so would be to lose a major aspect of the gospel. Churches today that are not deeply committed to being the one family of all nations at a global level and also at their local level are missing one of the central components of the good news. They are taking the easy road. Groups that are all or primarily one race, one people group, or one tribe are not fulfilling the gospel that God announced to Abraham and delivered through Jesus Christ.

"Once you were not a people," wrote Peter, "but now you are the people of God" (1 Peter 2:10). God has done the impossible. He has taken people of all nations and made them one family. Do you believe that? Do you live that out to your neighbors and relatives?

If you instinctively said "yes" to the questions above, then I urge you to ask yourself the questions below to see if your response was true:

- What group forms the basis for your identity?
- What group receives your highest loyalty?
- What group brings you security and comfort?
- What group do you trust the most?

This is challenging, I know. When Jesus called people to his family he stated categorically that "anyone who loves their father or mother more than me is not worthy of me; anyone who loves their son or daughter more than me is not worthy of me" (Matthew 10:37). The demand is forthright, the difficulty level unquestionable. That's probably why the very next words that Matthew records from Jesus are, "Whoever does not take up their cross and follow me is not worthy of me" (Matthew 10:38).

There can be no divisions in this family (1 Corinthians 1:10–13). We must bear with one another in love, and "make every effort," Paul pleaded, "to keep the unity of the Spirit through the bond of peace" (Ephesians 4:2–3).

We can tell who the children of God are, asserted the apostle John, and who the children of the devil are. The children of the devil are those that don't do what is right and who do not love their brothers and sisters (1 John 3:10).

Being the family of God is essential. Demonstrating God's wisdom and faithfulness to a watching world is of inestimable worth. "See what great love the Father has lavished on us, that we should be called children of God! And that is what we are!" (1 John 3:1).

I want to say something on a personal level here. Some will read this chapter and not feel that they have experienced this level of family in their current congregation, or maybe ever. Others will feel familial bonds with some pockets within the fellowship but not others. For some, those lines will be largely along racial lines. If you identify with that, I understand your frustration and I grieve with you. It will never be perfect in any church family. But being family is the very reason that God has put us together. We must not give up. We must not leave out of frustration. It was about 3 a.m. when the disciples saw Jesus walking on the water (Mark 6:48). They had been up all night rowing against the wind and the waves to go where Jesus asked them to go. What would have happened if they had grown weary and frustrated and quit rowing at 2:45 a.m.? They would have missed Jesus' incredibly faith-building miracle. Don't grow weary. If you haven't experienced the church as a family in the way that it should be, then I plead with you to be the change that you want to see. Build family; expect it; foster it; call others to it. And don't call it quits.

We must see ourselves as the new "race," to use Clement's wording. That must become our primary identity in the world. Our identity in Christ is so important that we will spend the next chapter focusing on the reality and implications of becoming part of the new creation in Christ.

Questions for Discussion

1. Why is it important to understand that Jesus called us to a family and not just to be part of a religious group?

2. Do you truly view your brothers and sisters as your family?

3. Do your passions and loyalties lie primarily with your national, racial, or familial identity, or with your identity in God's family?

4. What do you think is the biggest area of growth needed in your local church when it comes to embodying and embracing the reality of being a family and treating one another as such?

5. What group forms the basis for your identity, receives your highest loyalty, brings you security and comfort, and is the one you trust the most? If it is not your church family, why do you think that is?

Chapter 8

More Disciple than White

Paul was a bigot. He was a racialist. There's little question about that. Oh, I know that he was Saul when that was true, but the sentence has more impact when it starts with "Paul." Trust me, I tried it both ways. When we piece together the details that we have of Saul's early life in the first-century Mediterranean world, we start to get a picture of what growing up was like for him.

Paul biographer John Pollock describes Saul's early life:

> Gentiles were all around, and the columns of pagan temples dominated the marketplace. Ninevah of the Assyrians, Babylon, Athens, and Rome had combined to create Tarsus, and Paul was unconsciously the child of his Oriental-Hellenic world. In his youth it seemed remote, for although many Jews throughout the Mediterranean had been influenced by the Greek view of life, Paul's parents were Pharisees, members of the party most fervent in Jewish nationalism and strict in obedience to the Law of Moses. They sought to guard their offspring against contamination. Friendships with Gentile children were discouraged. Greek ideas were despised. Though Paul from infancy could speak Greek, the lingua franca, and had a working knowledge of Latin, his family at home spoke Aramaic, a derivative of Hebrew, the language of Judea.
>
> They looked to Jerusalem as Islam looks to Mecca. Their privileges as freemen of Tarsus and Roman citizens were nothing to the high honor of being Israelites, the people of promise, to whom alone the living God had revealed His glory and His plans...
>
> By his thirteenth birthday Paul...was ready for higher education.
>
> Tarsus had its own university... But a strict Pharisee would not embroil his son in pagan moral philosophy. (Such studies would have to come later.) So, probably in the year that Augustus died, AD 14, the adolescent Paul was sent by sea to Palestine and climbed the hills to Jerusalem.[38]

Paul was surrounded by Gentiles as a boy but would almost surely have looked down on them. The Jewish communities interacted with the pagans around them as little as possible, since they were unclean, did not fear God, and were not the people chosen to be the keepers of Abraham's promise. Clearly at one time in his life, Saul found his background and resume, so to speak, to be a great source of pride.

> *If someone else thinks they have reasons to put confidence in the flesh, I have more: circumcised on the eighth day, of the people of Israel, of the tribe of Benjamin, a Hebrew of Hebrews; in regard to the law, a Pharisee; as for zeal, persecuting the church; as for righteousness based on the law, faultless.* **Philippians 3:4b–6**

Saul didn't just value his Jewish heritage; he looked on others with disdain. In some of his letters, we get a picture of his level of zeal for his beliefs and his prejudice toward those who believed differently from him, as well as his willingness to violently persecute them.

With the death of Jesus, surely Saul and the other Pharisees thought that his motley group of followers would quickly scatter and disappear like so much dust in the wind. Until they didn't. They were brought before the Sanhedrin and threatened. When the disciples wouldn't stop spreading their good news, the stakes were raised. Not only were people starting to believe this gospel, the Jewish leaders were growing worried that they were going to be blamed for Jesus' death (Acts 5:27–28). Evidently, they wanted to shift the blame for that to the Romans. Standing before the Sanhedrin, Peter answered for himself and the others, "We must obey God rather than human beings! The God of our ancestors raised Jesus from the dead—whom you killed by hanging him on a cross." And there it was—the blame for Jesus' death. But he continued, "God exalted him to his own right hand as Prince and Savior that he might bring Israel to repentance and forgive their sins. We are witnesses of these things, and so is the Holy Spirit, whom God has given to those who obey him" (Acts 5:29–32).

Saul was almost assuredly there for that speech. He must have bristled in fury at this blasphemy. At some point, Saul broke with his teacher, Gamaliel, who had urged caution and a hands-off approach (Acts 5:33–39). Saul's immediate future would be anything but hands-off.

We don't have to speculate about Paul's level of bigotry and hatred for others. He was more than forthcoming in his own words:

I am a Jew, born in Tarsus of Cilicia, but brought up in this city. I studied under Gamaliel and was thoroughly trained in the law of our ancestors. I was just as zealous for God as any of you are to-day. I persecuted the followers of this Way to their death, arresting both men and women and throwing them into prison, as the high priest and all the Council can themselves testify. I even obtained letters from them to their associates in Damascus, and went there to bring these people as prisoners to Jerusalem to be punished.
Acts 22:3–5

For you have heard of my previous way of life in Judaism, how intensely I persecuted the church of God and tried to destroy it. I was advancing in Judaism beyond many of my own age among my people and was extremely zealous for the traditions of my fathers.
Galatians 1:13–14

I too was convinced that I ought to do all that was possible to oppose the name of Jesus of Nazareth. And that is just what I did in Jerusalem. On the authority of the chief priests I put many of the Lord's people in prison, and when they were put to death, I cast my vote against them. Many a time I went from one synagogue to another to have them punished, and I tried to force them to blaspheme. I was so obsessed with persecuting them that I even hunted them down in foreign cities.   Acts 26:9–11

Saul was there, approving of the violent murder of the Christian disciple, Stephen, as he was stoned to death for the crime of preaching the gospel publicly. If we read the accounts above, there obviously was a great deal of activity and persecution instigated by Paul after he watched Stephen die. After receiving permission from the high priest to expand his campaign, Paul headed for Damascus. Little did he know that he was about to experience something that would change his life forever. This violent blasphemer would be shown mercy (1 Timothy 1:13), and in an instant, his prejudice and bigotry would be forever transformed, as would his identity.

Paul's Conversion

You probably already know the story well. Paul tells it on three separate occasions in the book of Acts. He is on his way to way Damascus with murderous intent in his heart. Suddenly, a light from heaven flashes around him and he hears a voice saying, "Saul, Saul, why do you perse-cute me?" His life will never be the same. At first he is puzzled. He never persecuted any heavenly figure, only those infernal Christians. But when Jesus reveals who he truly is, the awful truth must seem to burn into Saul's reality. These people truly are the Messiah's people, the promised family. What had he done? When Jesus instructs him to go into Damascus and wait, there is no hesitation on his part.

Saul spends three days, praying and fasting and coming to grips with who Jesus was. He was the King after all. The gospel made sense to Saul for the first time. God's promises fell into place for him. We don't know if this full understanding came to him during those three days, but much of it must have. Ananias came to him and baptized him, and a new identity was born.

Saul immediately began to preach and proclaim the gospel of Jesus in the synagogues in Damascus. Eventually he would stop being called Saul, the name that had helped him to emphasize his Jewish identity, and would go by the more Greco-Roman-sounding Paul.

He quickly made his way to Jerusalem, and the shock must have con-tinued for both him and the other disciples. But it was there in Jerusalem that Paul first ran into the life to which he was being called. It was there that he was first touched by sacrificial love for the benefit of others. When he arrived in Jerusalem, the disciples were all afraid of him. Why would they not be? He had spent months trying to hunt them down, throw them in jail, and kill them. It is quite probable that many of them had known Stephen well. Yet Paul was allowed to move among the disciples and was accepted by the apostles and the church. It is even probable that included in that group of disciples were friends of Stephen and perhaps even Ste-phen's widow. Yet they showed Paul fellowship, forgiveness, and accep-tance. It must have convicted and encouraged him all at the same time.

Paul was no longer a stranger and foreigner to God's family. His trans-formation was as radical as it was quick. And it is no wonder, when we look at how Paul describes what happened to him as a result of his con-frontation with Jesus:

> *I have been crucified with Christ and I no longer live, but Christ lives in me. The life I now live in the body, I live by faith in the Son of God, who loved me and gave himself for me.* Galatians 2:19b–20

Paul saw the distinction before and after his entrance into the king-dom of God as being so sharp that the simile he turned to was that of death. He had died to his life, his identity, and what was important to him. He had laid down his will. He had laid down his agenda. He had laid down his opinions and preferences. They were gone—he was dead. Now, what was left was Paul's body as a vessel for the life of Christ. His desire was that when people interacted with him, they would feel like they were meeting Jesus in Paul's body. His life was now part of the kingdom, which meant that it was within the realm of the King's rule.

Have you ever thought about your own life in those terms? Can you point to the moment of your baptism and say, "Yes, at that point I died"? Have you laid down your life, your will, your agenda, your opinions, and your preferences? Is your whole life inside the realm of the King where his will is obeyed as the one with all authority?

Death to Bigotry

One day as Jesus was out traveling with his disciples, word came back to him that his dear friend Lazarus had been taken ill. Jesus didn't seem alarmed. He calmed his disciples, telling them that this sickness wouldn't end in death (John 11:4), and he was in no hurry to get to Bethany where Lazarus was. Then word came that his friend had died. Jesus' response? "Lazarus is dead, and for your sake I am glad I was not there, so that you may believe." This had to be confusing and rather upsetting. Jesus had said this wouldn't end in death and now it has, and on top of that he's telling them that it was for their benefit so that they could learn something. As they arrive in Bethany, Jesus confirms that Lazarus is dead and then calls him out of the tomb. Lazarus had died, but is now called by the King to a new life. It is in the next chapter that Jesus teaches them the point: "Unless a kernel of wheat falls to the ground and dies, it remains only a single seed. But if it dies, it produces many seeds" (John 12:24). "Anyone who loves their life," he continued, "will lose it, while anyone who hates their life in this world will keep it for eternal life. Whoever serves me must follow me" (John 12:25–26a).

To have the life of Christ, to be a citizen of the kingdom, demands that we first die. Bringing Lazarus to life was an acted-out parable of that truth. How do you think Lazarus lived the rest of his life? Do you suppose he did what he wanted and marginally obeyed the King? Or do you think he, like Paul, would have said, "I have been crucified with Christ and I no longer live"?

When Paul was "rescued from the dominion of darkness and brought...into the kingdom of the Son" (Colossians 1:13), it changed his entire worldview and identity instantly. It was Christ's love, he said, that compelled him because he was convinced that Jesus had died for all and called them to die to themselves in response (2 Corinthians 5:14). Why did he die for all? "He died for all," Paul elucidates, "that those who live should no longer live for themselves but for him who died for them and was raised again" (2 Corinthians 5:15). The impact of this was remarkable on every aspect of Paul's life. "So from now on," he says, "we regard no one from a worldly point of view. Though we once regarded Christ in this way, we do so no longer" (2 Corinthians 5:16).

Paul was completely transformed, and it suddenly changed everything about his identity. Look at what he says in Philippians 3:

> *If someone else thinks they have reasons to put confidence in the flesh, I have more: circumcised on the eighth day, of the people of Israel, of the tribe of Benjamin, a Hebrew of Hebrews; in regard to the law, a Pharisee; as for zeal, persecuting the church; as for righteousness based on the law, faultless.*
>
> *But whatever were gains to me I now consider loss for the sake of Christ. What is more, I consider everything a loss because of the surpassing worth of knowing Christ Jesus my Lord, for whose sake I have lost all things. I consider them garbage, that I may gain Christ and be found in him, not having a righteousness of my own that comes from the law, but that which is through faith in Christ—the righteousness that comes from God on the basis of faith. I want to know Christ—yes, to know the power of his resurrection and participation in his sufferings, becoming like him in his death, and so, somehow, attaining to the resurrection from the dead.*
>
> *Not that I have already obtained all this, or have already arrived at my goal, but I press on to take hold of that for which Christ Jesus took hold of me. Brothers and sisters, I do not consider myself yet to have taken hold of it. But one thing I do: Forgetting what is behind and straining toward what is ahead, I press on toward the goal to win the prize for which God has called me heavenward in Christ Jesus.* **Philippians 3:4b–14**

If Paul had been keeping a ledger in his early life, he would have thought he had a huge profit balance adding up in his favor. He was part of the right family and had the right pedigree. He had the right training and was taking the right actions. Even his zealous violence and persecution of the church were things that he thought were showing him to be in the right. He had much in his favor. That is, until he recognized that Jesus was the true King with all authority. This changed everything. All that he thought had brought him value had actually kept him from seeing the kingdom of God.

But like the men in Jesus' kingdom parables of Matthew 13:44–45, once he got a glimpse of the kingdom, nothing else mattered. He was willing to give up all those prestigious things because he saw them for what they were worth. His ethnicity, lineage, education—none of it amounted to a hill of beans. The only thing that he cared about was the resurrection life. He had gladly exchanged his life for that of Christ and wanted to expend every ounce of energy he had in living out his new identity.

Paul's change in behavior when it comes to Christians is obvious. When you go from hunting down a group of people to becoming one of them, and your first official act is to be lowered out of a basket to escape your former compatriots who are now hunting you, that's a big change. But his transformation toward the Gentiles was just as striking.

That journey, in fact, is remarkable. A group of people that he looked down upon and despised was now the object of his love and sacrifice. He was pelted with stones by people of Galatia at the instigation of his Jewish opposition. The assault was so violent they thought he was dead (Acts 14:19), but he got up and went back into the city, motivated by his concern for the young church. Paul repeatedly traveled around the Roman world, expending and endangering himself for these Gentiles. At one point, he acknowledged that his ministry was so challenging that he would almost prefer death, but he rejected it because that would not be the best for the predominately Gentile church in Philippi (Philippians 1:23–24).

His entry into the kingdom changed everything: He changed his name. He changed his commitment to the Law. He changed the focus of his life. He changed what he valued and pursued in life.

Paul's identity switch was not just personal; he also expected it of others. His comments in 2 Corinthians 5, concerning Christ's love that compels us to no longer live for ourselves, weren't just for him; he was writing that to all the disciples. All of us should leave behind our worldly viewpoint. "If anyone is in Christ," Paul says, "the new creation has come" (2 Corinthians 5:17). This verse has been a challenge to translate since it was written, because apparently, Paul was so excited that he didn't fully complete the sentence. If we were to translate directly what he wrote, it would read something like "If anyone is in Christ, new creation." Does he mean to say that the person has entered the new creation? Or that the new creation has entered them? Or that they are a new creation? Quite probably, he meant all of those. When we enter Christ, we enter an entirely new reality. Or have we forgotten that Paul also wrote, "You were taught, with regard to your former way of life, to put off your old self, which is being corrupted by its deceitful desires; to be made new in the attitude of your minds"; and, continues the apostle, "to put on the new self, created to be like God in true righteousness and holiness" (Ephesians 4:22–24).

What Forms Your Identity?

When I was a teenager I was part of several groups. I had my parents and my sister, of course. But I was also part of a group of friends. I was on sports teams. I was a member of various clubs and activity groups at school. I went to a youth group at our local church. I was a white person (I guess I still am). In a way, these categories were all part of who I was. Yet only one of those attachments truly formed my identity and produced my internal security, and so had my ultimate loyalty. At times, it might have been difficult to tell which one it was. I liked all of them and spent time with each group. There were things about each one that I appreciated and valued. But when push came to shove, if anyone from one of those other groups said something negative about my sister or my parents, it was on. That was my true source of identity. At the end of the day, I was a Burns. The Burns identity extended beyond my nuclear family. When my Aunt Sue married my Uncle Charles, a black man, he became part of the family. If a conflict had ensued for some reason, I would never have taken sides with a nonfamily white person against my Uncle Charles. He was part of my identity group, while they were not.

As you read this, you are probably part of many different communities and groups as well. You are part of a family, you have your work, your ethnicity, your neighborhood, perhaps a political ideology or party, and for most of you reading this, the kingdom of God. There are many other groups that could be added to the list. Which group defines you? Which group creates your identity? Do you get angry with other disciples because of their political beliefs or unfriend a brother or sister in Christ because they posted something on social media that supports the "Black lives matter" or the "All lives matter" philosophy? If so, what does that tell the world about your ultimate loyalty and identifying group?

Paul gets to the heart of it in 1 Corinthians 7:

> *Nevertheless, each person should live as a believer in whatever situation the Lord has assigned to them, just as God has called them. This is the rule I lay down in all the churches. Was a man already circumcised when he was called? He should not become*

uncircumcised. Was a man uncircumcised when he was called? He should not be circumcised. Circumcision is nothing and uncircumcision is nothing. Keeping God's commands is what counts. Each person should remain in the situation they were in when God called them.

Were you a slave when you were called? Don't let it trouble you—although if you can gain your freedom, do so. For the one who was a slave when called to faith in the Lord is the Lord's freed person; similarly, the one who was free when called is Christ's slave. You were bought at a price; do not become slaves of human beings. Brothers and sisters, each person, as responsible to God, should remain in the situation they were in when God called them.

1 Corinthians 7:17–24

As Paul addressed the spiritually immature and struggling group in Corinth, he wanted them to understand their true identity as citizens of the kingdom of God. Throughout this letter to the Corinthians, Paul is trying to help them understand what it means to live in Christ. When he expounds on the same topic in his letter to the Galatians (3:27–28), he says, "…for all of you who were baptized into Christ have clothed yourselves with Christ. There is neither Jew nor Greek, slave nor free, nor is there male and female, for you are all one in Christ Jesus." He is emphasizing that once you have entered the life of Christ, human distinctions that create worth or identity pale in comparison to your identity in Christ. We should neither exalt ourselves for them nor feel bad about them. We are in Christ, and that is the only important place to be. All other positions are merely tools to be used to bring glory and honor to Christ and places in which we can carry out his work.

If we don't have in mind that concept from Galatians 3, the passage in 1 Corinthians 7 can seem a bit out of place. Why would Paul include discussions on circumcision and slavery in a chapter that focuses on sex and marriage? It is because the real point of the chapter is about understanding who we are in Christ. He had been using the topics of gender and marriage to make his larger point about identity, and in verses 17 through 24 turns to two other hot-button issues of his day. Notice that gender, circumcision, and slavery are the three topics that he cites in Galatians 3 as not having any significance when it comes to identity in Christ.

Circumcision was an unmistakable divider between Jews and Greeks, especially in Greek towns where the men bathed and exercised naked. Many Jews in the first-century Greek towns were so embarrassed by this physical marker that they took to having surgeries to make it look like they hadn't been circumcised.

Slavery was a major part of life in the Greco-Roman world. The entire economy and social fabric was built upon it. We should note, though, that although it was still far from God's plan of freedom for all humans, this was not nearly as brutal and dehumanizing as the form of slavery practiced in the New World from the sixteenth to the late nineteenth century or the evil form of human trafficking and slavery still practiced in many corners of the world today.

Paul's remarks on both subjects should not be taken out of context. He is not writing about his personal feelings on these topics, nor is he laying down a biblical standard, that, for instance, slavery should be considered a positive thing. We must stay in the realm of identity in Christ, which is the point that he is making. Once someone comes to Christ, there should be no exaltation or shame over whatever position they were in when they were called. Men should not think themselves better than women, and being uncircumcised is not better than being circumcised (nor vice versa), or free better than slave. These are all human constructs and are null and void in Christ, where all are equal. The Christian need never be swayed by social pressures to "improve" themselves or change themselves. In Christ, we have all we ever need. This is what Paul means when he says that keeping God's commands is all that counts (this is deliciously ironic for a Jew who would consider circumcision to be doing just that). The whole of keeping the law, in Paul's mind, is to remain in Christ. In Christ, all of God's commands are kept, which is, of course, something that we could not do on our own power.

Here is Paul's point: Once you have entered Christ and stepped into the age to come available in the kingdom, that's what forms your identity. Don't obsess about the identity markers or position that the world has hung on you. Ethnic identities like circumcised Jew or uncircumcised Greek are unimportant when it comes to your worth in the kingdom of God. Even social statuses like slave or free do not define you.

Just like that, Paul has turned identity on its head. Does the world say you are a slave worth little to nothing? Well, you're free in Christ and no lower than anyone else. Does the world say you are free and valuable? You are a slave in Christ and no better than anyone else.

This has huge implications for the topic at hand. If we take the last five hundred years as a unit, there can be little argument that ethnicities defined as white have been viewed as superior and have had more power, while ethnicities defined as colored or black have been viewed largely as inferior and have had less power. In Christ that is all gone, every bit of it. Do you believe that? I don't believe that the gospel is going to change the way that is in the world. They will ebb and flow and vacillate, but division and oppression will remain in one form or another. The world talks a good game about diversity, but only the kingdom can truly bring it. Although we are not going to be able to change how the world operates all that much, we can live God's way in the kingdom and show that divisions can be done away with. We can become a group of people who are not defined by the labels the world wishes to tag us with.

If the world says you are lesser, then you are of inestimable value in Christ. If the world says you're pretty special, then you are just a humble servant in the kingdom. Paul's point is not to exalt one group while cutting another down to size. He is teaching here that the identities of the world lose their meaning once we have encountered the King.

Have you received historical benefit and opportunities because of the color of your skin? In Christ, there are no such benefits. Leave those at the door and work hard not to take advantage of them or bring an attitude of privilege into the body. Do you receive the short end of the stick in many ways because of the color of your skin? In Christ, you are exalted. There is no inferior or superior status here. There is no advantage or disadvantage. There is no privilege or lack of privilege here. In Christ there is no strutting around with racial pride but neither is there slinking about with guilt about the past or shame in the present.

Just a Disciple

I am not a white disciple. My wife is not a black disciple. We are disciples who happen to have been labeled by the world in a certain way; although me being white and she being black and the accompanying cultures that we were raised in are important to us, and do contribute to a certain amount of who we are and how we view the world. We are each proud of our earthly heritage. But when it comes to our standing before God and how we approach the important aspects of life, we are disciples first and foremost. Our experiences, our past, our heritage, our culture, our ethnicity, and a host of other things shape who we are. There's no denying that. They all contribute to making us the special individuals that we are. But when those things start to take precedence over our identity as kingdom citizens, it is a form of idolatry. We'll get into more specifics in the next section about some of the conflicts that arise in the body, but there seems little doubt to me that at least some of them come about when brothers and sisters exalt their racial or political identity above their kingdom identity. They subsequently see the world and interpret events through those lenses rather than from the radically unique kingdom perspective.

Isn't this what Paul meant when he spoke of knowing nothing but the power of the resurrection life of Christ? Paul well understood the importance of cultural expression and diversity, but those must be subservient to our true identity.

At one of the many moments during Jesus' ministry when large crowds were following him, as he so often did in those situations he brought out some of his most challenging teaching:

> *If anyone comes to me and does not hate father and mother,*
> *wife and children, brothers and sisters—yes, even their own life—*
> *such a person cannot be my disciple. And whoever does not carry*
> *their cross and follow me cannot be my disciple.* Luke 14:26–27

What was this all about? Some have compared it to Matthew 10:37 where Jesus talks about the need to love family members less than him. While there are similarities, I believe that these are two separate sayings with slightly divergent meanings. In Malachi 1:2–4, God explains to the prophet that he has accepted Israel as the people of the promise and the inheritance. He collectively refers to them as "Jacob" because they are the heirs of Jacob. He also explains that Edom, the descendants of Esau, he hates. This is inheritance language. God is not teaching that he hated a group of people; that would go against his nature (1 John 4:16). To "hate" in this context was about inheritance and identity. God is simply saying that Edom was not part of the fulfillment of the promise to Abraham. Paul uses this passage in Romans 9:13 in the midst of explaining why Jesus is the only path to the fulfillment of the promise. In that sense, God has loved Jesus and hated all other possible candidates to be the keeper of the endowment. Likewise, what seems to be Jesus' point in Luke 14 is that he is the only path to the promise. His is the only life that will lead to inheritance, and his is the only identity that carries value in this age and the age to come.

Let's return to Paul's letter to the Corinthians. He was passionate in his desire for these believers to understand that an obsession with our status, ethnicity, ideology, or anything else other than Christ is a demonstration that we consider our place in the present age to be far more important than it is. Paul brilliantly speaks to all of us, but not in a one-size-fits-all way. His words hit home for each of us as he challenges our worldly concepts of status and identity. Does the world see you as important? In Christ you are a member of the body with no more value than anyone else in the kingdom. Does the world see you as unimportant? Then in the kingdom you are valuable beyond words (1 Corinthians 12).

This is vitally important as we go forward. When we realize that we are members of one new race in Christ (Ephesians 2:14), we can move past the divisions of the world. We can embrace this new identity. After all, it is the only one that will last into the resurrection age. Since race is a social construct of man anyway, do you think it is a distinction that will matter in God's presence? When we allow this truth to envelop us and permeate our thinking, it releases us to be who God wants us to be in this life. If there are no racial divisions in heaven, then there can be none in God's kingdom, because it is the place where his will is done just as it is in heaven.

Where Are Your Loyalties?

Let's get down to brass tacks. What would happen if there was a race war in the United States? Let me be clear: I pray there never is. I don't think there ever will be, and I will do everything in my power to avoid such an unspeakable tragedy. But just for a moment, imagine that there was. Where would your loyalties lie? Would you refuse to take sides because you were a disciple, despite enormous pressure to do so? I believe most of us would, but would you? If you're torn even a bit, you may have just had something very important revealed to you about how you currently define your identity. It's something to think about.

We are all part of a new identity, a new family, and a new reality. In fact, as Paul addresses the largely Gentile congregation in Corinth, he addresses them as his brothers and sisters and reminds them about "our ancestors." They are now Abraham's seed with a mission to tell the world the good news that there is a new King who has all authority on heaven and earth.

There is value in knowing and appreciating my earthly ancestry, but it doesn't define me. If some white people did horrible things in the past, I can recognize that and admit it without a shred of guilt. It happened; it was wrong. Let's admit it. But it doesn't cause me shame. That's not where my identity is rooted.

Does the world define you as black, white, Hispanic, Asian, or another ethnicity? That is wonderful. Be proud of it. But don't let that define you. Who am I? I'm a Christian. Who are you?

Questions for Discussion

1. Did you have any forms of bigotry in your past that you have had to repent of?

2. Can you, like Paul, honestly say that you have died to yourself and no longer live?

3. Have you found yourself recently feeling tempted to be more loyal to your ethnic group or nationality than to your identity as part of God's family?

4. As a kingdom citizen, have you dropped your worldly identity, or do you find yourself hanging onto it?

5. How does your church family need to grow in exalting those who are humbled or oppressed by the world and humbling those among you who are exalted in the world's eyes?

CROSSING THE LINE

Section Three
Race and Culture in the New Testament Church

Chapter 9

Troubled Waters

I never planned to coach basketball. When I graduated from college with a degree in education and a passion for history, I knew that more than anything I wanted to teach high school history. I was hired shortly after graduation by a wonderful group of administrators at a high school in Milwaukee's central city. It just so happened that, in addition to a social studies teacher, they were also looking for a boys' basketball coach. When they learned that I had played a little bit in college and had extensive youth coaching experience, they decided to give me a crack at the position.

I had played a lot of basketball but had not experienced a whole lot of diversity growing up. Everyone on my basketball teams came from pretty much the same background and the same cultural world. That meant that it was usually pretty easy for us to get along. We understood each other. It was more of a challenge when I got to college. We eventually became friends, but it was a little more work since many of our backgrounds were so unalike.

But that did nothing to prepare me for my first year of coaching. We were about middle-of-the-pack talent-wise that first year, but I had my work cut out for me in more ways than I could have imagined. I thought it would be easy, like it was when I was in high school, since everyone was from the same city. Boy, was I wrong. Our school was unique in our conference in that it was the only school at the time that served a somewhat diverse neighborhood. We had black, white, Hispanic, Native American, and Asian students. To add to the mix, we also had guys who were affiliated with at least three or four major gangs in the city, most of which drew their boundary lines ethnically. We also had some guys who were not in gangs. The players on that team ran the gamut in about every way, and that made it much more difficult to bond than any team I had ever played on. They were a great group of kids and we eventually came together, but it wasn't easy. They had different values and varying loyalties, and did not trust each other much at the beginning. We had a lot of conflicts and there was a constant threat of them factionalizing into several groups, which, in effect, would have ripped apart the chemistry and unity that we needed to have.

I learned something from those early years of coaching, though: the more diverse a group is, the more challenging it is to be unified and get along. I think that's why division is so natural in our world. We separate by our differences and similarities because it is just simpler to be around those with whom we have things in common. The more we see things alike, the easier it is, typically, to congregate. As the old saying goes, "Birds of a feather flock together." The converse is also true. The more diversity present, the more difficult it will be to create community.

It has historically been next to impossible for our world to have both diversity and unity. We seem to be good at doing one or the other, but not both. We face ongoing challenges in this country and in the church to be both diverse and truly unified, but it is nothing that the early church did not face as well. It's often easy to consider the early church the golden era of Christianity, and I suppose in some ways we could make that case. But from the very outset, ethnic strife made its way into the church, and it continued to be a major problem for them. A case could be made, in fact, that it was the biggest cause of internal conflict within the church.

In addition to the comfort of knowing that we are not the only ones to deal with these issues, knowing that the first generation of Christians struggled with the topics of race and culture helps us to look for and find the solutions that they used to help them navigate through those choppy waters. As is often the case, the problems were mostly cultural, but they manifested themselves along racial and ethnic lines. What was true for them is especially true for us today. We will examine this idea more in subsequent chapters, but for now it will be sufficient to simply point out that many of the problems that we think are racially instigated because they tend to fall along visibly racial lines are actually issues of culture. That's good news, because cultures can be adjusted and transformed—although it takes great effort.

In the coming chapters, we will look at the biblical solutions for these potential divisions and then delve into an examination of culture and how cultural diversity can be used to build up a church rather than divide it. But first, it will be helpful to get an overview of the ethnic strife that was an ever-present specter in the apostolic church.

The Hebraic and Hellenistic Jews

As we have already examined briefly in previous chapters, one of the central aspects of God's promises to Abraham was that all nations would be blessed. At the heart of the gospel proclamation that Jesus was now the rightful King with all authority was that the time for the blessing of all peoples, Jew and Gentile alike, had come. As the Spirit poured out on the disciples at Pentecost in Acts 2, there were "God-fearing Jews from every nation under heaven." These were Jews that had been spread during the diaspora after the conquest of Israel and the destruction of the temple in the sixth century BC. The list given in Acts 2:9–11 includes Jews from a broad geographical range that stretches beyond the Middle East and into modern-day Asia, Africa, and even Europe. Despite their geographical dispersion, though, these Jewish communities were marked by amazing levels of religious and cultural fidelity. Despite their distance from Jerusalem, they maintained practices and beliefs markedly distinct from the cultures around them. They were no doubt influenced by the people groups around them where they had settled, but their similarities as faithful Jews gave them many points of commonality despite the differences created by physical separation.

As these Jews from all over the world were baptized into the family of the Messiah, the shattered mirror of humanity started to be slowly pieced back together. Although they were all Jews, it was a deeply symbolic event. The division of the nations was being healed just as Isaiah had proclaimed (Isaiah 2:2–4).

One of the marks of distinction, of course, of those first disciples of the King was their unity and devotion to one another (Acts 2:42–47). They behaved more like a first-century family than a religion of the day. They were devoted to the same spiritual practices no doubt, but also to creating community, being together constantly, and providing for each other. This was true unity. There would be no unmet needs in this new society. In writing Acts, Luke stresses that they were together "every day" and met together in public places and in one another's homes. The unity was idyllic and unmatched.

Yet there were obstacles that loomed on the road ahead. The church was growing; amazing things were happening; it was gaining attention throughout the region. But not just from those that believed. In Acts 4, the church encountered its first big obstacle. The Jewish leaders seized Peter and John and dragged them before the religious leaders in Jerusalem. After a rigorous questioning that may have taken hours, they strongly forbade the disciples from speaking or teaching about Jesus in public. I can assure you that they were not threatening a slap on the wrist if the disciples rejected their commands. This was serious stuff.

On their release, Peter and John returned to the other disciples, and they all prayed for boldness so that they could shake off these threats and get back to proclaiming the good news. They jumped that obstacle with seeming ease. And Luke then stresses again at the end of chapter 4 that they were unified, sharing their possessions, taking care of one another in sacrificial ways, and living out the unity of the kingdom.

Then chapter 5 starts and we get another obstacle. Were they really a committed family? Up to this early point in the story, Luke has described a community of believers that were all in. But Ananias and Sapphira were not. They wanted to give the impression that they were, but they proved that they were thinking of themselves separately from the body. They wanted to look like family but not completely commit to it. So they lied. The Spirit responded quickly. A message was sent to the kingdom people. To pretend to be part of this family while not really being so in your heart will kill you spiritually. The physical death that this married couple experienced was an acted-out parable of sorts. It was sending the message: just as they died physically, so you will die spiritually if you take the Spirit lightly. "Great fear seized the whole church" (Acts 5:11). That was an appropriate response. The message was received and another hurdle was jumped.

Then another obstacle arose that is detailed in the latter half of Acts 5. Persecution from the Jewish leaders came to the forefront again. The kingdom was spreading and the religious leaders were not happy about it or the fact that their orders had been disobeyed by this group of simpletons. So they dragged them back into the Sanhedrin and warned them again. This time they were so angry they were ready to put them to death for blasphemy and be done with it. An unlikely ally came to their defense. Gamaliel, one of the most respected teachers of that time, urged the council to leave the disciples alone. If their movement was from God it would be foolish to fight it, he argued; and if it was not, they would soon be scattered and gone. His wise words spared the lives of the Christians that day, but they were severely flogged and ordered once again to stop proclaiming the dangerous message that Jesus was the King. Another daunting obstacle was cleared. It was starting to seem as if nothing could slow down the word of God as it was trumpeted from the lips of every disciple.

Acts 6 opens with the information that "the number of disciples was increasing." The kingdom was expanding and even serious external persecution and internal rebellion of an Exodus quality could not slow down the spread of God's word. Until, it seems, we read the rest of verse 1 in chapter 6. The number of disciples was continuing to increase, the word of God was spreading rapidly, but then the brakes are seemingly slammed to the floor: "...the Hellenistic Jews among them complained against the Hebraic Jews because their widows were being overlooked in the daily distribution of food" (Acts 6:1b). Here is another obstacle—and don't overlook how serious this one was. Persecution and lack of commitment can hamper a church and beat it down, but there was far more peril inherent in this obstacle. It could have divided the church in two.

What would happen to the message of the gospel, the proclamation that Jesus was the King and that his rule was the promised blessing to all nations? What would happen to the message of reconciliation (2 Corinthians 5:18–21) between both man and God and between the nations if there were two ethnic branches of the church that could not get along?

It's easy to overlook the severity of this problem, but imagine that you were there and were a Hellenistic Jew, meaning that you were a Jew who grew up somewhere outside of Israel as a result of the diaspora. Even though they were all Jews with much in common, there were cultural differences between those who grew up in Jerusalem and the surrounding areas and those who were raised in a more pagan context. As a Hellenistic Jew, you had heard the good news of the Messiah and accepted it. You desired to be a member of this one family of all nations, the true descendants of Abraham. You were thrilled to be part of the fulfillment of Isaiah's great prophecy as the people of all nations began to stream into the kingdom. You were excited to see the love and care that disciples had for one another. All of you were together all the time and shared with anyone in need. This was unquestionably the reign of God in living action. It didn't even matter that the Hellenistic Jews and Hebraic Jews tended to live in different parts of the city. Even though your fellow Hellenistic Jews spoke Greek and the Hebraic Jews spoke Aramaic, and there were tensions between the two groups at times, none of those divisions had a place in the body of Christ. Maybe Hebraic Jews looked down upon the Hellenistic Jews everywhere else, but not here in the kingdom. You were one family and one body, and those distinctions no longer mattered in Christ.

You believed all that, but then some among you realized that the Hebraic Jews were getting more than their fair share of the distribution of food. Taking care of the poor and vulnerable was a hallmark and characteristic of the Jesus community, so no one had a problem with the fact that it was being done. It was the inequity that became concerning. The apostles were Hebraic Jews, and so it seems that the Hebrews were in most positions of authority in the church.

This shouldn't be a problem, right? These distinctions hold no mean-ing in Christ. Except that they do. Cultural differences are a beautiful and important part of diversity. They should be celebrated. That's part of the kingdom. What is not part of the kingdom is when those differences start to serve as our identities and become a source of division. They were one in Christ, but there was more work to be done.

Are you still imagining that you are a Hellenistic Jew at that time? Good. How would you have felt about this? What temptations would be making their way into your thinking? How about fear? Wouldn't you be afraid that the same prejudices and tensions that were a normal part of life between these two groups were coming into the kingdom? Maybe it wasn't that different after all. How about mistrust? Those leaders really are showing favoritism and tribalism. They are favoring their people over ours. How about anger? Something must be done. These guys don't really love us. They are just like everyone else in the world. They are trying to neglect and subjugate us. They want us to be second-class citizens. How about sedition and division? We can't keep being treated like this. They don't understand us and our pain, and they don't want to. We need new leaders. Or maybe we should just form our own community around Jesus and leave them to themselves. We can take care of our people and they can take care of theirs.

Persecution could slow down the church but not destroy its message. Internal lack of commitment and honesty before God were serious prob-lems that could derail the cohesiveness and effectiveness of the church, but they would not extinguish its message. But ethnic division? That would be an outright assault on the gospel. This was huge.

We will look at the solution they generated in the next chapter, but for now I want to highlight what Luke writes immediately following the resolution of this community cancer. He says, "So the word of God spread. The number of disciples in Jerusalem increased rapidly, and a large num-ber of priests became obedient to the faith" (Acts 6:7). The impression given is that growth had ground to a halt during this kerfuffle. How could the good news concerning the King of the family of all nations be a light to the world if they couldn't work out their own issues and were having ethnic wars? How was this any different than anywhere else? But once the solution was brought to bear, the word of God spread again. (Is this an important truth that we should consider deeply in our own contemporary context?) We can only speculate at this point, but it seems that these ac-tions and the aftermath led to the conversion of a healthy numbers of Jew-ish priests. Could it be that part of what drew these priests to the gospel was the fact that they were able to overcome ethnic tensions and division in a way that they had never seen before? Was that what led them to see that the Christian community really was the unique kingdom of God?

The Kingdom Borders Expand

The obstacles weren't over; more were on the horizon. With the internal issue abated for the time being, the church could get back to focusing fully on the mission to the world. This brought more conflict with the Jewish leaders, leading to the eventual stoning death of Stephen, one of the men who was a pivotal part of the resolution to the problem in Acts 6:1–7. Stephen's death led to a great persecution that was so violent and severe that it was beyond anything they had yet experienced. It led most of the disciples, except the apostles, to scatter throughout Judea and Samaria. Saul was indeed an intense and zealous man. His pogrom was a big obstacle. Or was it?

As a result of the scattering disciples, the Word was spread wherever they went. That's where Luke records the next big obstacle for the kingdom people. Some disciples had preached the Word to the hated Samaritans. The Jews despised Samaritans, who were an ethnic mixture of Jews and pagans that had moved into the land after the northern tribes were taken off into exile. The Samaritans accepted the gospel and were baptized, receiving the gift of the indwelling of the Spirit. But the Spirit had not come upon any of these Samaritans in order to enable them to do something miraculous; their spiritual gifts were limited in scope and served as visible verification that these people were part of God's new family.[39] This was apparently unique, which is why Luke recorded it. The reason seems to be that the Spirit knew that many Jewish Christians, both Hebraic and Hellenistic, would come together in their protest against the gospel being given to the Samaritans. They couldn't just become part of God's family, could they? So Peter and John came and confirmed what had been done. They laid hands on the Samaritan disciples and the Spirit came upon them in a miraculous way. The objections would have to be abandoned. God had spoken, and the Samaritans were clearly part of the kingdom.

Luke seems to break into his story of obstacles to share a bit of good news and a hint of what was to come. An Ethiopian (Cushite) official representing his queen had come to Jerusalem, quite possibly as a religious quest to see Jerusalem or learn more about Judaism. On his way home, he was reading from the prophet Isaiah and invited Philip to teach him what this was all about. He accepted Jesus as King and was baptized right there on the road. But why no special mention of the Spirit doing something like delaying the visible gifts until the people could see it and verify that they came from the apostles themselves? Why did the Spirit not do anything unique to confirm that even Cushites would be welcomed into the family? The most obvious explanation is that he was going back to Africa. He would, in a very real sense, be out of sight, out of mind. The gospel would spread in Africa without the immediate obstacle of ethnic barriers in the minds of the believers who still tended to believe that only Jews could be part of God's family and that if someone wanted to become a follower of Jesus they would first have to become a full practicing Jew, including circumcision and adherence to the Law. That wouldn't be a problem here, so he was baptized and sent on his way to spread the word of God. No miraculous display of the Spirit was needed.

After the amazing story of Paul's conversion in Acts 9, another obstacle presents itself in Acts 10. This would be one of the biggest the church had faced yet. Yes, the Ethiopian Cushite was brought into the kingdom, but he would not be in the face of the Jewish believers, unlike this Gentile. Cornelius was a God-fearer, which means that he adhered to certain aspects of Judaism but would not have gotten circumcised and become fully Jewish. When Peter came, at the urging of a dream, and preached the gospel to Cornelius and his household, it presented a major issue. Most Jewish Christians would simply not accept Gentiles into the family of God. They were ethnically impure pagans. How could they be kingdom citizens without becoming Jews? Even Peter had to have the Holy Spirit come to him personally in a vision before he would accept this.

"I now realize" declared Peter with the full implications of the gospel beginning to dawn on him, "how true it is that God does not show favoritism but accepts from every nation the one who fears him and does what is right" (Acts 10:34). Please don't miss just how controversial that would have been. Even Peter would have a hard time selling that to the folks back in Jerusalem. The Spirit took care of it, though. As Peter was preaching, the Holy Spirit preempted any arguments or objections. He came upon them miraculously just as he had come upon Samson (Judges 14:6, 19, 15:14) and King Saul (1 Samuel 10:6, 10), enabling them to do what they could not previously do to fulfill God's purposes. Suddenly they had the same sign of acceptance and verification that the disciples did on Pentecost and the Samaritans did in Acts 8. Peter's response is telling: "Surely no one can stand in the way of their being baptized with water. They have received the Holy Spirit just as we have" (Acts 10:47–48). Of course, he was referring to the miraculous sign of acceptance, because they would not partake of the Spirit being in them until they were baptized into Christ.

With that, the kingdom was fully realized in its implications for all nations and would never be the same. As we have already mentioned, however, that is the starting point for the hard work, not the end of it. The ethnic conflicts in the church would continue. There were other sources of conflict, to be sure (such as issues raised between rich and poor disciples), but clashes of culture, race, and ethnicity would be ever-present in the Christian communities.

More Diversity, More Problems

Acts 11–14 continues to chronicle a church that was rapidly spreading and becoming more diverse as it went. The mixture created complex situations, only some of which we understand today. Each new Christian community seemed to have Jewish believers and a potpourri of Gentiles, but the lines of culture and ethnicity weren't so simple. Sometimes there was tension between Jews and Gentiles. Sometimes it was between different Gentile groups. Sometimes the ethnic and cultural conflicts were between the church and those that would not believe.

The primary racial controversy of the early decades, though, was whether Gentiles had to follow the Law of Moses to be fully considered part of the family. Even though the Spirit had seemingly spoken in the incidents described in Acts 8 and 10, there were still great doubts and a large cultural divide. Many Jewish Christians, especially a large group in Judea, believed that God had accepted the Gentiles into the true Israel; but only Jews in Christ were the true Israel, which meant that Gentiles had to become Jews at the same time they entered the Messiah. This was a huge cultural shift demanded of the Gentiles, as they were being told that they had to follow Jewish practices in order to be considered true kingdom citizens.

This led to the council in Jerusalem described in Acts 15. Paul, Barnabas, and other believers went up to meet with the apostles, elders, and those who considered themselves both Pharisees and Christians. The latter group was demanding that the Gentiles be circumcised before being fully accepted. Imagine the intensity of this. Imagine a scenario today in which an influential group of disciples teaches and proclaims that only men can baptize people into Christ. Anyone who was baptized by a woman, claims this group, needs to be baptized again by a man in order to be a true Christian. Think of the chaos this would have the potential of breeding in the church, not to mention the conflict, the hard feelings, and the insecurities. This is something of what was going on in the first century, but it was even more intense and far-reaching.

For Paul and those that understood the gospel in the same way that he did, this controversy could not be more vital and central to the kingdom. Was this going to be a family of all nations or not? Was the message of the gospel that Jesus was King and all those from all nations who entered his life were part of the family of God? Was Jesus the sole entry point into the kingdom? Was he the fulfillment of the promises of God? Or was there a two-tier entry process where one also had to become a Jew, submit to circumcision, and adhere to the Mosaic Law?

While this may seem like a strictly spiritual issue, it was also deeply rooted in culture and ethnicity. And it tended to create division right down racial lines. It could get more complex than that at times, but that was the basic dividing line. Paul seems to have had two great fears about this as it relates to ethnicity. The first is that if Gentiles did have to become Jews, in effect, to be considered Christians, then the ethnic dividing line between Jew and Gentile still existed. The border may have opened a bit, but the separation was still there. The second fear was that the real-world effect of this would be to create two separate churches: a Jewish church and a Gentile church. If either of those things occurred, the good news would be deeply damaged. A central component of the gospel itself, that Jesus had created the one family of all nations promised to Abraham, would be destroyed.

With Acts 15, this larger question about whether Gentiles had to become Jews to be considered members of God's family was settled. We will look at the specifics of their solution in a subsequent chapter, but it is enough now to say that the issue was resolved. As Paul would declare in Galatians 3, "There is neither Jew nor Gentile, neither slave nor free, nor is there male and female, for you are all one in Christ Jesus" (Galatians 3:28). There would be no dividing line that would create two arms of the kingdom. There would not be a Jewish church and a Gentile church; there would not be one version of the kingdom for men and another for women; there would be no free community of believers and one for the slaves. We are all one in Christ Jesus. Paul would not abide the idea that there could be nominal unity at a universal level but separate communities along racial, socioeconomic, gender, or any other lines.

More Trouble on the Horizon

When I lived in Milwaukee I would take the same route every day to the school at which I taught. On my drive, I would pass several churches that never stated that they were all-white, but in practice, that's what they were. I also passed a Hmong church, a Pentecostal church that was almost entirely Hispanic, and an all-black Baptist church. I understand that there are complex societal reasons for much of this, but if we view it from a strictly gospel perspective, we should readily understand how much this would horrify Paul. This is no gospel at all; it is a corrupted version of the good news, one in which we have allowed ethnicity and culture to become kings rather than Jesus. Let me put it this way: when people of the world see this sort of paper unity, how could they possibly see anything other than a natural reflection of the very world that they experience and live in every day? How is this any different from the world?

Over the course of the last six years I have read dozens of books on cross-cultural ministry and the challenge of creating culturally diverse groups. The shocking thing to me, at least at first, was that the majority of the books I read that have analyzed the state of (mostly) American Christianity have concluded that the best thing for the future is for black and white churches to learn to communicate and work together better; but that it is impossible and ultimately a negative thing to try to have churches that consist of all ethnic groups. Paul would, no doubt, roundly disagree.

Once it was confirmed that the Jews and Gentiles would accept one another as full members of the family with no ethnic markers or distinctions necessary, that did not resolve all the tensions and difficulties. There would be ongoing things that needed to be worked through, differences and practices that others would have to learn to bear with and accept. For the remainder of the chapter, I will highlight two of those clashes that will help us to grasp some of the issues that the first-century church continued to encounter. That will then springboard us into the next several chapters, where we will look at the important actions that our earliest brothers and sisters took to help them in their quest to be the one unified family of all nations that God had called them to be.

There is a bit of historical uncertainty as to specifics, but it appears that around AD 48, a group of Jewish Christians centered in Jerusalem and known today as the Judaizers were throwing the Gentile Christian world into confusion. This was just before the council in Jerusalem described in Acts 15. They had been creating controversy among the disciples in Antioch, Syria, and Cilicia, and were now making inroads into the churches of the Galatians. As they had in these other places, these Judaizers were declaring to the Gentile-heavy churches that the gospel that Paul had preached to them was incomplete. They needed to follow the Jewish Law and Jewish cultures and customs. This threw Paul into a tizzy as he sat down to write the Galatians, possibly shortly before the Jerusalem meeting. In his letter, he charged the churches in Galatia with deserting him and "turning to a different gospel" (Galatians 1:6). Paul's response, known as the book of Galatians, is terse and direct. He gives them the charge to hold to the gospel that they heard in the beginning, no matter what. There are not tiers of ethnicity and culture in the kingdom. To believe that they must become Jews spiritually and culturally was to abandon the idea that all of God's promises are "Yes" in Christ (2 Corinthians 1:20) and that his sacrifice on the cross had destroyed the barrier between the two people groups (Ephesians 2:14).

In his effort to turn them from this corruption of the good news, Paul tells them of a recent conflict at his home church in Antioch. Antioch was a diverse and active church that was constantly growing and sending out missionaries to other parts of the world. Acts 13:1 hints at the diversity in the church there in its list of the prophets and teachers in Antioch. It shows an amazing cross-section of cultural and ethnic variety.

Into that mix came the Judaizers, presumably the same ones that were attempting to infiltrate the Galatian churches with their version of the gospel message. Cephas, the esteemed apostle Peter, had come to Antioch for a visit and joined in with the customs and cultural practices of this mixed but heavily Gentile-influenced church. He enjoyed unencumbered table fellowship with the Gentiles, which was important because in the Jewish culture, table fellowship was a sign and symbol of the age to come. To eat with someone was a deeply significant act that meant that you accepted them and would be together with them in the coming age.

Perhaps Cephas struggled with it, but more than likely he was simply putting into practice the principles that he had learned immediately preceding the baptism of Cornelius and his household: that God had not set any people group or culture aside as unclean and they are all on equal footing at the cross. So he moved seamlessly into the diverse cultures of the Antioch church.

Then the Judaizers came to town. Paul never says explicitly what Peter's thinking was in this situation, but it's possible that he did not want to offend the Jewish Christians and so he withdrew from table fellowship with the Gentile Christians. This was the apostle Peter, after all, so Barnabas followed his lead. Paul is adamant in his criticism. This was a pivotal moment in the church, and Paul confronted him publicly, challenging him with the implications of the true gospel. A gospel could not be accepted that would create two cultures or two ethnicities in the body of Christ.

The remainder of Galatians is Paul's response to this false, Judaizing version of the gospel and his corrections to the damage that it had done and could do in the future. He could not allow the Jewish culture to be seen as superior. Identity in the family was through Christ alone and there could be only one family in Christ.

Trouble Spreads to Rome

About that same time, maybe just a few months later, another situation was arising in Rome that is just as fascinating. Some sort of conflict had broken out in the great city, quite probably between the large Jewish community in Rome and the growing Christian church there that consisted of both Jews and Gentiles; although much of the leadership of the church may have been Jewish. History has not preserved the exact nature and scope of the problems, but according to Roman historian Suetonius, the Jews made constant disturbances at the instigation of "Chrestus," and the Roman Emperor Claudius issued a decree expelling all Jews from Rome. We do not know the degree to which this was enforced and whether it extended only to the central leadership or to all Jews. It did, however, affect both the Jewish and Christian communities (the Romans did not yet make a distinction between those two groups).

The impact of this decree on the church was profound. The Jewish Christian leaders, including Aquila and Priscila, were forced to leave the city. Going with them were quite possibly the rest of the Jewish Christians, or at least most of them. This happened in AD 49. For five years afterward, the church in Rome existed as an exclusively Gentile group. Surely many of the conflicts and difficulties of being a cross-cultural community greatly diminished overnight. They settled into their normal Christian routine, and the church continued to grow. If we read the letter to the Romans carefully, it would seem that some of the Gentile Christians, if not the whole church, felt that God had left the Jews behind and that Christianity would be an exclusively Gentile thing moving forward.

In AD 54, Nero became Emperor of Rome and shortly allowed the Jews back into the city. An influx of Jewish Christians now returned to the church, and culture clashes were soon to follow. This was almost the opposite situation of what was going on in Galatia, where the Jewish culture had the upper hand and was trying to impose its superiority and will on the Gentiles. In Rome, the Gentiles were dominant and were leaving little to no room for the consciences, convictions, and practices of the freshly returned Jewish disciples.

Shortly after Nero's edict and the reappearance of the Jews in Rome, Paul writes to a church that he had never before visited. His expertise in these culture conflicts and his ability to apply theology to them would be of great value.

It is easy for us to read about the conflicts that Paul mentions in the church, primarily in chapter 14 of Romans, and to skate past them as though they were minor issues, but that would be a mistake. These were deep waters. Topics like whether it was okay to eat meat sacrificed at a pagan temple would have felt like sin issues and maybe even salvation issues to many disciples. Observing sacred days and festivals and other cultural practices made up an important part of who they were. To have a large portion of the church go against these sacred beliefs and dearly held practices had to make them feel dismissed, oppressed, ignored, or unloved. Countless Jews had sacrificed their lives for the right of their fellow Jews to be able to enjoy these freedoms, and now these Gentiles who were supposed to be their brothers and sisters in Christ didn't even seem to care. It must have crossed the minds of each side that the other disregarded them, didn't understand the gospel, or was flat-out prejudiced and bigoted.

Paul writes a church in Rome that seems on the verge of splitting in two. The only thing worse than them splitting into a largely Gentile church and a mostly Jewish church would be if they did it and thought that it was just fine. His response is so helpful to us today that we will spend an entire chapter examining it.

To summarize, the first-century church faced their own set of complex and emotional ethnic and cultural bumps. This is part and parcel of a church that is built on the central truth of being one family of all nations. The more diversity you have, the more potential for conflict. In the chapters that follow, I will focus on the kingdom responses and solutions that the early church offered for solving their problems of culture and race.

Questions for Discussion

1. What is your response to this reminder of how many deep ethnic and cultural conflicts the early church had?

2. What do you think about the suggestion that ethnic and cultural divisions or conflict can potentially lead to stagnation and lack of growth in the body of Christ? What are the implications of that today?

3. Do you feel that there are any racial or cultural tensions or divisions in your church right now?

4. Do you agree with the claim that churches being divided along racial lines is an affront to the gospel?

5. What current events in society or in the church have the most potential to create conflict or division? What does your church do to respond to those threats?

Chapter 10

Choose from Among You: Validation

The first year or two of marriage was tough for my wife and me. It wasn't terrible; we didn't have a lot of fights, but we certainly didn't know what we were doing either. We weren't disciples yet, and we just limped along trying to figure it out as we went. We both readily acknowledge that if it wasn't for the kingdom of God, his guiding word, and the discipling and friendships that we had in the church once we became Christians, there is little chance that we would be married today.

Even after becoming disciples, things took time to change. They eventually did, and we have a wonderful marriage. But one of our issues in those early years was that I was sure that I was right—a lot. Actually, I was pretty certain that I was right about everything, even if I didn't always say it. That led to quite a bit of frustration for my wife. When she would see things and point them out, my instinctive response was to get defensive or justify myself. My view was that she never understood things. She never saw them from the right perspective. She never correctly analyzed my motives and actions. Or, if all else failed, she didn't say it in the right way. We didn't grow as we could have in our marriage because she was wrong so often, or so I thought.

Then one day I was studying the Sermon on the Mount and I came across Matthew 7:3–6. That's the passage where Jesus urges his followers to see the sin of others as little compared to their own. Don't look at the speck of sawdust in the other person's eye, he says, while you have a big plank in your own eye. You usually can't see it when you have something on your face. We need each other to point it out. Jesus never intended that kingdom people wouldn't point out one another's sin; he just knew human tendencies. He was well aware that when we strive toward holiness and living by God's will, it becomes too easy to look down our noses at others and grow irritated with their sin. It rapidly moves into the realm of hypoc-risy and being judgmental. So, by all means, help one another, but be fully aware of your own sin first. The best way to do that is to work together and point out each other's junk.

That hit home for me. I needed to grow in my humility. And the spe-cific part of my life that I needed to work on in order to do that was to lis-ten to my wife when she tried to point out things I needed to change. And even more important, I needed to assume that what she said was true. I stopped defending myself. I stopped explaining myself. I just listened and acted as though what she said was completely accurate, even when it didn't feel that way. I'm not saying I let her run roughshod over me. That's not her character at all, so I didn't need to worry about that. I simply resolved to trust her. I must be honest: much of the time what she said didn't feel right, accurate, or fair. But I acted as though it was, whether it struck me that way or not.

It may not surprise you to discover that I started to grow spiritual-ly like never before, simply because I listened to her perspective. I have found that she is right about my character and what she sees immeasur-ably more often than she is wrong. And even on the rare occasions when she is wrong, I believe that I still benefit from the process of humility that it takes to listen and to trust her way of seeing things and treat it with dignity and respect. I still have a long way to go. We both do. But the Holy Spirit has used us to help each other grow a great deal.

This Is Normal

This is a biblical skill that we don't see or experience much in the world. We become so convinced of our own beliefs and opinions that the only way we know how to interact with one another is to try to persuade others that they are wrong unless they agree with our opinion. Social me-dia has become a hotbed of this. Quite often someone will share their thoughts and perspectives about some important issue of the day. I have yet to see a response where someone else writes, "You know, that's not what I have experienced in my life. I don't see it that way at all. But I will trust what you tell me from your own experience and will act as though that is true rather than trying to argue you into seeing things my way." There is a time and place for discussion and debate, of course, but how much different would the world be if people were willing to do this?

As we discussed in the previous chapter, one of the earliest obstacles in the newly formed community of the Messiah's people surrounded the issue of caring for the poor among them. The early Christians definitely wanted to help those in need, but they tended to do that by taking care of everyone inside the new society of disciples and inviting others into this new world where people took care of one another, rather than by focusing on trying to solve or abate poverty out in the world at large. So the daily distribution of food to those among the churches who needed it was a big deal. Taking care of the widows who had few options available to them was a vital function of the community. The very acts of providing for one another's needs and caring for widows were strong signs to outsiders that they perceived themselves as one big family.

In the very midst of the community doing their best to love and provide for one another, Luke notes a problem. One of the things I love the most about the book of Acts is that Luke never tries to hide the struggles of the church. He is honest about their moments of victory and unwavering about sharing some of the low moments as well. The Greek-speaking Jews that shared a more Hellenist culture complained against the Aramaic-speaking Jews that shared a common culture from growing up in Judea.

While it is striking that Luke is so honest about their frustration and complaint, what is even more notable and perhaps surprising is the response of the church leaders. It is instructive, because this ethnic dust-up was perhaps a bit of a foreshadowing of the Jewish-Gentile clashes to come later, and it quite likely would have served as a blueprint, or at least the starting point, for resolving these inevitable issues.

With that said, let's examine the conflict between the Hellenistic and Hebraic Jewish Christians and find the important elements and principles that will guide us when we face similar situations.

The first thing that we should note is that this was not unique; it was not an example of an awful and dangerous sin like that described in Acts 5:1–11. When different cultures, ethnicities, and people groups come together to form one family, there will be conflicts and problems to work through. That is guaranteed.

When Paul wrote to the church in Colosse, he exhorted them to:

> *Bear with each other and forgive one another if any of you has a grievance against someone. Forgive as the Lord forgave you. And over all these virtues put on love, which binds them all together in perfect unity.* Colossians 3:13–14

That is decidedly challenging stuff right there. I call passages like this one "implied promises." When Paul urges them to bear with and forgive one another, it is an implied promise that they will have reason to. We will have conflicts. We will hurt one another. We will sin against one another. We will misunderstand others and be misunderstood. Count on it.

What can so often be overlooked is the context and Paul's train of thought surrounding this passage. In 3:1, he reminds the disciples that they have been raised with Christ and so should set their minds on heaven's will and not their own earthly will. They died to themselves and entered into Christ, after all (3:3). Because of this truth, as a community they should work together to leave behind the old ways of living and take up the life of Christ, which is an entirely new type of living (3:5–10). In Christ, he says, they are the one family of all nations; there is no division between Gentile and Jew or any other human distinction that can come into play in the body (3:11). "Therefore, as God's chosen people," says Paul, reminding them of their identity as God's family, "clothe yourselves with compassion, kindness, humility, gentleness and patience" (3:12). They are God's family of all nations, and these are the virtues they should strive for. But Paul is also a realist, and so he also writes verses 13–14. There will be conflict and they will have to work through it. As he starts to wrap up this train of thought, he declares, "Let the peace of Christ rule in your hearts, since as member of one body you were called to peace" (3:15). There will be skirmishes, but they cannot be allowed to divide the body.

I believe that one of the reasons Luke included this little incident in Acts is to remind us of that. Yes, conflict will come. It might come out of the ethnic and cultural identities that we were born into. Those are real. It is naïve and unrealistic to say that now that we are Christians those distinctions should no longer exist. They do. As we have pointed out before, we will often feel a natural level of comfort with those with whom we share culture. That will continue in the body, but it should not divide us and should grow less and less distinct over time. But the early disciples did not reach full unity by ignoring issues, covering them up, or acting like they were so accepting and "colorblind" that they had better not mention the problem lest they cause division. The fact that they had an ethnic clash was not the end of the world; it was a normal effect of applying the gospel. There was a division brewing. It was a problem. They named it and dealt with it openly and honestly.

Quick to Listen

James, the brother of Jesus, wrote his letter, I believe, not too long after the disciples from Jerusalem were dispersed because of Saul's intense persecution (Acts 8:1). He addresses his letter to "the twelve tribes scattered among the nations" (James 1:1). Perhaps he realized that in their scattering, they would spread the gospel wherever they went, and so one of the challenges they would face is that they would suddenly find themselves in community with people that were very different culturally. His advice to the family is as simple as it is difficult. "My dear brothers and sisters," he writes, gently reminding them of their familial connection to one another, "take note of this: Everyone should be quick to listen, slow to speak and slow to become angry, because human anger does not produce the righteousness that God desires" (James 1:19–20).

One of the most faithful companions to anger is justification. To justify ourselves is one of the strongest human drives. It is always at the ready, but especially when we are criticized or accused of something. "No, you've got that wrong." "That is not what I was doing." "You took what I said in the wrong way." There is a time and place for further explanation, but there is often a fine line between explanation and justification. Be slow with your mouth, says James. Fight the urge to justify yourself or show the other person why they are quite wrong about you and the events in question. Instead, we should be quick to listen.

That is exactly what the apostles did in Acts 6. Think of some of the justifications that they could have shot back with:

- "You are wrong. There is no favoritism here."
- "Stop being critical."
- "Don't play the victim."
- "Our job is difficult. No one could have planned for this, so we are doing the best we can."
- "Why don't you stop complaining and start helping?"
- "You are imagining things."
- "We are doing our best, and your complaints are certainly not helping the situation."
- "Maybe if there were not so many needy Hellenistic widows, we would not be in this mess."
- "You are being divisive and trying to create a controversy where there is none."
- "Okay, even if there is some truth to that, you pointing it out is only going to cause division."
- "We're sorry that you misinterpreted what is happening here and incorrectly thought that there was neglect."
- "You don't know the whole story or understand what is really going on."

I'm sure that there many more defenses that could have been offered, but amazingly we don't see any. The apostles did not offer one and Luke does not try to supply one.

Rather than offering up a justification, they listen to the complaint. They validate it. Validating the experiences and feelings of others is often crucial. Yes, there are times when someone needs to be gently challenged or moved past such things, but we should err on the side of listening rather than explaining.

The Twelve listened to the Hellenistic Jews and assumed that what they said was true. They realized that when one part of the body suffered, they all suffered (1 Corinthians 12:26), and something needed to be done. There was absolutely no attempt to turn this situation around on the Hellenistic Jews and accuse them of having bad hearts or of emphasizing differences that should not matter in Christ.

One of the most destructive things that can happen in a community is when one part brings up an area of neglect or needed growth and is not listened to, or the response is condescending. Allow me to provide a somewhat controversial example from the modern world. Many black Americans have cried out that although slavery is long in the past, Jim Crow laws have been expunged, and the President of the United States from 2009 to 2017 was Barack Obama, the average black person still has a tougher time in our society than do their white countrymen. Without getting embroiled in that debate right now, I will simply analyze one facet of the situation: the typical response to that from many white Americans is to discredit it. "You are incorrect," they often say, "racism is not an issue anymore. You have been fooled by the media, which has an agenda to continue the storyline of ongoing racism." Imagine how condescending it feels to have experienced and seen something your whole life, only to be told that you are not insightful enough to understand that you have not actually experienced it. There are always going to be different perspectives on any issue. I get that, and that's not my point. The point is that there is often very little listening and a whole lot of justification or dismissiveness.

While that is commonplace in the world, it should not be in the body of Christ. Let's say that a group of African American brothers and sisters approaches the leadership of their church and explains that they feel they are not represented fairly in the church leadership, or that almost all the musical and other cultural expressions in the church ignore their culture and music (I should point out that black disciples are not the only ones that face some of these slights. Whites can as well, although not as often; as can Hispanic disciples, Asian disciples, and other groups).

What can we learn from Acts in the response of the church to their issues? Validate their experiences. Don't try to justify. I find it interesting that we do not even read of an apology from the apostles. It is as if the assumption is, "Well yes, of course, we will have deficiencies. Thank you for pointing this one out; now let's get on with the solution."

Quick to Act

This leads into my next observation from this encounter over the care for the widows. After hearing the complaint and avoiding the tendency to defend themselves, explain away the issue, or turn it around on the complaining group; they took action. It was not hasty or reckless, but they got to it right away. One of the things that can be very harmful in bumps like these is that the leadership is slow to act. Maybe they don't see the problem. Maybe they don't know what to do. Maybe they don't prioritize it as a big issue, and it gets put on the back burner. Then nothing happens, and that leaves a lot of room for temptation.

How would the Hellenistic Jews have felt if the response was, "Oh, we certainly didn't mean to do anything like that. I don't think that's what is really going on here, but we'll definitely look into it and if they are being neglected, we'll figure out what we are going to do"? And if two years later, there was still no change? They would feel marginalized by that time, wouldn't they? The temptation would be to think that the divisions of the world still hold sway in the body of Christ. It is a bit counterintuitive when you think about it, but to render the divisions of the world impotent, the body of Christ must be sensitive to them and act as quickly as we can.

All indications in this passage are that the apostles immediately assumed that the complaint was true, with no counterargument, and moved toward a solution. It doesn't take much imagination to believe that the Hellenistic Jews felt valued and loved by their response.

Not Quick to Overreact

Yes, the apostles acted quickly, but they also didn't overreact. No blame was assigned here. If it wasn't intentional then none needed to be assigned; they just needed to resolve the problem. They responded appropriately by focusing on the specific situation. One sign of overreaction might have been if they directly took on this ministry themselves to show that they were taking the issue seriously. That might seem like a great solution and send a signal of how important this was, but it would have been reactionary. To do something of that nature would have involved losing sight of the bigger picture of their role as leaders. Instead, they were prepared.

When you expect conflicts to arise, you are far more likely to handle them appropriately and well. When you naively assume that they shouldn't occur and so are unprepared, that's when overreactions tend to happen. Imagine caring for a two-year-old for a weekend and assuming there will be no spills or accidents of any kind. You are likely to be sorely disappointed and find yourself overreacting when things do go awry. The apostles knew that they were not perfect. They knew the challenges for a transcultural people. They were prepared for trouble of some sort, and when that trouble came they acted efficiently and effectively.

Respect

What is on display in these seven verses in Acts is an incredible amount of respect. There is no patronizing of the Hellenistic Jews. There is no paternalism or condescension. There is only respect. What happened here is worth learning from. The Hebraic Jews were the dominant group. A group can be considered dominant in a larger group for a host of reasons, including a larger population, historical influence in the group, or holding a majority of the leadership positions. In some way, the Hebraic Jews probably fit the bill in all of those aspects. So they were the dominant culture in the church. (The term "dominant" carries no negative connotation. It simply notes that one subgroup has a greater power of influence in the overall culture of the larger group.) They could have easily cited their larger numbers or ignored the complaining minority. They did not do that, though. We have here an inspiring model of the dominant group listening to and respecting the nondominant group and treating them as equals. Let me be clear: I am not saying that this never happens today in the body of Christ and that the nondominant cultures or groups are always marginalized or ignored. But sometimes they are.

The apostles likely knew that if they went with their own perceptions or listened to the rest of the dominant group they would remain blind to the truth of the situation. If overlooking the Hellenistic Jews was unintentional, and all indications are that this was the case, then how would the Hebraic Jews know of the situation? They most likely did not know. If they wanted to defend their leadership, they would still not know. If they only listened to the dominant group's perspective, they would still be in the dark. They had to hear what the Hellenistic Jews said, assume it was true even though they had not seen it, and then show respect in their response.

Power Under

In Chapter 6, I suggested that the type of leadership power manifested in the kingdom of God is power under others rather than power over them. Jesus taught these men, "Those who are regarded as rulers of the Gentiles lord it over them, and their high officials exercise authority over them. Not so with you. Instead, whoever wants to become great among you must be your servant" (Mark 10:42–43). Peter learned that lesson well, writing later in his life telling leaders in the body to "be shepherds of God's flock that is under your care, watching over them—not because you must, but because you are willing, as God wants you to be; not pursuing dishonest gain, but eager to serve; not lording it over those entrusted to you, but being examples to the flock" (1 Peter 5:2–3).

Vividly on display in Acts 6 is a power-under approach. Leaders who are focused on their power will tend to defend themselves when challenged. These leaders did not feel the need to make themselves look good, to fix the situation themselves, or to make it appear as though the Hellenistic Jews were the real problem here rather than their own leadership. Instead, they gave the power in the situation to the nondominant group. It is not clear here whether they asked the entire church to choose men who would lead in this situation, or if it was the Hellenistic Jews who chose. I lean toward the latter. The seven names listed in Acts 6 are all very distinct Hellenistic names.

This would mean that the apostles gave the authority to right the situation to the nondominant group and, in fact, gave them leadership in this area over the entire congregation. They didn't feel the need to keep all the power amassed in their hands. What is equally amazing is that, apparently, the Hebraic Jews trusted the Greek Jews to lead wisely. Don't miss the otherworldliness of this. The dominant group listened to the nondominant group's complaints about being overlooked and, rather than justifying the situation or trying to fix it themselves, they trusted the nondominant group with the solution and the authority to fix it. And not just the authority over themselves, but all the responsibility for this very important ministry.

There is another significant point here worth considering. By circumstance, the Hebraic Jews had control of the power and probably the culture of the church. I feel confident that if we could go back and ask the disciples involved in this situation, we would hear that not one of them was overtly prejudiced toward the Hellenistic Jews. These were their brothers and sisters in Christ, and while they had differences, cultural and otherwise, they had probably worked very hard to ensure that there were no vestiges of bigotry in their hearts; they did not want, after all, the natural tension between the two groups coming into the church. That is good, but it does not change the fact that the Hebraic Jews benefited, as unintentional as it may have been, from holding the positions of leadership. What the apostles did, then, in releasing their authority and advantage was vital to a healthy culture moving forward. They leveled out the playing field to the extent that could be accomplished at that point. The intentional shift of power was immeasurably important.

Spiritual Solution

One of the other indicators that they did not overreact is that we are told that they chose men full of faith and the Holy Spirit. Yes, Stephen is singled out in that respect, but surely that does not indicate that the rest were not in the same category. That much is implied strongly. Stephen is specifically mentioned because the narrative is about to focus on his important confrontation with Jewish opponents.

A solution that quite often comes from the likes of the world when an inequity has occurred is that they resolve it by simply giving someone something they did not earn or are not prepared for. This is complex, and I'm not taking aim at any specific concepts or programs, merely pointing out that this isn't typically the best solution. I was in South Africa recently driving through the countryside with a friend. He explained to me how the governments in the area wanted to try to fix some of the problems of the past, so they were systematically taking farms away from white farmers and giving them to black Africans. The problem was that the blacks were not farmers, and the government did not train them well. The results have been problematic. Hopefully, that will be resolved in the future, but simply putting people in positions they are not ready for, even if they are not ready because of past complexities, is not a good solution.

The apostles did not appoint a bunch of Hellenistic Jewish leaders just to have some diversity in the leadership and to appease the complainants. There is no whiff of any appeasement here. They chose men who were qualified spiritually. It is true enough that they were sought out in response to this problem, and it was quite intentional that they were Greek Jews, but they were also qualified to be in those positions. For example, let's say a church in our fellowship has a music ministry that is almost exclusively populated by African Americans. Some of the white disciples complain that they would like to hear some music from their culture on occasion. The right response would not be to put me in the music ministry. I could not sing or play an instrument if my life depended on it. In fact, I have been banned from joining the music team on two continents. Lord knows I tried. Finding qualified people would be the order of the day, but finding qualified people from the nondominant group should be a priority if we are to follow the example from Acts 6.

They Acted Intentionally

This point may seem obvious, but it is worth outlining. As we can see, the apostles took action in this case. They didn't have to. They did not see the problem or they would have already addressed it. Perhaps they were tempted to feel that it was an inaccurate or unfair complaint, but they avoided that option. Whatever the case, they acted in a very intentional manner not just to resolve the immediate situation but to act in a way that was consistent with the kingdom and the age to come.

Even though they seem to have acted quickly (although we are not given a timeline with this incident), they were careful, measured, and intentional. They did not conform to the patterns of the world, but acted in a transformed way (Romans 12:2). They validated the complaints of the nondominant group. They respected their perspective and trusted their wisdom as well as their heart in the matter. They did not deflect or pass the buck. They displayed power under others. They empowered the group that did not have power.

In fact, that may have been the most brilliant aspect of this obviously Spirit-led decision. They could have simply fixed the immediate situation. That's probably what most leaders would have done. But they intentionally looked down the road at what they were becoming and what they wanted to reflect to the world. Imagine a visitor coming in and asking about the ministry of the daily distribution of food. The ministry itself would have impressed them enough, but try to think of their shock when they heard that the Hellenistic Jews held the authority to oversee food distribution for the whole body after complaining that their widows were being overlooked. The church was surely being a city on a hill.

We should not be afraid to deal with issues of culture and race head on and purposefully. Whether your congregation is overrepresented by one race or underrepresented by another, or the cultural expressions of the body are almost exclusive to one ethnicity, or there is a perception by one group that they are not adequately represented in leadership; these items will not change without intentionality. It is okay to state the problems, be honest about the needs in the community, and then through prayer and humility establish an intentional plan to counteract the things of the world. We are continuing to form something the world has never seen outside of the kingdom of God, and maintaining that family of all nations will take much determination.

They Got Back to the Mission

When we do have cultural or racial issues in the church, there is, I believe, a temptation to ignore them and hope they go away or just get them dealt with as soon as possible so that it doesn't cause a distraction. There is no hint of that mentality here. The leaders took the time to listen and then discuss the problem among themselves. They then formulated a plan that was in line with who they knew the people of God needed to be as one family of all nations. Dealing with the issue was not a distraction. To not properly address it would have been a distraction, and likely would have become a festering sore on the body.

Once the people had chosen their servant leaders, they presented them to the apostles. The apostles trusted their choice, praying over them and laying hands on them. And so "the word of God spread" (Acts 6:7). The word translated "spread" literally means "to increase" or "to grow." I believe there to be a bit of a dual meaning here. As a result of their God-glorifying actions, the word of God increased and was magnified to a watching world. But that also meant that the gospel spread and more people were added to the kingdom. Of all the stories that Luke could have included about the developing church, he chose this as one of them. That probably indicates that this was a pretty emotional and important issue in the church. It could have caused a split. Instead, it became a source of victory and growth. Once they had jumped this hurdle, they could continue with the mission of both being the good news and proclaiming it.

Sometimes issues like these are ignored or relativized by church leadership because they sincerely want to focus on growing the church and helping more people become disciples. This incident shows us that to deal with these conflicts is *part* of the mission and often will allow the church to continue to expand the gospel to all nations.

Questions for Discussion

1. Have you seen any instances in your church where you felt that one group or ethnicity was being overlooked in some way?

2. How has the church responded to those issues in the past?

3. What can you do in a positive and constructive manner to help with those situations in the future?

4. How challenged are you by the suggestion to listen to others and then act as though their perspective is true?

5. In what ways do you see power-under leadership manifested in your church family?

Chapter 11

I Opposed Him to His Face: Confrontation

It took us nearly two hours of weaving in and out of some of the most congested traffic I had ever seen before we finally arrived at the medium-sized airport in Luanda, Angola. It was a hot day and there wasn't much that we could do in the car to make it more bearable. I had forgotten a water bottle and felt parched, my mouth as dry as a July day in Death Valley. I was a bit anxious as we arrived, because some of the brothers from the church I was visiting in Luanda had warned me that the airport could be a bit dangerous for foreign visitors. They urged me to steer clear of the police if I could, and not to pay any bribes if I was stopped at any point during the process of getting to my plane. If I was confronted and refused to pay, I could very well end up in jail.

The wonderful brother who had acted as my driver and guide walked me up to the airport entrance and we said our goodbyes. After hugging one another, I was ready to turn around and make my way through this gauntlet that I had been thinking and praying about all morning. Suddenly, the brother barked out, "Stay right here, I have to go get something for you. Please don't leave." Before I could even respond, he had darted out the door and was gone. This was not in my plan. Rather than getting through this airport as quickly as possible, I now had no choice but to stand there and wait. As I nervously waited, I tried not to notice that I had not escaped the attention of the soldiers and police officers. As five minutes passed into ten and then fifteen, the officers became more numerous. They crept ever closer to me as they circled, and after some time, a few of them didn't even try to mask the fact that they were keeping an eye directly on me.

My mind darted back and forth: "Should I stay here or just go through to the security and passport area?" As much as I wanted to go, this brother had asked me to stay put. But with each passing second, I became less and

less inclined to follow his wish. After nearly twenty minutes, I was leaning against a pole and noticed that a police officer, complete with a fully
automatic rifle slung around his shoulder, was about thirty feet away and
staring directly at me without looking away at all. I felt completely vulnerable. I stood out like a flashing neon sign. In that particular moment, I was
the only white person that I could see, and it was pretty obvious to anyone
there that I was not from the great country of Angola. I didn't want the
attention of this officer, or any others, for that matter. The officers at this
airport did not have great reputations, and there was a known corruption
problem here. I didn't know which officers were good and which would
harass me, and I didn't want to know. I didn't feel like I could trust any of
them. I just wanted to be invisible and be left alone. For the first time in my
life, I truly wished that I wasn't white and wasn't American and could just
blend in with everyone else. It had never before been a conscious thought
that I was either of those things; I just was. Now, not only was I aware of it,
it was impacting me in a way that I did not choose.

The rising trepidation and feelings of angst had reached their boiling point and I decided to bolt. I would have to explain to my brother
in Christ later why I didn't wait for him. Just as I pushed away from the
pillar, I heard a nearly breathless voice behind me gasp out the words, "My
brother, I am here." It turns out that he had graciously bought a beautiful
Angolan dress for my wife and had to go pick it up. I thanked him for his
thoughtfulness and generosity and knew that my wife would love it. We
hugged again and off I went.

By the grace of God, I made it through security despite the icy glares
and probing questions, and then through more of the same at passport
control. Just when I thought things were good, I rounded a corner and
was instantly reminded that every person leaving Angola must go into a
private office with officials to be searched. They want to make sure that no
one is illegally taking any currency out of the country. The anxiety crept
in again because I had heard that this was the most likely place to be harassed, held up for a bribe, or even arrested. My thoughts were broken into
by a man who shouted at me in Portuguese, indicating that I should step
into the next available room. I said a quick prayer and moved forward,
dreading each step. As I entered the doorway, a man at a desk swiveled
around in his chair to face me, shouted, and shooed me out. I didn't want
any trouble, so I turned around to exit the room. But as I did that, the
burly officer who had directed me toward that office now shouted and
gesticulated wildly that I should indeed go in.

Now I stood frozen, not knowing what to do. "Here we go," I thought.

"I'm doomed." Then something amazing happened. The two officers began to argue with one another, which didn't immediately make me feel any better. But suddenly the large man who had initially ordered me to go in looked at me with an oddly agitated look on his face and brusquely asked me in broken English if I had any currency on me. I squeaked out a "no," and that was it. "Go," he shouted at me; that was the first English word I had heard in the airport since I had left my brother in Christ near the entrance. He pointed up the stairs to the international waiting room, and I bolted. To this day, I believe that God spared me from having to go into the interrogation room, but I didn't stay around to ask any questions as to what the problem was or why they let me, and me only, go.

The Benefit of the Doubt

As I got on the plane, I took some time to reflect. That was perhaps the most disconcerting experience I had had in my life, as brief as it was. I felt helpless and powerless. I had never in my life felt afraid of the authority figures around me; I had never felt that I didn't and couldn't trust those in authority. All of these officers weren't bad, but I couldn't tell and so didn't want anything to do with any of them. I had never before truly noticed that I was white in any significant way, much less wished that I wasn't. I don't think I had ever been in a situation where being white made me stand out in a negative way and drew attention that I didn't want. The feelings of impotence in those brief moments rattled me. I had been confronted with a different perspective, and it transformed my thinking in many ways.

Several weeks later I was sitting with a friend of my mine, a brother in Christ who is African American, and I was recounting my adventure. Granted, it's not the most epic story ever told and hardly the most dangerous or harrowing situation that a teacher of the gospel has ever been in, but it was significant to me. I felt like God had taught me a lesson in vulnerability at the very least. But it was during that conversation that it really hit me. "Wait a second," I slowly breathed out, "is what I went through a little bit like what black people feel in the United States?" He smiled and without hesitation said, "Every single day, brother. Every single day."

You don't have to agree with his sentiments. That's not what I'm getting at. We will never fully agree on things seen from varying points of reference. What I do want to focus on, though, is the importance of being open to a different perspective. We should be willing to give the viewpoint of others the benefit of the doubt.

In Chapter 9, I briefly outlined the ongoing conflict between the

Jewish concept of Christianity and the Gentile one. In this chapter and the following two, I will look at different facets of that conflict. Here I will consider Paul's letter to the Galatian churches.

There are actually two confrontations based on perspective that take place in the book of Galatians. One is the letter itself. Paul becomes aware of what has been taught to the believers in those churches concerning their ethnic identity and standing in Christ and confronts them on why they would accept such antigospel ideas. The other is a story that Paul tells within the story as he recounts how he confronted Peter on his prejudice and racism.

There is a delicate balance that we must strike in the body of Christ. On one hand, we need to confront racism, racialism, prejudice, and bigotry as surely as we would any other sins. If we see it coming into the church or see elements of it in our brothers and sisters, there need to be firm but loving discussions that call for awareness, change of perspective, confession, and repentance. We must admit that we are often unaware of our own biases (and we all have biases) and the way that we come across to others, so humility and a lack of defensiveness will go a long way. The conversations like this that need to take place in the church should be done with love and humility on both sides.

On the other hand, we must be aware that there is a growing worldliness when it comes to confronting these topics. We must avoid the worldly tendencies toward anger and bitterness when we think someone has acted wrongly concerning culture or race. There is a growing sense of a witch hunt in our society, where everything is labeled racism and it is thought that the dissenters should be hunted down and dealt with. I have said it before, but if our responses and solutions are not very different from the world's, then what would be the point of joining the kingdom? We cannot allow our feelings and actions to be dictated by the world's moods.

We must be willing to confront but also be ready to extend the benefit of the doubt. A full hundred years before Jesus was born, a Jewish sage and rabbi named Yehoshua ben Perachia wrote that each person should "make for yourself a mentor, acquire for yourself a friend and judge each person with the scales weighted in their favor."[40] He captures the essence of a practice that was common in Judaism and in early Christianity: Think the best of others. Give them the benefit of the doubt. We are so quick to assume the worst, but this is part of what Jesus meant when he urged us not to judge others (Matthew 7:1). We should train ourselves to think the very best until we know otherwise, and even then, we should act for the benefit of the other person and not because they angered or hurt us.

Before Christ, Israel thrived on their identity as God's chosen people. They were given much. They were given the Law, the prophets, and the inheritance as God's children. Along the way, however, they lost sight of a few things. The purpose for them being set apart was to be a light to the nations (Isaiah 49:6). But they lost sight of that and begin to shine the light on themselves, thinking that they were guaranteed salvation simply because they were born into the right race. They were Israel, Abraham's descendants, chosen by God, and that's all there was to it. So, for them, salvation took on strong racial overtones. Salvation was for the Jews, and the pagan nations were out of luck for the time being. We must understand the mindset of the first century or we will easily get off track in a book like Galatians and start to steer it toward meaning something different from what Paul was teaching.

With that said, let's go through Paul's letter to the Galatians to see how he confronts the racial and spiritual problems that had developed among them.

Galatians 1

After a brief opening to the letter (1:1–5), Paul jumps right into a passionate expression of disappointment. He cannot believe that they would allow a group of teachers from Jerusalem to come in and present a gospel that is so contrary to what they know about Jesus. We don't know much about this group that Paul calls the circumcision, other than the content of some of their teaching. How much they were connected to the church in Jerusalem, if at all, remains a mystery. What we do know is that Paul was incensed at the nonsense he felt that they were spreading to the Gentile churches. It appears that they claimed that Paul was trying to win the Gentiles' favor by only sharing the easy part of the gospel, but had left out that they were not the right race and so were not part of God's family or chosen people. If they wanted to be part of that, they needed to become Jews, which meant full circumcision and a life of following the Law.

What can easily look like merely a spiritual point, then, had wrapped up in it a great deal to do with culture and race. The people of God, in the mind of the Jews, was limited to one ethnic group, and that group was set apart by their food practices, following the Law, and circumcision. This is where the conflict came in. They really believed that for these Gentiles to be part of God's people, they needed to do the things that made one an Israelite. Paul, however, believed that the message of the gospel he received from the Messiah was good news for all humanity. Salvation was available to all nations and ethnic groups, not just one.

He makes it very clear in this opening chapter that he didn't invent this message. Neither did he receive it from someone else and twist it to his purposes. He was taught directly by Jesus himself. This was not what Paul was planning to do with his life. He was as zealous for the Law and ethnic Israel as anyone alive, and probably more than most, because he was willing to persecute the church that was preaching this nonsense that all people from all nations and cultures could be part of God's kingdom.

Galatians 2

After many years of proclaiming the good news of Jesus' kingship among the Gentiles, Paul went to Jerusalem at the behest of the Holy Spirit. He had not received his gospel from the apostles or any other man, but he was no renegade either. Unity in the body of Christ was as important to him as to anyone. So he took the opportunity to lay out in detail his message of the one family of all nations in Christ that he had spread to the pagan peoples, as well as the fact that he was not requiring circumcision or observance of the Law. Titus, an uncircumcised Greek, was there with him, and the apostles did not object. In fact, they did not see the need to add anything to Paul's teaching. They were in full support. They agreed that Paul had been gifted and called to go to the Gentiles and should continue to do that, while they would continue to focus on spreading the gospel to those in Judea. We should not see this division of labor as a strict ethnic barrier between two ministries. Rather, what Paul describes is their general area of focus. He would go to the Gentile nations, understanding that the mission field was primarily Gentile, but there were almost always Jews there as well. Meanwhile, Peter and the others would focus in Judea, which meant that most of their mission field would be Jews.

Paul wants to emphasize just how important it is that the kingdom of God is for all people, all nations, and all cultures, so he tells of a time when Cephas (Peter) visited him and acted in a way that was not consistent with the true gospel. We will analyze this confrontation below, so I will not say anything more about it presently.

Paul says that he died to the law so that he might live for God (2:19). We must understand his point. The only way into the family of God is by dying with the Messiah, and when we come back to life after baptism, it is his life that we now live. The Law could not accomplish that. The Law could only separate Israel and bring one ethnic group to God. In Christ, that barrier is destroyed and the kingdom is open to all. Paul introduces these ideas in chapter 2 but doesn't explain them fully until chapter 3. People are not justified, a term that refers to being declared in a right relationship with God (part of his family), through the Law. God's promise for a family of all nations must be fulfilled through faith in the life of Christ.

Galatians 3

Paul reminds the Galatian disciples that the gospel they heard involved the fact that Jesus was crucified and resurrected, in part, so they could enter his life, which meant that what was true for the King was true for his people. Being part of God's people was never about a single ethnicity or following the Law. It was about believing in God's promises. Abraham was not an ethnic Jew and had no Law to follow. He was declared to be in a right relationship with God because he lived by faith in God's promise. The way into the family of Abraham's descendants, then, has nothing to do with culture or ethnicity. Those who place their faith in Jesus, who is God's greatest promise, will be part of Abraham's promised family.

What about those that cling to the Law and their ethnic identity as their membership cards into God's family? They will find that the codes have been changed and they will be locked out. If one wants to keep the Law, then they have to do so perfectly, says Paul. Since that is impossible, it's a good thing that no one is justified in that manner anyway. Christ redeemed us from that limitation. "He redeemed us," declares Paul, "in order that the blessing given to Abraham might come to the Gentiles through Christ Jesus, so that by faith we might receive the promise of the Spirit" (3:14). Paul's major point here is not about earning salvation. It is about trusting in Christ to establish our connection to God versus continuing to follow a plan that exalts one ethnic group and shuts the others out.

Paul then explains the role of the Law. It came over 400 years after Abraham and didn't stand in opposition to the promise to bless all the nations, though it could easily appear that way. Inheritance in God's family was always connected to faith and not ethnicity, culture, or the Law. That was the mistake the Jewish people made. The Law was given as a temporary measure to keep Israel apart from the nations until the Messiah could come. That wasn't because it was ever part of God's plan to give the kingdom to one ethnic group. It was because of sin. The Law was like a state of quarantine during an outbreak. Israel was quarantined and kept from the other peoples until it developed the antidote to sin, which was the Messiah.

Thus the Law wasn't opposed to the great promise but was simply a measure that God used to get humanity back on track so that he could fulfill his promises. "So in Christ Jesus you are all children of God through faith," Paul declares triumphantly, "for all of you who were baptized into

Christ have clothed yourself with Christ" (3:26–27). The promise has finally been fulfilled. Ethnic distinctions and divisions that give more worth to one group than another evaporate in Christ. "There is neither Jew nor Gentile, neither slave nor free, nor is there male and female, for you are all one in Christ Jesus. If you belong to Christ, then you are Abraham's seed, and heirs according to the promise" (3:28–29).

Galatians 4

The time has come. God's family is now available to all humanity. He has answered "yes" to every single promise. People of every race and nation can come into the kingdom and be part of the good news for the whole world.

Once the Messiah has come, the Law is unnecessary. Paul understood the cultural power of the Law and never demanded that it be completely rejected (that would probably have been too much for those who had lived under the Law their whole lives), but he insisted that it cannot be required either. He finishes chapter 4 with a powerful metaphor to make the point that those in Christ are children of the promise and they should not let those that did not receive the inheritance convince them to come and live like they have no inheritance. We are not enslaved to the Law that keeps out the nations, so we must not act like it.

Paul's grand point in chapters 3 and 4 is that only in Christ did God create his promised multiethnic family. This was God's purpose all along. He has fulfilled his promise through Jesus and faith in him alone. The Law limits God's promise to one ethnic family. In Christ, all find equal footing and standing before God.

Galatians 5 & 6

In the last two chapters, Paul addresses what may have been a common Jewish objection to this idea that all nations could simply enter Christ and be part of God's family without the Law. How could they live as God's people and do God's will without the Law to guide them? The pagan nations were virtually defined by sin and disobedience to God. So, what would keep them from bringing that into God's family as the norm? The answer is simple: that's the role of the Spirit. The Holy Spirit will lead the nations into loving their neighbor and cultivating the true life of the age to come; or as Paul calls it here, "the fruit of the Spirit" (5:22). The Law is good but it doesn't enable people to live by the Law. The Spirit lives in us and transforms us, empowering us to live out God's will and fulfill the Law by sacrificially loving others. He does this occasionally through inner prompting, but quite often through the word of God, and even, at times, through the wise and Spirit-led counsel of others. In Christ and through the Spirit we can escape the obvious behaviors of the old humanity and live by the fruit of the Spirit as the new humanity or "race" of God's people. This, of course, doesn't mean that those not in Christ are inferior or less human than those that are being restored in God's image.

All the divisions, whether they be ethnic in nature or divisions between those who follow the Law and those who don't, are now irrelevant. None of that means anything, argues Paul; rather, "what counts is the new creation," that is, the Messiah's family of all nations, trusting in his life and Spirit as he enables us to love God and others. That is what God is doing in the world—that is what counts.

Getting to the Heart of the Matter

Paul did not mince words in his letter to the churches in Galatia. The enormity of the issues at stake wouldn't allow for him to beat around the bush or slowly get to his point. And yet we have to recognize that he was dealing with extremely touchy issues. It's difficult to get into much more emotional and passion-invoking matters than race, culture, family, identity, and salvation. And these were all rolled into one here.

There is little doubt that the Judaizers had divided the Galatian churches. We must never forget as we read Paul's epistles that these were real human beings that he was addressing. Yes, they were being formed into the Messiah's Spirit-led family, but they had struggles, feelings, and emotions like the rest of us. This circumcision group came to Galatia to teach and were allowed to do so, apparently, by the leaders. Many were apt to listen to them. But think about the fallout of what they were teaching: that the disciples in Galatia had been tricked by Paul, their spiritual father. He had only shared half the truth with them. And now, despite all that they had sacrificed and given up to follow Jesus and be part of his family, they were not, because they were not born into the right ethnic group. Ethnicity did matter, after all, even though Paul had told them that it didn't. The good news for those that were at one time "separate from Christ, excluded from citizenship in Israel and foreigners to the covenants of promise, without hope and without God in the world" (Ephesians 2:12), was incomplete, at best. They still hadn't done enough. They were not good enough. They were inferior. They were not of God's people.

Imagine the factions that formed. Think of the hard feelings and hurt that developed. How could their leaders support or allow this? How could my brother in Christ believe that? He supports these prejudiced policies?

It must have driven a spike right through the church. That's why Paul had to confront it head on. Matters that can cause division must be talked about and dealt with. To not talk about them out of fear of causing division is to allow the very thing that we fear. These men had come and stirred up dissension over things not based on the gospel.

As part of his confrontation, Paul enlightens them in chapter 5 about the life of the Spirit that is available for all people. At the beginning of chapter 6, he shows them what this will look like in their own painful situation. He has dealt with the issues very specifically, but he is careful not to name any names in chapter 6. There were probably people on both sides of the divide who felt the other side was in sin. Paul has laid out the truth but leaves it for them to work out how they will apply it in their specific situations.

If someone was in sin, forgive them, help them, restore them; but be careful that you don't get caught up in the same issues that they were involved in. We often view Paul's warning in 6:1 to "watch yourselves, or you may also be tempted" to be a warning not to get caught in the same sin. That's possible, but given the context, it's more likely, I believe, that he is warning them not to get entrapped with all this garbage that a brother or sister on the other side of the issue was embroiled in. That will lead to bitterness and getting entrapped in sin yourself.

Paul laid the boundaries for them: they are part of God's family in Christ alone. The Law cannot enact that. But he has still left a great deal of leeway, and that could lead to future conflict if they are not careful. Some may still have a conviction about following some or all of the Law, for example, and while they now understand that they can't require others to do so, they will follow it for themselves. Others, who do not share those convictions, might be hurt by that. How could they support or take part in this racism? Imagine you were a Gentile sister who lived near a Jewish sister who still felt that she should follow the Law and who had supported the teachings of the Judaizers. This would not be easy, would it?

Principles of Restoration and Reconciliation

In Galatians 6:1–5, Paul lays out six principles that can be applied to a body that has been divided over ideology, conflict, or the like.

First, he says to gently restore the person caught in sin (6:1a). This should always be the goal. We are to love one another and work toward restoration rather than removal. When issues get passionate, the first things that often go out the window are gentleness, respect, and love.

Second, Paul says to take care that you don't get trapped into the same passions, arguments, and issues as the person you are trying to help (6:1b). This will demand a great deal of patience and discipline, especially if you disagree with what the other person did, said, or believes.

Third, he urges them to carry each other's burdens (6:2). If they are going to be God's Spirit-led family of love, they must realize that they are all in this together. They cannot let false-flag issues like race become a divide. They must love one another and display the fruit of the Spirit even to those that have hurt them and sinned against God and the body.

Fourth, he disciples them to not think they are something when they are not (6:3). Avoid the temptation, Paul exhorts, to think that you are right, you know everything, and you have nothing to learn from or change in this situation. Don't put this all on the other person. You most likely have growing to do yourself.

Fifth, Paul warns that each person should test their own actions (6:4). In other words, he tells them not to think that they have done no wrong in this. Don't become fixated on the specks in the eyes of others. Deal with your own planks as well. How consistent were you with the fruit of the Spirit? This is important because people who believe that they are in the right often do not hold themselves to kingdom standards of love and patience in their responses to what they think is wrong. The early church believed that if someone struck you and you struck them back in defense, both acts were sin. That is true in conflict as well. If our responses are not rooted in love, it matters not how "correct" we are.

Sixth, the apostle tells them that each one should carry their own load (6:5). Yes, they are in this together and should carry each other's loads. They should work on the big issues as one body. But each person is still responsible for their own actions. Even if I believe that I am 5% wrong in a conflict and the other person is responsible for 95%, I can take responsibility to apologize and repent for my part.

In verses 6 through 10 Paul steps back and looks at the whole congregation once again. We don't know for sure, but if we follow his train of thought, it appears that some people were, to use a modern phrase, "voting with their pocketbooks." The primary topic in 6:6 is money. Some were angry. Others were hurt, frustrated, and had lost trust. And, it appears, they were not going to take part in supporting their leaders financially or in the economic life of the church. They could focus on investing their heart and money in fleshly things or things of the Spirit, says Paul. Yes, times had gotten tough, but they should not grow weary in doing good and supporting the family of believers.

With this letter, Paul has masterfully confronted all groups involved in the conflict. He has laid out the true kingdom perspective, which was probably different than either side in this situation had taken. But we should take notice of something very important. For Paul, the agitators expressed an "outsider" opinion, and he addressed this worldly thinking directly. But within the community of the churches in Galatia he does not take sides. He does rebuke adherence to the Judaizers' teaching, but other than that, he leaves the direction to the believers vague. He doesn't come in and say, "Okay, group A, you are clearly wrong here and you need to repent and apologize. Group B is correct in their view of the way that you have acted and needs to forgive."

The reality is almost always more complex. Because a false teaching was involved, Paul is blunt about that, but he carefully leaves room for everyone to own their own sin and take appropriate action. The life of the kingdom to which he called them had challenges for everyone, and Paul was content to leave it at that. He was not interested in their personal convictions or positions so long as these fell within the boundaries of the gospel and did not impinge on the freedoms of other brothers and sisters.

Paul's main objective in his confrontation with the saints in Galatia was that they understand the true gospel. That is his focus throughout the letter. He spends precious little time on the error other than to describe it briefly. Paul knew that when we grasp the implications of the true gospel, much of our worldly thinking will melt away. Much potential conflict in our contemporary Christian setting over matters of race and culture comes because of an incomplete appreciation for the good news and the kingdom. When we bring in other ideologies and political opinions rather than focusing ourselves on a kingdom outlook, conflict will ensue. That is precisely why Paul, in confronting the churches, lasers in on the gospel itself and what it will look like in their lives as they live it out.

Another Conflict

Within the context of this confrontation of the erring churches in Galatia, Paul describes the clash between Peter and him. This provides us another window into some important principles for confrontations.

It is impossible to know why Cephas (Peter) came to Antioch. It was likely several years before the writing of the letter. When he first arrived, he found a church that already had an established unity between Jew and Gentile believers. As I have already mentioned, Antioch was a widely diverse church and had apparently grown quite comfortable with that diversity. Jews and Gentiles were freely interacting with one another and sharing table fellowship. That is a strong indicator that they had a clear understanding of the fact that both Jews and Gentiles were free of the Law and were able to engage in observing it or not, as much as each one chose. Peter fit in seamlessly, which leads us to the conclusion that he agreed with this principle that was on display in Antioch. The vision given to him on the eve of his meeting with Cornelius had obviously had a great impact on his worldview. Peter did not follow the Law while in Antioch and freely enjoyed table fellowship with his brothers and sisters.

But then some brothers who had been sent by James came from Jerusalem. It is important to note that this took place before the meeting in Jerusalem that is described in Acts 15. We cannot know for sure why these brothers came and what their message was, but the most likely scenario is that word was getting back to Judea that Peter was in Antioch and was freely disregarding the Law and living seamlessly among the Gentiles. He was being all things to all people. This presented a serious problem in Judea. It would have confirmed the fears of some very conservative Jewish Christians and provided fuel for Jewish critics in their arguments that the Christian sects were opposed to the Law of Moses. This would have made evangelism much tougher for the Christians in Judea and quite possibly put them at a greater risk of being met with violent responses.

When the men arrived with their message from James, Cephas probably took the course of action that he thought was the best possible thing to do given the complexity of the situation. He withdrew from the Gentile brothers and sisters.

Paul cannot abide this decision. He was immersed in a Gentile world whereas Peter was not, and he had thought through the implications of such things much more than had Peter. Yes, Peter was trying to do the right thing, but in light of the gospel, it was the wrong thing. From a worldly perspective, it was a wise thing to do. Without intending to, Peter had applied a worldly solution to a uniquely kingdom situation. This is often dangerous and leads to tension and conflict. If we try to deal with matters such as culture and ethnicity within the kingdom using the old philosophies of the political left and right, we will run up on the rocks every time. Kingdom life demands kingdom solutions and responses. That is why, for example, we should openly discuss and deal with these matters even when worldly wisdom says not to talk about them because it will create strife.

Paul's solution no doubt would create some strife. But imagine what messages Cephas' initial response would have sent. Yes, it would have quelled some problems temporarily in Judea, but it would have established that the Gentiles, even those in Christ, were inferior. It would have reinforced the status quo. And think of how the Gentiles felt. Suddenly the esteemed apostle and elder would no longer take communion or fellowship with them at meals. That must have really hurt. It made them feel as though the kingdom was no different after all. The prejudices and divisions of the world really did count. When Peter applied worldly divisions and solutions to this kingdom situation, it made things far worse.

And because this was a public situation with far-reaching implications for all brothers and sisters, it had to be dealt with publicly. This wasn't just Peter involved. The other Jewish Christians in Antioch, even Paul's partner Barnabas, followed his lead. So Paul confronts the prejudice and racism head on. He calls out Peter's hypocrisy, as he was bringing in worldly categories and perspectives and was unwittingly reinforcing an antigospel worldview. That's the problem with these outside mindsets; they simply have no place in the kingdom. They are incompatible with it. We have to be very careful not to smuggle in political and worldly philosophies and dress them up as Christian ideas.

Typical Responses to Cultural Confrontation

As he was confronted on his behavior, there were likely several universal responses that Cephas initially had to deal with. This is speculation, of course; we don't know what went through his mind, but these are typical responses, and it is quite possible that they were also temptations for the apostle. When the dominant cultural group is confronted by a nondominant culture, it often causes stress because it is a situation that they are not used to. Here are some common specific stressors:

1. **Having it suggested that your viewpoint is racialized and not objective.** Paul surely implied that with Peter. People like to think that they are being objective and recoil at the idea that their behaviors and thought patterns have been conditioned by a racialized and divided world. We each like to think that we are free from that, so an implication from someone with a different perspective that this is not the case can often be hard to take.

2. **Hearing a divergent perspective from the nondominant group.** After the Judeans arrived, Peter only saw things from a Jewish perspective. To hear Paul share the nondominant perspective and apply gospel thinking must have been an initial shock and rather uncomfortable for Peter.

3. **Not being agreed with on your racial perspective by the nondominant group.** People do not typically love to be disagreed with, at least not initially. When you are in a dominant group, your perspective and thinking are

constantly reinforced as normal and right. Jews were not dominant in the world, but they were the culturally dominant group in the first-century church. Peter was suddenly confronted with a different way of thinking, and that must have been disconcerting. He could reject it out of hand or accept the fact that his take on things might not be the only valid one.

4. Learning that your behavior had a negative impact on others. People don't typically intend to harm others with their behavior. But sometimes, even seemingly benign or normal actions have that effect without you knowing it. In this case, Peter's behavior would have deeply wounded the Gentile Christians. He would have been faced with the choice to own that or to deny it and cite his intentions, rather than accepting a different perspective and hearing that he had hurt others. In this case, it might have put the Jerusalem Christians in a tough spot, even a dangerous one, but one that was consistent with the gospel life. Demeaning the Gentiles, though, to make the Judeans more comfortable, was not consistent with the gospel and so was unacceptable.

5. Acknowledging that the nondominant group has been harmed. This is never easy. Humans have a strong drive to justify our own behavior. We think acknowledging that we hurt others makes us a bad person. But it is important to be open to how others view our actions and to really listen. Often our "right and correct" thinking is harmful worldly wisdom and not loving kingdom wisdom. Would we rather be unloving toward our brothers and sisters over being "right"? Peter's initial thinking was "right" in that it would protect the Jews from further difficulty, but it was not in line with the gospel.

Peter's Response (I Think)

What we are never told in Galatians is how Cephas responded. The fact that Paul doesn't dwell on it further, and that he brought it up in the first place, surely indicates a positive response on Peter's part. Of course, later in his life, Cephas would refer to him as "our dear brother Paul," (2 Peter 3:15), so we can safely conclude that Cephas saw the proper perspective here, overcame any temptations toward defensiveness and justification, and repented quickly. Admittedly, the text does not say this directly, but I do think it is implied and so the following thoughts will be based on that assumption.

We can then assume and learn the following from Peter here:

1. He was willing to be challenged. If Peter had mounted some sort of counterargument, Paul would most likely have included it because it would have been instructive. The indication of the passage, then, is that Peter heard and agreed with Paul's perspective.

2. He was willing to be uncomfortable. Peter was seemingly quite humble in this situation. He allowed himself to be publicly called out in a way that challenged not just his behavior but also many of his views and assumptions.

3. He was willing to take responsibility. It is unlikely that he would have tried to pass the buck or justify his actions. He had stepped outside of the gospel and had hurt others. Every indication of his life and character that we find in the gospels would indicate that he saw his wrong and immediately took responsibility.

4. He was willing to act to remedy the situation. Again, Peter's character would dictate immediate action. We can safely assume that he quickly resumed table fellowship and brought a swift end to the harm that he was causing.

5. He was willing to note their differences. This may sound odd, but there were distinct differences between the Jews and Gentiles; not as far as it concerned their status in the kingdom, but their ethnic and cultural backgrounds did create dissimilarities. Sometimes to treat people fairly they must be treated differently. Peter realized that to truly be part of a society of no divisions, he would have to take intentional action to address the situation. If there was some weird situation where Peter would have had to stop eating with some fellow Jews for a time for the safety of other Christians, it would likely not have been a big deal. But it was a big deal when it came to Gentiles, as in this situation. He could not put the physical safety of others above equality in Christ for all disciples.

We cannot fix every problem in the world. Even if we wanted to, that would be an impossible task. Our job is to let the kingdom come into our lives as we do God's will on earth as though we were in his very presence. We can confront worldly thinking in the kingdom, and we can take action to cut out the divisions of the world that have followed us into the Messiah's church. We can confront one another when we see secular or racialist thinking that hurts others. Speaking as a white man, I can't fix the world or change what sin has done. But I can acknowledge it. I can even embrace that I have benefited in a worldly way from some of the racial attitudes that are prevalent and the systems that our culture is built on.

I have learned that there is often a benefit of the doubt that I receive in our society that my sons and wife do not. When we lived in an all-white area in Appleton, Wisconsin, driving the same streets at basically the same speeds and in the same vehicles, I was never pulled over once in five years. My wife was pulled over well over a dozen times for various reasons just to "check" on things. I can't fix that. I don't really need to try.

What I can do, what we all can do, is to live by the gospel and show the world a different way. We can respond with the kingdom when confronted with the world. And when nonkingdom thinking or actions make their way into the church—and they will—we can lovingly meet that challenge, deal with it, and strain toward what is ahead.

Questions for Discussion

1. When it comes to the issues discussed in this book, are there any areas where it is possible that you have allowed worldly attitudes to dominate the way you think or perceive things?

2. Have you ever been hurt by another disciple? How did you handle it?

3. Have you ever had another disciple tell you that you hurt them? How did you handle it?

4. Ask others in your life (or those with you if you are reading this in a group) if they see you as someone who is open to the perspectives of others.

5. Consider the six principles provided from Galatians 6:1–5. Of those principles, which do you feel is the area in which you most need to grow?

Chapter 12

For the Glory of God: Sacrifice

Paul and Silas had been on the road for some time when they saw the city of Philippi, in modern-day Greece, off in the distance. It was probably AD 51. They were filled with nervous energy at the anticipation of seeing what the Spirit was going to do this time. As they walked through the city streets it felt very familiar, even though they had never been to Philippi before. This was a Roman colony and shared a culture and ethos with many places where they had been before. There was no question that culturally, this place was Roman, only maybe more so than the average Roman city (Acts 16:12).

After a few days and some important conversions to Christ, the missionary duo continued to preach the gospel to everyone who would listen. After an encounter with a slave girl caused a serious conflict with her owners, Paul and Silas were dragged into the public marketplace so a complaint could be brought against them. They eventually found themselves before the city magistrates with an angry crowd pressing for their punishment and claiming that they were "advocating customs unlawful for…Romans to accept or practice" (Acts 16:21). This vitriol seems to go well beyond the circumstance that Paul may have messed up a tidy profit for one slave owner. What was he preaching and doing that was so countercultural?

A clue comes from the origins of the city of Philippi. As I mentioned in an earlier chapter, it was founded by retired Roman soldiers who had gained their citizenship as Romans. Although they lived far from Rome, the people of Philippi were very proud of their Roman-ness and Luke confirms that, drawing special attention to their being a Roman colony, the only city he describes as such in all of Acts, even though most of the places they went were Roman colonies. Philippi was very Roman in its culture and proud of it. And they didn't take kindly to Paul's gospel.

In a nutshell, the whole of Roman society was built on the idea of getting ahead. Roman culture was constructed around the fact that about three percent of the population was considered to compose the elite class. The elite class was split into Senators, Equestrians, and Decurions, the non-elite class into freeborn, freedmen, and slaves, in order from the highest to the lowest position in society. The lower you were, the more you had to obey those above you and the less freedom you had. The higher you were, the less you needed to bother with obedience and the more easily you could move toward more freedom. So obedience was not a virtue and neither was humility. Social climbing and earning honor in the eyes of others were not just valued, they were expected. Romans would do everything in their power to amass impressive titles and societal positions, to accomplish things that gained them attention, to show others how great they were, and to take advantage of every opportunity to get ahead. This was normal, and to do almost anything to gain esteem from others and move up the social scale was considered human nature and even virtuous.

Everything that Paul taught was running contrary to this. The gospel is just about the opposite of the above values in every way. Paul was proclaiming a message that Jesus is King, and that meant that there were no class divisions, that they need not climb the social ladder and advance socially to form an impressive identity. They didn't need Rome's power or citizenship to impress anyone or get ahead. They needed something radically different. What was it? I'm sure that Paul preached it, but his arrest by the magistrates gave him an opportunity to demonstrate it in a powerful manner.

Before Paul was thrown into jail, he was beaten severely. After a harrowing night in the lockup where he was able to bring a jailer and his entire household into the kingdom, Paul was released. Before he left, though, he informed the officers that he was, in fact, a Roman citizen. This was a huge problem for the magistrates, who could be put to death for having had a citizen beaten without a trial. The question for us is, why would Paul wait to declare his citizenship until after he was beaten and had spent a night in jail? He was hardly taking advantage of his rights or he would have done it beforehand to avoid the violent beating; something that he would do elsewhere (Acts 22:22–29). Why did he take the beating?

Before answering that, let's look at what Paul would write the Philippians a few years later. As you read it, keep in mind what I said above about what the normal mindset for a resident of Philippi would have been, and read Paul's words in that light.

Do nothing out of selfish ambition or vain conceit. Rather, in humility value others above yourselves, not looking to your own interests but each of you to the interests of the others.

In your relationships with one another, have the same mindset as Christ Jesus:

Who, being in very nature God,
    did not consider equality with God something to be
    used to his own advantage;
rather, he made himself nothing
    by taking the very nature of a servant,
    being made in human likeness.
And being found in appearance as a man,
    he humbled himself
    by becoming obedient to death—
        even death on a cross!
Therefore God exalted him to the highest place
    and gave him the name that is above every name,
that at the name of Jesus every knee should bow,
    in heaven and on earth and under the earth,
and every tongue acknowledge that Jesus Christ is Lord,
    to the glory of God the Father.   Philippians 2:3–11

Every word of this drips with anti-Roman-culture rhetoric. Be humble. Be obedient. Put one another first. Be like Jesus, who did not use his status to his own advantage. He made himself nothing. He made himself lower than he was rather than trying to get ahead. He suffered the most shameful death imaginable in Roman society. Be like him, says Paul. Put down your own rights and live for the benefit of others. But just so you don't think that Jesus was just a lowly slave who was unable to do anything else or incapable of standing up to the power of Rome, Paul says beginning with "Therefore," look who he really is. He is acknowledged by God to be the highest imaginable person. He did not have to do any of those things. He willingly sacrificed for our benefit.

What message would Paul have sent when he was being dragged off by the Philippian magistrates if he had taken advantage of his citizenship? Would the anger then have turned to the new Philippian converts? Apparently, Paul thought something of the sort would happen, so he took it upon himself. This was the gospel in living color. All that Roman culture said was important was rendered irrelevant by Paul's example. He was a living letter to them before pen ever touched paper to craft the letter to the Philippians. Just as Jesus had taken a status lower than his rightful one, so had Paul by not invoking his citizenship. Just as Jesus had sacrificed and given up his rights for their benefit, so had Paul. And just as God had exalted Jesus, showing that he was not at the mercy of Rome but had done this willingly and purposefully, so Paul declared after the fact that he was a Roman citizen who chose to suffer for the benefit of others and to put the gospel on display.

Loving Others Can Be Difficult

To love others, which is the central virtue of the kingdom of God, is to sacrifice for their benefit (1 John 3:16). I will give just two examples here that show that the primary way the apostolic church dealt with thorny issues of culture and ethnic clash was through the path of love for one another and a willingness to lay down their rights for the benefit of those around them.

I have already briefly mentioned the problems that led up to the council in Jerusalem in Acts 15. The basic question between the ascension of Jesus and the council in Jerusalem was whether God was going to have a singular ethnic family, or whether the promise to Abraham had always been that all ethnicities would be brought into his family. In other words, would it be a multiethnic family? In addition to that, what would be the uniform of that family? What would be the main architect of identity and culture within the family? Would it be Moses' Law or the life of Christ?

That the Jews of the first century had misused the Law and slipped into racialist attitudes is difficult to deny. Peter himself demonstrates that typical Jewish attitude as he begins to address those gathered in Cornelius' home with his cringe-worthy statement, "You are well aware that it is against our law for a Jew to associate with or visit a Gentile. But God has shown me that I should not call anyone impure or unclean" (Acts 10:28). Israel had twisted the Law from a protection against idolatry into a means to look down on others, and God was correcting that and fulfilling his promises all at the same time.

So, by Acts 10 the church has finally become the one family of all nations. Mission accomplished. The work was done and all that was left to do was let the masses come rolling in. Once they were taught that we are all one in Christ and that racial distinctions no longer matter in this family of the restored and reconciled humanity, the unity would flow and the problems would float away. Right? Not exactly. As the Gentiles began pouring into the church, that was the start of the work of being a multiethnic people, not the end of it.

We should continue to remind ourselves of two important realities as we look at the solutions to the ethnic clash found in Acts 15. The first is that Jewish Christians were the dominant culture in at least the first two to three decades of Christianity. They held the primary positions of power and had built the church. That means that there would always have been a temptation for them to foist on others the culture, methods, and practices that were part of their response to the gospel but not necessarily the gospel itself. There was always a danger of viewing the Gentiles and their ways of implementing the gospel as inferior. Of course, I'm not talking about sinful practices and responses, just cultural ones. The second thing to remember is that this was a highly charged and emotional issue that could have easily erupted and led to very hard feelings and even a split that would result in two arms of the church, a Jewish one and a Gentile one. That, of course, would be disastrous for the gospel of reconciliation.

Handling Cross-Cultural Relationships

There are several important principles in dealing with cross-cultural relationships in the church that we can find in the proceedings recorded in Acts 15.

The *first principle* is that the leaders of the church were aware that there was disunity and a growing ethnic problem in the church. Yes, the underlying cause was one of spiritual interpretation, but this was causing a cultural divide, and that's what we are focusing on here. The leaders saw it and dealt with it quickly. They didn't try to cover it up or hope that it would go away. There seems to be a remarkable willingness in the early church to be brutally honest and open about their own shortcomings. That is only matched by their unwavering energy to deal with those problems in light of the gospel.

The *second principle* that we should note is that they gathered all the parties together at the table, so to speak. Everyone was fairly represented and had a voice. Paul and Barnabas were Jews, but they had spent years working with Gentiles and being immersed in their perspective. They also brought other believers with them (Acts 15:2) who were undoubtedly Gentile. This was important. Everyone could feel heard and valued.

That leads into the *third principle*. Members of the nondominant culture, in this case the Gentiles, were treated with respect and dignity. That had not always been the case with Jew and Gentile relations outside of the church. They could not allow mistreatment of the nondominant Gentiles, even if it was unintentional. Unintentional prejudice and disregard are just as painful for the recipients as are intentional acts, by the way. Simply calling together this conference just to work out this issue showed the Gentiles that they had worth in the eyes of their Jewish brothers and sisters.

The *fourth principle* that we can glean comes from Peter's speech. He acknowledged the problem. He publicly declared that some in the church wanted to treat the Gentiles in an unfair and ultimately nongospel manner. They were equals in the kingdom, but cultural practices and expectations were creating an inferior class. That was incredibly insightful on Peter's part, no doubt inspired by the Holy Spirit. Cultural practices, which is what circumcision and the Law were, seem normal to the culture that engages in them. In this case, that was heightened because these cultural practices were rooted in the Hebrew Scriptures. But Peter makes clear that they are not binding on all people; they were now nothing more than cultural preferences. What makes this remarkable is that it is very difficult for someone immersed in a culture to see that their "normal" is just *a* way to do things and not *the* way. It's like a fish recognizing that it's wet. It wouldn't know that because wet is all it has ever known. It's not until the fish could experience being out in the dry world for a time that it would be able to appreciate what being wet even means. The council listened to Peter and others and was willing to step outside of their own cultural conditioning and see from a different perspective.

The *fifth principle* comes in the Jews' willingness to set aside strongly held convictions and practices for the benefit of their brothers and sisters. Of course, they would have been unwilling to set aside something that was central to the gospel and the kingdom. But as important as it was to them to keep to their ethnic markers found in circumcision, the dietary laws, and so on, they were willing to compromise. They were willing to see that they had to drop some of these things, like their table fellowship practices, in order to embrace the truth of the gospel that the Gentile Christians were their family. There were other practices they could continue, but they were willing to no longer require them or force them onto others. It was a huge shift, but they were willing to make the effort.

The *sixth principle* is that they each had to lay down some rights to remain one people. This means that the leaders had some requests for the nondominant culture as well. The biggest decision at this council was perhaps that the Gentiles would not have to be circumcised, as this was now considered a cultural practice that could be accepted or rejected. But they did ask the Gentiles to make some concessions. This was not hypocrisy or inconsistency. The Law was not binding on the Gentiles, but treating their brothers with consideration, respect, and love was. The items that they were asked to abstain from were all things that seemed normal and okay from a Gentile perspective. So as not to needlessly offend their brothers and sisters who were Jewish, they were to keep from eating meat sacrificed to idols, from blood rituals, from the meat of strangled animals, and from sexual immorality. All these had strong connections to the pagan temples and were part of normal life for Gentiles. For example, it might be difficult for us to comprehend, but in the Gentile world for a man to have sex with a boy, a slave, or a temple prostitute was not considered adultery or even wrong. These things were encouraged, so it would not have automatically occurred to Gentile converts that they were doing something immoral, and the cultural pull would have been strong to continue those practices.

The Jewish leaders were not thrusting a new law onto the Gentiles. They were not saying, "You need not follow the Law of Moses to be in Christ" and then turning around and saying, "but follow these particular laws of Moses." They were asking them to be willing to lay down some of their rights so as not to offend or hurt the consciences of their family members. We will discuss how this played out in the real world a bit more below, when we come to 1 Corinthians. At the end of the day, the tone of the letter that was sent out to the Gentiles was that "it would make things much easier on us Jewish Christians if you would adhere to these things." They were not sending the message that if they ate meat sacrificed at a temple that they would no longer be considered a brother; but just that it would make fellowship and unity unnecessarily difficult for their Jewish fellow disciples.

The *seventh principle* here is that they did not have to agree on everything to be unified. They did not need to do everything the same way and see everything eye to eye in order to fellowship together. There would be some areas where they should be sensitive and not needlessly offend their brothers and sisters or cause them to struggle. But they were also free to worship God through their own cultural language and preferences. This would mean that Christianity was not limited to one culture, one ethnicity, or one way of doing things. That is the beauty and brilliance of the gospel. It is transcultural and cross-cultural. It may look very different in different places, and it should, but it is still the same gospel.

The *eighth principle* is how they heard one another's perspective and genuinely listened. This was community at its finest. They respected one another. They worked together. They communicated at the highest level and hammered out an agreement that preserved dignity for everyone and was a compromise that both sides could live and thrive under. Compromise often has a negative connotation, but in cross-cultural ministry situations, faithful compromise for the benefit of others is a fruitful virtue.

I need to point out one more remarkable thing before moving on to the situation in Corinth. Despite the ongoing tension and troubles between Jews and Gentiles in the Christian family, Paul was traveling around the world collecting money from the predominantly Gentile churches, many of whom were poor themselves, for the brothers and sisters in Jerusalem who had fallen on hard times. The lesson here is that when we have every reason to be at odds with someone, the kingdom response is to bend over backward to love and serve them. That will do more to bring unity and peace than a million "right" arguments.

Conflict in Corinth

As we turn to Paul's letter to the Corinthians, we find the same basic cultural issue arising in Corinth. The same principles of mutual respect and love are here, but Paul adds to our understanding of these issues because he doesn't just describe the conversation or the compromise but helps the believers think through the situation fully. As the old saying goes, "Better to teach a man to fish and feed him for a lifetime than to give him a fish and feed him for one day." Rather than just telling them what to do, Paul wants to teach the Corinthians how to carefully consider these thorny issues when perspectives and cultures clash.

Paul's letter to the Corinthians is just one of a number of correspondences over a number of years that he shared with the church that he founded. In 1 Corinthians Paul deals with a number of problems that the church was having. The book can be divided into five major divisions, each primarily addressing one of these problems. The five primary topics that Paul deals with are 1) divisions in the family; 2) sex, relationships, and immorality; 3) food and idolatry; 4) church gatherings; and 5) resurrection of the dead. In each section, Paul describes the conflict or misunderstanding that the church was having. He then patiently proclaims the gospel to them and explains how it speaks to that specific issue. He concludes by showing them that the way they are living and the practices they have developed are incongruent with the gospel message and with kingdom life.

Although all the issues have a cultural tinge to them, I will focus on the third major problem that Paul addresses, that of food and idols, because it is the most overtly cultural issue of the five.

In the ancient Greco-Roman world, nearly all meat was initially brought to temples and sacrificed to the various gods; and then what was left would be sold in the marketplace. Jewish communities that did not have their own butchers would simply avoid eating meat altogether because they didn't want to appear to contribute to idolatry in any way, shape, or form.

In Corinth, this quickly brought conflict. Some in the church felt fine about eating meat from any source. They weren't worshiping these gods, they were simply eating. For others, though, this was deeply distressing. It felt like sin to them. It was supporting idolatry, and so if it felt immoral for them, then it must be sin for others. Surely, the primarily Jewish Christian group wondered how these other people could claim to be Christian and support such practices at the same time. The largely Gentile group held a very different view. Their freedom was being infringed upon. These other Christians were small-minded bigots. You can see how this would lead to division.

What about the letter that the Jerusalem council had sent out that asked for Gentiles to avoid food sacrificed to idols? It appears that the teachers in Corinth thought they knew better. This is a classic case of one church pushing out past their brothers and sisters around the world and thinking that they had a better understanding; they had learned more and couldn't be limited by such restrictions.

In the first four verses of 1 Corinthians 8, Paul quotes three separate slogans that were being taught or passed around in the church in Corinth:

1. We all possess knowledge (8:1a).
2. An idol is nothing at all in the world (8:4a).
3. There is no God but one (8:4b).

When we look at these three slogans together, we can understand their larger point. The Gentile disciples were knowledgeable enough to know that idols only had power if you believed in them. They are not real; only God is. Therefore, there is no good reason not to enjoy a piece of meat for supper.

Paul responds sharply. Yes, we all possess knowledge, but knowledge alone puffs up (8:1b). Yes, there is no God but one, but part of the truth of that one God is that he has revealed himself through the person of the Lord, Jesus Christ (8:6), which means that imitating Jesus is what determines our actions, not mere knowledge. This was a gentle push back toward the sacrificial love of Christ. In fact, every problem Paul cites points back to a lack of Messiah-type love, which is why Paul will eventually tie everything into his great crescendo in chapter 13 on love.

As Paul lays out his direction on this conflict in chapters 8, 9, and 10, he sprinkles throughout several important principles that will serve us well when it comes to being a multiethnic family in Christ.

First, not everyone is at the same place or has the same way of looking at things (8:7–8). That's not necessarily a bad thing. It's a normal part of being a community. Food does not bring us closer to God but, Paul implies, love does. Some are trying their best to serve God and maybe they don't understand everything as well as you do. But who is being more like Christ, the one that is trying their best to be faithful but has not quite worked out the fullness of the gospel, or the one who does understand the implications of the gospel, but then applies them with no love or respect for the perspective of others? Paul is brilliant here in that he moves the libertine side closer to the middle by beginning to lay out his call to sacrifice their rights for the benefit of others; and at the same time, he very gently demonstrates to those with a "weaker" conscience that there are a few things that they would do well to ponder which would aid them as they grow in their understanding.

The second principle comes in 1 Corinthians 8:9–13. Paul gets directly to the point as he says, "Be careful, however, that the exercise of your rights does not become a stumbling block to the weak" (8:9). The family of God and loving others are far more important than the rights that we suppose we have. Allegiance must be to Jesus, not our opinions or preferences. The main thing was that they needed to build each other up in serving Christ. Cultural, ethnic, and political issues must always take a back seat to that. If someone could watch your life and reasonably conclude that you serve Jesus and other gods because you were eating meat sacrificed to those gods, then spit the meat out. Paul says if that's the case, "I will never eat meat again" (8:13). But if there is no one around who could misunderstand or be offended, then have at it; enjoy your freedom.

There is inherent responsibility involved in this, of course. One brother must be sensitive and aware of what could truly be damaging to others. But the others must not abuse that and claim injury on every little thing that they don't like or prefer. That would be abusive. We must show great discernment and care for others on both sides.

In our day, we don't have too many issues over meat sacrificed at pagan altars, but there is a seemingly endless list of items that fall under similar principles and cause conflicts. I will use just one as an example. In contemporary society, we believe that we have the right to be heard, to speak our mind, to espouse our political beliefs, to see the world how we want to see it, and to declare what we think is true. Do we have those rights as Christians? I suppose. But what if our beliefs genuinely hurt other brothers and sisters? What if I am a Democrat and I discover that some brothers and sisters are genuinely hurt by this. They do not see how I can be a Democrat and support some of the things that Democratic politicians espouse. It becomes a stumbling block to them to the point that they consider leaving the church or are holding private grudges against me in their hearts. Or, what if I am a Republican and I discover that some brothers and sisters struggle with all those same things regarding my beliefs and actions?

Would I be willing to lay that down? Would I be willing, like Paul, to say, I'll never have another political thought in my life if it is going to hurt a brother or sister or impede someone from coming to the gospel? But wait, you might, say. We have a right to have political opinions and engage in politics. No doubt. And the Corinthians had a right to eat meat if they were hungry. Should they be more loyal to the gospel or to their stomach? Should we be more loyal to the gospel or to our opinions and ideologies? Are we willing to approach our rights with the same sacrificial heart that Paul had toward his?

For the Benefit of Others

In 1 Corinthians 9, Paul offers an extended exposition to explain the rights that he has as an apostle but lays down for the benefit of others. He points out that he has every right to be supported financially by the church, but he has willingly laid down that right for their benefit so that they do not ever have to question his motivations in preaching the gospel or muddy their relationship with the apostle (9:1–18). His teachings in 9:19–27 are so important that I will return to that passage in detail in the next section of this book.

Moving on to 10:23–31, Paul surrounds a practical example of a very real clash in culture with some important and timeless principles. First, I will consider the example. He imagines a dinner party thrown by an unbeliever with a disciple being invited as a guest. These parties were typically more accessible than they are today, and any passerby could easily see who was there and what they were eating. Paul has already made clear that if it bothered your conscience or tempted you to see a power in the very real demonic forces that take advantage of the empty worship offered to these fake gods and lifeless statues (10:14–22), then by all means, abstain. But if you recognize that all things belong to the Lord and it doesn't bother your conscience or cause anyone to think that you are serving other gods, then enjoy the meat. But if another Christian walks by, pointing out that it has been sacrificed to idols, then it obviously bothers them. In that case, says Paul, do not eat the meat. Sacrifice your rights to protect that person's heart and conscience. Paul freely admits that the conscience of the other person does not take away or judge your conscience; that is to say, it doesn't make it wrong for you to eat the meat. What would make it wrong is if it caused them to stumble. If no one struggles with it, then Paul has no problem with anyone else eating meat that has been sacrificed to idols. Of course, Paul strongly discourages them from ever going into the temples themselves or taking part in any of the pagan practices there.

We get the sense that Paul would ultimately like to get everyone to the point where they fully grasp their freedom in Christ and are no longer bound by cultural practices; but he is also a realist and understands that consciences take a long time to rehabilitate and heal. Sometimes they have been shaped so strongly that they never will come around. Those with very tight consciences can continue to work on that, but in the meantime, those that are not bothered should never grow weary in putting the interests of their brothers and sisters ahead of their own.

Surrounding this real-life example, Paul gives four principles that summarize his thoughts on cross-cultural relations in the church and serve as a summary for this entire chapter. He writes them in response to the slogan or statement that was, apparently, used by some in Corinth, "I have the right to do anything" (1 Corinthians 10:23).

Principle #1. Not everything is beneficial (10:23a). There are lots of things as disciples that we can do, but that does not make them beneficial kingdom activities. I can become very politically minded and opinionated, but is that beneficial from a kingdom standpoint? I can go to a vegetarian convention munching on a turkey leg as I walk about trying to share my faith. How beneficial would that be? We can easily lose sight of what's important if we don't keep the kingdom first. When we act out or hold to a particular ideology, is it beneficial for everyone in showing them the kingdom, or does it serve another purpose?

Principle #2. Not everything is constructive (10:23b). Some things serve no other purpose than to tear others down. With every action we take, we are either building up the kingdom or building up something else entirely. When we invest our passions in constructing things other than the kingdom or trust in nonkingdom philosophies, assets, or solutions, we invest in things that will not last (Matthew 6:19–21). Out heart follows the things in which we invest and that we truly treasure. Look at what stirs your anger, passion, fear, joy, happiness. That just might be the thing that brings you security and comfort. Are we constructing things other than God's kingdom?

Principle #3. Do not seek your own good, but the good of others (10:24). This principle speaks for itself. But as obvious as it might seem, it takes great discernment and a resolve to keep the kingdom and the gospel at the forefront of our passions. We have to make sure that it is truly the word of God that lies behind our beliefs, our solutions, our opinions, and our ideologies. Otherwise a very real problem that will quickly present itself in the body lies in different interpretations of who the "others" are whose good we seek. Paul, of course, is thinking of other brothers and sisters here, but some will point to passages where Jesus indicates that the outcasts, poor, and oppressed are those that should be our highest priority (Luke 4:18–20). This can be a difficult balance, but we will let Paul have the final word here: "Let us do good to all people, especially to those who belong to the family of believers" (Galatians 6:10).

Principle #4. Do everything for the glory of God (10:31). Paul says, "Whether you eat or drink or whatever you do, do it all for the glory of God." His direction is simple: Before you interact with brothers or sisters, consider whether your interaction will bring God glory. Before you decide to let yourself get upset about something, consider whether your emotions will bring God glory. Before you decide to advocate for something publicly, consider whether that position will bring God glory. And when you advocate for a position that you believe in, and it hurts or upsets another brother or sister, will your response bring God glory? Just because something is done in the name of justice for others does not mean that it is kingdom justice or brings God glory.

We can have all the talent, spiritual ability, knowledge, and passion in the world, but if it is not directed by a sacrificial love and willingness to lay down our rights for others, it will harm the family of God (1 Corinthians 13:1–3). Whenever we find ourselves in a difficult situation in the body because of culture, race, or any other reason, let us remember Paul's words to the Corinthian disciples:

> *Love is patient, love is kind. It does not envy, it does not boast, it is not proud. It does not dishonor others, it is not self-seeking, it is not easily angered, it keeps no record of wrongs. Love does not*

delight in evil but rejoices with the truth. It always protects, always trusts, always hopes, always perseveres. Love never fails. I Corinthians 13:4–8

Questions for Discussion

1. Do you believe that your church has an open ear to the concerns of the brothers and sisters, especially when it comes to racial and cultural issues?

2. Are you willing to lay down your rights and opinions for the benefit of others?

3. Can you be truly unified with those with whom you strongly disagree on nonsalvation issues? What do you do when you don't agree with another brother or sister?

4. Are you willing to sacrifice some of your political beliefs or opinions, or at least airing them publicly, for the sake of the gospel and advancement of the kingdom?

5. Are there any areas racially or culturally in the church where the actions of other disciples have caused you hurt or to struggle?

Chapter 13

Accept One Another:
True Diversity

On the night of February 26, 2012 Trayvon Martin, a seven-teen-year-old high school student, was walking back to the home of his father's fiancée. He had walked up to a convenience store for some refreshments during the half time of an NBA game he was watching. By now, you probably know the rest of this tragic incident. A neighborhood watch captain named George Zimmerman saw the hooded-sweatshirt-wearing individual and thought him suspicious. He was on high alert due to a number of recent break-ins in the gated community where he lived and patrolled. He began to follow Martin and continued doing so after police told him not to. At some point, Martin noticed that Zimmerman was following him. Zimmerman exited his vehicle, and an argument began that quickly escalated into a physical altercation. Accounts diverge as to who was the aggressor; but everyone does agree that the teenager was unarmed, while twenty-eight-year-old Zimmerman was carrying a gun. The whole incident began at 7:09 p.m. It ended at 7:16 p.m. when Zimmerman shot Martin, killing him.

News of this incident immediately went worldwide, and it sparked emotions and raised passions in nearly everyone who heard of the story. Almost overnight, most people in the United States, it seemed, split into two camps. Some were very supportive of Zimmerman and saw this as a case of self-defense and nothing more. Others were outraged. They felt that Martin had been killed because of prejudiced suspicions and stereotypes, because he was a black teen with a hoodie pulled up. The country was ripped apart by two very different ways of looking at the events and a sensationalist media that was more than happy to feed into the chaos to increase their ratings.

My own home was not immune to the divergence in perspectives. My wife and I grew up very differently. I grew up in an idyllic, midsized town known for its tranquility, its many parks, its blue-collar work ethic, and a middle-class lifestyle for most of its residents. The streets were safe and everyone was friendly. This, of course, shaped my outlook on life. One of the results from my upbringing is that I tend to trust people in authority.

Life for MyCresha was very different. Although we grew up in the same state, we lived worlds apart. She grew up in a midsized city, but it is situated right between Milwaukee and Chicago. It has its nice parts of town and some very rough parts. She grew up in those rough parts. Those neighborhoods are riddled with crime, poverty, and gang activity; and the city serves as a pipeline for all sorts of nefarious things traveling between the two metropolises on either side. Her upbringing shaped her outlook on life as well. For instance, it is hard for her to trust people simply because they are in authority. She was conditioned in many ways while growing up that trust was not always a safe course of action.

She is also a woman and a mom; and I hope you've already guessed, but I am neither of those things. So when the story on the Trayvon Martin case spread to every media outlet in the country, we each heard the narrative in our own way. She heard it as a mom with an incredible heart and love for all people, as someone who tends to see the world from the perspective of the underdog, and as someone who doesn't automatically trust the authorities or the system to get it right. I heard the story mostly from a pragmatic point of view, although there is no question that it was a heartrending tragedy.

Her view of it was simple: "He was a baby, and he was killed by a man with a gun." She didn't need to know much more than that. It didn't escape her that Trayvon was black, and it seemed to her that his skin color had to have played a role. Zimmerman didn't go out to shoot someone because they were black, she reasoned, but his biases and stereotypes caused him to perceive Martin as a threat and to approach him in that manner and treat him as a danger. That resulted in the death of a baby in her eyes! Understand, our oldest son was virtually the same age as Martin. At that time, he would often walk through the neighborhoods around our house in a hoodie that was pulled up over his head. Trayvon represented her son and it brought up a lot of emotion for her.

I, on the other hand, prefer to look at things logically. Yes, this was a tragedy. Any situation that ends in violence and death is due to sin, a win for Satan, and something that should be mourned. But I tend to process that all very quickly and move on to the practical far too quickly for my wife's liking.

Eventually Zimmerman was tried for murder, and before the verdict was handed down MyCresha and I had a discussion. She passionately argued that this grown man had shot down a baby and needed to be put in jail. I pointed out to her that she was reacting too emotionally (yeah, that always works well, right, husbands?). My point was simple: what I believed about the particulars of the case didn't matter; the Florida law, as written, gave Zimmerman the grounds to do what he did. My personal feelings were irrelevant. He was going to be found not guilty, and that was that.

Neither of us was inclined to change our position. As you might guess, that happens a lot in our household. We don't fight over these things. We don't get angry about them. But most of the time we have very different opinions about the important issues of the day. So, how do we love one another and live together despite these incredibly divergent points of view?

The Roman Controversy

That's the same question that Paul must have asked himself as he sat down to write the letter to the Romans. I described the problem in the church in Rome in Chapter 9, but I will summarize before looking at how Paul addresses the challenges that were presenting themselves there.

We don't know who planted the church in Rome or how it got there, but we do know that Paul was not directly responsible for it, yet he felt great concern for the brothers and sisters there and desperately wanted to go visit them. The church was a mixture of Jewish and Gentile believers, but then some sort of disturbance or series of disturbances broke out between the Jewish community in Rome and the Christian Jews. It was quite possibly an outbreak of attempted persecution of the Christians on the part of the Jews. The Emperor Claudius would have none of it and simply issued a decree expelling all Jews from the city of Rome. It is unknown if just the leaders of the communities left. It's probable that it went beyond that and most or even all of the Jews left. Whatever the extent, both Jews and Jewish Christians became refugees and left the Emperor's city. That was in AD 49.

For five years, the church in Rome was functionally Gentile. The culture and life of the church would have surely become increasingly Gentile and less Jewish in every way. We can speculate a bit that with most of the Jewish Christians gone and far fewer Jews in Rome, the number of Jewish converts slowed dramatically and may have even stopped; leading some to surmise that God had given the Jews their chance to enter his family and now that opportunity had disappeared and Christianity and salvation belonged to the Gentiles.

In AD 54, an exciting new Emperor named Nero took power and the people loved him, at least at first. In his first year in power he allowed the Jews back into Rome. This would have included the return of many Christians who had left five years previously. Among those who left under Claudius' initial decree were Aquila and Priscilla (Acts 18:2). After serving Christ by helping in churches around the region, they had returned to Rome (Romans 16:3), which no doubt added to Paul's interest in the community there.

This influx of returning Jews seems to have led to a fair amount of tension in the church. Things had no doubt changed in those five years. The makeup of the family was different. The culture and ethos had shifted. The leadership had become exclusively Gentile. When suddenly a wave of Jewish Christians came flooding back, what would be done with them? Would they resume the positions they held previously? Would they form Jewish house churches rather than integrate with Gentile house churches?

We simply don't know the minute details of the conflict, but we can be certain that much of it was based on cultural and racial clashes. This provided the primary occasion for Paul to craft his letter to the church. He covers a wide variety of topics and theology in what has often been called his masterpiece, but we should always keep at the forefront of our minds that his biggest concern and reason for writing was to heal the ethnic divide in the church. All the brilliant theology in this letter, which has so enriched our understanding of what it means to be Christian, was aimed at helping the church in Rome understand the implications of being God's multiethnic family. In the first eleven chapters, Paul lays out the theology and explanation for how and why God's people must consist of all ethnicities. In the remaining five chapters, he gets down to the practical implementation and ramifications of understanding who God has called his family to be.

The Gospel Explained

Admittedly, some of the material we will examine here overlaps with the controversies in Galatia and Corinth, but there are some important differences and nuances. And since the Spirit felt that it was important that we have several different angles on these tough ethnic issues and how the apostolic church approached them, it was apparently worth repeating a few things.

Paul begins his letter declaring in no uncertain terms that Jesus is King (1:1–4). This will frame everything else in his letter and help establish the identity of the believers. A gospel in the Roman world was a good news declaration about the reign of a king, and this was no exception. He reminds the predominantly Gentile church that they have been graciously called to belong to King Jesus (1:5–6). After expressing how much he desires to see them (1:7–15), Paul declares that he is not ashamed of the good news. Jews claimed that the good news that Jesus was King of the world was a scandal, and Gentiles thought it pure foolishness that someone could resurrect from the dead, let alone be the true king of anything (1:16). But, he says, this kingship announcement is for both Jew and Gentile, because in it is the fulfillment of all of God's promises (1:17).

With his introduction out of the way, Paul begins his main argument. In essence, he is answering the question, who are the people of God? Is it the Gentile nations? Romans 1:18–32 is his answer to that. In short, of course not. Who could even attempt to claim such a thing? That was an obvious point, but Paul is very cleverly teaching the disciples how to think about their ethnicity and kingdom citizenship.

After reading chapter 1, the heads of the Jewish Christians were probably vigorously nodding in agreement. Not so fast, Paul warns. Chapter 2 turns the tables. Ethnic Israel is not the promised family of God either. Gentiles are sinners, but so are the Jews who have the Law. They are no better just because they have circumcision and the things that set them apart, if they don't actually live as God's people. "A person is not a Jew who is one only outwardly" (2:28), the apostle concludes.

Chapter 3 then opens with the obvious question: well, "what advantage, then, is there in being a Jew"? The Jews, argues Paul, did have an advantage because they were given God's word, but even if they did not remain faithful to his promises, God will (3:3–4). So, while there were advantages to being part of ethnic Israel, that advantage was squandered. "Jews and Gentiles alike are all under the power of sin" (3:9). This is an important truth for us to grasp today. Some ethnic groups may have certain advantages in society, but they all stand on the same ground as sinners in need of a King. What the world says is important simply is not. Ability to stand securely in covenant with God as his people does not come through the Law (3:21); it comes through Jesus Christ (3:22). Neither Jews nor Gentiles have access on their own to God's glory and covenant status before him (3:23), but all can have this as they enter into Jesus (3:24). It is not the Law or the ethnicity of anyone that brings them standing before God. It is faith in the life of Christ (3:27–31). There is no disadvantage or advantage to being born into one ethnic group or the other.

Abraham's life is evidence that God's family was always defined and demarcated by faith. His obedience and faith were the entry markers into the covenant. Ancient Near East covenants, incidentally, were basically agreements between non–family members to treat one another as family. That was the cultural institution that God chose to express his relationship to Abraham. Abraham did not receive God's promises or live like they were true because of the Law (4:13–15). It was his faith in God's promises that did that (4:18–25). In short, neither ethnicity nor the Law had anything to do with creating and marking the boundaries of God's family. Those would later become temporary tools, but they were never the defining markers.

Paul turns to the Garden of Eden to demonstrate that we all must believe that we really can become members of God's family through Jesus Christ and by no other means (5:1–21). If that is the only means through which our sin is forgiven and we have entered God's family, then no other status such as ethnicity or religious works of the Law should play a factor in our identity or how we value others. Things that don't matter should not be a cause for division. In fact, humans are not as divided as we might think. Sin entered the world through one man, Adam, and because he was humanity's king, of sorts, what was true of the king became true of his people. We were all born in a fallen world with a desire to sin, and we all do. Putting our own desires first is idolatry, and the result of idolatry is death. In that sense, Adam's one act of sin put all of humanity into one fallen family (5:12–18). But Jesus has acted righteously and opened up a new family for all people to join. The effect of King Adam's sin is great and impacts his people, but the effect of King Jesus' righteousness is even greater and brings the life of the age to come to those who enter his authority (5:21).

In Romans 6–8 Paul is going to put the life of Christ on display as a way of saying, "This is what the promises God gave to Abraham really look like." One of the main objections to his gospel message that all people could enter into God's family through Jesus and live a life of faith and grace was that the Gentiles would have no Law to guide them. This would lead to chaos. Was Paul's argument that this was fine because they would just go on sinning in their Gentile ways that Paul described in 1:18–32, but God's grace would cover that all over? No way, says Paul. The Law is like crutches for a broken leg. Entering Christ is like amputating your old legs and getting a brand-new pair of perfect legs. The emphasis in chapter 6 is that baptism institutes a death and a burial with Christ; and when we are raised to a new life, it is his life that we now have, not our old sin-riddled existence. Being in the realm of grace does not mean that you can do whatever you want because there is no Law to provide boundaries. The new boundaries are the very life of Christ. That is our identity and reality. In exchanging our life for Christ's, we become slaves of God (6:22), and that is a good thing. The wages of sin is death (6:23), whether you have no border fences or the Law is your border fence. You are still in your sin either way. So if your identity is the Jew or Gentile self that you were born into, you are in a lot of trouble. But the gift of God is the life of the age to come that is found only in Christ (6:23) as he becomes our new identity.

The primary point of chapter 7 is that the Law and the corresponding argument that one needs to become a Jew in order to be part of God's family has a fatal flaw. The Law cannot change your behavior; it can only show you where you went wrong. It is a bit like using printed-out Mapquest directions in the early 2000s. If you got lost, they could only serve to show you that you were not in the right place; they had no power to guide you to your proper destination the way modern GPS does. Paul has taken six chapters to thoroughly make the point that Jewish ethnic identity as defined by the Law could not be the uniform of God's people. Ethnic Israel could not be the fulfillment of God's promises, because the Law can only divide the nations and show them they are in the wrong, but it cannot lead them to the salvation of the kingdom. Of course, it took Paul a mere fifteen verses to demonstrate that same truth for the Gentiles, but that was a much easier case.

Chapter 8 is a picture of the fulfillment of promises that the Law, whose shortcomings are described in chapter 7, cannot bring. Those in Christ have the Spirit to guide them toward the realm of God. The Spirit has brought us into God's family (8:14–16), but following the Spirit will lead into conflict with the world and subsequent suffering (8:17); so persecution and criticism should not lead to the conclusion that the Roman Christians were on the wrong path, but that they are on the exact right one. This path is worth it (8:18) because it leads to and anticipates the renewal of all creation that God is bringing about in Christ (8:19–22). The multiethnic family of all nations is a strong sign of that renewal and restoration. And not just a sign; it is part of the renewal itself. The powerful truth of being in Christ is that this is God's final and complete fulfillment. To have a family in Christ being conformed to his image has always been God's plan (8:29), and nothing shall replace or separate that family from the eternal covenant with God (8:32–39).

One of Paul's greatest desires, as he begins in chapter 9, is that his countrymen, ethnic Israel, would turn to God's solution in the Messiah. But, he is careful to point out, it's not as though God has failed to keep his promises. He promised that the blessing for all nations would come through Abraham's descendants, but the promise was not given to all his descendants, only part of them. Just as the inheritance passed from Abraham to only one son, and from that son, Isaac, to only one of his own sons, Jacob, so the inheritance has passed over ethnic Israel and gone to one of Abraham's descendants (9:7–13). For, says Paul, in one of the most important verses in the whole letter toward helping us understand his greater purpose and focus, "not all who are descended from Israel are Israel" (9:6b). The nation of Israel was not chosen to inherit the promises, and they have no right to complain about that. God chose them for their role as those who would forfeit the initial inheritance as his people; but that left them no more disadvantaged than Egypt or any other pagan nation (9:14–29). Israel willingly rejected God's Kingship and found themselves outside of God's people. That has led to the deeply ironic truth that the Gentiles have found God's covenant promises (righteousness) through faith in Christ, and ethnic Israel has not because they insisted that the Law and their racial identity were enough for them to be part of the kingdom people (9:30–33).

Paul wishes that ethnic Israel would be saved (10:1), but he knows that this is unlikely for the collective because their great zeal for God has been placed on the wrong things and not on the Lordship and Kingship of Christ (10:2–4). Anyone who submits to Jesus as King and declares him the true Lord will be saved (10:5–13) as part of his people. Paul finishes chapter 10 with a flourish wondering how Israel missed all this. Moses (10:19) and Isaiah (10:20) both prophesied, he declares, that he would be found by those that were not his people, but his people would disobey and reject him (10:21).

Just as the Jews might have gotten overexcited after reading 1:18–32, before Paul brings them back to earth with the next six chapters, so the Gentiles might have been overexuberant at reading chapters 9 and 10. "Yes! This is just what we have been claiming. God has moved on from ethnic Israel and we are now his people, so the few around here that are in Christ should fall in line and do things our way."

"Did God reject his people?" No way, Paul says clearly. His point in chapter 11 is that while being an ethnic Jew does not automatically place one in God's family, the door is still wide open for Jews to enter through Christ. Paul hopes that the numbers of Gentiles streaming into the kingdom will wake up Israel and make her people jealous (11:11) so that at least some of them will come to their senses and be saved (11:14). He reminds the Gentiles that they should not denigrate the Jews but should recognize that they were the root of the tree and be grateful for them as their ancestors (11:17–21). If Jewish people drop their unbelief in Jesus as King, they will be brought right back into the multiethnic family of promise just as readily as the Gentiles were (11:22–24). Ethnic Israel has been turned over to their own sinful desires (hardened) just as Egypt had been, and now Gentiles were flocking in (11:25). Paul's point is dense but simple: most ethnic Jews will reject God's plan, but he has promised that Israel will be saved, and as Jews and Gentiles enter the Messiah, that promise is fulfilled. This is how all Israel will be saved. Israel was always to be a family of all nations, and "not all who are descended from Israel are Israel." The Jews might be persecuting Christians right now, but God has not given up on them. Entry into the elect family of God is still theirs if they will only accept his mercy (11:28–32).

Paul has spent a great deal of time explaining to both Jew and Gentile who they are in Christ. Neither has a claim to the family of God based on their own merit or ethnicity. But neither has a disadvantage either. What matters is that they have both been shown God's grace and mercy in different ways. And now they must realize that any action or mindset that works against displaying the glory of God's manifold wisdom shown through his people of all nations is a monstrous problem. The path to his promises could not have come through Gentiles following the Law and becoming Jews, because then God's family would still comprise only one nation. It could not exclude the Jews, because then it would not be of all nations. A new family, a new ethnicity has been formed, but it MUST consist of all the divided nations. And that is who they are. With all that dense but incredibly necessary theology explained, Paul can get to the real heart of the matter: how can they live together when they have such very different cultures and perspectives on what it looks like to be a disciple of Jesus?

Living Together as One Family

In chapters 12 and 13 the apostle gives relevant and practical teaching to the whole body, instructing them how to think and act as one. In chapters 14 and 15, he will turn to helping them navigate specifically through the cultural divide that has broken up their fellowship.

On the heels of all the theology of who they are as the great fulfillment of the one family of all nations in Christ, Paul says appropriately, "Therefore, I urge you, brother and sisters, in view of God's mercy, to offer your bodies as a living sacrifice" (12:1). This, he says, is true and proper worship. In light of the ongoing context, it's hard not to imagine that at least some of what Paul has in mind here is that a good part of what is being sacrificed is ethnicity-based identity. God wants our whole selves to identify and act as his children. But it will require an incredible amount of work not to conform to the molds of sin and division that the world is constantly trying to squeeze us into. Rather, we must transform by intentionally renewing our minds in Christ. The Spirit will lead his family (8:14–16) to a new identity, a new purpose, and an uncommon unity (12:2). Paul urges them not to think of themselves more highly than they ought (12:3), which is likely a corrective on seeing themselves as individuals and separate from the body. We form one body, he reminds, and "each member belongs to all the others" (12:5), a sharp and poignant reminder for a fellowship in a bit of turmoil.

There is nothing more unifying than recalling that you are all on the same mission, and so Paul spends the remainder of the chapter reigniting those memories within them. If they think they have nothing in common, they would do well to remember that they are all hating what is evil, being devoted to one another, honoring one another above themselves, being patient in affliction, staying faithful in prayer, blessing those that curse them, honoring those of low position, spurning revenge, and much more. Living the disciples' life together is far more unifying and identity-forming than any ethnic or racial alignment ever could be.

In chapter 13, Paul reminds them that, in the kingdom of God, they are creating an alternate society and way of life to which everyone is invited. They are not revolutionaries bent on overthrowing the powers that be. The right response to acknowledging Jesus as the King cannot be, "And now all other forms of authority and rule must go." God has allowed governments in the kingdom of the world to be a limiting and organizing force. That doesn't mean that they are godly or that Christians should throw in their lot or identify with them, or put their hope in them, but they should respect them as much as possible. The disciples' primary ethic in the world is not political power but to love their neighbor as themselves (13:9). This is vital, because the arrival of the age to come is creeping ever closer.

Paul makes an incredibly important point in 13:11–14 that should not be overlooked. Even though it is night and the kingdoms of darkness rule (a situation in which we still find ourselves today), the day is coming as surely as the sun rises in the morning. The resurrection age will arrive soon. In the meantime, disciples are not to live as though it is nighttime. Our way of life, identity, community structure, purpose, and values should look as different from the world's as day does from night. When our solutions are drawn from the world or look very much like those of the world, why does the world need the kingdom of God? If it just offers the same sort of tired answers that they could find in any rally, town hall meeting, or political convention, what is the point? I know I keep repeating that same general idea, but it usually takes most of us several times before something fully sinks in, right?

Navigating a Culture War

As Paul arrives in chapters 14 and 15, he directly addresses the divisions that had surfaced in the multicultural church in Rome. Since virtually every church in the world is multicultural in one way or another, the principles that Paul provides in this section are incredibly helpful for us.

Before looking at the principles, however, I want to remind you once again just how deeply emotional these issues were for the disciples of that time. Their conflicts were deeply rooted and complex. They were from ethnic groups with a history of conflict in the world including hundreds of years of persecution and deaths, and more violent struggle was in the future. They clashed over issues of identity and matters that were based on sincere conviction or history, often things that would feel like sin if people did or did not engage in them. This was no small thing that Paul was dealing with. The stakes were high.

What is striking as Paul helps the believers to navigate through this minefield of dangers threatening their community is that he never demands that one side see themselves as in the wrong or urges them to drop their convictions and practices to appease the other. That might be how the world handles things, but Paul points to a very different way—the kingdom way.

Principle #1 – Accept Those with a Different Perspective (14:1–9)

These Jewish and Gentile Christians grew up in different cultures with divergent perspectives of history that caused them to interact with and perceive the world in very different ways. Was one right and the other wrong? Perhaps that is the wrong question. Following Jesus is less about the right way and the wrong and more about a journey toward Christ.

The goal for God's people on that journey is to understand that we are all on different points along that path and that consciences take a long time to train. They don't change overnight. Paul urges acceptance of those who are weak. Paul doesn't use the term "weak" the way that we might, meaning that these were people with shaky faith or who were uncommitted. He means that their experiences have rooted them to a reliance on convictions that are not absolutely necessary to their faith, but not opposed to it either.

Some felt that it was sin to eat meat sacrificed to idols; others felt that it was ridiculous not to. We must remember that there was a long history of persecuted Jews dying rather than betraying the food laws. To eat tainted meat would not only have felt sinful, but also like a denouncement of those who had died long ago defending the faith. Some felt that it would be wrong for them not to honor the Sabbath. Again, this was a deeply rooted element of their identity and way of life. Why would they turn their backs on that when there was no scriptural demand to do so? But that would have felt incredibly difficult to hold to when others felt no such loyalty. You can imagine the challenge of creating a community with these divergent convictions.

Paul's answer is that each should follow their own convictions. This doesn't mean that each person can create their own elements of faith, accepting or rejecting whatever they would like. Of course, there are limits. Divergent perspectives and actions still need to be rooted in Christ and God's word, but there is a great deal of leeway within the body of Christ. Each person belongs to the Lord, and while we must work together, having different convictions because of differing experiences is acceptable. We might wish for Paul to give a clearer answer here, but what if it is less important for us to be in lockstep uniformity in every way and more important to the character of our communities that we learn to love one another despite the differences? That is certainly more challenging and able to produce more Christlike compassion and empathy. This, then, is what Paul means when he calls on Christians to be like-minded (Philippians 2:2).

This is both encouraging and challenging for us today. In the church, we find liberals and conservatives, black, white, and all other ethnicities. Some are passionate about racial injustice. Others think that this distracts from the work of bringing people to Christ. Some think one of the biggest problems in our country today is racism. Others believe that racism is bad but is not a major issue and is one that is largely fabricated by a predatory media. There is an incredible temptation to argue and think that we must convince one another on these issues, or shut the other side up. If that doesn't work, then we simply must part ways because the beliefs of "those others" are too painful or too disturbing. I have seen this happen. Maybe you have too. Our first-century brothers and sisters were just as tempted to move toward those supposed solutions as we are. But we belong to one another (12:5). Together we live for the Lord and die for the Lord (14:8). Rather than exalting our convictions to the dividing line, Christ must be all in all, and as important as our passions are, they must be subservient to our loyalty to him and to the body.

Principle #2 – Don't Judge Your Brothers and Sisters (14:10–18)

It is Rome, AD 55. You are a Christian who takes your role as a disciple of Jesus very seriously. You are passionate about the call to be holy and separate from the world. You are surrounded by pagan influence, thought, and practices everywhere you move in this bustling metropolis. You want to revere Christ and bring him glory in everything and will not compromise with the constant Roman temptations of idolatry that are wrapped up into almost every facet of life. So you do your best to avoid these sins completely. Since there is no butcher around that sells meat that has not been sacrificed to idols, you will partake only of vegetables, cutting yourself off completely from sin. You are invited over for a dinner party with a few married couples who are also disciples. They are preparing meat that has obviously come from the pagan temple down the road. From their perspective, though, everything in the world belongs to God. And yes, they desire to be holy too, but they believe firmly that men and women are not made unclean by what goes into them, but by the words and actions that come out. They have no interest in restrictive religious demonstrations that have no true power or meaning. They are tired of being criticized and looked down upon by those who don't seem to fully grasp the freeing power of the gospel. You can see the problem here. Both sides would begin to frown upon and judge the other. How can you have community like this?

It's simple, says Paul; not easy, but simple. Do not judge others or treat them with contempt. Rather than passing judgment, assume that they are doing what they are doing out of genuine conviction. Yes, he points out, there is nothing inherently wrong with eating meat that is unclean, but if that truly bothers someone, put love for them over your opinions and even over your "rightness." Maybe it's silly to others, but don't speak of it negatively and don't let others do it either. If we read verses 10–18 carefully we see what a fine line Paul is walking. Both sides have reason to be confident of their conviction, even if one is not in full grasp of the truth of the gospel. Neither side should feel bad about their genuine convictions, but they should not demand that the other one change their behavior either.

This is simple, but still very thought-provoking. What if we have one sister who feels passionately that racism must be spoken out against and justice must be had for all, while a certain brother feels that most of the issues of so-called racism today are interpreted as such by those who want to generate instances of racism to divide us politically? Do they have to argue? Do they have to convince one another? They need to listen to each other, no doubt. They need to have the heart to suffer when one part suffers

(1 Corinthians 12:26). In so doing, they may very well come together and formulate a new understanding and appreciation for both perspectives. But what do we do when that doesn't happen? Can the white conservative brother who feels that his black sister does not fully understand what is really going on in the world respect and support her outlook and passion without labeling her as a race baiter? Can she respect and support him without labeling him as a racist?

The fine line here, of course, is between perspective and actual sin. To harbor racism or support such things is wrong, and clearly sin. But it is also a problem to exalt one's racial identity over and above the kingdom and become so passionate about certain issues that it is difficult to tell the difference between your opinions and positions and those that we find in the world. A true kingdom perspective will, at times, overlap with philosophies found in the world but will never run directly parallel to them. This will take great spiritual discernment and maturity. But understand that the issues Paul was dealing with were just as emotional, just as historical, and just as divisive as our issues today. In verse 16 he urges them not to look at what their brothers and sisters are doing, think they made a huge mistake, and curse the church or their brothers and sisters as unclean or sinners. It is easy, when it comes to issues of race and culture, for us to do something similar and give up. But that would be as foolish for us today as it would have been for them.

Principle #3 – Pursue Peace (14:19–21)

The challenge for the disciples in Rome was that each side could genuinely look at the other and think they were wrong. But, Paul says, do everything in your power to pursue peace and to build one another up. The kingdom is more important than our positions. Love trumps convictions on nonsalvation issues, and even then, love for God and one another is always supreme.

The challenge for us too is that we can look at one another and genuinely think the other is wrong. I will again use the example of racism. One disciple believes that it is sin and must be confronted wherever possible. Another believes that our job is to create a kingdom community where racism does not exist, so it is unnecessary to try to address every instance of it in the world. Just build up the kingdom, they believe, proclaim the gospel, and invite those that suffer in the world into this new community. As close as those positions are to one another, they can often feel worlds apart, and division looms.

Yes, prejudice is a sin and should be confronted in the church. But what if you truly believe another brother or sister is prejudiced and they just can't be made to see it? Can you still love them and work toward peace? If not, then is something other than the kingdom your true priority? Our first-century brothers and sisters would know the challenge of that well, but they faced it, and so must we.

Principle #4 – Keep It to Yourself (14:22–23)

"Whatever you believe about these things," commands Paul, "keep between yourself and God." I don't believe he is talking in general about their own personal beliefs, because those would have been visible and obvious. Instead, he is referring to what they believe about what others are doing. Keep that between you and God. In the meantime, don't judge them; love them and work for peace. Paul does offer a word of encouragement for those that are on the freer side of things. You are not condemned, he says, because you approve certain foods and do not see that as being opposed to a holy life. But don't put others in the position described in verse 23: do not look down on them or think that they are a lesser Christian because they have different convictions and perspectives.

There is an important likelihood here that we rarely consider or fully contemplate the implications of. What if God wants these many different perspectives and convictions in the church? It would be easy for a church to be unified and love one another if everybody had the same background, saw the world in the same way, practiced their discipleship identically, and held to the same convictions. But what would that really demonstrate to the world? The world can do that; they can be united when there is uniformity. But can we hold to deeply different beliefs and still be the unified body of Christ?

Listen, I have deeply passionate beliefs about the issues raised in this book. I have spent years studying and experiencing them and have talked to thousands of people on the subject. These have all shaped my outlook and understanding. I wish everyone believed as I did. I truly think there are some brothers and sisters on both sides of the spectrum who are just wrong, are closed-minded, and have not wrapped their heads around the full ramifications of their kingdom identity. Some of the things that other disciples have said or done when it comes to issues of race, racism, ethnicity, and culture have made me angry. I would be lying if I didn't admit that. I see the challenge of us all living together in community as one family. But this is what brings God glory. This is what marks the kingdom as different from the dominion of the world. Jesus had a Jewish zealot and a tax collector who worked for Rome among his disciples. They could not have been more opposed. Yet they embraced the kingdom together and worked through their differences. I'm sure they transformed many of their ways of thinking, but I suspect that deep contrasts remained until the day they died. Yet they were unified and loved one another. Can we do the same?

Principle #5 – Bear with One Another (15:1–4)

This principle would not be that effective or important if we just stopped at "bear with one another." That would be fine, I suppose, but it would not get us very far to simply grit our teeth and endure the boorishness and faulty thinking that we are sure each other are guilty of. This would create communities where we smiled into one another's faces while secretly fuming and disliking many people we see, especially those with differing perspectives. But the apostle urges that our motivation be to love one another and build each other up, rather than trying to please ourselves. Simply bearing with others can be very self-focused. Paul calls for genuine others-focused behavior. We seek their best interest and not our own.

Our mindset must be focused on the good of others. That can be difficult in communities with multiple cultures and perspectives, but it is our goal. Before we formulate opinions, reject another viewpoint, get angry with a brother or sister, or post something on social media, we should think about building up the body. Christ did not seek to please himself and neither should we.

Principle #6 – Have the Mind of Christ (15:5–6)

Just as Paul called the Philippians to others-focused behavior because of the example and pattern of the Messiah (Philippians 2:1–8), he does the same here. God is not brought glory by us all thinking the same and pressuring every single believer into one great monolithic perception of the world. God's incredible otherworldly wisdom is put on display when a bunch of people with all different backgrounds and ways of seeing things are willing to set those aside when they would divide anyone else, and remain faithful to God and loyal to one another because we have the incredible treasure of the kingdom. "His intent was that now, through the church, the manifold wisdom of God should be made known to the rulers and authorities in the heavenly realms" (Ephesians 3:10).

Principle #7 – Accept One Another…With a Twist (15:7)

Paul began this section with the call to accept one another, and now he repeats that principle but adds an important enhancer. Don't just accept one another, accept one another as Christ accepted you. That's a higher standard, isn't it? Jesus sacrificed for us while we were his enemies in full rebellion against him. He died for us "while we were still sinners" (Romans 5:8).

When the world cannot agree, it tends to divide into camps. For this reason, we continue to see much division and strife even at a time when there are ever-increasing calls for diversity and coming together. Unity in the body will not come by us all thinking alike. That is both naïve and immature thinking. Unity is a sham without diversity. But diversity without unity is a ticking time bomb. It is only by living as the King did and loving as he does can we accept one another as he accepted us.

Principle #8 – This Is Bigger than You (15:8–22)

It helps to remember that being a multiethnic family that consists of all nations and more cultures than we can count has been part of God's plan and promises from the beginning. It's hard to be a family with people so different from ourselves. It can be excruciating to have to lay down our lives and pet beliefs for the benefit of others. It can seem beyond our abilities to put loyalty to God's kingdom and what he is doing through his people ahead of our own passions and the issues that we support. It can be unbelievably difficult to find the balance between advocating for justice and defending the oppressed, and maintaining unity in the body. There are no easy answers.

But this is God's plan. He has created a new humanity out of all nations. "May the God of hope fill you with all joy and peace," wrote Paul, "as you trust in him, so that you may overflow with hope by the power of the Spirit" (15:13).

Principle #9 – The Mission Depends on This (15:23–33)

Paul tips his hand to another of his purposes in writing this letter. He was passionate about proclaiming the good news everywhere. He needed the church in Rome to get their act together so that they could provide him support as he spread the gospel to Spain and beyond (15:24).

It seems that when God's people are not unified among the nations as Isaiah prophesied (Isaiah 2:2–4), then it does hinder the mission. We saw that alluded to in Acts 6, and Paul hints at it here again. In Deuteronomy, God urges Israel to be his obedient people, "for this will show your wisdom and understanding to the nations, who will hear about all these decrees and say, 'Surely this great nation is a wise and understanding people'" (Deuteronomy 4:6). The mission is always about showing God's wisdom and glory through the lives of his people.

One of the great strengths of the gospel lies in its ability to create a diverse family. Our fellowship of churches has always embraced that. We should be proud of that and praise God for what he has done. We simply cannot allow worldly identities and issues to turn a strength into weakness. Too much depends on it.

Questions for Discussion

1. Do you consider yourself open to the perspectives and opinions of others, or would you describe yourself differently?

2. What is the primary factor in determining your opinions and convictions on racial, cultural, social, and political issues?

3. Is there anyone in the body that you dislike, bear a grudge against, or avoid because of their beliefs, opinions, or convictions? What does Paul's teaching in Romans and the other letters we have looked at direct you to do in these situations?

4. What are your personal challenges when it comes to not judging and being unified with brothers and sisters who have strongly held convictions that are very different from your own?

5. What does it mean to accept one another as Christ accepted you?

Chapter 14

The Way of the Cross:
Self-Sacrifice

In his biography, *A Long Walk to Freedom,* famed apartheid activist Nelson Mandela describes a time when the Antiapartheid Movement was not gaining much traction despite a great deal of effort. Mandela was a young man and still formulating his beliefs and tactics. He describes a speech in 1952 in which Chief Albert Luthuli put forth important principles. The speech was entitled "The Road to Freedom Is Via the Cross." Luthuli was a deeply religious man who ingrained this simple truth into Mandela. It was at this time that Mandela began to realize what was wrong with the freedom movement in South Africa. The leaders had not been willing to sacrifice. They wanted freedom without self-sacrifice. Mandela learned the same lesson that Mahatma Gandhi and Martin Luther King Jr., among others, had learned well: to obtain freedom from oppression, you must be willing to take the suffering on yourself rather than trying to push it to others.

This is the precise problem with many of the political movements today that want to impact the world, relieve the suffering of the oppressed, end racism, and many other worthy causes. They want victory, but they don't want the pain. They want to make others feel the agony and discomfort. They want to transfer the hurt back to those that they feel have caused it, or to the masses that are not directly responsible but have remained silent, in hope that transferring some discomfort onto them will induce them to act on behalf of the cause. It will not work. It never has. Putting the pain onto others rarely, if ever, results in large and lasting change. The reason is fairly simple: pain usually causes a negative backlash. If you hurt me, my instinct will be to hurt you back. The cycle of violence and hurt then continues on and on until one side is simply destroyed and can no longer hurt back. This is the power of the sword in full effect.

But these three great champions of change in the twentieth century, Gandhi, King, and Mandela, all demonstrated the wisdom of self-sacrifice. What should not surprise us is that all three of them cited the teachings and influence of Jesus as one of the major components of developing their worldview. The way of the cross, the way of self-sacrifice, was a central element of the greatest life that was ever lived. He taught this idea constantly, and even more important, demonstrated it in his own life.

The Great Sermon

Nearly two thousand years ago, Jesus addressed a group of disciples on the side of a mountain, delivering a sermon that changed the world. Of course, everything about Jesus' life, death, and resurrection changed the world; but the ideas presented in the Sermon on the Mount were so revolutionary and so otherworldly that most people in the last two millennia simply have not known what to do with them. Some have suggested that they are nothing more than ideals that cannot be obtained. Many others have watered them down to the point that they are so comfortable, they become nearly meaningless.

Matthew, who recorded this particular speech, highlights the fact that Jesus gave this lesson from the side of a mountain. There are several points in Matthew's gospel where he draws attention to the parallels between Jesus and Moses, and then demonstrates how Jesus is greater than even Moses. The Sermon on the Mount is one of those moments. Just as Moses stood on Mount Sinai and gave Israel the commandments of the Lord, teaching them how to live as God's people, so did Jesus. But Moses' laws were limited to the present age. Israel was a physical nation, with physical boundaries, physical battles, and physical enemies. The kingdom of God under the New Covenant was just as real but had a whole new reality wrapped inside it. Jesus opened access to the life of the age to come. No longer would humans be bound to the values and responses of the present age. We can now live by the values of heaven. We can do God's will on earth as it is done in heaven (Matthew 6:10). For this reason, the kingdom is not less than physical, it is more than physical. We can now get to the real root of the issues. The realm and boundaries of the kingdom are spiritual rather than limited by the physical. This means that our battles and enemies are also on a spiritual level. When we hear that, I believe some of us are tempted to think that "spiritual" means unconnected with the real world, but that could not be further from the truth, as we shall see.

The Sermon itself, found in Matthew 5–7, is a work of art. It is constructed in a typical Ancient Near East format called a chiasm. A chiasm is a literary device that structures a passage, whether short or long, in an inverse fashion. So it starts in a pattern such as 1, 2, 3, and then inverts and restates or expounds upon the ideas as 3, 2, 1. Examples of this style of structure can be found throughout the Scriptures, both Old and New Testament.[41] The pattern of the Sermon looks like this:

Introduction (5:1-2)
   A – The poor in spirit (5:3)
     B – The mourners (5:4)
       C – The meek (5:5)
         D – Hunger and thirst (5:6)
           E – The merciful (5:7)
             F – The pure in heart (5:8)
               G – The peacemakers (5:9)
                 H – The persecuted (5:10)
                 H – Persecuted but visible (5:11-20)
               G – Peacemaking (5:21-26)
             F – Pure in heart (5:27-37)
           E – Merciful to all (5:38-48)
         D – Hunger for God not man (6:1-18)
       C – Living under control (6:19-34)
     B – Mourning over sin starts with you (7:1-6)
   A – Recognizing your need (7:7-11)
Conclusion: Summary & warnings (7:12-27)

The whole speech is Jesus' description of what the life of the age to come will look like when lived out in the present age. It starts with abject humility (poor in Spirit) and total reliance on God, asking him for everything we need to live like this. If we look at the Sermon in this structure, that means that the bottom line H, above, is the heart of the speech. At the center of the life of a disciple will be persecution. And that gets even more challenging when we realize that the corresponding explanation of being persecuted is that we are to be salt and light. The biggest thing those two items have in common is that there is no mistaking when they are present. They are noticeable. And so should be the lives of Jesus' community. Yes, it will elicit persecution, but we must shine like a beacon in the darkness.

Just about midway through the Sermon, we find the section that I will focus on for our purposes here. In the beatitudes, Jesus says that those who will operate in a state of blessing are those that are merciful. Mercy means to treat someone better than they deserve. It shows them a higher option than they would have otherwise thought available. In the corresponding expansion of the concept of mercy, Jesus expounds upon exactly what this might look like among his followers. His words in those eleven short verses will continue to change the world if we take them seriously. With that said, for the remainder of this chapter, we will seek to apply Jesus' teaching in Matthew 5:38–48 to the modern situations of culture and race in our fellowship of churches and in the world.

An Eye for an Eye

The standard of the Old Covenant was "Eye for eye, and tooth for tooth" (5:38). To our ears this sounds violent and harsh, but it was actually quite merciful for its day. It limited vengeance and justice to fair standards. If someone poked out your eye, you were to seek a fair level of justice, not a punitive one. It was "eye for eye," not "their entire head for your eye." As much as people tend to recoil at the level of brutality that is presumed in this standard, it is exactly the standard that most people expect today. It is, after all, the best you can do if employing the solutions of the world.

We see it embodied in many popular slogans: "I want what's coming to me." "No justice, no peace." "Fair is fair." "I want my fair share." "Justice for all." These all embrace or imply the simple level of justice and fairness for everyone embodied in an eye for an eye. This is what most people want, and it seems reasonable.

Except for one inconvenient fact. When injustice abounds, suffering of some kind must take place to right the wrong. I will use the example of a pie. Let's say we have a scrumptious pecan pie cut into eight pieces for Thanksgiving dinner. There are eight of us present, but two people have greedily scooped up two pieces each for themselves. That leaves six people and four pieces of pie. The fair solution, of course, is to take one piece each from the people who have two. That's fair. We are not, after all, taking both of their pieces and punishing them. We are just taking one piece so that justice can be done for all. But what if they don't want to give up their pie? What if they feel that they earned that pie or worked for it? In the real world, people do not tend to want to give up their pie. Conflict ensues.

That leads us to consider the two primary responses to conflict. There is strength and justice, or weakness and the status quo. We can fight for what is ours or for justice, but that perpetuates conflict and often makes it worse. It rarely brings true solutions to any situation. Or we can allow the injustice to happen, but appeasement and looking the other way is not really a positive option in the long term either.

When it comes to the racial divide in our country, it seems to be growing. Maybe that's not true, but it sure does not seem to be getting any better. The racial and cultural conflicts continue. How do we respond? Some disciples are passionate about it and demand justice. They want the path of strength. Others don't see it as such a problem and think that it doesn't need to be addressed, especially not in the church. This is the route of the status quo. When faced with true conflict, I believe we must avoid both responses. We must spurn both justice and the weakness of following the status quo.

Does it sound odd to your ears to hear it argued that we not seek justice? After all, isn't one of the central virtues of disciples of the kingdom that they are the people who stand up for the oppressed and afflicted? Yes, but the pursuit of the world's justice is almost always destructive, and quite often it creates as many problems as it solves. We have a crime problem so we throw everyone in jail. That's justice, but it creates a whole new set of issues. We don't like a new governmental policy so we throw our lot in with those who are protesting and fighting. But that often perpetuates enmity and doesn't deal with the root. Keep in mind, I am not arguing that society at large implement this life. Jesus gives no indication that this life is for anyone other than his small band of followers on the narrow road (Matthew 7:14). Justice was an important pursuit under the Old Testament Law, as Jesus noted (Matthew 23:23), but the time of the Old Covenant was limited to the solutions of the present age. With the kingdom of God came new possibilities, new solutions, and a new concept of God's justice rather than man's.

Seeing injustice in society, such as racism, for example; and responding by saying that as disciples we will stand up for the oppressed and fight with them until justice is served just might be a fool's errand, in my opinion. It is to employ the methods of the world. If it does work, it will create a whole new set of injustices and problems. Why limit ourselves to the world's solutions if there is a better way?

I'm not saying that we don't stand up for the needy, oppressed, and outcasts. God's people should stand up and fight for them. The question is, how?

The Way of Mercy

What did Jesus mean in the first part of Matthew 5:39 when he said,

"Do not resist an evil person"? It cannot mean, "Do nothing, and just let evil have its way." New Testament scholar N.T. Wright translates this verse in his Kingdom New Testament Translation, "Don't use violence to resist evil!" I think that's closer to what Jesus was saying than the NIV implies. This is a broad-reaching principle, because there is physical violence, yes; but there are many other types of violence. Jesus forbids any of them for those trying to make a kingdom impact. His point was to not use the weapons of the world. Jesus offers an option that is quite remarkable, and was virtually unheard of and virtually untried before he stepped foot onto this earth.

> But I tell you, do not resist an evil person. If anyone slaps you on the right cheek, turn to them the other cheek also. And if anyone wants to sue you and take your shirt, hand over your coat as well. If anyone forces you to go one mile, go with them two miles.
> Matthew 5:39b–41

If someone in that culture walked up and slapped you, presumably with their right hand, they would have to backhand slap you to make contact with your right cheek. That gesture sent an unmistakable message that was meant to demean the recipient. Obviously, Jesus is using this example as a paradigm for teaching his followers how to interact with the world in which they live. How will you respond when someone demeans and attacks you? You could fight for justice, in the many different forms that could take. You could hit back. You could try to ruin the person's life. You could sue them. Or you could take the other approach and, in weakness, just let them do it. Let them demean you or run roughshod over you or others. How will you respond?

Now, before we begin to think that this section applies only to personal attacks, insult, or injury, keep in mind that Jesus has already called for his disciples to be peacemakers (5:9), which will call us into situations beyond just protecting ourselves. It will call us into conflict on behalf of others in all types of situations. With that in mind, I ask again, what is your response?

Will either of the responses that the world can put forth really accomplish anything? Worldly justice might stop the behavior for the moment, but it perpetuates the idea of strength solutions. Human justice is simply one form of human power and strength exerting its will over another. It may be the right power, but it is power nonetheless, and so it does little to change the real problem. Weakness avoids conflict but reinforces the power game. To speak broadly, strength solutions put the pain of conflict and justice on the perpetrator, but don't really benefit them. Weakness keeps it on you, but does no true good to the perpetrator.

Jesus says to turn the other cheek. That is a well-known saying, but what does it mean? Don't fight back, but don't just run or take it either, he says. Step up; look the person in the eye. It will help if we keep in mind that we are acting for their benefit and not our own. We are showing them mercy, not searching for justice. When we face them and show them the other cheek, they very well might slap us again. That could happen. You could get hurt. But what just happened? We took the pain onto ourselves. We have shown them a completely different way. This is the way of the cross; it is the cross in action.

Jesus gives two other specific examples to help make the point crystal clear. If someone is trying to rip you off or seek their own perception of justice and sues you for your shirt, you would normally have two options: fight for justice or give in. But here comes Jesus' new way, which sounds crazy. Take your cloak, which would not only serve as your coat in cold weather but also your blanket at night, and give that to the person that is already trying to harm you. These cloaks were so important in that culture that it was considered off limits to sue for someone's cloak because that could put them in serious danger without it to keep them warm. Just give it to them, says Jesus. To fight the lawsuit would not demonstrate the kingdom even if you gained justice. To do nothing does not show them the kingdom either. But to go beyond what you have to, showing them that you are not a victim, but are willingly sacrificing for the benefit of someone who was just trying to harm you? That is unheard of. That's something the world had never seen before. And just so we're clear, this might cause a very unpleasant night for you without a coat. Yet you have demonstrated the life of the age to come by taking the suffering upon yourself and showing them the way of mercy.

His third example came from the humiliating world of subjugation. The Romans were an occupying force in the land of Israel, and they wanted to send the message of their power in many ways. Jesus references one of those methods. A Roman soldier could enlist any Jewish person at any time to carry his gear for up to one mile. The Jews hated this. It reminded them daily that they were not truly free in the world. They could fight for justice, but the chances of that accomplishing any change were close to none. They could just put up with it. That was probably the easiest route, but that would not bring about change either. Or, says Jesus, you can go the mile and then willingly offer to carry the gear another mile. What was a position of subjugation a minute ago has just become one of power under. You have taken the pain onto yourself and shown this soldier mercy. You have sacrificed for his benefit.

This way of the cross, the path of mercy, has the real power to change things. Whenever people have turned to it or stumbled upon it, they have made real and lasting change in the world. The Christians of the first, second, and third centuries believed this and lived it, and the world shifted under their feet. Men who were not completely or firmly kingdom minded, like those mentioned at the beginning of this chapter, discovered that the kingdom path works. It changes hearts and transforms people.

In first-century Rome a practice called "exposure" was common. It was the abortion of its day. If someone had an infant they did not want, could not afford, or could not care for, they could lay it outside and allow it to die. The children usually died, but were occasionally taken by those who wished to use them as slaves, often for sexual gratification. The Christian community could have fought this; they could have demanded justice. Or they could have just thrown their hands up in the air and accepted that it was a problem too big for them to have an impact on. Instead, they took the pain on themselves. They took these children into the Christian community at their own expense and raised them as part of that community. Granted, that is not the worst pain that could be taken upon yourself, but it does demonstrate their lifestyle of sacrifice for the benefit of others.

Some people have tried to limit Jesus' words in this passage to apply only to religious persecutors. But that simply does not hold water. It is a real stretch, at best, to claim that these three examples are restricted to cases of religious oppression. These were everyday examples from real life, of conflict between two people, legal conflict, and national conflict. Jesus brilliantly covered a broad range of scenarios with three short illustrations.

You Have Heard

"You have heard," continued Jesus, "that it was said, 'Love your neighbor and hate your enemy'" (5:43). This was the wisdom of Jesus' day. They all would have heard this sentiment. And so have we. This is part and parcel of the way the world typically operates. We will love those that love us. We will love those that act like a neighbor and respect the laws. We will love those that act like decent human beings and act in culturally acceptable ways. But if you go outside of that, then all bets are off. Then we can call you an idiot. We can post nasty things about you on social media, especially if you are a public figure. If you are an oppressor or a bigot, then you deserve all the harsh words and harsher treatment you get.

Our society is inundated with the "hate your enemy" philosophy. It just makes sense—why would you do anything different? These are people that are trying to bring harm to you. They are trying to hurt others or oppress people. At the very least, their ideas can bring injustice or damage, and so we feel justified in hating them.

Let me ask a simple question. As a whole, are Christians today perceived as people who love their neighbors and hate their enemies? I think if we are honest, that might be how we are perceived. It might not always be true, but it might be accurate much more often than we would hope.

What if our level of love for others was determined solely by how much we loved our worst enemy? We live in a culture where people constantly cry out for more tolerance and love, but they don't mean it. What they mean is to tolerate and love those whom you find acceptable. As soon as someone steps outside of those bounds, forget it. Before we take on an air of condemnation about the hypocrisy of the world, we must ponder: are we all that different? Have we unwittingly accepted the ideology of loving our neighbor while allowing ourselves to hate our enemy?

But I Tell You

The responses of the world come naturally. It's easy to hate those that perpetrate wrong or hate others. But what does that change? Martin Luther King Jr. rightly acknowledged in a 1957 sermon that "returning hate for hate multiplies hate, adding deeper darkness to a night already devoid of stars. Darkness cannot drive out darkness; only light can do that. Hate cannot drive out hate; only love can do that." Injustice is an act of causing pain to others. As I said above, human justice is an attempt to right that wrong, but most often it includes efforts to lob the pain back at the one who committed the injustice. In this world, violence is met with violence; and hate with hate of a different kind, but hate all the same.

Yes, said Jesus, the world will tell you to hate your enemy. "But I tell you, love your enemies and pray for those who persecute you" (Matthew 5:44). Please don't fall into the mistake of thinking that this sounded any less crazy to Jesus' first audience than it does to us. To be honest, this is stupid stuff from the world's perspective. If you go around sacrificing for the benefit of your enemy, you might really get hurt, or even worse. Why would anyone do this?

To tell the truth, I have to agree with the world that it makes no sense. I need to either hit my enemies back or just leave them alone (is it still cool to say "shake them haters off"?). But to do good to them? To love them? To pray for the very people that are persecuting me? If my goal is to stay safe or create a world where justice reigns, then this is very foolish behavior. It's why I believe that Jesus intended this only for his kingdom people and never intended in any way for nations of the world to be part of the kingdom. People of all nations, yes. But not the nations themselves as a corporate identity. How could a country feasibly love its enemies? No, this gets us nowhere toward simple justice. It is, once again, a description of the kingdom in action. It takes the suffering onto oneself. I've talked about that a lot in this chapter, but what does it accomplish?

Allow me to return to the pecan pie. How can we find justice if two people each have two pieces and now there are six people with only four slices left? It cannot be to split the pieces. That would not be justice, because now we would have people with half a piece. That's better than nothing, I suppose, but it's not justice. Short of forcing our will onto the two and taking pieces from them (which they may or may not have acquired legitimately—it makes no difference in this illustration), we must simply come to the realization that justice cannot be found in this age. Once injustice has been released, it is like toothpaste squeezed out of the tube. It is not going back in there. The kingdom solution is for the people of God to step in and hand our piece willingly to those without. Now they have tasted justice and the unjust have, possibly, seen a new way to live. This is more than sharing out of our surplus; this is sacrificing for the benefit and wholeness of others. Jesus did not give a few spare minutes of his time to help us out. He laid down his life. That is true love (1 John 3:16). That is the way of the cross.

In the world of racial divides, I see precious little of this kingdom approach anymore. That is true even among well-meaning disciples who want to stand up against this sin and protect those whom they believe are being oppressed. It's the right heart, but the wrong approach. So, what does the kingdom applied look like in these situations? I don't know. Each situation is different. This is not a rule book; it is the principle. It's not the methods; it's the mission. We are called to be a sacrificing-for-the-bene-fit-of-others type of people in every situation. We need to seek to go be-yond justice and allow people to see the kingdom of God in action. That will stand out far differently than the most finely tuned argument on so-cial media or the most intense street protest that could be concocted by man. The world has seen all that. I'm not saying that well-thought-out statements or protests are wrong. It is the intent that matters. What does the action seek? Simple justice or the kingdom?

Be Perfect

We are to live by this kingdom ethic, says Jesus, so that we may be "children of [our] Father in heaven" (5:45). Children in the ancient world were expected to live by the values and character of their father, and God's family was no different (Ephesians 5:1; John 5:19). God will eventually re-store all things and bring perfect unity and harmony back to his creation, so in that sense it will be the time of ultimate justice. But in the present age, even God does not enact justice across the board. He has the right to and the ability to, but for our sakes, he does not. The sun shines and the rain falls on both the deserving and the undeserving. In other words, God loves his enemies. And, of course, the cross is the ultimate demonstration of that. But he acts at his own expense for the benefit of others every day.

Jesus asks a series of questions that are biting in their challenge: "If you love those who love you, what reward will you get? Are not even the tax collectors doing that? And if you greet only your own people, what are you doing more than others? Do not even the pagans do that?" (5:46–47). If he hasn't already driven us far away from the responses of the world, these questions serve as the final push.

The people and nations of the world can get along with those that agree with them and support their causes. That is not unusual in the least. And I'll admit, and I'm sure you will confirm, that there is a strong grav-itational pull toward those that agree with us. It makes us feel good. It confirms our own instincts, culture, and wisdom. The others? They are dangerous and foolish. Why would I want to put up with them for one more second? I know all their tired and destructive arguments. I will not subject myself or others to their venom, hypocrisy, or ignorance any lon-ger. Destructive people should be removed from our lives. This wisdom does not come from Jesus, by the way.

He leads us in the opposite direction: Sacrifice for the benefit of those that would take from you. Love your enemies. Be stunningly different in your lifestyle and solutions to the problems that we face in the present age. None of this is designed to get us ahead or lead us into comfort or safety. I eventually had to come to the nauseating truth that Jesus was dead serious when he said, "Whoever wants to be my disciple must deny themselves and take up their cross daily and follow me" (Luke 9:23). He was calling for the repeated willingness to subject ourselves to death for the benefit of others just as he did. That's the direction in which he lived and died, and he requires that we follow him there.

Are you prepared to love someone who has harmed those you love?

Are you ready to show kindness to someone who thinks you are less than human or has shown you nothing but bigotry? Are you up for demonstrating gracious patience with someone who denigrates beliefs to which you hold dearly? Will you sacrifice for the benefit of people who have only brought harm to others? If the answer to any of those questions is "no," are you sure that it is Jesus you are following?

Jesus concludes this section with these daunting words: "Be perfect, therefore, as your heavenly Father is perfect" (5:48). Is he serious? How can he possibly expect this? Before we completely lose it and come to the conclusion that he didn't really mean any of this after all because it is impossible, let's take a moment to consider what he was saying. The Greek word here for perfect is *teleios*. It can mean perfect, but in the sense of "complete" or even "fully mature." Jesus is not saying that we must be as flawless as God. That truly is impossible. What he is saying is that God is our standard. He is complete in loving his enemies. There is no one that is left out. There is not a category of those that God loves and another that he does not love. He has the benefit of everyone in mind, so that is our standard. There is no one outside of this call to love.

The only means that a Christian has to destroy an enemy is to love them until they become our friend. They may not, but that is the only option we have available to us in the kingdom. If someone has flesh and blood, they are not our enemy. We may be theirs, but they are not ours. They are to be loved.

Far too many Christians seem to have missed this in our fight against evil and injustice. We should stand up for the oppressed. We should fight for them. The question is not "if," but "how." Is it going to be with the tools and weapons of the world? That is often the case, is it not? We scream for justice now. I get it. I have too at times. I forget sometimes that this will typically change very little, and it certainly will not transform the world. Human justice sounds good; it sounds fair. But it perpetuates the very darkness that it seeks to escape.

You may have been sinned against and faced intense bigotry, hatred, or racism. Those who consider you an enemy may have wronged you intensely. Now you know whom to love, not whom to hate. You know whom to pray for. You may have seen people hurt those you cherish, or someone has angered you with what you feel is dangerous thinking. Your only rightful biblical response is to do everything in your power to love them. I know this is incredibly hard, but it is our mission as kingdom people. My first instinct was not to love the people who treated my son so awfully when he was in high school, but those are the very people that I must pray for and find a way to love.

Too many of us have dropped our kingdom directive in the name of fighting against racism or some other social cause. That is not to make light of these things. We should fight against them—fiercely. But we must ensure that we are fighting with the weapons of the kingdom of God and not those of the world (2 Corinthians 10:4–5). We must do everything in our power to use the methods of the gospel and not the ideas from the kingdoms of this world, even what we think are the very best ones.

I believe firmly that the degree to which the people of God will be a light to the nations and transform the world by showing them a different way to live is the exact same as the level at which we embrace the way of mercy. Are you prepared? It is a narrow road.

Questions for Discussion

1. What do you think about the assertion that kingdom people should seek more than mere human justice?

2. How do you feel about sacrificing for those that are violently opposed to what you believe or value?

3. How would you go about loving someone who hates you?

4. Is there anyone that you would have a very difficult time loving?

5. For you, what is the most challenging aspect of the way of mercy?

CROSSING THE LINE

Section Four
The Power of Culture

Chapter 15

Culture Clash

Last summer I took my son and nephew to our local swimming pool and waterpark. It's a large facility that has several pools, medium-sized water slides, rock-climbing courses over the water, a zip line that lands in a pool, and a plethora of other fun water adventures and games. The boys love this park, and once we found some empty chairs and placed our stuff on them, they went racing off to their favorite pool. The one they went to is large and open and usually has a good number of people in it but is rarely overpacked to the point where it is no longer fun because you can't really move around. On one end is a basketball hoop that sits just a few feet above the water so that people can play water basketball if they like.

As the boys jumped into the water, I sat on the side of the pool, dangling my legs in the crisp blue liquid, enjoying the contrast of the warm sun on my back and the cool water on my feet and legs. To my right was a group of black teenage boys that had taken over the basketball hoop at about the same time we arrived at the pool. They were whooping it up and having a blast, playing a game of Twenty-one. To my left was a group of white teens who were equally enjoying themselves while playing a game of Marco Polo. After a short period of time, however, I began to notice something. There was a palpable vibe among the adults that were in and around the pool. Almost all the adults in the area were white, with just a few exceptions. I could tell that something was amiss. Many of them looked very uncomfortable, and quite a few were visibly irritated. Then I looked again and realized that all the people that seemed to have a problem were white. Not all the white people were upset, but everyone who was demonstrably upset was white.

I wondered to myself what was going on, what the problem was, so I sat there and observed for a bit. The group of black teens was being loud, talking a bit of trash to each other, playing, dancing, and getting in and out of the pool in a rather demonstrative way. They weren't harassing or interacting with anyone else. In short, they weren't doing anything wrong. Yet the situation grew more and more tense. The white teens were also playing, getting in and out of the pool, and laughing and having a good time. Their interactions were just as good-natured, and a bit more subdued, but not much. They too, were doing nothing wrong.

But many of the adults around the pool area were growingly disconcerted. Dirty looks and frustrated faces were all around. A few parents eventually left the area with their children, but one parent went and complained to a lifeguard. Not a single askance look went toward the group of white teens. Eventually, nothing came of it. The lifeguard apparently chose not to confront the group. My nephew joined in on the game and I jumped into the pool and stood by the group, mildly interacting with them so as to turn away the negative attention of the adults who were irritated.

Race or Culture?

Scenes like this play out all the time. Sometimes the kids are a little less innocent than this group. Other times, the racial mix might be different, but it does seem that this situation is representative of what happens most often. There are probably many more such interactions that never result in any confrontation or tension, but many do. The question I pondered for a while that day was, why? What was it about that group that caused a problem for so many parents? They weren't endangering any smaller kids. They were cussing a bit, but so was the group of white kids, so that couldn't have been it.

Of course, many would be quick to put forth the idea that it was because they were black and the adults were white. Could that really be the cause? Call me naïve, but I just don't think that too many, if any, of those parents looked at that group of young men and harbored ill will toward them because they had what we would call black skin. I doubt that many of them viewed those young men as an inferior level of human being and were worried about their children being in water that had been tainted by their presence. Those attitudes existed in the past, but they are, I hope, rare today.

I think this is true across the board. The legacy of the curse-of-Ham theology is mostly gone. The repugnant philosophies that black people are lesser evolved and closer in genetics to apes has been thoroughly refuted. Very few people look at other humans and are repulsed by the color of their skin.

Yet there are unquestionably racial tensions in our country today that tend to run along these lines of black and white. Why? What causes that?

I think my little experience at the pool illustrates it. It was a culture clash. There were two distinct cultures on display at that pool. And even though we are often unaware of it, culture is a powerful force in our lives.

Culture is "a socially learned system of knowledge and behavioral patterns shared by a certain group of people. In other words, it is a way of life to which a particular society adheres."[42] Every single person has been conditioned by a culture. In fact, you have probably been conditioned by many different cultures, some of them very big and shared by many people, and others microcultures shared by just a few. Nations can develop a unique culture. Ethnic groups often have their own culture. But smaller geographic regions, cities, and even neighborhoods can have a culture. Within some of the bigger and more influential cultural groups such as your nation and ethnicity, families develop their own cultures, as do individual households. Even gender groups can have a unique culture. Each of these micro- and macrocultures work together in a complex web to shape who you are, what you value, what you find acceptable, and so on.

Before I continue, I feel that it is important to note that many times culture and race are inextricably linked. This makes culture clashes more intense because they are tied to the skin color of those involved and all the history that relates to that. From the perspective of those boys, had they been aware of what was going on, it would have felt like prejudice. I'm not saying that it wasn't. But the root cause was not directly the color of their skin; it was the content and expression of their culture. Culturalism or cultural elitism can be just as damaging and wrong as racial bigotry. It is a form of bigotry, in fact. I'm not trying to minimize anything here but simply to identify the problem so that we can see similar dynamics in our own lives, perhaps, and deal with them. The good news is that race-based prejudice is often owned once pointed out. People are quite often unaware of their own cultural bias, and once aware, can be much more open to dealing with it.

I have had the opportunity to travel around the world quite a bit to teach the gospel. Every time I leave the United States I am reminded just how strong my cultural conditioning is as an American. I am suddenly thrust in with travelers who have very different expectations of personal space, standing in line, and how much food makes up an adequate meal. Not all Americans share the same cultural standards in everything, but there are many elements of how we think that have been shaped by our American culture. I was in an airport a few years back waiting for my flight when I observed a number of Americans, including myself, who were all scrunched up in our tiny airport seats, trying desperately to get comfortable. Meanwhile, a group of Chinese passengers were laid out on the floor, sound asleep. Without even realizing it, our culture has conditioned us to believe that floors in public places are dirty and not appropriate for lying down, but the Chinese culture has no such inhibitions. We were uncomfortable for no good reason other than that our culture had taught us not to do something. Mashing into a chair just felt more normal.

That is perhaps the greatest power of culture: it teaches us what normal is. Is it respectful to look at someone in the eye when you are speaking to them, or is it rude and confrontational? Do you shake hands, bow, or hug someone you are greeting for the first time? When conflict arises, do you confront it immediately with a loud voice and demonstrative body movements, do you avoid the situation altogether, or do you only hint that there might be a problem? Is pork an acceptable food, or does the idea of eating it disgust you? Are fruit bats an acceptable food, or does the idea of eating that disgust you? Should special moments like communion or special days like Easter be honored in quiet reverence and composure, or should they be times of jubilant celebration that borders on revelry? Is it important to show up for family events and appointments with friends on time, or is that not so vital? When a meeting is gathered, who should speak first? Does your personal opinion matter or is it what the majority of the group believes that will determine what everyone holds to and does?

All these things are determined by culture. It is incredibly powerful in the way it shapes our lives. Culture is a shared system of norms that dictates what is acceptable and pleasing to a group of people. The most powerful and unseen aspects of our culture are learned long before we are even aware that there is such a thing. These expressions are seamlessly integrated into our belief systems about how the world operates and how we interact within that world. This is why some cultures, for instance, are musically inclined and some are not. It's not that certain people groups are genetically born with more rhythm or the ability to sing better than others. Some groups, however, grow up around singing and dancing before they can even talk or walk. They learn the moves and the songs, and music is integrated into every part of life and even the way they think and view the world.

The first few years of my marriage were an adventure in cross-cultural discovery. Here's but one example. My wife would often ask me to scratch her back. But she would just come right out and say, "Would you please scratch my back?" That was annoying. How rude. You don't just ask someone a question like that directly. You have now obligated me to say yes, with no option to decline the request. This is an aggressive and selfish behavior. Of course, I didn't think through all of that each time she did things like that; I just felt it, strongly. I didn't know why I was feeling that way. I just did. It wasn't normal, at least not in my mind. So I just had to accept that my wife was pushy and rude. What she should do is what I would do. If my neck hurt, I would not just ask that she rub it. I would politely mention that my neck hurt quite a bit today, and may even add to the subtle request by rolling my neck around a bit and rubbing it myself to demonstrate the severity of my discomfort. Now, this was a proper social request. She could then pick up on the cues and had the opportunity to accept or decline the request. It was all so simple.

But it wasn't. She would never rub my neck when I did that. I know! I can feel your outrage and I thank you for your support. Not once did she answer my "request" in the affirmative and actually rub my neck. Again, I just had to learn to accept it. Until one day I was reading a cross-cultural ministry book for a class I was taking and I nearly fell off the couch. It was describing my marriage to a T. It was then that I realized that we were part of very different cultures. In being married together we had formed some aspects of a new culture in our household, but we still had deeply ingrained cultural practices and expectations that were worlds apart.

I came to understand that my wife was not being rude or selfish at all. My way of thinking was not normal, but it wasn't abnormal either. It was cultural. After we talked about it, I realized for the first time that in her culture, to ask directly for what you wanted was considered respectful, and to hint for something was thought of as manipulative and would not be rewarded by the community. In my culture, asking directly was aggressive, bullying behavior. It wasn't that one of us was right and the other wrong. We had been enculturated differently.

Confusing Culture and Race

There are some aspects of some cultures that can be wrong and sinful. I am not talking about those things. We definitely do need to examine our cultures at the door when we become Christians to see if some of our dearly held cultural beliefs and practices are at odds with the gospel. But there are many simple cultural expressions that are not wrong at all, although they are very different from those of other cultures and can lead to conflict.

My younger son got more time around my relatives for a few years when he was in primary school than he did his mother's extended family. I was on a trip to Africa, and while I was gone, my wife took him with her to one of her family reunions in another state. He was extremely quiet and withdrawn for most of the day. When they got home, she asked him why. He proceeded to tell her that her family was loud and aggressive, not like dad's relatives. "What are you saying?" she asked him. "Black people," he responded, "are kind of scary." As she chuckled, she reminded him, "Son, you're black."

That little conversation reveals several things. Did you notice how color, black in this instance, was used to identify culture? They were not talking about anyone's skin color or racial features. This conversation was all about culture, not race. While skin color can sometimes identify certain cultural beliefs and concepts, it can be misleading as well. This is what people are referring to when they accuse a white person of "acting black," or malign someone in the black community for "not being black enough" or "acting white." Those are statements of culture and have nothing to do with race, not really. What we think are racial divides that are deep and maybe impossible to overcome are actually issues of culture. That's the good news, because we can learn skills to bridge these gaps. We will look at several of those in the next chapter.

What happened at the pool was definitively a culture clash. The group of boys playing basketball were loud and aggressive. They were challenging one another and being very demonstrative. They were using slang words that were quite normal in their cultural experience. But everything they were doing was countercultural to the people around them. That made their benign behavior feel threatening. Meanwhile, the group playing Marco Polo was doing the very same things but in the context of their culture, which made sense to the people around them. Their behavior was culturally acceptable to the adults. I must admit that for a brief moment I was irritated by the behavior of the black teens. But I have a lot of experience with different cultures and was quickly able to translate their behavior and see that they were doing nothing wrong. That shows how powerful cultural conditioning can be, though. It still felt abnormal to me in the moment until I thought through it.

Turning the Tables

If we could suddenly switch out all the adults present with adults that were either raised in or familiar with what I will call here the black culture, no one would have batted an eye. This raises another issue. If the adults around the pool at that moment had been black and did not see anything wrong with the black teens' behavior, would they have been offended by the white teens?

Of course, I don't know exactly how a group of any other adults would have acted in that situation, but my feeling is that a group of black parents would have acted differently. But why? The answer illustrates a truth about dominant and nondominant culture. It can, of course, be quite complex, but broadly speaking, there does tend to be a white culture and a black culture in our country. Historically and numerically speaking, this broad white culture is the dominant one in the United States. It is what is considered normal. There are four elements that tend to be true (though not in every case) that are important for us to understand when it comes to dominant and nondominant cultures. The first is that dominant cultures tend to be unaware that they have a culture. They don't have to think about it much. This has been historically true in America because most of us are so isolated geographically from other countries and cultures. The dominant culture often does not have to interrelate as much with nondominant cultures, and so they start to think of their own ways of interacting with and viewing the world as normal. On the occasions when they do interact with another culture, rather than viewing it as a viable and legitimate culture that is different from theirs, they tend to think of it as wrong, silly, or something that just makes no sense.

The second thing is that the nondominant culture is typically very aware of their own cultural identity as well as that of the dominant culture. The nondominant culture comes in contact with the dominant culture more so than the other way around. That is not a condemnation of the dominant culture. It is just reality.

That leads into the third point, which is that the nondominant culture is more likely to know how to operate within the dominant culture, if they choose to; whereas most members of the dominant culture are more likely to be ignorant of the nondominant cultures around them and be quite awkward in operating within any of those cultures. This leaves them feeling very out of place and unaccepted when they find themselves in a situation where the style of interaction of a nondominant culture is suddenly the prevailing one at the moment.

The fourth point concerns the reactions when these two cultures come in contact. The dominant culture does not tend to understand the nondominant; so they are easily upset and offended by it, finding it to be weird or not acceptable as "normal" behavior. It does not occur to them that their way is "a way" to do something rather than "the way." On the other hand, nondominant cultures either withdraw and submit their culture to the dominant one, or they can get very defiant and cling to their cultural norms. This can come across as overtly aggressive and threatening to members of the dominant culture.

Interpreting Culture

This information has important implications for a church family that seeks to include a diverse mixture of cultures. Church families will eventually create their own culture within the life of the community, but that will always be a cauldron of the various cultural expressions and behaviors that the various people groups bring in with them. Each church will usually have a dominant culture and one or more nondominant ones. The goal is to increasingly work toward all groups represented in the church to have an equal seat at the table, and to be a community that is persistently intentional about embracing, recognizing, and celebrating all nations and their cultures.

It is quite possible for a church to be multiethnic but not multicultural. That means that they are visually diverse, with people from many different nations or ethnic groups, but with a cultural life that is dominated by one group, who are almost always unaware that this is the case. In the introduction, I mentioned that a number of black brothers and sisters have commented that they love their brothers and sisters but often feel that they must act white to be comfortable in church life. This is what causes that dynamic. I should mention that this is not true of all congregations in our family of churches. There are a few in the United States where the African American or some other culture aside from the typical white one is the dominant force. And there are a few that really have reached the level of cultural plurality.

The challenge here is that quite often those in the dominant culture are unaware of their own cultural uniqueness and oddities and just think that the way things are done in the church is the normal Christian way to do things. Couple that with the fact that changing the culture of a group and opening it up to other cultural expressions is something that only the dominant culture can bring about. They must recognize it, be open to it, and be deliberate about diversifying the ethos of the group. In the next chapter we will look at ways this can be done.

To restate the case, one of the main causes of conflicts between individuals is culture. This goes well beyond ethnicity and race. People of the same race can have divergent backgrounds and experiences. It is even true that two people could be of the same ethnicity, grow up in the same town, and share much of their culture in common but have distinctly different microcultures in the homes in which they grew up, and so still have many differences culturally.

Of course, many culture clashes happen because the actions or preferences of one person seem weird or unintelligible to another. Yet the most common problem in cultural conflicts is in interpretation. When my wife directly asks me to scratch her back, I immediately tend to interpret her request. We all do that. But most of us are unaware that there are at least two levels going on simultaneously. The first is obvious: what do the words that she said mean? The second level is not so obvious: what is the underlying meaning behind her words? When it comes to the first level, I hear her words and understand that she wants me to scratch her back. But the adventure begins at the second level. I also interpret that she is being aggressive, rude, and does not care to give me a choice. It feels like an imposition and like she is being controlling. So I come away with a very negative impression of her behavior even though all she has done is make a simple request.

But why do I have that negative response to an innocent question? Because I have interpreted her actions by what they would mean if I undertook them. Since my cultural background has subtly taught me that to directly ask for something from someone is insensitive and imposing upon them, if I did it, that's what it would mean, so I assign those same motivations to my wife.

This happens all the time. The white parents at the pool observed the behavior of the black teens and interpreted it according to what they would be feeling if they acted that way. But they completely misinterpreted the event, just as I did with my wife. The question to ask is not "what would I mean by that action?" but "what did she mean by it?" That's a whole other question. In her cultural context, my wife was being direct and respectful, and would be mostly unaware that I am interpreting her behavior any differently than she would. And that's how conflict arises.

Imagine a spiritual mentoring situation with two brothers discipling one another. One brother's cultural background has taught him to be very direct and to the point. You don't beat around the bush because that does not help people. You don't try to sugarcoat things. You say it straight out and then deal with it. To him that is both kind and loving. His friend, however, grew up very differently. For him, innuendo and hinting are the order of the day. To look at someone directly and say something, especially something with negative connotations, is aggressive, threatening, and unkind. So the first brother disciples the second brother on something, being very candid and forthright as he does it. He is loving his brother in Christ the best way he knows how. But the second brother interprets it as harsh and walks away thinking that his brother is unkind, uncaring, and unloving. He has got to get out of that discipling relationship because it is damaging him. Was this a spiritual problem or a cultural one? Quite often, it's the latter. Someone can walk away thinking another disciple is harsh or just a poor disciple, but what really happened is that neither of them were able to interpret the situation culturally.

It's important to emphasize that cultural differences and conflicts can happen between people of different nationalities. They can happen between people of different ethnicities. They can happen between people from different regions or socioeconomic statuses. They can happen between people of different genders or generations. They can also happen, especially on an intimate personal level, between people who share all those things in common. But the more cultural differences and variances you have between two people, the more potential there is for conflicts.

For years, my wife and I muddled along, doing the best we could. We went to marriage retreats. We read all the marriage books. We got constant discipling and mentoring in our marriage. And we grew and became more spiritually mature. But we still struggled. Conflict would arise often, and while we never had bad fights or nasty arguments, there was constant friction. It went beyond just nonverbal expectations or the way we approached one another. It was much more far-reaching than that.

Here are just two examples. We had very different notions about who family was. We both agreed that the church family was our priority. There was no question about that, so that led to a great deal of harmony in many respects. We both agreed that our household was our priority, so no problem there. But after that, things got a bit more dicey. I was raised in a loving family, and I still love my family. But our culture was very much built around the idea that once you reached a certain age and were able, you moved out and formed your own family and identity. We can maintain our bonds of affection, but it's not a problem to move farther away from the rest of the family to live as your own family unit. When I married, we became a new family unit in most respects. We are still connected in some ways to the other family units, but we no longer think of ourselves as one unit with them nor do we operate that way. My parents are one unit. My family is another. My sister's family is yet another, and so on. We will help one another if needed and see each other often, but we are expected to do everything we can to make it on our own and not need that. We love each other very much, but we are separate families with separate resources.

My wife was raised with a completely different view of this. Family is always one family. It does not matter how far away they live—which is usually not very far—how old they are, or how many people are involved; family is family. They see their resources, whether it be time, money, or anything else, as being one pool. If you have it, the whole family has it. If a need arises, it is your responsibility to take care of it as much as it is the responsibility of the person in need to do whatever they can.

I can't say one is right and the other is wrong, but in the early days of our marriage we were each convinced that our way was the correct and only way to approach family. In fact, we were each somewhat unaware of the other's viewpoint. It's just not something you think to discuss before forming a new household, because it is just assumed. You can imagine all the fun that ensued when these two worldviews collided. It was a struggle for us because the actions and attitudes of the other just felt wrong.

Another cultural conflict arose over our view of time. Sociologists classify cultures into two broad categories of time classification (although these can be broken down into many more). There are monochronic and polychronic cultures. Monochronic cultures see time as linear. Time is here and quickly gone and cannot be retrieved once wasted. They tend to focus on one primary activity at a time and value orderliness. They believe that there is an appropriate time and place for everything and do not appreciate interruptions. Time commitments are taken very seriously, and changing plans is not looked upon kindly. In addition, these groups tend to place high value on private property, personal space, and individualism.

Polychronic cultures are just the opposite. They tend to see time as cyclical. It comes around again and again; there is plenty of time, so there is no rush. Multiple things can be done at the same time, so distractions and interruptions are not a problem. Plans can be changed willingly and easily. People and relationships are more important than schedules, so there is a high premium placed on relational time, irrespective of the clock. Relationship is far more important in these cultures than tasks or objectives, and they tend to place high value on group and community activity.

Have you identified yourself in one of those two groups? Without a doubt, I was raised in the first culture and my wife in the second. You can probably already imagine the great adventure of trying to combine those two ways of thinking. When we were first married, this was painful. My relatives would throw a Christmas party that basically went like this: The party begins at 4 p.m. The food table opens up at 4:15 p.m. Conversation and mingling will last until 5 p.m. At that time, there will be crafts and activities for the kids. As the clock turns to 5:30, it is time for the annual reading of "The Night before Christmas." Gift exchange happens at 6 p.m, and the party is over at 6:30; see you next year. That's a bit exaggerated, but not much.

But then we would go to be with my wife's relatives for a holiday lunch. We arrive around 11:30 a.m. and no one is there yet. By 1:30 most everyone is there, but there are still a few people on their way or running to the store to get something. By 2:30 the kitchen has begun to hum and the hanging out with one another is just getting going. Fast-forward to 6:30 or 7:00 and we still haven't eaten. That's right, we haven't eaten yet! This was supposed to be lunch. The worst part is, no one seems to care.

It drove me nuts. I'd keep checking my watch, getting more and more irritated with each passing second. I'd ask my wife when we were going to leave. She interpreted this as rude and to indicate that I didn't like her relatives. Meanwhile, to me, the actions of her relatives indicated a lack of concern for others and an inability to organize. I didn't realize that we were placing value on different things. In my culture, gathering together is an objective that still needs to respect time. In hers, fellowship is priceless and cannot be bound by time. In case you were wondering how that goes, I now bring snacks with me when we go to be with her folks.

This effect has often been embraced by black Americans who have jokingly referred to it as CP time (colored-people time). In Africa I have heard it referred to as African time. Not all white people, of course, are monochronic, and not all black people have a polychronic view of life. But these differences are very real.

While some of these situations may sound humorous, they can easily create disharmony in a diverse community. They created rifts between my wife and me and our relatives, because her relatives would sense my tension at the lack of a schedule and interpret that to mean that I disliked them. Or my wife would run to the store before my relatives' Christmas party and she would come an hour late. That indicates trust, closeness, and family in her culture. In mine, it demonstrates disdain for others. So imagine the sparks that can fly when one group interprets another's actions based on what their own motivations would be for those same actions.

Culture and the Church

When a church community shares the same culture, many of these problems are avoided. But what happens when you get a mixture of monochronic and polychronic folks together as one church family? A worship gathering starts at 10 a.m. Half of the church is there while the other half is on their way. Those that are present immediately assume that those that are not are uncommitted, uncaring, selfish, disorganized, or a host of other negative causations. They then chide those that show up "late." There can be, after all, no other way of looking at this; there is no excuse for being late. When chided, the polychronic folks are immediately hurt. The unspoken cultural message that has been unwittingly sent to them is that this is a business arrangement and not one of family or deep fellowship.

It is often cultural disparities like this that lead a portion of the church to tout what a great family the church is, while others feel that it is anything but.

There are many other examples that we could delve into. Some cultures find it rude to just show up at someone's house, while others find that this communicates closeness and family connection. Some find it rude to take food away from a dinner party, while others find it offensive if you don't. The list is nearly endless of all the ways that we can clash culturally in a diverse community.

What about musical tastes? Of course, it is obvious that groups of people value a range of types and styles of music. But it can go well beyond that. Some cultures find it inappropriate and rude to express themselves by moving around, dancing, and showing joy in various other ways during singing and worship. Others find it restrictive and not worshipful to fail to do those things.

When we misunderstand one another's culture, all sorts of problems develop. It is natural for most people to gravitate toward those that share their culture and understand certain aspects of the world in the same way they do. Now, I love being around people groups from around the world and experiencing other cultures. That's especially true of worship styles. But I have to admit that when I've been traveling for a while and interacting with people from cultures that are foreign to mine, and then I suddenly run into a small group of Americans, I can be magnetically drawn to them. I feel more at ease; I understand where they are coming from and they "get me" easily without having to do a bunch of interpretive work (and I'm not talking about language here).

This can happen even within a single church body. I have watched as my wife, without realizing it, has found herself in a circle after church "chopping it up," as she would say, with three or four other black sisters. There is a whole different cultural world going on in that circle than the one normally displayed in the church. On one occasion, a white sister actually inserted herself to ask if they were upset or if everything was okay. She misinterpreted the volume and intensity of the conversation to be something negative. In fact, they were having a blast. These cultural huddles are not wrong to form, but it can be dangerous for any group to create a dynamic where others don't feel welcome or comfortable, or if the huddles become long-lasting cliques. The solution is not to ask people to all act a certain way. A delicate balance must be struck so that we forge communities that are inclusive to everyone but where people can be themselves and express themselves in an authentic manner without others taking offense at that. Being intentional about drawing others in and teaching them your cultural norms can go a long way, and this is especially true for the nondominant cultures.

The work of diversifying our corporate culture needs to be done on both sides, but more of the work often lies with the dominant culture. If they see their cultural behaviors as "normal" and those of others as "changes," then the reaction often becomes, "Why do we have to change and do it that way? That's not normal and I don't like it." But it doesn't occur to them that others are always bending their cultural expressions to that of the dominant culture. There has to be give and take, and usually it is the dominant culture that needs to do a lot more giving. In the next chapter we will look further into practical solutions and steps forward in creating a truly multicultural community.

Questions for Discussion

1. Are you aware of your own cultural beliefs, practices, expressions, and oddities?

2. Do you identify more with a monochronic or a polychronic culture? How does that affect you in day-to-day life, especially in the church?

3. Take a moment to analyze yourself. Are you ever guilty of gravitating toward people of your own culture and having much less to do with those of other cultures?

4. Do you have a tendency to be judgmental about the cultural expressions of others?

5. How much effort have you put in toward becoming familiar with the cultures of others? How much work are you willing to put in from here on out?

Chapter 16

Pliable Culture

My wife and I attended the twenty-seventh annual Dr. Martin Luther King Jr. Holiday Breakfast in Minneapolis. I was not planning on going. I had just arrived back late the night before from giving a biblical teaching weekend in another state. My wife was going to attend the event with our younger son, but they had also been out of the state on a different trip and did not get back until 2 a.m. He was too tired to leave so early, so I took his ticket and went with my wife. Since I was not planning on going, I had not paid much attention to what the event was or what would be happening at it. I was envisioning a small, intimate affair with a couple hundred people, at most, in attendance. I knew that the widow of Medgar Evers, the Civil Rights Activist who was assassinated in 1963, was speaking at the event, but that was it. What I did not know was that it was a semiformal event with over 2,000 people attending, including the governor of Minnesota and many other national and state dignitaries. Additionally, it was televised across the state of Minnesota.

Being unaware of all that, I threw on some khaki pants and a sweater and we hopped in the car well before sunrise to make our way downtown to the Convention Center where it was being held. As we arrived, I immediately noticed that virtually every other man I saw was in a suit and dressed very smartly. I instantly felt underdressed. It was only then that I noticed that my wife was in a very lovely, formal black dress. I turned to her and informed her that I felt a bit underdressed, to which she replied, "Uhh, yeah."

"What do you mean, yeah?" I retorted.

"Of course, you're underdressed," she said.

"What do mean, of course?" I queried a bit irritated, but still joking, mostly.

"When my people get together for an event like this," she replied, referring to the fact that the audience at this event was overwhelmingly

African American, "we're always going to be dressed up."

"Whaaat?" I screeched, aghast, "Why would you not tell me that?" I couldn't believe that she had left this little nugget of information out, and I was also a bit surprised that this part of her culture had somehow escaped my notice.

"E'rbody knows that," she volleyed back.

"Obviously, I didn't. This is information that would have been good an hour ago," I shot back.

She deadpanned back at me, as she slowly turned back my way, "You're grown; I just figured you were going to do what you wanted to do."

"But," I sputtered back, "I would have told you if you were underdressed. Now I feel weird."

"Don't worry about it. I wouldn't," she responded and then glibly finished, "But my people are always going to dress like a Sunday morning at something like this; you should know that."

What we have here is a culture clash on many levels. How many different layers can you spot here? First of all, it was not my assumption that a breakfast event at 7 a.m. would involve dressing up in suit and tie. It was obviously hers. Second, notice her playful identification with her "people." There was a good-natured ribbing going on that there were cultural dynamics in play within a group that was very familiar to her, and that although I have spent twenty years learning, I still do not know all the ins and outs. Third, she didn't say anything to me about my underdressing. That still feels wrong to me. To her, it felt like the right thing to do. If someone wants to be nonconforming to the norms, then they should do that. I feel more pressure to conform to the norms that are in play and would want someone to tell me if I am stepping outside of them. I could even mention the cultural assumption that Sunday morning attire is very dressy clothing. That is not the church culture I grew up in.

There were all kinds of potential conflicts there. It's a good thing that we have been married for nearly twenty years now and can laugh about things like this. In case you missed the tone of that conversation, the whole thing was genuine, but also lighthearted and playful.

Learned Behavior

As I detailed in the previous chapter, a culture is a shared and learned system that creates norms and is integrated into the lives of those who are part of that culture. Since culture conditions us and informs almost all aspects of life, including the many subtle areas of human interaction and what we believe to be acceptable behavior, it can often be a source of conflict. Much of the conflict that we have in society today that is deemed to be racial conflict is actually cultural. That is good news, I suppose, because race and ethnicity are inherent qualities that cannot be altered, but culture is learned and can be changed. If race really were our dividing line we might be in trouble, but culture can be trained and interpreted from one cultural "language" to another.

This is not limited to just society at large. Most of the conflicts within church life that would be classified as being ethnic in nature are cultural. For the most part, our society, and certainly our fellowship of churches, has moved past prejudice over someone's skin color or ethnic identity. We don't believe that darker skin is the sign of a curse from God or a marker of being lower on the evolutionary ladder. The conflicts that we have tend to be caused by cultural differences. The good news, as I stated, is that culture is learned, and so we can learn to overcome many of these conflicts. The challenging news is that most humans tend not to have learned the skills of cross-cultural communication, so they easily fall prey to the pitfalls of culture clash. And these cultural conflicts in our movement, and anywhere really, go well beyond just ethnicity. I would take a guess that a good seventy-five percent of the conflict that arises in our churches is caused by cultures crashing into one another.

As I noted in the previous chapter, perhaps the biggest pitfall in cultural communication is the act of interpreting the actions of another by the standards of our own cultural norms; that is, by what we would have meant or intended had we taken those actions. Often, there is an extremely different intent behind someone else's actions than there would be if we had taken that same action, but the failure to understand that leads to judging and conflict. Rather than properly interpreting what the person was doing or intending to communicate, we walk away with a very different idea and think they are wrong, mean, rude, or acting inappropriately.

Cultural skills are vital in our fellowship of churches. I would argue that they are among the most important skills that we can learn as we embrace and move forward with life together in the diverse and multiethnic family that God has formed in Christ. We want to be culturally competent. In fact, in a family of all nations, it is indispensable that we be just that. It is worth repeating the idea that a group can be ethnically diverse but not culturally diverse.

We can easily find situations where people embrace other skin colors without embracing or even having a clue about other cultures. This can become explosive when a white person, for example (although it can go in any direction), acts in a culturally dismissive or demeaning way without realizing it and is then incorrectly called a racist by a person of color. The white person then defends themselves by pointing out that they have an adopted black child or have many black friends. But neither realizes correctly that skin color is not the issue at all; culture is. And you can still be clueless about causing cultural conflicts or engaging unintentionally in offensive behavior no matter how many black, Hispanic, and Asian friends you have. Ethnic diversity does not equal unity. The broad road to destruction (Matthew 7:13) is quite diverse. Plantations in the Old South were ethnically diverse. We must strive for cultural inclusion as well as ethnic diversity. Being "colorblind" is dangerous because it is really to be culture-blind.

All Things to All People

The church in first-century Corinth was diverse in many ways, including their culture. This contributed to their tendency toward division. The church was dividing over preferences in teaching styles, according to the possession of spiritual gifts, and economically, just to name a few areas. And their cultural backgrounds and expressions were adding to the tumultuous situation. Paul understood that and gave them, in a few short verses, some of the most important spiritual advice when it comes to cross-cultural diversity that we could ever learn:

> *Though I am free and belong to no one, I have made myself a slave to everyone, to win as many as possible. To the Jews I became like a Jew, to win the Jews. To those under the law I became like one under the law (though I myself am not under the law), so as to win those under the law. To those not having the law I became like one not having the law (though I am not free from God's law but am under Christ's law), so as to win those not having the law. To the weak I became weak, to win the weak. I have become all things to all people so that by all possible means I might save some. I do all this for the sake of the gospel, that I may share in its blessings.*
> I Corinthians 9:19–23

Of course, it looks as though Paul is talking solely about bringing people to salvation in Christ. But we will miss much if we think that all he is saying is that he will do whatever he needs to do to help people come into the kingdom. He does convey that desire, but also much more than that. He wants this to be the constant mindset and lifestyle of disciples.

This is part of a passage in which Paul is teaching the church about the need to lay down their rights in order to love one another. If it harms my brother, Paul teaches, then I will never do that again. Love trumps our rights. He demonstrates this by showing his own willingness to sacrifice his rights for their benefit. In chapter 9, he thoroughly lays down a defense for the right for apostles and other workers in the church to receive financial support from the churches that they serve. "Do not muzzle an ox while it is treading in the grain," he says, invoking a principle from Deuteronomy 25:4. In other words, a worker has the right to compensation and support. He could ask for support from them, but he had not and would not. Paul was adamant that he provided for himself while he was with them and continued to refuse support from them for himself while he was traveling.

This raises the question: why would Paul not take money from the Corinthian church to support himself? The book of Philippians makes clear that he was willing to take money from other churches. So why not Corinth? There were two issues in play. The first is that of the role of teachers in the Corinthian culture. In Judaism, it was a great honor for a student to learn from a teacher. The goal of the student was to closely follow the teacher wherever they went and learn to be like them. Imitation was the name of the game. In the Greco-Roman culture, however, especially in the area around Corinth, there was a patron-client mentality attached to teachers. Groups loved to have important teachers come in and would support them lavishly as they taught. But this was meant to put the teacher into obligation. The students were the patrons and he the client, and he now owed them. Although he was the teacher, they would dictate his schedule and even what he taught. The students, in a sense, became the boss, and the teacher was indebted to them. The second issue is that this congregation was spiritually immature. Because of that, Paul evidently feared that they were yet unequipped to overcome this aspect of their culture and would apply it to him, taking on the posture that he was in their debt and now owed them certain favors and would need to toe the mark and do what they asked him to do. Because Paul understood their culture so well, he was unwilling to take money from them. This was his way of protecting them in the situation. He didn't want them to think they could own him, nor that he was in this to get rich and be supported in a lavish lifestyle the way the other teachers were in their culture.

Paul's mode of operation was to adapt himself to the culture in order to best serve its members with the gospel. He was not being sneaky or disingenuous. He was being culturally aware and sensitive. In the verses above, we can find at least seven important principles that Paul brings to the surface for the disciples in Corinth, and for us.

First, he did not have to do this. He was free in Christ and under no obligation to change himself culturally. What Paul means is that there is nothing wrong with his cultural expressions and tendencies. He could go on serving the Lord in the ways that match up with his conscience and be perfectly fine. Of course, there are things that we must all change when we submit to Jesus as King, but a large portion of our cultural conditioning and expressions are fine and good. Paul understands that.

Second, the gospel was his goal. He didn't have to give up his rights, in that they were not sin in and of themselves. But the gospel message that Jesus is King, and the truth that all nations will come into his service, did obligate Paul to love his brothers and sisters. Thus, the gospel trumped his rights to be comfortable in his own culture. He willingly laid down his rights "to win as many as possible" (9:19). Paul does imply that there is a choice here in the sense that someone could decide not to take up the mission to love and help save others and remain locked into their own preferences and ways of doing things. Love is always a choice. That's what so amazing about it. We don't have to love. But if we are to follow Jesus, then we will love and we will lay down our rights.

Third, Paul adapted himself, not the gospel. Paul's gospel never changed. There were times in his life when he would change some of his language or his approach based on the culture and background of the group he was addressing, but he never changed the content of the gospel. Methods can change; the mission does not. But what Paul primarily changed was himself. He became like the Jews to win the Jews. He became like Gentiles culturally, to win them. He was very careful around those with sensitive consciences. Paul was willing to change his own behavior and give up his preferences for others. He understood this to be an aspect of sacrificial love. And because it is an aspect of love, it is like love in the sense that if we are all engaging in it, that is so much the better and the community runs optimally, but if we wait for equity in being loved or wait for the other person to start, then there are going to be problems.

Fourth, Paul was very aware of the cultures with which he came in contact. He learned about and understood these cultures. He knew when to challenge them, but he knew how to adapt to them as well. That is a tremendous skill and takes a lot of effort. Learning about the cultures and expressions of other groups of people is not always easy. It takes time, adaptability, and resolve. Paul was willing to learn and grow constantly so that he could stay on task with the mission.

Fifth, Paul was willing and able to adapt himself to multiple cultures.

Whoever he was with at the moment, he could speak their cultural language. This made him infinitely more effective in spreading the gospel. We cannot become so focused on the mission and saving people that we pay no attention to being culturally sensitive, aware, and adaptable. Refusal to grow in this area like Paul did will hamper the gospel.

Sixth, Paul was motivated by his love for them and not his preferences. He wanted to save as many people as possible. He tells them that he will adapt his culture and rights in any way because his motivating factor is his love for others, not his own comfort level.

Finally, Paul wanted to share in the blessing of the gospel. At least part of what he means here must include belonging to a multicultural family. Paul didn't see that as a curse. It was part of the blessing. Learning to adapt to and appreciate the many different approaches to life and the gospel in a diverse community was the good stuff for Paul. He celebrated it, and so should we.

The Many Avenues of Cultural Expression

There are many ways that this diversity will be expressed in the life of the church. We have different preferences in music. One group likes more traditional folk hymns. Another likes more lively gospel music. Some will want reverentially slow music. Others will desire to "whoop it up." Churches have split over music preferences, forgetting that all singing in worship is ultimately for God. It is important to understand, however, that music is like the language of culture. For many, it is how they communicate and express themselves. Imagine if you went to worship gatherings week after week and only every three or four weeks heard one prayer in a language that you understood, and everything else was unintelligible for you. This is a bit of what it can feel like to those who do not hear God worshipped in the music of their natural culture. We can learn to grow and appreciate the music of other cultures, but sometimes we just won't be able to. So, what happens in that situation? You can stand there and begrudgingly sing along without truly engaging. But we must do better than that. Just remember, if you find the church singing a style of song that you dislike or that feels unnatural for you, there are brothers and sisters who feel that same way when singing your favorite songs. Now imagine how they would feel if the church only sang the songs you like. Give yourself to God and your brothers and sisters in *every* song. Get out of your comfort zone.

I have noticed that singing in the many different African cultures tends to be an affair that involves the whole body, not just the voice. It is very much that way for my wife and her cultural background. Me? Not so much. The 90s R&B group, Snap, once sang that "rhythm is a dancer," but for me rhythm is an enigma. I would prefer to stand still when I sing and not expose my awkward lack of ability to sing and clap my hands at the same time, or to move in any controlled fashion. But I am committed to enjoying music of all cultural styles and I will fully give myself to them when they come (although this is often to my wife's chagrin). We should be willing to not just tolerate cultural expressions like these, but to celebrate and invest in them. It is important.

Language is another significant area of cultural diversity. Many of our congregations have people for whom English is not their primary language. It makes sense that most of our US churches operate exclusively in English. If that is the dominant language, it should be that way. But incorporating other languages into songs, prayers, and welcomes, even if there are not many others who speak that language, is important. It demonstrates that we give value to all nations and all languages, just as the Scriptures do (Revelation 5:9), and that we really are a diverse family. It shows that we take being a multicultural community seriously and that there is a place at the table for everyone. When songs are sung in a language other than English, however, it is important to have the words displayed in English so that we can know what we are singing. In the end, this is another vital way that we can communicate the values of our multiethnic family in Christ.

We don't often think of cultural differences in clothing, but there are many. The biggest divide in the United States when it comes to clothing styles over the past thirty years has been whether to dress casually or more formally for worship gatherings. I am convinced that each person should wear whatever they feel comfortable with when it comes to this question. And while it might look strange, I believe there is benefit in having one person "on stage" wearing a suit, and the next person that comes up wearing jeans. That diversity will make every guest feel comfortable, knowing that someone else is dressed like them and that they are not inappropriately over- or underdressed.

But there is a growing area of concern here. Where we live in the Twin Cities, there is a large Somalian population. Most of them are Muslim, but whether Muslim or not, they tend to be very conservative in their dress. Somali women typically wear head coverings and loose fitting dresses that go from neck to toe. I have talked to folks who have expressed their inability to even consider worshiping God in an environment where the women were dressed immodestly, compared to their standards of modesty. This brings up an interesting dilemma, doesn't it? Most American Christian woman would adamantly defend their right to dress how they please. Some of what I have seen at church over the years borders on immodesty, even by American standards. What are we going to do in cases like this? Would we defend that right even though it could very well mean that some will never feel comfortable coming into our community? Would we be willing to radically change the way we dress so as to win as many as possible? I'm not necessarily advocating head scarves here, but even when it comes to that, would we be willing if it was potentially standing in the way of people coming into the kingdom? Paul called the church in Corinth to make sure that the women wore head scarves, presumably so as not to offend the cultural sensibilities of those around them. Are we willing to become like people to win them?

This next one might be the area that has the most potential for conflict and misunderstanding: communication. One person has been culturally conditioned to speak directly and bluntly, believing that this is the most respectful form of communication. Another has been raised to deal with things indirectly in an effort to allow the other person the opportunity to avoid shame. This is just one example of cultural communication styles that could clash. The possibilities are almost endless. Are we willing to learn about, understand, and respect others' communication styles? Are we willing to do the work to come together and learn how to effectively communicate with one another?

Say, for example, you have a small church planting. Ten people on the mission team only speak Spanish. Ten only speak English. What are they going to do? They could stay within their own language circles and have little to no true communication with one another. But the effect of this would be immense. It would, in effect, create two churches in one. What a situation like that necessitates is that each group, or at least one of the groups, put in the effort to learn the language of the other. This illustrates the work that we need to do culturally with one another. This will often be true between different ethnic and racial groups, but again, it will not be limited to that. In some cases, we might be of the same race and from the same state as someone and still have certain important cultural differences, especially in communication styles.

There are many other examples that we could discuss in relation to the body of Christ, but the ones above should suffice for our purposes.

The Challenge of Cultural Versatility

Cultural diversity and fluidity are not always going to be easy. The precepts Paul lays out in 1 Corinthians 9:19–23 can be extremely challenging at times. Paul recognized this and addressed it:

Do you not know that in a race all the runners run, but only one gets the prize? Run in such a way as to get the prize. Everyone who competes in the games goes into strict training. They do it to get a crown that will not last, but we do it to get a crown that will last forever. Therefore I do not run like someone running aimlessly; I do not fight like a boxer beating the air. No, I strike a blow to my body and make it my slave so that after I have preached to others, I myself will not be disqualified for the prize. I Corinthians 9:24–27

There is a reason that Paul follows his sentiments in verses 19–23 with this higher call. He launches some important thoughts on spiritual discipline. To be an athlete requires training and self-mastery, says Paul. But athletes competed to earn a laurel wreath that would soon be gone. The Christian life, and especially the life of the community, earns a blessing that will last eternally, and it takes an equal amount of training and self-mastery. Paul says that he doesn't want to waste his efforts. He wants to be disciplined, intentional, and effective. He recognizes that sharing the gospel is a challenging mission, and doing so in the manner he has just described, namely being all things to all people, requires hard work. We will not by accident become diverse cultural communities that reach out to all groups and types of people. And we certainly won't stay that way without intense effort, ongoing communication, and continual growth.

To be the most effective multicultural churches that we can be, I believe we need to instill the following five values in our membership. They must be understood, thoroughly taught, emphasized, repeated, and shared.

First, we must value diversity. As common sense as that sounds, not everyone does. Some people really like their way of doing things and are uncomfortable with trying new things or with change. They simply don't understand why we can't just do things the way they've always been done, the "normal" way. It doesn't occur to these dear brothers and sisters that when a church is worshiping with one consistent style of music and expression, communicating through the same common formats, holding the same types of events, and so forth, according to what the dominant group prefers, many other people are being forced into unnatural cultural situations. They are constantly bending and stepping outside of what is most familiar and comfortable to them. That will start to wear thin after an extended period of experiencing unwillingness by the dominant culture to be fluid in their expressions and communication. This is another example of what black brothers and sisters mean when they say that they often feel that they must "act white" to fit in. That is all about culture; it is a demonstration of the opposite of being multicultural.

There is another side point to this that will catch the attention of the evangelists among us. A church that is well trained in cross-cultural communication and embraces diversity is a church that will reach larger segments of people more quickly. Visitors will feel invited and accepted immediately. When people know how to interact with them without needless offense, that will make a difference. When they hear multiple languages employed in many gatherings, even if it's not their language, that will make a difference. When they not only see visual ethnic diversity, but also experience true cultural diversity, that will make a big difference.

This all requires patience, of course. These values will not just appear overnight. As Paul knew, it takes time, perseverance, and much hard work.

Second, we must undertake cultural self-assessment. The more we are aware of our own culture, the better off we are. It is challenging to be culturally fluid and diverse when we are not cognizant of our own cultural uniqueness and peculiarities. Remember my earlier illustration: a fish will never know what wet is until it gets out of the water for a while. Only after experiencing dry land and air will it be able to appreciate that it has been immersed in liquid its whole life. For us, the best way to see our cultural restrictions, boundaries, and preferences is to spend significant time in another culture. If that's not possible, we can find people from other cultures and ask them what they see about our personal culture and the church culture that we have created. In addition, it is important in general to be as aware as possible and examine ourselves to see how many of our assumptions and practices are rooted in culture and could feel restrictive or foreign to others. If so, then we can determine if we are willing to see our cultural expressions as something that we are prepared to reexamine for the benefit of those around us.

If we look at our churches in the United States, the blunt reality is that most of them are culturally white. We tend to do things in a "white" way. Teacher Gordon Ferguson notes that in the early days of our movement, "the leaders were nearly all white; and the practices of the church were generally the same as in any predominately white church." He goes on to note that there was nothing wrong with that approach at first but that we have been slow to adapt to and include other cultural styles of worship and community in our fellowships.[43]

Third, we must develop awareness of how cultural differences influence interactions. Was that conflict I just had a result of culture? How about my dislike of the music at our last worship gathering? Did I keep in mind that when something is uncomfortable for me, it probably feels like home to others? When we explore diversity as a community, I may not enjoy every aspect of that, although I do love other cultures besides my native one; but at the very least I can rejoice that it is nourishing the soul of another brother or sister. I was worshiping with our rather large sister church in Nairobi, Kenya a few years ago, on a Sunday morning. They sang a song in which each verse represented the style and culture of a different tribe in Kenya. Each verse was accompanied by a dance that was from the cultural life of that tribe. It was a joy to experience as brothers and sisters near us would excitedly announce to me that this dance and verse was from their tribe. It was among the most memorable experiences I have ever had as I watched Revelation 5:9 in action with "persons from every tribe and language and people and nation."

Fourth, we must incorporate cultural understanding into the life of the church. Half the battle is simply being aware of the dynamic of culture and knowing that we have an ethos that feels natural to us, but is foreign to many others. The willingness to be aware of our own culture and that of others, and to learn, will go a long way. As I have said before, this will not happen without intentionality. It will need to be taught and retaught. We will need to ask many different people to contribute and share their perspectives. When a new disciple moves into town from a different church culture, ask them what they see about the culture and diversity within the church. Visit other churches and learn from them.

Fifth, we must be willing to modify activities and aspects of the community life to make them culturally diverse. This need not be a source of conflict. If we all embrace Paul's heart in 1 Corinthians 9:19–23, this will become a joy and the source of great adventure. Would you want to eat the same exact food for every meal for the rest of your life? Would you want to watch the same movie every Friday night until you pass on? I wouldn't. As the old saying goes, "Variety is the spice of life." Get excited about doing things in new ways and hearing input from new sources. Don't make changes just for the sake of change, but be willing to question everything that the community does to evaluate whether there are mere cultural expressions that can be explored or altered.

Exploring Culture

With these five values of cultural diversity set out, there are some main areas of culture that can be explored. I mentioned some already but will repeat them for the sake of emphasis and add a few new thoughts.

Communication. As I have said already, this is the area with the biggest potential for conflict. But it can also be exciting to learn how others communicate. For instance, is the idea of communication to be direct or to insinuate and let someone else discover what you are saying in a nonthreatening manner? What simple cues do other cultures use to communicate respect? I have learned from my wife that for most people in the black culture in which she was raised, it communicates respect to refer to older women by their first name with the very necessary "Miss" in front of it. So you might spend the afternoon with Miss Myrtle or have a d-time with Miss Crystal. To simply call an older person Myrtle or Crystal feels disrespectful to my wife. It feels weird to me to use "Miss," but I have learned that it demonstrates great cultural respect when I can remember to do it. I have a Nigerian friend who lives in the United States and felt disrespected in almost every leadership meeting. What we eventually discovered was that in Nigerian culture, the oldest man in the room, which was him during these meetings, was always given the opportunity to speak first. He was rarely afforded that honor and without initially realizing it, it rubbed him the wrong way.

Space. What is the appropriate distance between people when speaking? That all depends on culture. Should you be close or a few feet apart? Should you hold hands when you talk or not? These physical expressions can be important. A friend of mine recently told me that there was a problem in the churches that were planted in India several decades ago that resulted from our fellowship's cultural tendency to hug one another. In India, he told me, hugging is considered an intimate act of a sexual nature. So you can imagine the confusion that resulted for visitors who felt like they were being sexually harassed at every meeting of the body. Instances like that are probably less frequent, but it is vital to keep an eye out for such differences.

Social structure. Is the base understanding of the community that it is a group with one identity, or a collection of individuals? The biblical answer to that is clear, but it's often not that simple. Many white Americans, for example, have been culturally conditioned to view the individual ahead of the group. This carries into the church in ways that we often never even notice. Is it okay for someone to show up at your house unexpectedly and come in for a few hours, or would that annoy you? Your answer might well demonstrate whether you have a group or individual orientation. I can tell you that this has been one of my wife's great struggles as a disciple over the years. She was raised in a very collective culture. People came in and out of her grandmother's house throughout the day, no invitation needed.

To her that feels like love, family, and community. When people don't act that way in the church or subtly send signals that it would be appreciated if when you came over, you had an appointment or time set up because otherwise they are unprepared for guests and get flustered, that does not feel like family to her. The only way to know things like these is to have ongoing and deep conversations where we can share our feelings and work toward mutual benefit in constant light of being all things to all people.

Time orientation. What can we do when some disciples are strictly monochronic and others are polychronic? Not running by the clock feels monumentally disrespectful to some, but to be a slave to it feels like antifamily legalism to others. There is no easy answer here. It will take compromise. I don't think the solution is to have an open starting time for worship gatherings, for instance. Stating in the weekly announcements that Sunday gatherings will now start somewhere between 10:05 and 10:30 will just not work. But I do believe that we can find ways, especially during less formal gatherings, to understand and enjoy the strengths of both cultures. As I described in the previous chapter, I used to get deeply annoyed when going to events with my wife's relatives because of their lack of clear starting and ending times and a lack of discernable structure to the events themselves. It can still be a struggle, but I have learned to appreciate the strength of simply enjoying and being immersed in one another's company with no regard for the clock or feeling the need to rush and get to the next thing.

Public interactions. This is always a fun one in my family. My wife comes from a culture that is perfectly comfortable with exuberant, animated, and loud interactions in public. It is the norm. For me? Not so much. Somewhere along the line I learned that you should be as quiet as possible in public; this is how you show respect to others. For me, it feels rude to be demonstrative or to shout across an open space. In many other cultures, that is just not the case. Put those two perspectives together and you can imagine the sparks that can fly.

When you go to a movie these days, the previews are rife with reminders to keep quiet and turn off your phone. This makes sense to me. It is respectful of others and the right thing to do. It didn't occur to me that this was simply a cultural expression that is often forced upon others who do not share that same perspective. At the risk of sounding like I am stereotyping, I will almost bet you that if you go to a movie theater in a predominately African American area, that sound restriction will not be adhered to as strictly. My wife likes to talk during movies. It took me a long time to get used to that. Okay, I admit it—I'm still not used to that.

This phenomenon can have big implications in our fellowship if one set of expectations is always subtly enforced or expected. Can people be loud and demonstrative in ways that feel comfortable to them without others feeling violated or disrespected? I think we can, but again, it takes intentionality.

Expression of sacred moments. Should communion be a quiet time for reverent meditation, complete with soft music to aid in that reflection? Or should it be a raucous celebration of the banquet of the Lord and an anticipation of the age to come? Neither is prohibited in Scripture, and both could find justification in the purpose and meaning of the Lord's Supper. So when we exclusively engage in one style, has it ever occurred to us that this might be a lack of cultural diversity? Should important gatherings like Good Friday, Resurrection Sunday, or Christmas Eve be formal, reverential events that bespeak the magnificence and mighty nature of the Almighty and what he has done for us? Or should they be celebrations that are full of exuberance and emotion? Once again, our practices might be more culturally conditioned than we realize. And they just might be tipped very heavily in the direction of one form of cultural expression at that.

Power distance. Cultures can have great differences in how members accept, reject, or respond to power that is distributed unequally. High-power-distance cultures encourage conformity to hierarchy and authority and believe that everyone has a place and should respect that authority. The authority structure and power of individuals does not need to be justified or validated; it just is the way it is. On the other hand, low-power-distance cultures believe in an equal distribution of power and they tend to question or rebel against inequities of power. Like the other areas, when a community includes people of varying degrees of both these broad cultural categories, conflict can ensue.

Principles for Cross-Cultural Life in the Body

Cultural diversity can be a source of great conflict, but it can also be a great victory and serve as a light to the world. For the remainder of this chapter I wish to provide a few simple principles that will aid us in our cultural sensitivity and diversity, along with some helpful questions that will direct our steps as we travel down these winding paths. Before we begin, though, I will return to Romans 14 and 15 and provide an overview of general principles, in list form, that directly relate to our approach to cross-cultural life in the body. Because we are looking at them from a slightly different angle, these principles will vary a bit from those that we gleaned in Chapter 13, but will overlap some as well.

Cross-Cultural Principles in the Body

1. Accept the cultural expressions and perspectives of others as valid (Romans 14:1).
2. Do not treat the cultural expressions and perspectives of others with contempt (14:10).
3. Do not put up stumbling blocks for others (14:13).
4. Build one another up rather than tearing down (14:19).
5. Give up your rights rather than force your perspective on someone else (14:21).
6. Put the interests of one another first (15:1–6).

With these broad principles in mind, let's take a look at ten simple, practical reminders for cross-cultural life in the body of Christ.

Reminder One: Give the benefit of the doubt. If someone does something that you find unusual, odd, inappropriate, or even offensive, hold off on judging their motives. The natural inclination for most of us is to jump to a negative conclusion. That person is rude. They are thoughtless. They are selfish. They are strange. They are stupid. Part of the traditional Jewish culture is to train oneself to think the most positive options available about someone or another situation until you are certain of what happened. Let's learn from that. Think of how many conflicts and hurt feelings could be avoided if we assumed that someone who just treated us rudely was perhaps acting appropriately in their cultural context. It never hurts to assume the positive when we don't know the facts.

Reminder Two: Look for what an action means in that culture—not in yours. This is vital and doesn't need a whole lot of explanation. Do not judge the actions of others by what they would mean or how they would feel in your culture. Try to understand how the actions are perceived in their culture, and you might see an entirely different perspective.

Reminder Three: Allow each other to make mistakes. Being gracious is always the best policy. We will be insensitive. We will mess up. That has to be okay if we are going to maintain a loving community. Most of the time, someone is completely unaware that their actions or beliefs are hurting you. And even if they are aware but are so dogmatic that they believe they are right, to the point that they are rigid and unwilling to change, remember that Jesus called us to love even our enemies and those with whom we ardently disagree.

Reminder Four: Be sensitive. Do your best to be aware of the needs and cultural sensitivities of others. This is simply another form of putting the interests of others ahead of your own. When we are all seeking to accommodate and encourage one another, a community will thrive.

Reminder Five: Don't be so sensitive. This is not a contradiction of the previous point. Be sensitive to others, as much as it depends on you, but work very hard at not being overly sensitive yourself. If someone offends or ignores your cultural sensibilities, the first step is to try not to be provoked by it. That's not always possible, and it won't take away the need to have conversations and help educate others, but it is an important starting point.

Reminder Six: Reserve judgment. Reminder one was to hold off on assuming or perceiving things negatively before we know the whole story. Here I refer to the times when we do know what is going on. There have been times with my wife and me in our cross-cultural life together that one or the other will observe some cultural expectation or practice of the other's family and jokingly remark that it is just wrong, and our own culture is better. What we joke about, some take seriously. All cultures are prone to sin and evil expressions; I'm not talking about that. I'm talking about judging the practice of another culture as wrong, stupid, or backward, when what we really mean is that it does not suit our taste or preference. There is a big difference, and it is an absolute must that we recognize that.

Reminder Seven: Don't assume that your point of view is normal or correct. This is intimately related to the previous reminder. But it is such an important skill that I feel that I need to set it apart and mention it directly. I stated before, and it bears repeating, that our culture is *a* way to do things, not *the* way. We can impose our cultural expectations on others in ways that we don't even imagine. I watched a discussion between a white man and a black man on race and culture on a talk show a few months ago. The African American individual began to get passionate about his perspective and raise his voice. He was not committing any moral outrage, but he was acting in a manner that the white host and white guest did not appreciate. He was told, in so many words, that he should not be so emotional and that they should be able to talk about race in an intellectual manner without strong feelings. But it never occurred to them that this was their cultural expectation. That's not necessarily the way that many cultures in West Africa, for instance, would talk about important issues. It does not tend to be the way that much of the African American culture discusses such passionate topics. The two white people were unaware, I'm sure, that they were assuming a stance of cultural superiority, deeming that their cultural expression was the right way to do things. Is it? Maybe. Maybe not.

This is really important for us to understand. People of nondominant cultures are constantly reminded in subtle, and sometimes not so subtle, ways that they are not doing things correctly. The dominant culture is almost always unaware of this, but it happens nonetheless. So a white talk show host tells a black guest to calm down. What the guest heard, although he probably couldn't have described exactly why he felt that way, is that his cultural way of handling passionate discussions is wrong and unwelcome. He heard, "Your culture is lesser than mine, so you need to play by the rules of 'society.'" Of course, the host is entirely unaware of all that and is not doing this intentionally. But the message is sent, all the same. This is then not perceived by the guest as what it truly is, a cultural issue, but is most likely felt to be a denunciation of his race. It seems like a "black and white thing." Frustrated by all this, but still not totally cognizant of why, he comments that he is tired of racist society trying to bully his people. The white guest and show host are flabbergasted because they didn't feel they were being prejudiced at all. What was not an issue of race has now become one.

Reminder Eight: Be proactive. Don't wait until misunderstanding or conflict occurs. Take the initiative. Be the change your community needs. Start the conversation. Respectfully ask for ongoing education for the church so that you can be prepared for many of these issues before they happen. It will never eradicate the gaps. My wife and I have been together for twenty years, and we still have culture clashes on a regular basis. But we are proactive. We communicate often, and as a result we have greatly conquered the gap between us.

Reminder Nine: Get out of your comfort zone. Being diverse will demand much of all of us. We will need to have awkward conversations. There will be times when we do things that are new or don't put us at ease. At every turn, we will need to be willing to step out of our normal routines, ways of doing things, and what brings us comfort. But in so doing, we just might find that exciting new options open up to us in the ever-diversifying family of God.

Reminder Ten: Relax. These can be sensitive and passionate issues, but we can choose to approach them together with a sense of excitement, adventure, fun, and even playfulness. When we understand that we are in this together, we can give each other permission to mess up, ask questions, learn, and explore without fear of being jumped on when we make a mistake. This doesn't have to be awkward and a negative experience the way that it often is in the world. Remember, these cultural identities and expressions are secondary to our mutual identity in Christ, so that removes much of the fear when exploring these deep areas of human interaction.

Important Questions

I want to finish the chapter with five questions that we can ask ourselves that will help guide us through many of the cross-cultural interactions in which we will find ourselves in the body of Christ as well outside it.

Question 1: What are my cultural beliefs or behaviors in this instance? Self-awareness is key. When we know our own cultural conditioning, we can avoid judgmental attitudes and unintentionally forcing others to play by our cultural rules. When we know ourselves, we can be far more gracious and adaptable to others.

Question 2: Does the Bible call me to a specific, new way of thinking here? We want to do everything for the glory of God (1 Corinthians 10:31) and in light of his word. Perhaps the prime directive, to borrow a term from Star Trek, is to become all things to all people. This means that cultural adaptability and acquiescence should be our default mode. That right there will often call us to new ways of thinking and acting; but we should always be on the lookout to run every belief, practice, custom, assumption, or opinion through the prism of God's word. We might just find that some of our dearly held cultural practices don't match up with our citizenship in God's kingdom.

Question 3: What are the other's cultural beliefs or behaviors in this instance? Once you are aware of your own culture and have considered Scripture, you can consider what another's cultural expression is and how you can understand it, adopt it, or work with it, as is appropriate to the situation. Learning another culture, though, takes time. Don't assume you understand something without verification from someone of that culture. And never forget that the best way to learn a culture is to ask as many respectful questions as you can. A word of warning: If you're the one being asked the questions, be as patient and gracious as you possibly can, even if you think the questions are not the most finely crafted ones in the history of humankind.

Question 4: This time ask this question in light of the other culture, not yours: does the Bible call me to a specific, new way of thinking here? How does the Bible direct me to think about them and their actions? I know that I am to lean toward adapting to suit their interests whenever possible, but that does not mean to accept everything blindly. Just as I consider my actions in light of Scripture, so must I consider theirs. What happens, you might ask, if you are attempting to bend to my cultural preferences at the same time that I seek to bend to yours? Well, that's a wonderful problem to have, isn't it?

Question 5: Am I willing to ask respectfully, "What did you mean by that?" This is one of the most important practical steps that you and I can take in seeking cross-cultural fluency. Rather than assuming or judging, we simply need to take a moment and ask, "When you did that, what did you mean by it?" More often than not, you'll discover that the other person intended to be considerate because what they did, what they said, or how they said it, is acceptable in their cultural context. For instance, I can be very sarcastic in my responses to many situations. This was normal for me while growing up. My wife does not so readily understand or appreciate sarcasm. She can easily take offense at it. I've learned not to use it so much around her, but every now and then it will slip. Rather than assuming I was being mean, she has learned to either interpret it in the best light, or ask what I meant by it. That has saved us much grief over the years. When I know how another person intended something, I can translate it properly and not take offense.

To truly be able to do this, though, we have to create an environment where we give one another permission to ask this question or ones like it. Talk about it as a church and decide that it will always be acceptable to ask, "What did you mean by that?" Agree that it will also be tolerable to explain how that action would be perceived in your own culture, whether it be rude, dismissive, or something similar. When we are willing to be open and honest and not take things personally, we can demystify this process and bring glory to God with our unity. And always keep in mind that a multicultural church will start in the living room. The more we intertwine our lives together, the more truly diverse we will be and the more God will be brought the glory.

Questions for Discussion

1. Have you ever misinterpreted the actions of others or had them misinterpret your actions? What role do you think your respective cultures played in that misunderstanding?

2. Are you willing to be flexible in your culture in order to help others in the body of Christ?

3. What can the dominant culture in your body do to improve diversity, communication, and unity?

4. What can the nondominant cultures in your body do to improve diversity, communication, and unity?

5. How proficient do you feel your church is at cross-cultural communication? What are some positive steps that the leadership could take to help the body improve in their understanding of one another?

Chapter 17

Forging Ahead

We had a few minutes before the team bus left for a long ride to our basketball game that day, and I was fooling around with some friends in the hallway area in between our locker room and the doors where the bus was waiting. I was a freshman in college and we were running up and down the steps chasing each other around; what could go wrong? Until it did. I was making one last dash away from my friend. I determined that I could leap down the last small flight of steps, pivot quickly and run through the foyer to the outside doors to the bus before my friend could catch me. She didn't stand a chance. Until she did. As I neared the bottom of the stairway on my leap, my left foot didn't quite clear the last step. My foot caught and my left ankle rolled quite severely, all my weight coming down in force on the joint. I knew instantly that I had broken the lower part of my ankle, but I wanted to play in our game that night. So I lied. I told our trainer that I had turned the ankle a bit and needed it taped, but I pretended that the pain wasn't that bad. I gutted it out and played on a very painful joint. Turns out, I probably shouldn't have done that, as I caused it to fracture more and created some bone chips in my foot. That ankle would continue to bother me for the next several years, and I rebroke it twice and had a couple of surgeries. During that time my doctor told me that it would be a problem for the rest of my life.

A few years after college I slowly picked up the hobby of running. After a few years more, it turned into distance running and regularly participating in marathons. During the past eighteen years of running, I have strengthened my ankle and other joints an incredible amount just from the steady beat of mile after mile. Amazingly, my ankle no longer causes me problems. It affects me, but it doesn't slow me down anymore. To this day, I can still feel an occasional bone chip in there through the skin of my foot. The flexibility in that ankle is permanently about twenty-five percent less than in my other ankle. So, yes, it will always affect me because of the past. But I have overcome that. I found ways around the pain in the early days. I have worked around the decreased flexibility, and there are certain things that I will never try because I know that it would be too risky for that ankle. But as I write this today, it is strong and it gets me where I need to go.

Overcoming the Past

What has happened in the past will have an effect. There is no way that it cannot. That is a truism of life. We should never get into a position where we want to ignore the past or just leave it back there and pretend that it doesn't impact us today. We don't want to be victims unable to overcome what has hurt us; instead, we can learn from it. We can overcome and compensate for the past, but it will continue to affect us, especially if we don't deal with it. I have seen friends of mine continue to struggle with character sins in their lives, and it seems that, at least in part, it is because they will not deal with things that happened in their past. They have convinced themselves that it doesn't matter now and they can just move forward. Moving forward is good, but it can only happen once we have truly dealt with our history. In Philippians 3, Paul says that he will forget what is behind and strain toward what is ahead (3:13), but that is because he has already come to terms with his past, learned how it affected him, and discovered how to overcome it (3:4–11).

We need to be aware of what sin has done to the world and to us as individuals. The world has been steeped in sin since the Fall in the Garden of Eden. Sin and division have damaged people and societies right down through the ages. In Christ, we can overcome the effects of sin, but the impact of it will still follow us into the church. We must be aware of the world's damage and division in the life of the church, or it will ruin us. We cannot pretend that sin does not exist, nor can we imagine that sins of long ago won't continue to create problems. Sins will have long-lasting impact (Exodus 20:5).

Think of your own experience as a Christian. When you triumphantly rose from your baptismal waters, were you completely sanctified and holy? Did the impact of all the sin in your life immediately melt away into the water? I'm going to go out on a limb and guess that that is not what happened. You made an important decision to turn your life over to Christ. You received the Holy Spirit who would help guide you through the process of transformation, but there was still a lot of work to be done, wasn't there? There still is. You didn't immediately get rid of pride, lust, anger, resentment, and selfishness. You didn't instantly become impervious to the consequences of your earlier sin. With the Spirit's help, you have learned to put those sins to death, some quickly and others slowly. You have devised strategies to compensate for or overcome the effects of your previous sin. But all that will never completely go away in the present age.

So it is with division. The effects of division in this world are many and they are powerful. Because division is rooted in idolatry and selfishness, it is one of the most devastating sins in the world. It has ripped apart humanity since the beginning. Division has finally been dealt with in Christ, but that doesn't make it magically go away in the church. Jesus leaves us to work out the reality of life in his kingdom. We must learn to deal with and rid ourselves of the past sins of our societies and our part in them and learn how to move beyond the scar tissue from that sin, which still runs throughout our community. There is no question that we can do this. But there is much striving ahead of us.

As we strain toward what is ahead for God's people, I will suggest a number of strategies that will help us to bring about racial unity in the church. These suggestions will be aimed at what you as an individual can do. After that, I will put forth some suggestions for what church families can do together to continue to build healthy, thriving, multiethnic communities. Finally, I will bring the book to a close with some opinions regarding things that might be helpful to avoid in the future.

What Can I Do?

I am always puzzled when I hear someone say, "Well, that's just the way I am." It seems like a conversation ender to me. It's an assertion that they are unwilling to change or feel that they are unable to change. I try to gently remind people in those situations that there is only one "I AM," and it's not me or you. The rest of us are a "will be." We need transformation and growth. In fact, that is at the heart of what it means to be a Christian. We have been freely given the identity of Christ and now we spend the rest of our lives learning what that means and how to grow into this suit of clothing that is way too big for us.

When it comes to being Christlike and growing as partners in the one family of all nations that God has created, here are some things that I think we can do to continue the process that the Spirit has begun in us.

1. Pray constantly. Not much happens without prayer. Do you pray for racial, ethnic, and cultural reconciliation every day, or at least on a regular basis? Pray for it in the church. Pray for the divisions in the world. Pray that they will see their need for the solution that God has given in Christ, the only place that they will ever find the true and lasting solution to division. Pray for those that agree with you. Pray for those that disagree with you. Pray for those that you believe have been victimized by the systemic evil in the world. Pray for those that you believe perpetrate evil or are unjust. Pray that God will help you see things from a kingdom perspective. Pray before you speak. Pray for guidance and for God to show you what you can do in addition to prayer. If these are issues that are deeply on your heart, then I suggest that you consider a time of fasting and praying for repentance and growth, both regularly and in the face of particularly challenging situations. There is nothing more powerful and effective than prayer. Do you believe that?

2. Display the kingdom. Every problem the world has is because of sin. Fallen humans put our own interests first and do our own will rather than God's. To accept the good news of Jesus as King and to live by the values of his kingdom is the only true solution for the world. We must never lose sight of that (Luke 9:60; Acts 8:4). We can be active in different ways, but in the end, all roads must lead back to showing people what the life of the true kingdom looks like and how it can change the world, one heart at a time. Many are proclaiming things other than the kingdom a whole lot more often and louder than they do God's kingdom and his church. It is amazing to be part of a fellowship of all nations, tribes, and languages that love one another. Shout that to a watching world. It's rare. Embrace it and be proud of what God has done.

I believe that there is a real danger of turning a strength into a weakness. One of the great blessings and strengths of our family of churches is the diversity that God has given us. We must cultivate this and strengthen it. It sets us apart as we live out the gospel. We cannot allow the divisions of the world to seep into the church and divide us. We cannot drift into being churches that are culturally monotone and no longer cherish the ethnic and cultural diversity that God has given us. We must recognize that it will be challenging and that this is precisely where Satan will attack us. We must flee from division and embrace the strength that God has bestowed upon us. Rather than it being a source of tension and despair, it should be one of the things that we point to when we talk about the miracles that God has wrought among us. Don't turn the light on us as though we are something great. It's not about us. But don't be afraid to boast in the Lord for creating one family of all people groups. It is amazing, and people need to know that the solution to division is out there.

3. Consider cross-cultural training. This can take many shapes, whether formal or informal. But the more you can learn about cross-cultural communication and about other cultures, the more effective you will be for and in the kingdom of God. There are many helpful books and other resources that will assist growth in this all-important area.

4. Have conversations. I am under no illusion that this book will be the primary catalyst of growth or change in our churches. I hope that it helps point in the right direction, but the real power comes through the guidance of the Holy Spirit. I believe he will primarily work through conversations with one another. "Everyone should be quick to listen, slow to speak and slow to become angry" (James 1:19). The more we talk and find common ground in Christ, the more we will become the people that God wants us to be. The most important and effective conversations will take place in your living room and around your dining room table; in other words, the best talks will be with those you have invited into your life. Panel discussions and social media outlets are not the most effective forums, though they do have their place.

5. Love your friends and your enemies. If you think a brother or sister is bigoted, not listening, or unloving, love them. If you think someone is deluded, subjective, and emotional, love them. If you think someone is a victim, love them. If you think someone is a perpetrator, love them. If you think I am wrong, love me. If I think you are wrong, I will love you. Jesus knew that Judas was going to betray him and yet none of the other disciples had a clue. That shows that Jesus loved all his disciples, including Judas, the same. Regardless of whether someone is your friend or your enemy, the world should see no distinction in your kindness, patience, and love for them. That's challenging, but it is at the very heart of what it means to be a follower of Christ.

6. Sacrifice for your enemies. If you think someone is a perpetrator of violence or racism, go volunteer in their world and find a way to love them. That's true discipleship. You want to go love those you view as victims or whose perspective you share? Good, do that. But even the world does that (Matthew 5:43–48). Go help, volunteer with, and build bridges and relationships with those that you think are in the wrong. That's big boy and girl stuff. If you support the brave policemen in our world but think there are too many out-of-control policemen, go volunteer with them and get to know policemen on a heart level. Make a difference in their lives.

If you think that the problem is with those who protest what they see as injustice, or those that are so angry that they instigate violent reactions against authority, then maybe you should go volunteer in areas of unrest, the parts of the city that are in turmoil, or wherever appropriate to the situation. Love, help, and support those that you disagree with. Double your efforts of love and reaching out to those whom you violently disagree with. That's what will really stand out to the world and show them the true life of the kingdom.

If it is another brother or sister with whom you disagree, you can avoid them, ignore them, argue with them, try to shut them up, or even just "tolerate" them. You can do that, but it's not godly. Guess who is the first person that you should be having over for dinner and to lavish love on? And it should not be to try to change their mind, but simply to love.

7. Remember that freedom comes through self-sacrifice. Freedom for others comes through the power of the cross. Jesus lived that message out his entire life. So did Paul. Men like Dr. Martin Luther King Jr., Gandhi, and Nelson Mandela learned it. We will never enact change or bring freedom by putting the suffering on others, even if we think they deserve it. We will likely never bring much change by refuting or shooting down their arguments or beliefs. If that were the case, Jesus would have come and put everyone else on the cross. If you want to really foment change, be prepared to bring the sacrifice onto yourself. This is perhaps the largest missing piece of many groups today that want justice: they are yet unwilling to take the sacrifice on themselves. As Jesus' people, this is our calling every single day (Luke 14:27).

8. Renounce all forms of violence. God's kingdom is a kingdom of peace (Isaiah 2:2–4). If it uses the weapons of the world (2 Corinthians 10:3–4), then it is not being his kingdom or being like Jesus. Jesus never used violence against other human beings (and no, the acted-out parable of judgment in the temple was not violence and harmed no one). This is incumbent upon all disciples. We should be against violence, reject it as a strategy, and not support it as a viable alternative for God's people. We must not only reject violence as an option for ourselves but also stand against violence toward others, both past and present. We are ambassadors of the kingdom, and it is a grave problem if we represent it as a kingdom that embraces force. The kingdoms of the world have that as a sanctioned weapon to keep order, but it is not an option for the kingdom of God.

9. Work for justice. As soon as I say that, I must remind us of two things. The first is that we should always be fighting for kingdom justice as our primary concern (Proverbs 20:23). Working toward societal justice is fine as long as we keep it in perspective and don't let it derail, endanger, or take priority over our kingdom mission. The second is that Christians should "fight" for others, but I firmly believe that it must be in the form of the cross. It will require self-sacrifice rather than seeking worldly justice.

Please do remember that your obsession must be for the kingdom and not for human fairness. We can strive for that but will never achieve it outside of the full coming of the kingdom. We will have very different perspectives, but I remember how crazy some people went when they believed that O.J. Simpson was escaping justice and how they decried the legal system. That's the way many people feel when they see videos of what they believe is definite, unprovoked violence or killing and, because of their experiences, have a hard time trusting the justice system. Others implicitly trust authorities and the justice system because of their experiences. Be gracious with one another and create space in your worldview for differing perspectives. Don't be guilty of extrapolating someone else's view to unfair conclusions. For example, it's never a good thing to be disrespectful or resistant to authority figures, but because someone feels that this should not be a crime punishable by gun shot, does not mean that they support violence toward policemen. And just because someone tends to support policemen does not mean that they are prejudiced. We may have to admit that our cultural and historical backgrounds on these issues are so different that we might never see eye to eye. That incongruence can at no time be allowed to take precedence over our kingdom identity, unity, or mission.

It is, I believe, important to keep in mind that for many who have been hurt and scarred by racism and prejudice, they must do something. It is a conscience issue for them. I don't think it is ever helpful to imply that they should ignore that and only be about the kingdom, leaving social issues alone. For them, that is an important part of the reality of the kingdom in their lives. These are our brothers and sisters, and they need us to be with them on this. If we do nothing to deal with the ongoing impact of racism, it can easily tempt them to think, "Well, you have your fair share of the Monopoly money and now you don't care about anything else or the people that have been wronged." Is that an entirely kingdom perspective? Perhaps not. But it is much like those who had sensitive consciences toward eating meat sacrificed to idols. If it hurts my brother, I will take the loving action every time. Love trumps rights. We always want to work toward the fullest kingdom perspective we can have, but we must understand that it is a process and we are in this together. To paraphrase Dr. Martin Luther King Jr., we may have all come into God's kingdom in separate ships, but we are in the same boat now.

10. Accept one another. This is primarily for disciples and how we interact with each other. Accept differing perspectives and respect them. Be open-minded and listen. Don't grow weary of doing good. Go back to Romans 14:1–15:7 often. These were important issues over which they violently disagreed and yet Paul called them to respect one another and to pursue unity, knowing that they might never agree. Your stand on an opinion issue, no matter how strongly you might believe in it, can at no time come before your unity with and love for your brothers and sisters in Christ.

11. Keep politics in its place. Far too many Christians come to their opinions or worldviews based on their upbringing, their culture, or because someone in the media or on the Internet made a convincing argument. Whenever you hold an opinion, simply ask yourself if it is rooted in Scripture. Every position we hold should be Scripture-informed. Many disciples forget or ignore this. But it is also possible for two disciples to hold differing opinions and both feel that they have come to their position based on their understanding of the Scriptures. In those cases, we must defer to accepting and loving one another. Political solutions have some benefit, but they only go so far and will never have answers to the deep issues and sins that divide society. To exalt them over the kingdom is a grave mistake.

12. Make unity the priority. If Christians can't be unified despite differences, and if they start to fracture and divide or devolve into arguing and blocking one another on social media sites, then we have lost already (1 Corinthians 6:7). It is worth restating: unity and respect for one another are more important than your opinions.

13. Validate the experiences and pain of others. I have never been sexually harassed or whistled at as I walked down the street, and I've never seen it happen to a woman. That doesn't mean it doesn't happen. How demeaning would it be if I told women who have experienced harassment that those things don't happen anymore? Hear each other out. Ask one another what they have gone through. Sometimes we can spend too much time letting worldly sources form what we think. Don't let your experiences or what your favorite news channel or website tells you cause you to discount what many others have experienced in their lives. You may still see things from a different viewpoint, but be empathetic and try to see things from the place of others.

14. Consider that you may not be right. I am certain that I have said things in this book that not every reader has agreed with. I understand that. There are things in this book that are not correct. I just don't know which parts. I have done my best, but I'm not always right. Have you considered that when it comes to your opinions and perspectives? These situations are complex and often experience based. Statistics and facts are only so helpful, because they must all be analyzed and often are interpreted in differing ways. It is far better to listen to one another without having already made up our minds and to put the interests of one another ahead of our own opinions or preferences. And if you believe vehemently that I am in the wrong on some parts of this book, or most of them, then I can expect an amazing night of hospitality at your house soon, right?

15. Forgive lavishly. We will need to forgive one another (Colossians 3:13). Count on it. In the body of Christ, we will hurt each other, offend one another, mess things up, blow it, and get on each other's nerves. Conflict doesn't mean that we have failed. Division does. When Paul and Barnabas had a sharp conflict, the church didn't try to hide it. It was recorded forever in the book of Acts. But they remained unified and focused on the mission. You may find that you need more formal conflict resolution. If that's the case, seek godly, spiritual leaders who can help with that in a biblical way. Be humble, though, and follow the biblical principles during that process. That means if you do have a sharp disagreement, don't scurry off to gather allies against your "foe." The very first thing you should do is to get together with the other person and try to work through it as brothers or sisters. Only when that has failed should you seek to bring in others to help. Keep in mind that Jesus was very clear as to how he feels about our unwillingness to forgive others (Matthew 18:21–35).

16. Spend time with those that think differently than you do. If you cannot agree on these issues, go share your faith together, pray together, encourage one another, and pray for each other. Remember that you have Christ in common, and that will always outweigh all your differences.

What Can We Do?

Change starts with the individual, but it must permeate the group or it will only go so far. Churches can do much to facilitate and encourage growth as a multiethnic family. There are many congregations among our family of churches around the country that have already taken great strides in the areas of culture and race. I will offer suggestions here, many of which we have already implemented or are working toward in my home church in Minneapolis-St. Paul. This list is by no means exhaustive, and I'm sure that in the near future, churches around the country will add to it with their great ideas and initiatives that they have successfully implemented. The suggestions below are intended more as idea-starters than a specific list to be followed. Your church may find some of these ideas directly helpful, but since each situation is unique, the ideas and solutions employed will need to be as well.

1. Teach thoroughly on the kingdom of God. The more we understand God's all-encompassing kingdom and the way of life intended for its citizens, the more we will be prepared to seek God's rule first in every area of our lives and to meet the challenges, problems, and temptations of a complex world that is stuck in darkness. Many of the problems and conflicts that I have seen between disciples when it comes to issues of race and culture are rooted in a lack of understanding and embracing the radically otherworldly way in which we are to think and live as God's kingdom people.

2. Teach and preach periodically on the issues of race, culture, and ethnicity. Highlight how the early church dealt with and responded to these struggles and the ways in which we can apply scriptural principles to our contemporary matters. This cannot just happen once. The topics are too complex and the perceptions far too deeply rooted for us to "get it" in one attempt. When we combine points 1 and 2, we begin to address the roots of the situation. This will be the catalyst for change. The remaining suggestions should flow from a growth in our understanding of God's kingdom and his plan for his multiethnic family.

3. Encourage diverse and multiethnic preaching and teaching. We should seek to go beyond just teaching on these topics; we need to hear a potpourri of perspectives, backgrounds, and races. Some churches are already doing this and are well prepared for it. Others need to work to reach this level. It is incredibly necessary that we hear the voices and influence of many cultures.

4. Work toward a multiethnic leadership. Changes in diversity will be most effective when the leadership and most influential opinions in the community are diverse. I do not advocate simply putting people in positions of leadership based on external qualities. However, if we are to be a family that comprises all nations and people groups, then that should be reflected in every aspect of our community. I'm not talking about quotas and getting caught up in numbers or statistics, but about having a mindset that seeks to raise up and maintain a diverse leadership group. If your church is not there yet, be honest about it. Ask for patience, prayer, and support from the body.

Two years ago, the leadership team of the Minneapolis-St. Paul church humbly and boldly stood up before the church and acknowledged that all the ten core members of the leadership group were white. They declared that while they believed God had raised every man up to that position, they also recognized that a lack of ethnic diversity in the leadership group was not a representation of the multiethnic family of God that we are striving to be. They asked for patience and prayer, and the church graciously and exuberantly stood behind them. Since then God has added two nonwhite leaders to that group, men who are spiritually qualified, very capable, and have helped in the journey toward reflecting God's multifaceted glory.

Often, a lack of diverse leadership reflects the damage done by the past sin of our society. It will take time, effort, and intention to overcome that and reverse the negative influence and patterns of the world.

5. Provide cross-cultural training. Each member should pursue appropriate learning and growth on their own, but the church as a collective should take a leading role in providing training and resources for the congregation in cross-cultural relationships, communication, and life. Without ongoing education in such matters, rooted in biblical truth and principles, the body will never function as well as it could. Before we think that this is a worldly endeavor, we should remember that the book of Romans, particularly chapters 14 and 15, to give just one example, is a clear case of Paul providing cross-cultural ministry training to the disciples.

6. Facilitate discussion. Ongoing discussion and communication are necessary to the diversity and growth of the body. Many of these conversations will be informal, but they should go beyond that. The church leadership can provide safe and directed opportunities for members to share perspectives and learn about one another's experiences and culture.

Whether done in a small group format or a larger setting, it will provide disciples an ongoing opportunity to discover and grow.

7. Organize regular opportunities to highlight celebrations of all cultures, languages, and nations. Many churches already do something like this. We are one family of all nations, and it can be important to regularly stress that and rejoice over it. In Minneapolis-St. Paul we have Simunye Sundays. "Simunye" is a Zulu term that means roughly, "We are one." We have a stirring time of reveling in expressions of worship in song and dance from cultures around the world. We pray in many languages. We have lessons from outside speakers that celebrate what God has done through the gospel. The highlight of the day is the meal where people bring dishes from around the world and we feast together. It is a highpoint of the year. It doesn't just provide an enjoyable worship experience; it reinforces our identity as the multiethnic and multicultural people of the King.

8. Create a committee or group to champion the cause of diversity. In Minneapolis-St. Paul we call this group the Acts 6 Committee. The needs for each city are different, and the way that each functions will vary widely based on context. But these groups can be valuable sources to pick up on needs or trouble spots in the body and alert the leadership, as well as to organize future events and suggest ongoing training, teaching, or communication that needs to take place in the church. It also provides an outlet and an opportunity for constructive influence for those that have expertise in the areas of cultural and ethnic issues.

9. Develop all-nations evangelism teams. Examine the makeup of your body. Is it diverse? Does it represent the people groups that are prevalent in your community? Our mission is to take the gospel to all nations; but remember, that term refers to people groups. It is our calling to bring the people groups back together in the kingdom of God. We are sometimes fooled by our racial diversity, not realizing that we have entire ethnic groups in our community that are completely unrepresented in our local congregation. Minneapolis-St. Paul is a diverse church body, but there is also a large Somali population in our area and, although we have many African American disciples and a healthy number of African disciples, we have no Somali members of the family. Some cultures, Somali being one of them, present specific challenges when sharing the gospel with them. A person must be proficient in certain aspects of their culture so as not to immediately offend them or cause them to shut down any opportunity to experience the kingdom of God.

We are working on a plan to reach out to the Somali people in our community. We have already had a guest speaker come in and teach us about the Somali culture, and we have plans to develop a team of people who have specifically been further trained to share the gospel with this group in the hopes of winning them for Christ. Endeavors like this take time and will not work or be necessary for every church, but it is something to consider in your local context if the need is there.

10. Develop or maintain a diverse music ministry. Music is the language of culture. It is also one of the most obvious indicators of a community's commitment to cultural diversity. If we tell visitors that we are a family of all nations and cultures, that message can fall flat if they hear a steady beat of one type of music. Sometimes churches think that their musical worship is diverse, but it is truly only diverse within one cultural type. Many of our churches excel in this area. Others have room for growth. I urge you not to overlook or neglect it. Don't let your music ministry be just a reflection of who you are now as a community, but of who you are called to be. This might call you beyond where you are, but as people "from every tribe and language and people and nation," let the music and all elements of worship be a constant reflection of God's manifold wisdom.

11. Utilize a Bible study that highlights the multiethnic family of God. When I became a disciple in 1999, a study on discipleship really demonstrated for me what set the church that I was visiting apart from any I had ever seen. While that topic remains indispensable, I believe that the issue of being called to be the family of all nations is one of the things, if not the top thing, that will shine a light and help people differentiate between the true gospel and lesser versions of it. Dr. Martin Luther King Jr. famously quipped that Sunday at 11 a.m. was the most segregated hour of the week. That is still mostly true today. Many church groups do not reflect the full glory of the gospel in this area. We have an opportunity to let the light of the kingdom shine. Why would we not? I would encourage us to get a Bible study on this topic into the hands of all members. Beyond that, I would urge that each church consider incorporating such a study into their primary study series for people learning to become disciples. I have created one such study that can be found in Appendix A. Others may write a better study in the future, but this will at least serve as a sample or an inspiration.

Things to Consider Avoiding

Before I bring this book to a close I want to offer my opinions, and they are just that, on a few things that we as disciples would do well to avoid in our relationships with one another. Discernment needs to be applied to all these things, but my hope is that they will help us to sidestep some common pitfalls in our cross-cultural communities.

1. Avoid "lives matter" rhetoric. The phrase "Black lives matter" has come to the forefront in recent years. I refer to it as a separate issue from the political action group of the same name, which I will not consider here. By itself the phrase represents the truth of the very real fear of many black Americans that their lives have not always been treated with the same respect and justice as have the lives of others. The responsive phrase, "All lives matter," feels demeaning to many of our black brothers and sisters and is not particularly helpful, as it ignores the obvious point that the original phrase does not call into question anyone else's value, but seeks confirmation that all lives are equal. If my house were on fire and the firetruck came, I would want them to spray water on my house. It would be inappropriate if a neighbor got upset because the firemen weren't also spraying water on their house because, after all, all houses matter. Yes, but my house is the one on fire right now, and it needs the attention. With that said, because the whole concept has become sadly controversial, I might recommend that the disciple simply find other language to express the important truths that need to be heard without ever disparaging the original phrase. That is not to deny the truth behind the statement "Black lives matter" or to negate the hurt it expresses, but simply to recognize that given the heated environment, more effective ways to communicate these truths might be found.

2. Don't charge people with reverse racism. If we are going to use correct language, what most people call "racist," is prejudice, bigotry, or racialism. Racism is a system of power and oppression. In that sense, black people and other people of color in the United States can rarely be in the position of being racist. They can, of course, be prejudiced or bigoted. Every race and ethnic group has people that are prejudiced and bigoted. If someone is trying to point out the struggle they have experienced or felt living under a system that is racist in their opinion, it is not helpful or particularly accurate to counter that with charges of reverse racism. Yes, all groups have bigoted people, but that is largely unrelated to the topic of systemic racism in the United States.

3. Don't make accusations of white supremacy. This is another loaded phrase that is often used for shock value but is not helpful in mature discussions, especially coming from disciples. If, for example, you are discussing affirmative action with someone and they believe it should be removed, it is not constructive to charge them with advocating white supremacy. There is so much that is negative associated with that term that it has become a pejorative and is sure to shut down any productivity in a conversation.

4. Don't say, "I can't be prejudiced because I have black friends." If you ask African Americans, most will tell you that this is one of the most demeaning sentiments out there. I have had incidents during which I found myself thinking in a prejudiced manner in spite of the fact that the rest of my household is black. A lot of these things are deeply ingrained in places we don't even realize. Anyone can be prejudiced whether they have many black friends, have adopted mixed children, or are black and have white friends. This type of statement is usually put forth as a defense. It is better, I think, not to be defensive and to hear out what people are saying. Yes, you have black friends. But yes, you may have been unintentionally thinking in a prejudiced manner or acting in a bigoted way. You may have no problem with skin color but be quite elitist in your cultural views and acceptance of other perspectives. Be quick to listen and slow to speak.

5. Don't call everything or everyone racist. It has become increasingly popular to call "racism" at almost every turn these days, as though everyone is racist and everything is an example of racism. Overusing a term saps it of its power and effectiveness, not to mention that people often mean prejudiced rather than racist. Not everything is racially motivated, although there is no question that racial issues run deep in our country and impact much of everyday life. Be judicious about using these terms, and if you do feel that it is necessary, it should be to educate and be constructive rather than as a pejorative used out of frustration.

6. Don't tell black people to "just get over it" when referring to their feelings about racism or even slavery. It is dismissive and ignores the fact that you may not understand the depth of someone's pain over the impact that it has had on their family. It is true that as a disciple they should begin to view these topics differently, but for some that takes time, and condescending responses will never help speed up the process.

7. Don't say you don't see color. I understand the sentiment behind this, but many people who say it don't realize the frustration and hurt that it often causes. If you spent your whole life in a society that sends subtle messages that your skin color is not the norm, and often that it is lesser, you might start to understand. Only now are dolls being made with diverse skin colors. Go buy a pair of "nude" pantyhose. That doesn't look like the shade of any person of color I know. People have worked hard, despite society often sending an opposite message, to be proud of the color that God gave them. I do see color. I see all the colors and shades that God gave to his people. The physical and cultural diversity in the world is amazing. We should see it and celebrate it. When someone says that they are colorblind, they mean well, but to other ears it sounds like that person wants to ignore the fact that society often sends messages that their skin color is inferior.

8. Don't use the term "white privilege." This is another hot-button phrase. I don't believe it is helpful, though, because it is usually misunderstood and it tends to shut down conversations. The phrase refers to the fact that society was built on the assumption that the white culture, and by default, white people set the norm for behavior. It doesn't mean that all white people are rich or have had everything given to them. It means that they will typically receive the benefit of the doubt and will be accepted and understood wherever they go. It means that their skin color is not going to immediately cast them into a negative light or stereotype. I have come to understand the truth of this. As I have said previously, I can do things in this country that my black sons cannot. I get the benefit of the doubt in many situations that they do not. It does not mean that they cannot overcome those things, but it does mean that they need to overcome certain things that I never had to deal with.

Because the term is so misunderstood, though, I recommend finding other ways to express the truths behind it without using that specific phrase. When you use it, you might be referring to the privilege of coming from the dominant culture, but people will think you mean something else and become defensive. Using the term "white privilege" just leads to confusion and often elicits a negative response. There can be exceptions to this, but for the most part it is wise to avoid terms that can be easily misconstrued and will shut off many people to the truths you wish to discuss before they even fully hear them.

9. Don't generalize. It is typically not helpful to say, "All white people…," or "Why do black people…," or "You people always say…," or "Why do whites…" or any other universal characterization of an entire group. It is almost always going to be untrue, and it is intellectually lazy as well. As a side note, just avoid the phrase "you people" altogether. It is dismissive and offensive.

10. Be very wary of social media. Social media can be used for positive endeavors, but it can also become extremely negative. People often say things there that they would not say in public or to people's faces. Many people are very sensitive and can only hear opinions that agree with how they think. The social media format is very prone to being misheard, misunderstood, or taken out of context. It is not the place for debates among disciples on sensitive issues. "Be wise," wrote Paul, "in the way you act toward outsiders" (Colossians 4:5). Social media is the ultimate window for outsiders. What we write can be seen instantly by anyone in the world. For some reason, we tend to forget that. I have seen disciples have very unfruitful arguments, display ungodly attitudes or thinking, and start unfriending other disciples over political or racial topics. They have forgotten the mission. Social media is a powerful tool, and I'm not saying to completely disregard it; I'm saying that we should remember that we are always on the mission of displaying the light of the kingdom and God's reconciling justice for the world. Think and pray before you post.

11. Don't harbor attitudes. If you are upset with something that a brother or sister in Christ said or did, the first step is to pray about it. Then you can think about whether you need to talk with them or not. First, consider if when you talk to them it will be for their good (Ephesians 4:29) or just to air your own frustrations. Whatever you say to them should be crafted so that it benefits them and helps them to be more like Christ. That might take a little time, but don't take too long. If there are people in the fellowship that you avoid or would not spend time with, then sin has its foot in the door. How long before the body of sin attached to that foot barges its way into your life?

12. Don't say, "You just don't get it." I understand that some conversations can be frustrating, but phrases like this are a failure on your part. We are called to be patient with one another. Sometimes people are not going to think the same way. That calls for love and forbearance. But dismissive phrases of this nature belittle others and make you look angry.

13. Don't say, "I give up." Sometimes it might be best to quietly let a situation cool down for a time. Like the previous phrase, however, this one demonstrates a level of frustration and ungodliness that is not helpful. It is one thing to say, "Perhaps we need to let this issue lie for a while and just figure out how to love each other like Christ loves us"; it is quite another to send the message that you are giving up on the other person.

14. One more thing. My wife and her best friend have requested that I add one more thing to this section. Don't walk up and touch or ask to touch a black woman's hair. Just. Don't. Do. It.

Questions for Discussion

1. Which suggestions for individual disciples do you most need to work on?

2. Which suggestion do you think the largest number of disciples in your local congregation need to implement?

3. Which suggestions for churches does your church most need to put into practice?

4. Which area in the suggestions for churches is already a strength for your church?

5. Which suggestion in the section on Michael's personal opinions is the most helpful to you?

Appendix A

Bible Study:
God's Promised Family

Genesis 12:1–3
- Approximately 4,000 years ago, God promised Abraham that the sin of all people groups would be dealt with (blessed) through the family of his descendants.
- The promise was, in essence, that there would one day be one family that consisted of all nations that would be reconciled to God.
- Q: Are you a descendant of Abraham?
- Q: If not, what does that mean for your salvation?

Isaiah 2:2–4
- Well over 1,000 years after Abraham, God repeats the promise he made to him, using different terminology but applying the same truths and principles. This points ahead to the people that he would create when the Messiah would inaugurate the kingdom of God (the mountain of the Lord).
- Q: What are the characteristics mentioned of this people?
- Q: What parts of this description of God's people sound appealing to you?

Mark 3:31–35
- In many ways throughout his ministry, Jesus announced that he was fulfilling the promise to Abraham to have one family of all nations.
- Q: Who does Jesus define as being part of his family?

Luke 13:28–29
- Jesus confirms that the people of the kingdom of God will include people from every part of the earth and from all nations.

- Dr. Martin Luther King Jr. once said that Sunday at 11 a.m. was the most segregated hour of the week.
- Q: What do you think he meant?
- Q: Why do you think we see so much division and segregation in the world if God's promised family was to consist of all nations?

Galatians 3:7–9, 26–29

- Q: What must we do, according to these verses, to become the descendants of Abraham?
- Q: How does Paul define the gospel in verse 8?
- Q: What becomes of any negative connotations of ethnic or any other differences for those in Christ?

Ephesians 2:12–19

- Paul taught the Ephesian church that Jew and Gentile were brought together into this family of all nations. This was God's plan all along—it was the fulfillment of the promises going back to Abraham.
- Paul was teaching them that they could not separate ethnically and become distinct churches or groups, because that would destroy the gospel message that they were to reflect.
- Q: Why must a church be ethnically diverse?

Revelation 7:9–10

- This is the picture of God's people.
- Q: What is significant about the group described?
- Q: Do you believe that it is God's will for his people to be a united family and to be racially, ethnically, and culturally diverse?
- Q: Why is this all so problematic for churches that are exclusively or almost entirely composed of one race?

Appendix B

Poem

The following is a spoken word poem that my younger son, Elijah, wrote and performed at school in February, 2017. It shows a perspective that I appreciate and think is worth sharing.

Who am I? Why do I look this way?
Am I black, am I white; what does society say?
My mom is what society calls black. She is from the state of Wisconsin. No, wait.
Her people are from a much farther place than that. Her roots are in Missouri. No, wait.
Her people go farther back than that. Her roots are in Mississippi. No, wait.
It goes farther back than that. Her roots are in a slave plantation and I'm not ashamed of that.
I'm proud that our people survived lash and chain, beating and pain. But wait.
Her story goes back farther than that. Her roots are in Africa, from where I just don't know.
Once they were brought to the slave fortress on the coast, well...it gets fuzzy before that.
But whenever she goes, Africans say "there is no doubt" you are Hutu, from the East.
So maybe I'm Hutu, but whatever it is, right now I'm still a beast.
My dad is what society calls white. He is from the state of Wisconsin. But wait.
It goes back farther than that. No, wait, it doesn't, his people are from Wisconsin and that's that.
But no it's not. They have a story too. They came on ships across the ocean blue.
His people came from Scotland on those boats. The only difference between my mom and dad is that his folks came without chains and on their own.
So, who am I? Why do I look this way?
I am what society calls mixed, but I don't see it that way.
I'm not half and half. I'm not a cup of coffee.
I'm all white and all black.
God made me that way. I'm proud of both. And we'll let that be that.

Notes

1. Some of the Slave Codes included allowing slave owners to retrieve their runaway slaves even from free colonies; African slaves were barred from carrying guns; interracial marriages or relationships were outlawed; and it was illegal for slaves to learn to read. Many of these Slave Codes were carried into the Jim Crow period in the post–Civil War South on a de facto basis.

2. Munn and Company (ed.). "Pygmies of the Congo." *Scientific American*, 5 Aug. 1905, 107–108.

3. Newkirk, Pamela. "The Man Who Was Caged in a Zoo." https://www.theguardian.com/world/2015/jun/03/the-man-who-was-caged-in-a-zoo. Accessed 12 Dec. 2016.

4. Darwin, Charles. *The Voyage of the Beagle: Journal of Researches into the Natural History and Geology of the Countries Visited During the Voyage of H.M.S. 'Beagle' Round the World, Under the Command of Captain FitzRoy, R.N.*, 1845. London: Wordsworth Classics Reprint, 1997, 196, 203–204.

5. Hart, Drew G. I. *Trouble I've Seen: Changing the Way the Church Views Racism*. Harrisonburg, VA: Herald Press, 2016, 82.

6. Weldon, Tim. "Study: Graduation Rate Gap Exists Between Black, White Males." www.csg.org/pubs/capitolideas/enews/issue6_3.aspx. Accessed 14 Dec. 2016.

7. Daly, Cullen, Louis Foglia and Greg Chen. "Wealth: America's Other Racial Divide" (video). http://money.cnn.com/video/news/economy/2014/12/14/the-economy-in-black--white-animation.cnnmoney/. Accessed 14 Dec. 2016.

8. Steele, Shelby. *The Content of Our Character: A New Vision of Race in America*. New York: Harper Perennial, 1990, 125.

9. Chalabi, Mona. "The 'War on Drugs' in Numbers: A Systematic Failure of Policy." https://www.theguardian.com/world/2016/apr/19/war-on-drugs-statistics-systematic-policy-failure-united-nations. Accessed 16 Dec. 2016.

10. Blum, Edward J. and Paul Harvey. *The Color of Christ: The Son of God and the Saga of Race in America*. Chapel Hill: The University of North Carolina Press, 2012, 20–21.

11. Cleveland, Christena. "Why Jesus' Skin Color Matters." http://www.christianitytoday.com/ct/2016/april/why-jesus-skin-color-matters.html. Accessed 20 Dec. 2016.

12 . An Afrikaner is typically a South African person of mainly Dutch descent. Most of the Dutch arrived in Africa in the seventeenth and eighteenth centuries.

13. Hays, J. Daniel. *From Every People and Nation: A biblical theology of race*. Downers Grove IL: InterVarsity Press, 2003, 34.

14. Ibid., 40.

15. Ibid., 44.

16. Ibid., 45.

17. Wieland, Carl. *One Human Family: The Bible, Science, Race & Culture.* Powder Springs, GA: Creation Book Publishers, 2011, 73–100.

18. Hays, 67–69.

19. For a fuller discussion of the interaction between the Cushites, Egypt, and Israel, see: Yamauchi, Edwin M. *Africa and the Bible.* Grand Rapids, MI: Baker Academic, 2004, 35–75.

20. Ibid., 84.

21. "What Is the Meaning of Esau, and Does This Make Him the White Man?" https://www.scriptureincontext.com/what-is-the-meaning-of-esau-and -does-this-make-him-the-white-man/. Accessed 21 Dec. 2016.

22. Harper, W.R. *Amos and Hosea,* International Critical Commentary. Edinburgh: T & T. Clark, 1905, 192.

23. Mays, J.L. *Amos,* Old Testament Library. Philadelphia: Westminster, 1969, 157.

24. Hays, 118.

25. Yamauchi, 146–147.

26. Ibid., 130–138.

27. Hays, 145.

28. Ibid., 177–178.

29. Emerson, Michael O. and Christian Smith. *Divided by Faith: Evangelical Religion and the Problem of Race in America.* New York: Oxford University Press, 2000, 24.

30. Crawford, Wes. *Shattering the Illusion: How African American Churches of Christ Moved from Segregation to Independence.* Abilene, TX: Abilene Christian University Press, 2013.

31. Turner, William Lofton, et al. "An Open Letter to Members of the Churches of Christ." www.christianchronicle.org/article/an-open-letter-to-members -of-the-churches-of-christ, 30 Aug. 2016. Accessed 23 Dec. 2016.

32. Boyd, Greg. *The Myth of a Christian Nation: How the Quest for Political Power Is Destroying the Church.* Grand Rapids, MI: Zondervan, 2005, 46–48.

33. Tertullian. *Ante-Nicene Fathers, Volume 3.* Peabody, MA: Hendrickson Publishers, 2004 (Reprint of 1885 edition), 45.

34. Davies, Mark. "Refusing the Hand of the Empire." www.oneworldhouse .net/2016/12/28. Accessed 13 Jan. 2017.

35. The text here refers to "nation," but that term was thought of differently in the ancient world. Nations were not the geopolitical states that we think of today, but were largely great and powerful families. The ideas of nation and family were closely linked.

36. Clement of Alexandria. *Ante-Nicene Fathers, Volume 2.* Peabody, MA: Hendrickson Publishers, 2004 (Reprint of 1885 edition), 268.

37. Justin Martyr. *Ante-Nicene Fathers, Volume 1.* Peabody, MA: Hendrickson Publishers, 2004 (Reprint of 1885 edition), 167.

38. Pollock, John. *The Apostle: A Life of Paul.* Colorado Springs, CO: David C. Cook, 2012, 18–19.

39. After the Christian communities were more established and developed and the New Covenant Scriptures were eventually recorded and spread throughout the Christian world, the visual verification in the form of the Holy Spirit coming upon people became less and less necessary and eventually faded from being the normative experience.

40. Mishnah, *Pirkei Avot* 1:6.

41. For a few examples, see: Burns, Michael. *The People of the Coming Age.* Spring, TX: Illumination Publishers, 2014, 6–8.

42. Lo, Jim. *Intentional Diversity: Creating Cross-Cultural Ministry Relationships in Your Church.* Indianapolis, IN: Wesleyan Publishing House, 2002, 23.

43. "Coming to Terms with Terms." www.blacktaxandwhitebenefits. Accessed 4 Feb. 2017.

www.ipibooks.com
Illumination Publishers

It was too late to turn back. . . .

   With a sinking heart, Johnny realized that he would have to go back down through the crypt. There was a high, spike-topped iron fence around the estate, and he didn't feel up to scaling it. But as he turned back toward the dark doorway of the chapel, he saw something. Someone was coming down the steps towards him with arms outstretched. A figure in a yellow raincoat. A figure with hollow mummy eyes and a withered mummy face and clawlike mummy hands. . . .

"Another lovely, funny, frightening thriller readers will thank Bellairs for . . . Marvelous surprises for everyone except the villains."   —*Publishers Weekly*

DISCOVER THE TERRIFYING WORLD OF JOHN BELLAIRS!

Lewis Barnavelt Mysteries

The House With a Clock in Its Walls
The Figure in the Shadows
The Letter, the Witch, and the Ring
The Ghost in the Mirror
The Vengeance of the Witch-Finder
The Doom of the Haunted Opera

Johnny Dixon Mysteries

The Curse of the Blue Figurine
The Mummy, the Will, and the Crypt
The Secret of the Underground Room
The Spell of the Sorcerer's Skull
The Drum, the Doll, and the Zombie
The Revenge of the Wizard's Ghost
The Eyes of the Killer Robot
The Trolley to Yesterday

Anthony Monday Mysteries

The Dark Secret of Weatherend
The Treasure of Alpheus Winterborn
The Mansion in the Mist

THE MUMMY, THE WILL, AND THE CRYPT

JOHN BELLAIRS

Frontispiece and maps by
Edward Gorey

PUFFIN BOOKS

PUFFIN BOOKS

Published by the Penguin Group

Penguin Books USA Inc., 375 Hudson Street, New York, New York 10014, U.S.A.

Penguin Books Ltd, 27 Wrights Lane, London W8 5TZ, England

Penguin Books Australia Ltd, Ringwood, Victoria, Australia

Penguin Books Canada Ltd, 10 Alcorn Avenue, Toronto, Ontario, Canada M4V 3B2

Penguin Books (N.Z.) Ltd, 182–190 Wairau Road, Auckland 10, New Zealand

Penguin Books Ltd, Registered Offices: Harmondsworth, Middlesex, England

First published in the United States of America in 1983
by Dial Books for Young Readers
Published in Puffin Books, 1996

9 10 8

Copyright © John Bellairs, 1983
Frontispiece and maps copyright © Edward Gorey, 1984

THE LIBRARY OF CONGRESS HAS CATALOGED THE DIAL EDITION AS FOLLOWS:

Bellairs, John. The mummy, the will, and the crypt.
Summary: Twelve-year-old Johnny Dixon and his friend Professor Childermass
look for the hidden will left by an eccentric cereal tycoon who wished to
make life difficult for his heirs after his own death by suicide.
[1. Mystery and detective stories.
2. Inheritance and succession—Fiction.] I. Title.
PZ7.B413Mu 1983 [Fic] 83-7223
ISBN 0-8037-0029-6

Puffin Books ISBN 0-14-038007-8
Printed in the United States of America

For Candice,
a fellow writer and a good friend

CHAPTER ONE

❧ ● ❧

"Professor, can we go home yet? My feet feel like they're gonna fall off."

"No," said the professor firmly. "We can *not* go home yet. We still have two more rooms full of pictures to look at, and then there's Mr. Glomus's office. No doubt there are art treasures in there. And if you are ever going to become a cultivated young man, you are going to have to learn to appreciate great art. So come along. You can rest your tired feet later."

"But, Professor . . ."

"But me no buts, John. If an old coot who's pushing seventy from the wrong side can keep on his feet, so can you. I'd hum a marching song for you, but I'm afraid that guard over there would not be pleased. I'll give you another two minutes to rest, and then we'll have to move on."

Johnny's voice was a despairing wail. *"Two minutes?"*

"Yes, two minutes. And I'll be counting them on my watch. So relax while you can."

Johnny Dixon and Professor Childermass were sitting on a padded bench in a room full of oil paintings by seventeenth-century Dutch masters with names like Rembrandt and Ruysdael and De Hooch. For hours they had been tramping through the rooms in the vast Glomus mansion—rooms full of the paintings, suits of armor, weapons, and art objects that H. Bagwell Glomus had collected during his long life. Mr. Glomus had been able to collect art because he was rich. And he had gotten rich by starting a cereal company.

A real health nut, Mr. Glomus had invented a cereal drink called Glomar. It was black and looked like coffee, but it was made out of wheat. Even though Glomar tasted terrible, people bought it because they wanted to stay healthy. Later Mr. Glomus invented Oaty Crisps, a cereal that was sort of like Kellogg's Corn Flakes. Oaty Crisps really caught on, and soon Mr. Glomus was able to build a large cereal factory in the town of Gildersleeve, Massachusetts. The factory was right across the street from Mr. Glomus's mansion, and Johnny and the professor had toured it earlier in the day.

Johnny sat still and tried to relax while the professor glowered at his pocket watch, mentally ticking off the seconds. They were an odd pair, these two. Johnny was twelve. He was pale, blond, and freckled, wore glasses, and was rather shy. The professor was short, his nose was red and pitted, and he had muttonchop whiskers that sprouted wildly from the sides of his head. The professor looked crabby, and he actually did have a rotten temper. But he was also a very kind man. He lived across the street from Johnny and his grandparents, and as strange as it may seem, he had become the boy's close friend.

Johnny needed friends. He had a bad habit of avoiding other kids his own age, and after a year of living in the town of Duston Heights, Massachusetts, he had only just begun to change. Most of the time—when he was not at home curled up with a book—Johnny preferred being with the professor.

"Well, time's up! On your feet!" The professor barked out this command and stood up. He stuffed his watch into his pants pocket and turned to Johnny.

"Oh, okay!" Johnny groaned. Wincing, he dragged himself up into a standing position.

However, the professor was not in a sympathetic mood. "What's the matter, John?" he said, in a dry, sarcastic tone. "Is it arthritis or tetanus or frostbite?"

Johnny gave the professor a dirty look. "When this is over with, I want a hot fudge sundae," he muttered sullenly. "Can we go get one?"

The professor smiled as he thought of hot fudge. As Johnny well knew, chocolate was one of the professor's obsessions. "Yes, indeed," he answered, nodding agreeably. "I was planning to do that. There is a wonderful ice cream parlor here in Gildersleeve, and they make big gloppy calorie-filled hot fudge sundaes. We will go there —*after* we visit Mr. Glomus's office. So march!"

Mr. Glomus's mansion was built like a castle, and his office was at the top of a tower at the northeast corner. Johnny and Professor Childermass had to walk down a corridor, up a flight of marble steps, down another corridor, and up a curving flight of cast iron steps before they finally got there. The furnishings in the large circular room were heavy and gloomy. There was a grandfather clock and two heavy mahogany cabinets with glass windows. Mr. Glomus's desk was made of paneled oak, and it looked as if it weighed a ton. On top was a clock made of black marble. The chairs were massive, with black leather upholstery, and there was a dark green rug. A row of narrow windows ran all the way around the room, and in the top part of each one was a piece of colored glass. Since it was a sunny day, the light that came in threw circles of red and purple and green and blue light on the floor, the only cheerful things to be seen.

As Johnny and the professor entered the room they suddenly realized that they had walked in on a guided tour. Clustered together near the desk was a small group of elderly men and women. The guide, a rather bored-looking young woman with a portable loudspeaker in her hand, was rattling off a speech that she must have memorized. Her voice had a singsongy rise and fall, and from the expression on her face she might as well have been talking about the price of beef in Argentina.

". . . and so, in the year 1936, although he had acquired great wealth and built up a thriving business, Mr. Glomus became depressed. He worried and stayed awake nights and began acting strangely. His family doctor advised him to try new things to break out of his rut. So Mr. Glomus began to study demonology and witchcraft, reading all the great books that have been written on this rather sinister subject. He took a trip to Europe and came back with some objects that had once been associated with the practice of witchcraft. Some of these may be seen in the small cabinet by the grandfather clock, including the so-called magic mirror that once belonged to Dr. John Dee, the sixteenth-century sorcerer. But, alas, in spite of his newfound hobby Mr. Glomus continued to feel depressed. And on the evening of November 13, 1936, Mr. H. Bagwell Glomus left his office—this very office that you are standing in—and he went home and drank a mixture of strychnine and cognac. The next morning his servants found him dead on the floor of his bedroom."

Several people gasped. The professor smiled knowingly and nudged Johnny in the ribs.

"Pay attention," he whispered. "This next part is really interesting."

"On the morning following Mr. Glomus's death," the guide went on, "a sealed envelope was found on his desk. In the envelope was a note that revealed the startling fact that Mr. Glomus had *not* left a will!"

There were more gasps and cries of "Oh, no!" and "How 'bout that!" One old lady with a raspy, irritating voice spoke up and said, "What happened to all his moolah, then?"

The guide coughed and looked pained. "Mr. Glomus's . . . uh, his money was divided up among his heirs according to the laws of the Commonwealth of Massachusetts. But this is not the end of the story. It seems that soon after Mr. Glomus's death some odd notes were found in his diary. The members of the Glomus family have deduced from them that a will does indeed exist. And they think that Mr. Glomus left behind clues to its whereabouts. The clues are supposedly right here in this very room!"

Immediately everybody in the group began gawking, turning their heads this way and that. But with a smug smile on her face, the guide went on.

"A great effort has been made to keep things in this office *exactly* as they were on the day Mr. Glomus died. And Mrs. Annabelle Glomus, Mr. Glomus's widow, has offered a reward of $10,000 to anyone who can figure out the hiding place of the will." The guide sighed. "Puzzle experts—people who know about cryptograms and codes—have been brought here from all over the world in an attempt to figure out where the mysterious will is hidden. Many have tried, but all have failed. It is generally thought, though, that the clues are to be found among this rather odd collection of objects on the library table over there. If you will all follow me, please."

With a lot of shuffling and whispering, the group followed the guide across the room to a large walnut table. The tourists talked a good deal among themselves about the objects. Some of them snapped pictures. Poor Johnny kept trying to get a good look at the table, but he couldn't see a blessed thing. He was blocked by several people, but most of all by a tall and very fat man who wore a New York Yankees baseball cap.

"Now, then," said the guide, smiling politely, "this concludes our tour. There is another group due to arrive in a very few minutes, so I must ask you to follow me downstairs to the main hall, where souvenirs may be purchased. Thank you."

Muttering and snapping still more pictures, the group filed out of the room. Johnny and the professor stepped aside to let them pass. Now the two of them were alone, with no one blocking their view. Johnny looked around. Although he could peer at the tantalizing objects on the table now, he decided to save that for last. With the professor following close behind, he started on a little tour of the room. There was Mr. Glomus's desk, with its gloomy marble clock and some pens and pencils laid out in a neat row on the dusty green blotter. Johnny's gaze traveled along the curve of the wall, past the grandfather clock. Between two windows was a china closet, and next to it stood the cabinet with the witchcraft collection in it. Farther along the wall were some paintings in heavy gilt frames. One showed a sunset scene in the White Mountains of New Hampshire. Another showed the Hudson River near West Point. Then there were some chairs, a marble bust of Mr. Glomus on a fluted column, and finally the library table with its peculiar assortment of objects. Johnny walked up to the table and stood with arms folded, looking down. At the front of the table was a big sign that said DO NOT TOUCH. Behind the sign in one corner of the table was a very handsome walnut-and-ivory chess set. It stood on a polished wooden board, and the pieces were all lined up the way they are at the start of a game. Next to the chess set lay an old, yellowed Greek newspaper. It was folded neatly in half so that the top part of the front page showed. The large black letters at the top told—Johnny figured—the name of the newspaper:

ΕΘΝΙΚΟΣ ΚΗΡΥΞ

The second word in the title had a circle drawn around it in red ink. The third item on the table was an old, weathered signboard. It was shield-shaped, with a fancy scalloped border at the top. Johnny could see two rusted screw-eyes sticking out of the top of the board, and he figured that the sign had once hung from a crosspiece on a post or on an iron bracket of some kind. The lettering on the sign was faded, but it could be read. It said YE OLDE TEA SHOPPE. That was it—there was nothing else on the table.

The professor stood watching Johnny with amusement. "Well?" he said in a raspy, needling voice. "Have you figured out where Mr. Glomus's will is? You've had oodles of time."

Johnny gave the professor an exasperated glance. "Aw, come on, Professor! You know darned well that nobody could figure this out! Not even if they had a million and a half years to do it!"

The professor grinned and rubbed his chin. "I will admit," he said dryly, "that the puzzle is a tough one. What possible connection can there be between a chess set, a Greek newspaper, and a sign from somebody's tea shop? Of course, there may not be any connection at all. What I mean is, if I were you, I wouldn't beat my brains out over this ridiculous puzzle. As the young lady pointed out, Mr. Glomus was a bit sick in the head at the end of his life. He may have just wanted to irritate his relatives by holding out the possibility that there was a will after all."

Johnny was about to open his mouth to say something when a mean-looking woman with narrow hornrimmed glasses appeared at the door.

"You two will have to leave now," she snapped. "Didn't you hear what the guide said? There's another group due in."

The professor turned to her with a malicious gleam in his eye. He hated bossy, officious people. "Is it your job to be nasty and impolite?" he asked. "Or are you just doing what comes naturally?"

The woman's mouth dropped open, and while she stood there looking astonished, Johnny and the professor walked out past her and down the stairs. As they went, the professor began to chuckle in a self-satisfied way.

A few minutes later Johnny and the professor were sitting in an ice cream parlor that had old-fashioned wooden booths and Tiffany glass lampshades and a marble counter and even a jukebox. The jukebox was playing "Come On-A My House," a song that the professor hated, and he flinched now and then while digging into his hot fudge sundae. Johnny was having a tin roof sundae, which is a hot fudge sundae with peanuts on top. And as he slurped and munched and crunched he felt at peace with the world. But Johnny liked puzzles—chess puzzles and picture puzzles and Chinese puzzles and all the other kinds—and so his mind kept drifting back to Mr. Glomus's office and the mysterious array of objects on the table.

The professor was a shrewd man, and he could tell from the expression on Johnny's face that he was still wrestling with the problem. "Come on, John," he said. "Give it up! It's a puzzle that can't be solved. It's like the Mad Hatter's riddle: *Why is a raven like a writing desk?* There isn't any solution."

Johnny popped a fudge-covered peanut into his mouth. He chewed it slowly and stubbornly. "Professor," he said thoughtfully, "what do you think would *really* happen if somebody found Mr. Glomus's will?"

The professor shrugged. "The law divided up Mr. Glomus's estate among his heirs. His wife and his two worthless sons got some money, and so did his two surviving brothers, and his sister. If a will turned up, there'd be fights in court and yelling and screaming, some reshuffling of the money, and then a lot of hatefulness and ill will. It'd be like setting off a bomb in a fireworks factory."

Johnny laughed at the professor's description. But then he paused. "Hey, wait a minute! If it's gonna cause so much trouble to find the will, how come Mrs. Glomus wants to find it?" he said.

The professor licked his spoon pensively. "Well," he said slowly, "I don't know much about Mrs. Glomus, but I suspect she is one of these fussy, finicky types that think everything in life should come out neatly, with straight edges and all. Rich people are *supposed* to leave wills, and so it may really gripe her to think that her late hubby didn't leave one. Or maybe she's just greedy. She may not be satisfied with the money she got under the present arrangement and may be gambling that she'll get more if a will is found. I don't know. But if I were her, I'd leave things the way they are. If a will is found, she may lose her ten thousand dollars, and more besides."

Suddenly the professor jumped up. "See here, now! I've had enough of chewing over the affairs of the Glomus family. It's time for us to pay up and hit the road, because I have mountains of papers to get through tonight. Term papers! *Arrgh!* Reams and reams of indigestible nonsense! But they have to be done, I suppose. Come on, John. Let's get a move on."

Later, as the car roared on through the twilight toward Duston Heights, Johnny sat slumped in the front seat with his eyes closed. It had been a busy, exciting day, and now the motion of the car, the droning of the motor, and the whiz of passing cars were putting him to sleep.

CHAPTER TWO

✦

It was a few weeks later, a chilly night in late September. Johnny was walking home from a Monday night Boy Scout meeting at the Methodist church, wearing his new Boy Scout uniform with the red neckerchief and the bright red-and-white numerals *112* sewed on the right shoulder. For months the professor and Johnny's gramma and grandpa had been trying to persuade him to join. They were worried that Johnny was too much of a loner, and they wanted him to break out of his shell and make some friends. And so he had finally signed up with Troop 112. The first meeting had not been much. Before the scoutmaster showed up, the boys spent their time horsing around, playing games of Steal the Bacon (using a knotted towel for the bacon) and throwing the cakes of Ivory soap at each other that they were supposed to be carving into little animals and things like that. But when the meeting started and things quieted down a bit, Johnny decided he liked the scoutmaster and most of the other boys too. He was stubborn about changing his mind, but he was beginning to think that maybe—just maybe—this Boy Scout business was a good idea.

As Johnny walked on, all sorts of thoughts came crowding into his mind. He thought about his mother, who had been in her grave for over a year now. He thought about his dad, who was flying a jet for the Air Force, over in Korea. The year was 1951, and the Korean War was raging. Mr. Dixon didn't have to be over there, because he had already served in the Air Force in World War Two. Besides, he was the only surviving parent of a dependent child. But he had volunteered anyway, because he liked flying. Johnny did not understand why his dad wanted to do such a dangerous thing. He didn't understand why the Americans had to go help the South Koreans fight the North Koreans and the Chinese Communists. But he did know one thing— he knew that he was scared. Sometimes before he went to bed at night Johnny would imagine seeing his dad's jet plane hurtling through the sky. Suddenly it would burst, exploding in flame and smoke, with pieces flying everywhere. Johnny would close his eyes and shudder. He worried about his dad a lot. Sometimes when the mail arrived on Saturday afternoons, Johnny wondered if there was an official U.S. government telegram in the pile, a telegram that began *We regret to inform you.* . . .

Johnny wished that he could stop worrying about his dad and just go along with what the professor had told him: There was one big rule in life—the things you worried about never happened, and the things that happened were never the ones you expected. Not that this bit of advice helped Johnny much. It simply meant that he spent more time guessing at what the unexpected disasters in his life would be.

When Johnny started up the walk toward his front door, he was suddenly hit with the chilling feeling that something was wrong. Quickly he glanced toward the big bay window. The window was dark. This was odd, because usually at this time of night Gramma would be in the living room watching TV. The Dixons were poor, and they hadn't had a television set until recently, when Professor Childermass had bought them one as a present. At first Gramma had been suspicious of this newfangled invention, convinced that the rays it emitted were harmful. But before long she was a regular TV addict, watching the *Kate Smith Hour*, Milton Berle, and soap operas like *Search for Tomorrow*. But no gray aquarium glow hovered about the walls tonight. Johnny wondered what Gramma was doing.

Oh, well. She might be up to any number of things. She might be lying down upstairs with a headache—she had had a lot of headaches lately, for some reason. She might be making fudge or a lemon meringue pie in the kitchen. She might be in the bathroom. So Johnny shrugged and started up the steps. *Slam* went the screen door. He walked across the porch and opened the front door. Now he was in the long, musty-smelling hall that ran from the front to the back of the house. With a strong sense of foreboding, Johnny opened the door to the living room and peered in. It was dark. Johnny could see various shapes: the rounded bulk of the brown armchair, the boxy shape of the television set. And as his eyes got used to the dark, he saw his grandmother sitting, rigid and still, on the couch. Her glasses glimmered faintly, but she was not moving a muscle. Terror clutched at Johnny's heart. *What was the matter with her?*

Johnny swallowed several times. When he finally spoke, his voice was weak. "Gramma?"

"Hullo, John. How're you?" Gramma sounded dull and lifeless, like a recording.

Not knowing what to say, Johnny hovered in the doorway. Then Gramma spoke again, unexpectedly, in the same flat voice.

"You're home from school early, arncha? They letcha out early, did they?"

Early. It was nine o'clock at night. Gramma had gone crazy. Or else she was drunk. But, no, she was death on liquor, wouldn't even stay in the same room with people who were drinking. Johnny felt sick. How had this happened? What could he do? He wanted to run out the door yelling and screaming. But instead he stood rooted to the spot. Suddenly he heard footsteps behind him. Somebody was coming up the walk. The sound broke Johnny's trance, and he dashed down the hall to flip the switch that turned on the porch light. When he stepped out onto the porch, he saw his grampa and Professor Childermass. Even in the pale light he could see that their faces were grim and haggard. And Johnny knew in a flash that they too knew something was wrong with Gramma.

The screen door opened, and the two old men entered. Grampa walked slowly forward and put his hand gently on Johnny's shoulder.

"Johnny, we hafta talk to you," he said quietly.

Johnny followed the professor and Grampa through the house to the kitchen. Grampa switched on the kitchen light, closed the door, and went to the stove to turn on the gas under the teakettle. Johnny could see now that Grampa's eyes were red-rimmed, and there were wet streaks on his loose, leathery cheeks. He had been crying.

The professor stood in the middle of the room with his arms folded. He stared hard at the floor. "John," he said, "there is something the matter with your grandmother. I'm sorry you had to come upon her alone like that, but I was across the street with your grampa. He was . . . well, he was terribly upset, as you might imagine."

Johnny's eyes were wide with fear. And now his voice trembled as he spoke. "Professor, what is it? Why . . . why's she actin' that way?"

The professor looked forlornly at Johnny. He opened his mouth to speak, but all he said was "My cousin . . ." Then he snapped his mouth shut suddenly and turned to stare at the wallpaper. His face became a frozen, secretive mask.

Johnny wondered for a second, but then it hit him. He knew what the professor had been about to say: *My cousin Bea died of a brain tumor.* Many times Johnny had heard the professor talking to Grampa about how Cousin Bea had had a brain tumor, only Doc Schermerhorn diagnosed it as bad teeth, so she died. A brain tumor. It sounded so horrible, so hopeless. Johnny hoped that the professor was wrong.

Grampa gently put his hand on Johnny's shoulder. "We called the . . . the hospital," he said in a broken, tearful voice. "The ambulance is comin' to get her."

Johnny looked dully at Grampa. He waited for Grampa to take his hand away, and then he walked over to a kitchen chair and slumped into it. He felt stunned, as if he had been hit on the head with a baseball bat. He couldn't cry. He couldn't feel anything or think anything except *This isn't really happening. It's not real.* In spite of what the professor had said, the things you are afraid of sometimes really *do* happen. And when they do, it feels worse than any nightmare.

The red electric clock over the stove buzzed, but

there was no other sound in the room. Finally the professor coughed. He turned and took Grampa firmly by the arm.

"Come on, Henry," he said in a low voice. "I know it's not going to be any fun, but we have to get Kate ready to go. The ambulance'll be here any minute. The sooner the doctors examine your wife, the sooner they can start fixing her up. She may not know why we want her to go, but . . . well, I don't expect she'll give us a whole lot of trouble. Are you with me?"

Grampa nodded. Then he opened the kitchen door, and he and the professor went out. Johnny followed them timidly through the dining room and the front room to the parlor. The professor went into the darkness, and a few minutes later he came out with Gramma holding on to his arm. She shuffled along uncertainly, and Johnny noticed that she was wearing her blue cloth slippers, the ones with the little blue felt rosettes. Her stockings were wrinkly and saggy, and her face was blank. She looked as if she did not have the slightest idea of what was happening.

The ambulance arrived. It stood in front of the house with its red light flashing. Two attendants got out and took a wheeled cot out of the back of the vehicle. They helped Gramma down the front steps, gently eased her onto the cot, and wheeled the cot out to the ambulance. Gramma was lifted inside, and the rear doors were closed. The big white vehicle roared away, its siren screaming. The professor watched it go for a second, and then he went across the street to get his car—he was going to drive Grampa to the hospital. As he was about to leave the house, Grampa turned to Johnny and asked him if he wanted to go with them. But Johnny said no, he would stay home. He stood in the doorway watching as the car backed out of the driveway and rolled away down the street.

While Gramma was in the hospital the days passed in a blur for Johnny. During school he had a hard time keeping his mind on his work because he was thinking about her so much. He told Sister Mary Anthony, his eighth grade teacher, about what had happened, and she asked the whole class to pray for Johnny's grandmother. And each day, after school had let out, Johnny went into the gloomy, echoing church next door and lit a candle in front of the Blessed Virgin's altar. Kneeling at the altar rail, he prayed that nothing bad would happen to his gramma.

Finally the news came. Yes, Gramma had a brain tumor. The doctor at the hospital explained to Johnny and Grampa that there were two kinds of tumors, benign and malignant. A benign tumor was just a little lump in the brain. It might grow, but it usually wouldn't do any harm. A malignant tumor would grow and eventually kill the patient. Unfortunately you couldn't tell if a tumor was benign or malignant until you actually operated and took it out. The doctor was an honest sort of person, and he laid it on the line: It was going to be a dangerous operation, especially for someone as old as Gramma was. Something might go wrong, or they might not get all of the tumor out. Everybody would just have to sit tight.

Grampa drove Johnny home after the session with the doctor. Neither of them said a word until the car had stopped in the driveway and Grampa muttered, "Gotta go fix supper." Then he got out of the car, closed the door, and loped off toward the house. Johnny watched him go. Grampa looked utterly defeated. His shoulders sagged, and his head hung. Tears came to Johnny's eyes, but with a snorting sound and a shudder he forced the sobs down. He got out of the car and was starting to walk down the driveway to the garage when he heard someone call.

"John! Over here!"

Johnny turned. It was the professor. He was standing in his front yard with a golf club in his hand. The professor played a perfectly terrible game of golf, but he kept at it anyway. Sometimes he practiced his swing in his backyard with a little plastic practice ball. The practice swings didn't help his game any, but—as he often said, sourly—he had chopped some lovely big holes in his back lawn.

"Johnny! Come here a minute. Can I talk to you?"

Johnny walked back up the driveway and across the street.

"Yeah, Professor? Whaddaya want?" The tone of his voice showed how rotten he felt.

The professor smiled sadly. "Is it as bad as all that?" he asked.

Johnny nodded gloomily. "It sure is. We talked to the doctor and he said—"

"Yes. I know. I called up the doctor earlier and got a full report. It's awful, I know, but . . . well, let's hope everything will turn out okay."

"Fat chance," said Johnny bitterly. He was in such a black mood that he did not want to be cheered up, and he did not want the professor to be painting fake rosy pictures for him.

"John," said the professor gravely, and he walked closer to the boy. He put his arm around him and smiled in a pained way. "I think you need to get away from here. I think you need to go on a vacation."

CHAPTER THREE

❦

Johnny was stunned—stunned, shocked, and angry. It was as if the professor had said, *Come on! Let's throw a party!* When he tried to speak, Johnny found that all he could do was splutter and stammer.

"Professor, I . . . I mean how could you . . . with, with, you know. . . ."

The professor was unmoved. He did not act as if he had said anything outrageous. "I mean it, John. It may sound a bit unlikely to you right now, but . . . well, tell you what. After supper I'm going to be making a cake, and I'd appreciate some kitchen help. Why don't you come over after you've eaten, and I'll explain my immodest proposal, okay?"

Johnny just stared at the professor. He was genuinely puzzled. He knew that the professor was not a hard or unfeeling person. Maybe when he had explained what he had on his mind, it would all make sense. "Okay," he said hesitantly. "I'll . . . I'll come over later." And Johnny turned abruptly and walked back to the house.

Supper that night was really pretty awful. It was another example of grampa's horrible cooking: the hamburgers were not only overdone, they were charred. Instead of mashed potatoes there was a slice of Wonder bread. And the canned peas had been cooked so long that they tasted like mushy green spit wads. After one bite of the hamburger Johnny went out to the kitchen cupboard and brought out all the sauces and condiments he could find: A-1 sauce, ketchup, mustard, and Heinz 57 sauce. And with the aid of these he managed to choke the food down. Grampa never said a word all through the meal. It was painful just to look at him. As soon as he could, Johnny excused himself and went across the street.

When Johnny arrived, the professor was all done up in one of his chef's outfits—a big white apron and a puffy white hat. On the kitchen table were boxes of flour and sugar, a bottle of milk, a can of baking powder, and some tiny bottles of vanilla extract and artificial food coloring. In front of the professor was a big green crockery bowl with some creamy yellow cake mixture in it. When he saw Johnny, the professor looked up quickly and grinned. Using a big wooden spoon, he began to stir the batter.

"Now, then," he said brusquely, "where were we? Ah, yes. I was trying to convince you to go away for a while. Do you want to know why? Well, it's all very simple. You're not doing your gramma any good by being here. You may think that you are, but you're not. If you go to visit her in the hospital, you'll find that she's in a rather strange state. And after the operation she'll be sleeping a lot. When you're at home, you'll see that your grampa is not much fun to be with. The two of you will just sit around making each other moody."

The professor paused. He dipped his finger into the raw batter, came up with a big sticky glob, and put it in his mouth. The professor had a passion for raw cake batter. "So, John," he went on as he stirred, "I think you should go somewhere. As you know, next week is Massachusetts State Physical Fitness Week."

Johnny was dumbfounded. What was the connection between Physical Fitness Week and going on a vacation? Between October 1 and 7 the kids in all the grade schools in the state would go to lectures and slide shows and movies and panel discussions on physical fitness instead of attending classes. In Duston Heights there would be special events like relay races and baseball and tug-of-wars every day out at the athletic field. All this left Johnny cold. He was not a big athlete. He could just barely play softball, but not well enough to please the tough kids who ran things on the St. Michael's

School playground. At all other sports he was a complete washout. And so he was expecting to spend Physical Fitness Week standing on the sidelines and watching other kids have fun.

"Yeah," Johnny said sullenly. "I know all about Physical Whoozis Week. What the heck does that have to do with going someplace on a vacation?"

The professor held up a gooey forefinger. "It has this to do with it, my fine feathered friend! As part of the big whoopy-doo of this wonderful week a group of Boy Scouts from this area is going to take a bus trip up into the White Mountains, to a scout camp near Lake Chocorua. When they get there, they're going to spend a glorious, delightful week hiking along mountain trails and singing around campfires and having a grand time. You'll enjoy it—I know you will. And it'll be a million times better than moping around at home. What do you say, eh? Can I twist your arm?"

Johnny looked doubtful. The whole thing sounded like it would be fun, but, well, he didn't think he ought to be having fun right now. It would be like going to a movie on the afternoon of someone's mother's funeral.

"I don't think Grampa would want me to go," he said.

The professor snorted and added a handful of sugar to the batter. "Oh, yes, he would. He might deny it, but at this point I think he'd be extremely glad to have you somewhere else for a short time."

Johnny picked up the measuring spoons and clacked them together. He was really torn. He liked the Boy

Scouts, and he loved the White Mountains. And hiking was something he could do.

"It'd cost a lot of money, wouldn't it?"

"Oh, I'll pay for it," said the professor, shrugging carelessly. "What's the use of having money in the bank if you can't do something nice with it? Now, come on. Be a good sport and say yes."

Johnny was still uncertain, and since the professor had decided that no more good would come of coaxing and wheedling, they agreed that Johnny would think about the professor's plan until tomorrow.

Johnny stayed and helped the professor with his baking. The cake came out perfectly, and after the professor made Ma Perkins's Own Spice Frosting, the two of them sat down to gobble. Then the professor went back across the street with Johnny and half of the cake on a plate inside an aluminum cake carrier. Johnny went up to his room to read while the professor sat down to talk to his old friend Grampa Dixon. He wanted to visit with Grampa to cheer him up. And of course he also wanted to do a little persuading.

A few days later, on Sunday, October 1, Johnny was riding northward in a school bus full of Boy Scouts. In the metal rack above his seat was a backpack, his cardboard suitcase, and his sleeping bag. Johnny was wearing his Boy Scout uniform, and all around him were other boys in uniform. They had just finished singing "Ninety-eight Bottles of Beer on the Wall," the song that is calculated to drive bus drivers out of their minds. Now, while most of the boys were talking and laughing and pestering each other, Johnny sat quietly, staring at the ring binder filled with notes on his lap. On the seat next to him was an illustrated guidebook from the Glomus mansion. He was working on the Glomus puzzle, trying to make sense out of the objects on the late cereal king's office table. He didn't really expect to solve the mystery; this was just something he had brought along to pass the time. As usual, Johnny was approaching the whole thing logically, trying to list all the qualities of the objects on the table, but oddly enough, logic wasn't helping him much.

CHESS SET
Material: wood and ivory
Arrangement: just the way it is before a game starts.
Design: Staunton

NEWSPAPER
Language: Greek
Material: coarse paper known as newsprint
*Lettering of headline: large black letters in Greek
    alphabet. Word circled in red is ΚΗΡΥΞ. It means
    "herald." Whole title ΕΘΝΙΚΟΣ ΚΗΡΥΞ
    means* NATIONAL HERALD.

SIGNBOARD
Material: wood. Don't know what kind.
*Notes: Wood is pretty beat up. Probably was
    outdoors for a long time. Blue letters say*
    YE OLDE TEA SHOPPE.

Johnny looked glumly at the orderly list that he had made. No, it was not much help. On the other hand, he was proud of what he had been able to find out about this curious collection of things. The guidebook had helped a lot. It had a close-up color picture of the table with the puzzle on it, and another close-up photo of the Greek newspaper. The professor had told Johnny the meaning of the Greek words. And Johnny himself had added the information about the Staunton design. Johnny was a chess nut, and he knew that the Staunton design was the most common. All this information was fine, just fine, except for one tiny little thing: It didn't bring Johnny any closer to solving the puzzle.

Johnny sighed. He picked up the guidebook that lay beside him and began to leaf absentmindedly through it. He looked again at the picture of the table with its mysterious collection of objects. This was all he had to go on. It would have been nice if he could have popped back to Gildersleeve, where the mansion was, before the bus trip began. But Gildersleeve was forty miles from Duston Heights—the trip would've taken too much time. Still, it would have been nice to have another look at the clues. *Clues, shmooze!* he said to himself as he slammed the book shut and threw it back down on the seat. The professor was probably right. The puzzle was a cruel, pointless joke. It could not be solved and was not meant to be solved. It was just something that Mr. Glomus had whipped up to drive his family crazy. Why was Johnny so interested in this idiotic puzzle, anyway?

Was it just because he liked difficult mental challenges? No, there was something else too: There was the reward. Ten thousand dollars for anyone who could figure out the hiding place of the will. He would use the money to pay for Gramma's operation. Johnny knew that operations were expensive. Gramma and Grampa were poor.

There was one more reason why Johnny was going after the will: Like a lot of people, he was always hoping that someday he would get to do something terribly distinguished and exciting, like finding a lost city buried under the sands of Egypt. The Glomus will was like a lost city to Johnny. If he found it, he would get a reward, he would become famous, and he would be able to do something wonderfully generous and kind for his grandparents. What more could anyone ask?

Johnny gazed dreamily out the window of the bus. The mountains were getting closer. In the distance, on the horizon, he could see long rumpled gray and blue lines. Lazily Johnny leaned back in his seat and wondered what the week at Camp Chocorua would be like.

CHAPTER FOUR

❧ • ❧

Lake Chocorua looks as if it had been intended by God to be a mirror for noble Mount Chocorua. And Mount Chocorua deserves a mirror, because it is a mountain that has *presence*. It stands out. Most of the White Mountains of New Hampshire have been worn down by millions of years of wind and weather into gently rounded, tree-covered humps. But at the top of Mount Chocorua a sharp horn of rock thrusts up into the sky. When Johnny first saw it, the mountain was at its most beautiful. It was the height of the fall foliage season, and the maple trees that grow on the mountain's sides were lit up with brilliant reds and oranges. Johnny looked up and hoped for a day when the wind wouldn't blow, so that he would see Mount Chocorua perfectly reflected in the still waters of its own special lake.

The bus followed New Hampshire State Route 16 past the mountain and the lake onto a dirt road that branched off from the highway. It crossed a rickety wooden bridge until it came to a wooded area where rich people had their summer homes.

In a clearing in the middle of a big patch of wooded land stood Camp Chocorua, which consisted of four two-story log buildings and a flagpole. Johnny and the other boys were assigned their bunks in these buildings. That night a fire was made in the big brick fireplace in one of the dormitory buildings, and the boys and the counselors gathered around to sing songs and tell ghost stories and eat popcorn and drink cider. The next day the camp routine would begin.

On Tuesday morning, after breakfast, Johnny was hiking up a dusty road with a group of other boys. Everybody was in uniform, and Mr. Brentlinger, the head counselor, led the way. Mr. Brentlinger was a big, hulking, rather kindly man who loved to sing songs. As they tramped along, raising clouds of yellow dust, they sang "We're on the Upward Trail," "The Happy Wanderer," and the ever-popular Army hiking song, "Sound Off!" It was a warm day, and Johnny was happy. Here he was, with kids who talked and joked and played games with him. It felt good, and he didn't want it to end.

Around noon the hikers stopped for lunch. The place

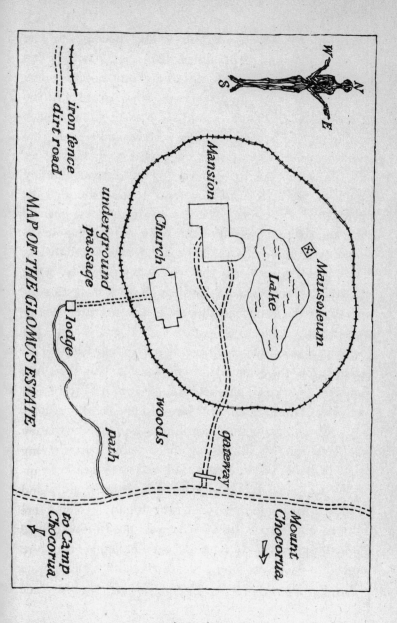

MAP OF THE GLOMUS ESTATE

⊢—⊢—⊢ iron fence
= = = = dirt road

Mansion

Church

underground passage

□ lodge

path

woods

Lake

⊠ Mausoleum

gateway

Mount Chocorua →

to Camp Chocorua ↓

N W E S

where they stopped was interesting because of the strange collection of buildings that stood nearby. The boys were standing on the rim of a gently sloping ridge. On their left the ground fell away fairly steeply. In the valley below them they could see a small stone church by a quiet lake, a grove of willow trees, and a grim gray stone mansion with clusters of spires, minarets, turrets, and funny bulbous domes. And in the distance Johnny could see the high rusty iron fence that surrounded the grounds of the estate. There were iron gates, chained shut, and a rutted disused road that wound away from the fence right up to the road the boys were standing on. The place where it met the road was marked by a big stone arch. Monster heads and leering human faces were carved on the arch, and there was also a name: STAUN-TON HAROLD.

Johnny stood with his sandwich in his hand as he gazed up at the arch. *Staunton Harold*. The name was familiar, somehow, but he couldn't for the life of him say why. Hmm. Staunton Harold. Had he ever known anybody named Harold Staunton? Nope. Not that he could remember. He shrugged, sat down on the low stone wall that bordered the road, and started eating.

"Looks like Dracula's castle, doesn't it?" said a boy who was sitting on the wall near Johnny. Johnny had noticed him before, because he was so odd-looking. He looked like somebody who had been pulled at from both ends. His face was long and droopy, and his ears stuck out. He had a long, blunt-ended nose and greasy, curly black hair. His gangly arms hung down, and his legs were long too. His feet were enormous. The shoes he was wearing were the kind that kids call gunboats. The boy was eating a huge ham-and-cheese sandwich, and when he stopped chewing, his mouth curled up into a friendly, sarcastic grin.

"What's your name?" he asked.

Johnny smiled shyly. "John Dixon. What's yours?"

The boy grimaced. "Byron Ferguson, believe it or not. But I wish you'd call me Fergie, on account of nobody in their right mind wants to be called Byron." Fergie took another bite of his sandwich. He chewed meditatively and jerked his thumb at the cluster of buildings. "You own this place?"

Johnny stared for a second, but then he realized that the kid was joking. "Oh, sure," he said, grinning. "It's all mine, and I'm Count Dracula. I eat and chew with the lower intestinal tract! I bite the head from the body and suck the blood! Born in Madagascar in 1892! Shot dead and come to life again!" This last part was a sideshow barker's routine that Johnny's dad had memorized and recited so many times that it had worn a groove in Johnny's memory.

Fergie laughed and spat bits of sandwich across the grass. "Where the heck'd you learn *that*?"

Johnny shrugged. "Oh, I know lots of things like that. I know poems and weird facts and all kinds of stuff."

Fergie turned to him suddenly. There was a gleam in his eye. "What happened to the Colossus of Rhodes?" he asked.

Johnny was startled. All he knew was that the Colossus of Rhodes was a huge bronze statue that had been one of the Seven Wonders of the World at one time and that it wasn't around anymore.

"Time's up," snapped Fergie. He grinned triumphantly. "Don't know? Well, it fell down during an earthquake and got sold to a Saracen junk dealer."

Johnny's eyes narrowed. He was not going to take this lying down. "Name the eight guys who killed Julius Caesar," he said.

This one stumped Fergie. He said he didn't know, and Johnny proudly rattled off the eight Roman names. Fergie looked at him with admiration, and Johnny realized that they were going to become friends.

Fergie and Johnny talked a blue streak to each other all during the rest of the hike. Johnny told Fergie about the professor, and about his dad, and Gramma's upcoming operation. At dinnertime that night the two boys met outside the door of the dining hall so they could get a seat together and talk some more. Tonight dinner consisted of hot dogs on buns, potato chips, baked beans, and "bug juice"—otherwise known as Kool-Aid. Soon Fergie and Johnny were seated across from each other at one of the long tables. They talked about baseball. Since Johnny wore glasses, he was naturally an expert on bespectacled players. Dom DiMaggio was a special favorite of his, and he had been to Red Sox games at Fenway Park, where the kids chanted:

> He's better than his brother Joe,
> Do-mi-nic Di-Mag-gi-o!

Next the boys went on to players who had other disabilities. Like Monty Stratton, who pitched with a wooden leg, and Mordecai Brown of the Cubs, who had only three fingers on his pitching hand. But in the midst of all this odd-fact fun, Johnny suddenly grew thoughtful and silent.

Fergie stared. " 'Smatter? Somethin' on your mind?"

"Yeah. I keep thinkin' about that name on that stone arch. It . . . well, it kinda reminds me of somethin'. I dunno what, though."

Fergie shrugged. "Well, it'll come to you in the middle of the night. That's what my mom always says."

Johnny mumbled "Yeah" and went on thinking about Staunton Harold. Later, after dinner, he went to the rec room with Fergie and played a couple of games of chess. Then, around ten, he dragged his weary, aching body up to his room. Johnny had a double room that he shared with a fat, obnoxious kid named Duane Eckelbecker, or "Double-decker" Eckelbecker, as he was known. When Johnny walked in, he found Eckelbecker sprawled on his cot, reading a comic book.

"H'lo, Duane," he said.

Eckelbecker grunted. He flipped a page and went on reading.

Johnny sat down on his cot and picked up the blue binder that had his Glomus puzzle stuff inside. He reached over to the bureau drawer and dug out a sheaf of letter paper and some envelopes. Then, using the blue binder as a desk, Johnny started writing. He wrote a letter to his grandmother in the hospital and another to his grandfather and one to the professor. In his letter to Grampa, he asked if Gramma was okay and when the operation was going to be. Then he folded the letters neatly, put them into the envelopes, and got out the address list that was tucked into a pocket inside the front cover of the binder. But just as he was beginning to address the first letter, he stopped. His pen halted in midstroke.

He had thought of something.

Quickly Johnny flipped open the binder. His eyes traveled down the page. *Chess Set . . . Design: Staunton.* Then, farther down the page, Johnny found the word in the Greek newspaper that was circled in red. The word *ΚΗΡΥΞ*, which meant "herald."

Staunton. Herald. Staunton Harold.

What did it mean? Was it all a crazy coincidence? Johnny's mind began to race madly. Then suddenly he jumped up. There was something he had to know. Eckelbecker looked at Johnny with sluggish curiosity as he raced for the door, opened it, and slammed it behind him.

With the binder still in his hands, Johnny ran downstairs to the dining room. The huge room was mostly dark, but a fire was crackling in the big brick fireplace, and shadows danced over the trophies and drinking mugs that littered the stone mantelpiece. In a big leather armchair before the fire sat Mr. Brentlinger. His legs were stretched out comfortably in front of him, and he was puffing on a big briar pipe. When Johnny saw Mr. Brentlinger, he paused. He was scared of counselors and teachers and policemen and other grown-ups who had authority over him. On the other hand, he knew that Mr. Brentlinger was a very nice, easygoing guy. And Johnny also knew that he would go out of his mind if he didn't find out the things that he wanted to know.

Cautiously Johnny walked forward until he was standing near the armchair. He coughed, and suddenly Mr. Brentlinger became aware of his presence. He turned his head and spewed out a long, thin stream of pipe smoke.

"Hi, John. It is John, isn't it?"

Johnny nodded tightly. "Yes, sir. That's my name."

"I thought it was. Well, John, what can I do for you?"

He's gonna think this is crazy, thought Johnny. But he plunged ahead. "Uh . . . well . . . Mr. Brentlinger, could . . . could you . . . I mean, would you happen to know the name of the people who own that old mansion that's near the place where we ate our lunch? You know, with the towers on it and the little church next door to it? I was just kinda . . . well, interested in knowing."

Mr. Brentlinger turned and looked at Johnny. He laughed and shook his head. "Well, now! That *is* a strange thing to be asking. Were you hoping that the place was haunted or something?"

Johnny squirmed and clutched the binder tightly against his chest. He began to think that it had been a mistake to bring it with him. What if Mr. Brentlinger wanted to see what was inside? Would he laugh and decide that Johnny was a Grade-A lunatic? "I just wondered if you knew," he mumbled. Johnny could feel his face turning red.

Mr. Brentlinger looked at Johnny sympathetically. "I wasn't trying to make fun of you, John," he said gently. "I just couldn't resist having my little joke. Actually I think I do remember who owns that place. It's the family that owns the cereal company. You know, the people that make Oaty Crisps and all that other gunk. They have a really weird name. It's Glomfield or Glimp or something like that. Anyway, it was the old man, the founder of the business, that built the place. It's falling down now—the mansion, I mean, and I keep wondering what they're gonna *do* with the place. I wish I could remember that name for you. Hmm . . . hmm . . . let me think a bit. . . ."

Mr. Brentlinger went on hmming and puffing at his pipe. Johnny stood there in the darkness, trembling. He felt cold all over, but he also felt wildly triumphant. He had doped out the puzzle—part of it, anyway. Could he be wrong? Johnny didn't think so. The lost Glomus will was out here, out in that old mansion—or somewhere near it maybe. Johnny wanted to do eighteen things at once. He wanted to rush out and find a phone and tell the professor what he had discovered. He wanted to tell his new friend, Fergie, and he wanted to be out at the mansion, prowling around.

Mr. Brentlinger's voice broke in on Johnny's thoughts. "Nope, I just can *not* come up with that name! Anything else I can do for you, John? John? Are you there?"

Mr. Brentlinger turned his head and peered into the darkness behind his chair. Johnny was there, all right. At least his body was there. His mind was out among the crumbling stones of the Staunton Harold estate.

"Huh?" said Johnny, startled. "Uh . . . yes, sir . . . er, I mean, what did you say, Mr. Brentlinger?"

Mr. Brentlinger chuckled. "Never mind. So is there anything else I can do for you?"

"Uh . . . no. No, sir," Johnny said. He felt flustered, and he was looking for an exit line. "You told me what I wanted to know, so . . . so I guess I'll go up to bed now. Thanks a lot."

"Don't mention it. Sleep tight."

Johnny went up to his bedroom, but he did not go to sleep. He felt like a wound-up spring. Mechanically he put on his pajamas and went down the hall to brush his teeth and wash his face. Then he came back and crawled into bed, where he lay tossing and turning all night while Eckelbecker snored like a chain saw. If the human brain were a machine with an on-off button, Johnny would have shut his mind off, and he would have gotten some sleep. But he kept thinking about the objects on the table in Mr. Glomus's office. That signboard—what did it mean? Was the will hidden in a teapot? Johnny tossed and turned and moaned.

Finally the room got lighter, and Johnny heard the bugler blasting away, playing reveille outside his window. It was time to get up.

CHAPTER FIVE

꘎•꘎

Somehow Johnny stumbled through the early morning routine at Camp Chocorua. He washed up, pulled on his clothes, combed his hair, and staggered out to the flag-raising ceremony that always began the day. The skin of his face felt prickly, and he was nervous. But one thing was perfectly clear to him. Before the morning was over, he had to get to a phone so he could talk to the professor. He was dying to tell him about the discovery he had made, and he also wanted very much to know how Gramma was doing.

After the flag had been raised, the boys were dismissed. The orderly khaki-and-red lines broke up into a mob of boys running madly. Johnny tried to fight his way up to the flagpole so he could catch Mr. Brentlinger before he got away, but it was like trying to go up a staircase when everybody else is going down. Stubbornly battling his way forward, he finally reached it, just as Mr. Brentlinger was leaving.

"Mr. Brentlinger? Sir? Can I talk to you for just a minute?"

The head counselor turned and eyed Johnny curiously. He chuckled and shook his head. "Okay, Dixon, what is it now? I think I oughta charge you a fee for services above and beyond the call of duty."

Johnny was flustered. He paused and pulled himself together so he could ask his question. "Sir . . . I'd . . . I'd like to use a phone, if I may. I need to make a long-distance call, but it'd be a collect call. It wouldn't cost the camp any money."

Mr. Brentlinger looked pained. "Oh, God. You *would* ask for *that*! Dixon, look. There's kind of a problem about phones. This whole deal of having the camp open for this week, it was, well, kind of a spur-of-the-moment idea. The place was all shut down, and we had to turn the lights and the gas and everything back on. And you know how there's always something that doesn't get done? Well, the phone didn't get reconnected. Sooo . . . we're out here without a phone. How about that?"

Johnny's heart sank. He felt helpless and horribly frustrated. What was he going to do now?

"*However*," Mr. Brentlinger added, "there is a solution to this dilemma. In about five minutes I have to make a trip into town to mail some letters and make a few phone calls of my own. I use the public phone at the Squam House, which is the hotel in town. Mrs. Woodley knows me, and she'd be glad to let you make a call. So would you like to ride in with me?"

Johnny nodded happily. His problem was solved.

"Town" turned out to be Kancamagus Center, a small village about two miles down Route 16. It had a few side streets with comfortable-looking white clapboard houses, and a main street with a post office, a couple of stores, a gas station, a movie theater called the Scenic, an Odd Fellows Hall, and a white wooden church with a stubby square steeple. These buildings stood along one side of a grassy village common. On the other side of the common was the Squam House. It was a long, two-story structure with green shutters and a porch that ran across its entire front. There were rocking chairs on the porch, and there was a white sign by the steps. The sign said TOURIST ACCOMMODATIONS. *Reasonable Rates*. B. Woodley, proprietor.

Mr. Brentlinger and Johnny went to the post office first. Then they walked across the common to the Squam House. The lobby was deserted except for a young man who was sitting in an easy chair, reading a newspaper. As Johnny passed the man he stopped short. He had seen the man before. But where? He couldn't for the life of him remember. Even though Johnny had always been taught that staring was impolite, he couldn't stop himself. At first the young man tried to ignore him, but finally he put his paper down and gave Johnny a dirty look. He had pale blond eyebrows and frazzled reddish hair, hooded eyes, and a receding chin. He looked secretive, and he looked mean.

Johnny glanced quickly away and walked across the lobby to join Mr. Brentlinger, who was standing at the desk and talking with the proprietor, a fussy-looking old lady with her white hair pulled back in a bun. As she talked the lady pointed off to her left. There was the phone, a scarred black thing in one corner that stood on an antique table with bowed legs. Next to the phone was a skinny blue glass vase that looked like it would tip over if you breathed on it, and there was a funny little stool to sit on. Johnny almost groaned aloud. He had expected a regular phone booth with folding doors. He had wanted to make this a very private conversation, but that was not going to be possible.

Mr. Brentlinger told Johnny that he could use the phone for a long-distance call, as long as it was collect. Also he had to keep it brief, as Mrs. Woodley did not like to have people tying up the phone for too long. So Johnny went and sat in one of the easy chairs in the middle of the room while Mr. Brentlinger made his calls. He was staring aimlessly around the room, when— quite suddenly—he realized that the unpleasant young man was staring at him over the top of his newspaper. And the stare was not just curious, it was hateful. Johnny was startled. What did this creepy-looking guy have against him? Nervously Johnny snatched up an old copy of *Yankee* magazine from a little table and hid behind it.

Time passed. Finally Mr. Brentlinger was through with the phone, and Johnny got to use it. Soon the phone was ringing down in the professor's house in Duston Heights.

When the professor answered, he was in an exceptionally crabby mood. He had been defrosting his refrigerator, which was something that he absolutely hated to do. For about an hour he had been putting pans of boiling water inside the refrigerator and poking at the ice with his Knights of Columbus sword, while cursing loudly, fervently, and picturesquely. Now waves of crankiness were sweeping over him, and he was trying hard to make himself cheerful again.

"Hello," he snapped. "Who is it?"

The voice at the other end was timid and apologetic. "It's me, Johnny. I . . . I need to talk to you."

"John, why the devil are you whispering? Are you involved in a conspiracy? Is the FBI after you?"

Johnny explained that he was sitting out in the open in a hotel lobby.

"So what?" rasped the professor. "Do you have government secrets to pass on? What the blazes do you have to say that's so private?"

Johnny swallowed hard several times. His face got red, and the palms of his hands were sweaty. When people crabbed at him, he always became very flustered.

"I . . . I j-just wanted to t-talk to you for a m-minute," he stammered. "Is . . . is that okay?"

The professor calmed down. He knew about Johnny's problems, and he was sorry he had been such a bear a moment before. "Go ahead," he said, mildly. "I'm listening. Shoot."

"Well, I . . . first of all I just wanted to know how Gramma is. Have they operated on her yet?"

"Yes, they have. She had her operation on Monday night, and she is doing reasonably well, considering her age and everything. The doctors think that they got the whole tumor out, and it was malignant, I'm sorry to say. I'd be lying if I said that I thought that everything was going to be rosy from now on: there may be problems."

"Problems?" Johnny's heart sank.

"Yes, problems. There's always the possibility that the doctors didn't get the whole tumor out, and if that was the case . . . well, it'd be pretty bad. Also, there's your grampa. He's still fairly depressed, and it may be some time before he's his old bouncy self again. So there! I've given you the news, and it's mostly good. Do you have anything else that you want to discuss with me?"

Once again Johnny was hesitant. He looked around nervously and then said in a loud whisper, "I found out something about Mr. Glomus's will!"

The professor groaned. He clenched his fists and struggled against the urge to chew Johnny out. "John," he said through his teeth, "you are supposed to be *en-*

joying yourself! You are supposed to be tramping about on woodland paths among the autumnal splendors of the White Mountains! What on *earth* are you doing thinking about dear old Mr. Glomus's will?"

Johnny explained. He told the professor about the arch that said Staunton Harold, and he told him why he thought the puzzle on the table fit in with it.

". . . and so I think that will just has to be on that old estate somewhere," Johnny went on breathlessly. "Don't you think I must be right?"

The professor was silent for so long that Johnny was afraid they had been cut off.

"Professor? Hello? Hello? Are you there?"

"Yes, I'm here," said the professor in a strained, testy voice. "But if I were *there*, I'd be driving you into the ground like a tent stake! John, this puzzle solution of yours is terribly ingenious, but it is absolutely cockeyed! *Please* put it out of your mind and go back to hiking and . . . and whatever else you're supposed to be doing! Do you hear me?"

"But the place out here really does belong to the Glomuses!" said Johnny desperately. "It—"

"I don't care if it belongs to Nebuchadnezzar or Czar Nicholas the Second!" roared the professor, cutting him off. "Let us change the subject! Enjoy yourself! Go out and hike till your feet are sore! Collect autumn leaves and put them into albums! Do anything, but please get your mind off that idiotic will! That is an order!"

"Yes, sir," said Johnny, meekly. He wanted to argue,

but he knew it would be no use. So he promised the professor that he would really try to enjoy himself, and then he said good-bye.

After Johnny had hung up, he looked around. First he turned toward the chair where the creepy young man had been sitting. He was delighted to see that the man was gone. Then Johnny noticed that Mrs. Woodley was standing, stock-still, behind the hotel desk. She was glowering at him. Johnny wondered if everybody in this hotel was crazy. First there was the young man, and now this old bat was making ugly faces at him, even though he hadn't done anything. Johnny happened to glance at the skinny blue glass vase that stood next to the phone. *She thinks I'm gonna smash it*, he said to himself. He had half a mind to knock the vase over and then catch it quickly before it broke, just to see what Mrs. Woodley would do. But most of all he wanted to get out of this creepy hotel as quickly as he could.

Johnny hurried across the lobby, down the front steps, and out into the autumn sunshine. As he crossed the common he thought about the phone conversation he had just had. He felt frustrated, but in an odd way he also felt relieved. He was glad to know that Gramma's operation was over, and that it had been a success. As for the puzzle business, it was true that the professor had not taken him seriously, but at least he had said what he wanted to say. And maybe the professor was right after all. Maybe Johnny should just forget about

Staunton Harold and the Glomus will, shove the whole stupid mess out of his mind.

Mr. Brentlinger's station wagon was parked outside the post office, but Mr. Brentlinger was not there. Probably he was still shopping or chewing the fat with some friend of his. Johnny started to get into the car and wait for him, but as soon as he opened the car door, he noticed something lying on the seat. It was a small square of heavy white paper with ragged edges. Carelessly Johnny picked the paper up and turned it over. What he saw was an old-fashioned black-and-white woodcut. It showed some young men drinking in a tavern. Outside the tavern door stood a skeleton. It held a spear up over its head, and it looked like it was getting ready to throw the spear at the young men. Underneath the picture was a little two-line poem, printed in old-fashioned lettering. It read:

> While Youth do chear
> DEATH may be near

CHAPTER SIX

❧•❧

Johnny sat rigid and still. He felt cold creeping over his body, as if he were slowly turning into a block of ice. The square of paper had been left on the car seat by someone who wanted him to find it. The drawing was familiar to him—in a hazy way. He had seen it in a history book somewhere. And its meaning seemed very clear to Johnny: It was a death threat. But who was threatening him? And why?

Suddenly Johnny looked up. Through the windshield he could see Mr. Brentlinger walking down the sidewalk toward the car. Johnny made a very quick decision. He scrunched the drawing up into a ball in his hand and stuffed it into his pants pocket. He really did not want to discuss this with Mr. Brentlinger or to be told that the drawing was just an ad for a Halloween dance or a free gift from somebody's funeral parlor. He had had enough of calm, reasonable advice from the professor. All he wanted was time to think and figure out what to do.

When the station wagon pulled into the parking lot at Camp Chocorua, Johnny thanked Mr. Brentlinger, got out of the car, and ran up to his room to get his baseball glove. Johnny had seen the kids playing softball as he rode back along the road toward the camp. He loved to play, even though he was not very good at it. And he was always hoping that somehow, mysteriously, he would turn into a better fielder and hitter. Now as he raced through the long grass his mind kept coming back to the evil thing that was wadded up in his pocket. He had to tell somebody about it or he would burst. He couldn't call the professor again. So then who . . .

As he jogged nearer to the mob of yelling, gesturing boys Johnny began to grin broadly. He waved excitedly. There was Fergie.

Fergie was sitting in the long grass, looking absolutely nonchalant as he chewed on a tufted weed. He was on the team that was up at bat. It was a chilly day, and so he was wearing an old scruffy gray sweat shirt with CYCLOPS ATHLETIC CLUB printed in white block letters across the front.

"Hi, Fergie," said Johnny, slumping down on the grass. Johnny tried hard to smile, but when he thought of the wadded paper in his pocket, his smile turned to a tense frown.

Fergie looked at Johnny curiously. "Hey, what's the matter with you? Did you bet on the Germans to win the Second World War?"

Normally Johnny would have laughed, but he was not in a very jokey mood. He dug his hand into his pants pocket and pulled out the piece of paper. Carefully he uncrumpled it, smoothed it out on his knee, and handed it to Fergie.

"I found this in the car when I went downtown with Mr. Brentlinger. I think it's a death threat."

Fergie squinted at the crumpled drawing and laughed. "A *death threat*? Are you out of your jug? This is one of those things from that book, whatsitsname, that the Pilgrims made so kids would learn their ABC's. I looked at it in the library once. This one's for the letter Y. What made you think it was a death threat?"

"Somebody left it on the seat where I was sitting in Mr. Brentlinger's car. Doncha see? They're after me on account of I know where the will is, and . . ." Johnny paused and stared at the ground. He bit his lip and felt his cheeks getting red with embarrassment. He had been running on because he was excited and scared, and he had not stopped to think that this would make absolutely no sense to Fergie. And now Fergie would probably decide that Johnny was weird. He would get up and walk away, and that would be the end of their friendship.

But that was not what happened. Fergie was staring at Johnny, but it was an interested stare. There was a gleam in his eyes and a faint curling smile on his lips. "He-ey," he said slowly, "are you mixed up in something? You can tell me, I won't rat on you. Come on."

So Johnny started to tell Fergie about Staunton Harold and the lost Glomus will and the table with the weird collection of objects on it. While they talked there was a lot of yelling and screaming going on behind their backs. Fergie's team was knocking the cover off the ball. Pretty soon the bases were loaded.

"Hey, Fergie!" somebody yelled. "You're up!"

"Oops. 'Scuse me! I'll be right back," said Fergie, and he scrambled to his feet. He picked up a bat and loped toward the plate. As Johnny watched, Fergie got ready to hit. The pitcher barreled the ball in, and Fergie swung. It was an awkward, lunging swing, and he missed. Johnny felt sympathetic and got ready to cheer Fergie up when he struck out. But then the ball came whizzing toward the plate again, and Fergie swung and connected. *Wok!* The ball sailed upward in a high, beautiful arc. It flew out over the head of the center fielder and came down in some bushes at the far end of the field. Fergie raced around the bases as all the boys on his team whooped and cheered. After he crossed home plate, Fergie stumbled back to where he'd been sitting before. He sat down, crossed his legs, and smiled modestly.

"Natural ability," he said, brushing an imaginary

speck of dust off his sweat shirt. "Okay, now. You wanna tell me some more about this trouble you're in?"

So Johnny told Fergie the rest of what he knew and what he guessed. He told him that he thought the lost Glomus will must be out at the estate called Staunton Harold. Fergie listened to all this thoughtfully. He nodded sometimes or shook his head, and now and then he would say something like "Hot dog! How about that!" or "Boy, that old guy must really have been out of his jug!" "Out of his jug" was one of Fergie's favorite expressions.

Finally Johnny was finished. He folded his arms and glanced nervously at Fergie. "Whaddaya think?" he asked.

Fergie was quiet a second before answering. "I think you're the only kid I know who's ever had a death threat handed to him. Honest! I never heard of it happening before!"

Johnny felt confused and kind of angry. First Fergie had said that the picture wasn't a death threat, and now he said that it was. Was he trying to be funny? "It's not like the Congressional Medal of Honor," he snapped back. "I mean, I might get killed."

"Yeah, you might." Fergie said this in an abstracted, dreamy way. It was plain that his mind was elsewhere. As Johnny stared at him anxiously Fergie hummed and gazed off into space. Suddenly a light came into his eyes. He snapped his fingers and turned to Johnny. "Hey!" he said. "You know what we oughta do?"

"What?"

"We oughta sneak out of our rooms tonight and go see if we can find a way to get into that Statler Harrison place. Whaddaya say?"

"It's Staunton Harold," said Johnny severely. He hated to hear people mispronounce names.

"Statler Hilton, Staunton Harold, what's the difference?" said Fergie with an irritated shrug. "Come on, answer the question. Do you wanta go or don't you?"

Johnny hemmed and hawed. He had a holy terror of violating rules and regulations, and camp regulations said that you couldn't leave your dormitory between lights-out and reveille. "We can't go," said Johnny fretfully. "If we get caught, they'll throw us out, and my grampa and gramma'll really feel awful if that happens."

Fergie snorted disgustedly. "Oh, come on, Dixon! Are you gonna spend the rest of your life wrapped up in a blanket in your bedroom? The only way to have any fun is to break the rules sometimes! Come on! I'll meet you at eleven P.M. out by the flagpole. There's a path over there," Fergie said, pointing off toward a mass of bushes near the tennis courts, "and it leads out toward that road. You know, the one we were hikin' on when we saw the old place. We'll just go out an' peek at the old dump an' come right back. Who's to know? You'll be in bed before anybody knows you left. Whaddaya say?"

Johnny still looked hesitant. "Eckelbecker'll turn me in if he finds out I've gone out."

Fergie looked grim. "You tell that lard bucket that

Byron Q. Ferguson told him to keep his trap shut unless he wants to have his ears tied into a bowknot behind his head."

Johnny was torn with indecision. The professor was always telling him that he ought to be more adventurous. Maybe he ought to quit worrying and live a little. "Oh, okay!" he said finally. "I'll be there."

At about five past eleven that night Johnny was standing out by the flagpole, waiting. It was a chilly, raw night with a fine mist in the air, and he was shivering as he peered up at the overcast sky. He was wearing his Notre Dame warm-up jacket over his pajama tops, and he also had on his blue jeans and his heavy socks and tennis shoes. He looked off toward the log buildings. So where was Fergie? Had he chickened out in spite of all his brave talk? But then Johnny saw a shape moving toward him. Fergie was sprinting across the wet grass, carrying something in his hand. Suddenly Johnny realized what it was—a flashlight. And then he felt very stupid: he had a flashlight, but it was in his suitcase. He had been so nervous and flustered about this whole deal that he had forgotten to bring it.

Fergie arrived, panting. "Hi!" he whispered. "Glad you didn't cop out on me. You bring a flashlight?"

"I don't have one," said Johnny untruthfully. "Is . . . is that all right?"

"Naw," said Fergie, grinning. "You get three demerits an' no supper tonight. Sure it's all right! Stop bein' such a fussbudget! This flashlight here is one of those super-duper sealed-beam jobbies. It shines for miles. So don't worry. Let's get started."

Fergie and Johnny jogged off into the drizzly darkness. After a couple of minutes Fergie switched on the wonderful sealed-beam flashlight. The effect was quite dramatic: A long bar of pale light shot out into the gloom. As Johnny watched, Fergie moved the beam back and forth. It lit up the hump of the pitcher's mound on the baseball diamond, and then it moved slowly across the mass of bushes beyond the field. The beam picked out a cleft in the wall of shrubbery.

"Aha!" said Fergie. "Aha, and other expressions of delight! Come on! We've got it knocked!"

The two boys marched on. They reached the edge of the wide grassy field and plunged into the gap in the bushes. It was a narrow path, and they had to go single file. Fergie went first with the light. Wet leaves slapped across Johnny's face, and he put out his arm to fend them off. His head was sopping wet now, and water was running down his neck. He thought about his gramma, and how she believed that if you got wet out in the rain, you might die of pneumonia. Poor Gramma! Johnny hoped that she was really going to get better. Silently he said a Hail Mary and an Our Father for her.

After what seemed like hours of slopping along through wet underbrush, the boys came out onto a road covered with wet gravel. Johnny had a vague idea that they were walking through a forest, but when he looked up, he couldn't tell where the trees ended and the sky began. Fergie's light slashed out through the mist like a sword. Neither boy spoke.

Johnny began to brood about the mysterious place that they had set out to explore. The old mansion was evil-looking, even in bright sunlight. What would it be like at night?

Fergie grabbed Johnny's arm. "Hey! What was that?" he said sharply, and he sounded alarmed.

Both boys halted and stood dead-still, listening. Off to their left they heard noises. *Crunch, crunch, crackle, crunch.* Somebody—or something—was thrashing through the wet underbrush. Johnny wanted to run. But he had his pride; if Fergie was going to stand his ground, then so would he.

"Hey! What the heck d'ya think *that* was?" Fergie was trying to sound brave, but Johnny could hear the trembling in his voice.

"I dunno. Maybe it was a dog."

"Naw. Too much noise for a dog. I'd say it was a hunter, only any hunter who was out here on a lousy night like this would have to be out of his jug. Some old bum maybe."

Johnny didn't think it was a bum. In his mind's eye he saw a Frankensteinish creature dripping green slime from its horny paws. Any minute now it would come charging out of the darkness at them, uttering strange cries and lusting for their blood.

Suddenly the noise in the underbrush died away. Fergie took a deep breath and let it out.

"Hot dog!" he said, grinning. "He must've gone away." Fergie chuckled. His old jaunty, swaggering self was coming back. "Let's move it! It's just a little ways down the road to the old place."

On the boys hiked while the wet gravel went *squrch*, *squrch* under their feet. The mist turned into a steady drizzle. Johnny kept straining to see, but he could not make out much except more road and vague leafy shadows crowding in close on either side. Finally, though, as they started down a hill, the close shadows of trees and bushes fell away. The long beam of Fergie's flashlight swerved to the left and picked out the heavily ornamented stone arch, with its swags and urns and columns. They were there. They had reached Staunton Harold.

And standing under the arch, waiting for them, was a man. He wore a yellow rubber raincoat and a black rubber rain hat with a wide floppy brim. Under his armpit the man held a flashlight, and in his hands was a rifle—pointed straight at Johnny and Fergie.

CHAPTER SEVEN

❧ • ❧

The drizzling rain kept falling. The still beam of Fergie's flashlight shone straight at the menacing figure's face. Even with the brim of the rain hat partially hiding the face, Johnny knew who it was immediately. It was the young man with the bug eyes and receding chin who had glared at him in the lobby of the Squam House.

Shifting the gun in his hands, the man took a step forward. "Okay, you two," he said nastily. "Just you hold it, right there! Now, would you mind tellin' me what you're supposed to be doin'? Huh?"

Johnny was terrified. He had a sudden vision of himself and Fergie lying by the roadside, shot full of holes and covered with blood.

Fergie, however, was made of sterner stuff. He stepped forward and challenged the man angrily. "Hey, you, what do you mean pointin' that gun at us? This's a public road. We ain't done nothin' wrong!"

The man looked at Fergie thoughtfully for a second. He looked down at the rifle in his hand. And then, amazingly, his whole attitude changed. "*Darnit!*" he yelled disgustedly, and he threw the rifle down on the ground. "Darnit all anyway!" He tore off his rain hat and threw it into a mud puddle. Then he sat down on a piece of carved stone that stood in the grass near the arch. "Go ahead!" he said, wringing his hands and staring gloomily at the ground. "Do what you want! Steal my gun! Break into the house! Make fun of me! See if I care! I try to be tough, but I just can't do it!"

Johnny and Fergie were totally stunned by this dramatic turnaround. They looked at each other, and then Fergie stepped forward.

"We don't want your dumb gun," he said. "And we're not gonna break into anybody's house. We just don't like to have people threatening us." Fergie pointed off into the darkness. "That house over there—is it yours?"

The young man nodded glumly. "Sort of. It belongs to my family. My name is Chadwick Glomus, and my grandfather was good old H. Bagwell Glomus. Or Grampa Herbie, as he was known in the family. I have too much money, and a lot of time on my hands, so every now and then I come up to this old place and look for Grampa Herbie's will."

Johnny was astonished. He had figured that he was the only one in the world who knew that the puzzle in Mr. Glomus's office pointed toward this place. Without pausing to think, he said excitedly, "Hey! How'd you guess that—"

The young man gave him a sour glance. "Oh, I'm clever. Very clever. And I gather you worked out that part of the riddle too. When I saw you at the hotel, I figured that you had come up here to search for the will. You see, I was working in the gift shop the day you visited my dear grandfather's cereal factory. You were babbling a blue streak about the puzzle to that old man you were with, and so I figured you might be on to something."

Johnny gasped. So that was it. He *had* seen the man before!

The young man smiled unpleasantly. "I hope you find the will, and I hope it turns out that everybody in the Glomus family has been cut out of it. I hope that Grampa Herbie left his dough to the Christian Scientists or the Red Sox or a home for retired organ-grinders! I hope nobody in my family gets a red cent!"

Fergie looked at the young man strangely. "Why don't you like your family? What's the matter with them?"

The young man put his hand over his face. "Oh, don't ask! Don't ask! But if you really want to know, the main reason why everybody is such a mess is Grampa Herbie. He was one of the most awful people you'd ever want to meet in your life! Always harping on the importance of a balanced diet. Chew your food thirty-two times before you swallow it! Did you know that a bowl of Oaty Crisps contains ninety-three percent of your recommended daily allowance of iron, riboflavin, and niacin? *Yaargh!* And then, at the end of his life, to start messing around with black magic the way he did! And to top it all off, that insane puzzle about the will!"

The young man shook his head and winced. "Ow! I wish you hadn't gotten me started on my family. I think it's giving me a headache!"

Agin Johnny and Fergie glanced at each other. They both felt sorry for the young man, but right now they wanted to go back to camp. They had decided that their adventure had reached a dead end, and they needed some nice, polite way of saying good-bye.

"Uh, we . . . we better be gettin' back to our camp," said Fergie, with a nervous glance over his shoulder. "If the counselors find out we're not in bed, they'll really blow their tops."

The young man looked very unhappy. At first he had seemed threatening, but now he merely seemed strange, wistful, and more than a little bit lonely.

"Oh, please don't go yet!" he pleaded. "I'm sorry I pointed that gun at you! Look, if you stay just a bit, I'll show you something."

Fergie wrinkled up his nose suspiciously. "Yeah? What?"

"It's a secret passage that runs under the fence and comes up inside the chapel next to the big house. The tunnel is a big Glomus family secret, but I'll let you in on it."

Johnny felt very nervous about this. He had always had it drummed into his head, ever since he was little, that you never went anywhere with strangers. And this was a stranger who was stranger than most.

The young man looked at Fergie and Johnny, and read their thoughts. With a pained expression on his face he got up and fished his rain hat out of the mud puddle. He shook it a few times and jammed it back onto his head. "Please believe me!" he said in a pleading, sad voice. "I'm not a murderer! I can't even shoot squirrels! That gun is empty. See for yourselves!"

Fergie took a few steps forward and picked up the gun. He slid the bolt back and pointed the beam of his flashlight in the chamber. Then he slammed the bolt back into place and handed it to the young man. "Yeah, you're right," he said, nodding. "Okay, look. I'll level with you. We were just gonna peer through the fence at that old dump over there and then hightail it back to camp. But if you wanna show us somethin', we could stay for, oh, maybe about half an hour." Fergie paused and turned to look back at Johnny, who was just standing there fidgeting. "That okay with you, John baby?"

Johnny glanced fretfully over his shoulder. He had mixed emotions. He was afraid of getting caught if he stayed out too late, but the idea of a secret passage really excited him. It was the kind of thing he had always dreamed of finding.

"I guess we could stay for a little while," he said hesitantly.

And so it was settled. The young man turned and walked back toward the stone arch, motioning for the other two to follow him. They headed along a narrow muddy path that ran down a little slope and off into the woods. As they tramped along, Johnny found that he was getting really nervous, but he was also getting really interested. He wondered what the passage would be like.

On they marched, over masses of soggy leaves, while water dripped all around them. Finally they came to a small clearing where Johnny could see the dark shadow of a small building. It seemed to be a funny little cottage of some kind. Fergie swept his flashlight beam upward, and Johnny saw part of a slate roof, a brick wall, and a little window with diamond-shaped panes. A door was set in a fancy stone arch. Over the arch was a stone banner with the inscription *Health Is Wealth*.

"This is one of those cute little outbuildings or lodges that you find around big estates sometimes," said the young man as he fumbled in his pocket for a key. He turned it in the lock and gave the door a good hard shove. Then he disappeared inside. Johnny and Fergie hesitated for a second and then followed him into a musty-smelling room with no furniture in it. Built into one wall was a very fancy marble fireplace. It was covered with stone knobs carved to look like the tiny heads of children. They were smiling and apple-cheeked, and were slurping cereal from bowls. Over the mantel was a mildewed oil painting of good old Mr. Glomus himself, with a box of Oaty Crisps in his hands.

The young man laid his rifle on the mantel. Then he grabbed one of the carved heads and twisted it. Johnny heard the clanking and clattering of hidden weights and chains. And then, as the young man pointed the beam of his flashlight into the dark mouth of the fireplace, Johnny saw the back wall of the hearth slide up. A low opening was revealed, with steps leading down.

The young man folded his arms and stared calmly down into the dark opening, laughing harshly. "Good old Grampa Herbie really thought of everything! If you're out shooting quail and a thunderstorm hits, you duck in here. And then you can scoot right over, zippity-zoo, to the chapel without getting your head wet. And now, if you've got a few minutes more, I'll show you part of the passage."

But before starting out, the young man did a strange thing. He stepped back, reached up onto the mantel, and took down a candle and a book of matches. Then he poked around in the darkness for a few minutes and came up with a long knobby bronze candlestick. Humming tunelessly, he screwed the candle into the holder and lit it.

"Whaddaya need that for?" asked Fergie. "You've got a flashlight, doncha? Or did your batteries run out?"

"The batteries are Everready batteries and will last for centuries," said the young man dryly. "This is for something else." His face suddenly grew grim and hard. In the candlelight it looked like the face of a gaunt and cadaverous ghost. "Have you two heard about the Guardian?"

Johnny stared. This was something new to him, and to Fergie too.

"Don't know, eh?" said the young man tauntingly. "Well, kiddies, the Guardian is something my irresponsible grandfather whipped up when he was fooling around with the black arts. He called it up out of the depths, out of the void, and it's still here, wandering around this old estate. The Guardian can be anything: It might be a pool of moonlight on the floor, or a chair, or smoke drifting in the air. And if it catches you . . . well, one of my great-uncles was caught by it. Afterward they buried him in a hurry." The young man paused and grinned unpleasantly. "Do you know what a mummy looks like after it's been unwrapped? Just a dried brown husk that used to be a human being, with holes for eyes? Well, that's what Great-Uncle Platt looked like after the Guardian got him. And I'll tell you something else you may not know. Three people have disappeared in this area in the last five years. No bodies were ever found, but I'll bet you—dollars to doughnuts—that the Guardian got them too."

Fergie's eyebrows went up. He was pretty suspicious about all this. "So, if there's this monster down there," he said, "why are we goin' on down to meet it? Is it monster-feeding time or what?"

The young man stared stonily at Fergie. "You can make fun all you want, my friend," he said grumpily. "But what I'm telling you happens to be true! And in answer to your question, the Guardian isn't there all the time. But I suspect that it will come for you if you get too close to the will. I have this candle. If an evil presence is near, candle flames burn blue. That's what Shakespeare says, and it happens to be the truth. So come along. . . ."

Fergie and Johnny looked at each other. Neither of them believed a word the young man was saying.

"Yeah, sure, let's go," said Fergie, with a jaunty leer and a devil-may-care shrug of his shoulders. "If you don't mind about monsters, neither do we."

The young man smiled a crooked, mocking smile. With the candlestick in one hand and a flashlight in the other, he bent over and stepped down into the narrow opening. Fergie went next, and Johnny came last. Down a dark, damp-smelling staircase passage they went. Johnny counted twenty-three steps to the bottom. Then the floor leveled off, and the passage grew wider. They were in a stone tunnel where three people could walk abreast. Fergie flashed his light around, and Johnny saw, at the top of an arch they were passing under, a smiling stone cherub and the carved motto *Mens sana in sano corpore*, which means "a sound mind in a sound body." Over by one wall of the tunnel some junk was piled up.

"Charming place, isn't it?" said the young man as they walked along. "I understand Grampa Herbie originally wanted to make this a little subway line, with a pneumatic-powered car and all. But he lost interest when he found out how much it would cost."

They walked on. In places there was a strong smell of earth, and Johnny noticed that pieces of the ceiling had caved in. Sometimes the walls were slick with damp, and here and there Johnny saw streaks of yellowish-green niter oozing down over carved corbels and columns. Every now and then he glanced at the flame of the candle that the young man was carrying. It burned sluggishly, because the air in this underground place was rather stale. But it did not burn blue.

Finally they stopped. Before them was a nail-studded wooden door set in a stone arch with a zigzag molding around it.

"End of the line," said the young man with a little sigh. He turned to face the two boys. "This door leads to the crypt under the chapel next to the big ghastly old house. You two must have seen it from the road. But I don't think we ought to go upstairs. No, I wouldn't want to take the responsibility if anything happened to you two. Let's head back."

Johnny was disappointed. He had not believed any of the young man's warnings about the Guardian and he wanted to see the inside of the spooky old chapel. Also he had a funny idea that was lodged firmly in his head:

If he could only get onto the grounds of the estate, he would be able to figure out the rest of the Glomus puzzle.

Fergie protested and Johnny wheedled, but the young man was quite firm. So, back they went and up the narrow stairs into the dusty little room where the journey had started. The young man blew out his candle and set it on the mantelpiece. He twisted the carved knob, and the stone slab at the back of the hearth came bumping and grumbling back down. Then, taking the rifle again and tucking it under his arm, he led the boys out of the lodge, locked the door, and slid the key into a hole in one of the carved ball-flowers over the door. And now the three of them were tramping back along the muddy path through the trees.

When they reached the gravel road, the young man stopped again. "Gentlemen, I am going to take my leave," he said, bowing stiffly. "My car is parked not far from here, and I gather you two can make it back to camp all right. I'm so glad I had a chance to entertain you. And if you ever think of me, remember that there are things in this world that are better than having lots of money. Like having all your marbles, which I don't seem to. Good day. It's really been, as they say."

And with that the young man wheeled abruptly and marched off down the road.

"Weird," said Fergie, shaking his head. "Weird is the word for that character."

"Yeah, but he was kind of nice, anyway," said Johnny thoughtfully.

"Uh-huh," grunted Fergie, and he screwed his mouth up into a distrustful frown. Then the two explorers turned and began walking quickly back toward camp. For a few minutes the only sound was the pattering of rain and the crunching of gravel under the soles of their shoes. Then suddenly the air was split by long, loud, hideous yells and shrieks.

Johnny and Fergie stopped dead in their tracks. The yelling had come from the stretch of road that the young man had just been heading for. The two boys did not discuss what they ought to do. Instead, they turned around and set off running, pell-mell, in the direction they had come from. Johnny was not a great runner, but he ran hard, determined not to be left behind in the dark. Suddenly the two of them stopped, breathless, in the middle of the road. The jumping, bouncing beam of Fergie's flashlight had picked out something. On the rain-soaked gravel lay two objects: One was a rifle, and the other was a flashlight. The flashlight was still on, and it cast its long, narrow beam out across the gravel of the road. On the handle was a raised oval medallion that bore the gold initials *CG*.

CHAPTER EIGHT

꧁ ● ꧂

Horrified, Johnny looked at Fergie. Fergie was staring down at the rifle and the flashlight, still breathing hard from the long run. Abruptly he stopped to pick up the flashlight. He flipped it over to Johnny, who was so surprised that he almost dropped it.

"Here," said Fergie. "Now we've each got one. Come on. Let's get headed back to camp."

Johnny was flabbergasted. He stood there opening and shutting his mouth. Finally he managed to speak. "You mean . . . you mean you're gonna just . . . just . . ."

Fergie hesitated. For a second he stared off into the darkness, and there was fear in his eyes. Then he laughed harshly. His lips curled into a cynical and knowing smile. "Yeah," he said, "we're gonna *just*. We're gonna mosey on back and get some sleepy-bye, if we can. Look, John baby, don't you see what happened? He dropped his stuff here in the road. Then he yelled bloody murder for a coupla minutes, an' then he lit out into the woods. He's probably out there right now, laughin' at us. You didn't *believe* all that junk about a monster that turns people into mummies, did you?"

Johnny was silent. Up until now he had not believed the strange young man's stories, but he was beginning to have second thoughts. Johnny looked down at the chrome-plated flashlight he held in his hands. It looked expensive. And there was the rifle lying there too. "Maybe you're right," he said slowly, "but . . . well, would he really have left this stuff just layin' here?"

Fergie shrugged. "Why not? He's rich as Croesus, so he can buy himself more rifles and flashlights, can't he? Besides, he's got a screw loose. Crazy people do crazy things."

Again Johnny was silent. It seemed to him that Fergie was being very reasonable and logical. All the same, he had his doubts. Finally, with a weary shrug, he said "Oh, okay! Let's go on back."

"Right," said Fergie, nodding. Then, on a sudden impulse, he tucked his flashlight under his armpit and cupped his hands to his mouth. "NIGHTY-NIGHT, CHAD BABY!" he yelled. There was no answer. But then, the boys didn't expect one.

Fergie and Johnny did not try to take the rifle back

with them. They left it lying on the rain-soaked road and slogged on back to camp. At the flagpole they parted, and each one ran back to his own building. As he slipped in, closing the door softly behind him, Johnny noticed the clock in the downstairs hall. It said five minutes before two.

Johnny didn't get much sleep that night. He was still terribly keyed up, and he lay tossing and turning for a long time, until—around five A.M.—he dozed off, and had a dream about Mr. Glomus chasing him through an endless tunnel. And then, before he knew it, reveille was blowing again, and Johnny crawled out of bed to face another day.

When he came stumbling into the dining hall for breakfast, Johnny felt like one of the walking dead. For two straight nights he had gone without much sleep, and now it was beginning to get to him. He shuffled along the cafeteria line, sliding his tray over the stainless-steel bars. As he was staring blearily at the bins of scrambled eggs, he heard the women behind the counter talking to each other.

"Hey, Edna!" said one, "didja hear that thing on the radio? About the guy that got lost last night?"

"No, I didn't. So what happened?"

"Well, it was the same like all o' the others. He just disappeared! They found his gun layin' in the road out near that old mansion—you know the one I mean. An' then they found his car parked up the road, with the keys in it. I betcha they never find him! Remember old Mrs. Spofford an' Charley Holmes an' that bum—what was his name, anyway? They never found none of 'em! An' I bet they never will, either!"

Johnny was wide awake now. He stared so hard at the woman who was telling the story that she noticed him and suddenly clammed up. "Milk or Kool-Aid?" she asked in a toneless voice as she shoved a plate of scrambled eggs and bacon at Johnny.

Mechanically Johnny took a glass of milk and moved on down the line with his tray. His brain was racing madly. So it hadn't been just a tall tale. Chad really had disappeared, and there were others who had gone before him. Distractedly Johnny looked this way and that. Ah, there was Fergie waving and motioning for him to come and sit down.

Scuttling sideways, Johnny made his way down the narrow aisle between two rows of tables. He put his tray down, climbed onto a seat, and immediately began talking.

"Guess what!" he said breathlessly, "I just listened to those two women up there at the counter, and they claim that that guy we met really *has* disappeared! And there's others who've been missing too!"

Fergie looked at Johnny scornfully. "Aw, come on, Dixon! Those two old bags'd believe anything they heard."

"You . . . you mean you don't think—"

Fergie laughed and shook his head vigorously. "Naah,

I *don't* think! Really, Dixon, you're one of the most superstitious kids I ever met in my life! Look. That guy was a crazy, right? He was playin' a joke, an' then maybe he screwed up an' he really *did* get lost. An' you wanna know what else I think? I think he's the one that left that weird picture in the car for you. It'd be just like him. He's really out of his jug! So don't worry about him—he'll turn up, one way or the other."

"Uh-huh," said Johnny weakly. He was not convinced by what Fergie had said, but he didn't feel like arguing. He remembered the awful, agonized screams they had heard. Johnny felt sorry for Chad. He really had kind of liked him. And then, suddenly, it occurred to him that they shouldn't be talking about last night's escapade at all. What if some creepy kid like Eckelbecker heard them and turned them in? Anxiously Johnny shot a glance at the kid who was sitting across the table. But he did not seem to be paying any attention to Johnny and Fergie. His eyes were on his plate, and he was busy stuffing scrambled eggs into his mouth.

Fergie elbowed Johnny in the side. "Don't worry about him," he said, snickering. "His ears are fulla strawberry jam."

At this, however, Eckelbecker did look up.

Days passed. Johnny learned Indian lore and made a belt out of little interlocking pieces of leather. With the other boys he hiked for miles and miles, and on Saturday he got to climb Mount Chocorua. It was a long, exhausting climb, and near the top it got scary because the path skirted the edge of a drop-off. But Johnny made it to the top like everyone else, and it gave him a great sense of accomplishment. He had done something courageous and difficult that he wouldn't have been able to do a week or a month ago.

At the last fireside folk sing on Saturday night Johnny stood proudly with the other Scouts as they sang:

> Softly falls the light of day
> As our campfire fades away
> Silently each Scout should ask
> Have I done my daily task?
> Have I kept my honor bright?
> Can I guiltless rest tonight?
> Have I done and have I dared
> Everything to Be Prepared?

Johnny felt the warmth of the fire on his face, and he felt friendly toward the other boys around him. He was sad about leaving, but he would be glad to see Gramma and find out how she was doing. Then he thought about Chad Glomus. He had never been found. For days search parties had been combing the wooded areas around Mount Chocorua, but he had not turned up. Johnny wondered if he should come forward and tell about what he and Fergie had seen. But to do that, Johnny would have had to admit that he had been out in the woods running around after taps. And he was scared of getting into trouble.

And there was something else on Johnny's mind too. It was the whole business of the Glomus will and the baffling collection of clues on the table. Johnny was absolutely convinced that he had figured out the first part of the puzzle, that the will was out at the estate called Staunton Harold. But beyond that point he was stuck. And come Sunday he was going to be even more stuck because he'd be back in Duston Heights and the secret hiding place of the Glomus will would be far, far away from him. Even if he ever solved the riddle of the sign from the tea shop, he would probably never get a chance to test his theories—or collect that lovely ten thousand dollar reward.

Sunday arrived, and Johnny packed up his things, shook hands with Mr. Brentlinger, and said good-bye. Then he climbed aboard the big black-and-yellow bus with all the other Scouts. He was really sorry that he had to go, and as the bus pulled away from camp there were tears in Johnny's eyes.

But on the ride back, he had a good time. He got a seat with Fergie, and the two of them really talked up a storm. For the first time Johnny discovered that Fergie lived in Duston Heights! The two of them had never met because Fergie lived over on the other side of town, and he went to public school. Johnny wondered at first why Fergie had been so closemouthed about where he lived, but it gradually dawned on him that Fergie was poor. He and his family lived on the third floor of a triple-decker apartment house down near the railroad tracks, and Fergie's father sold mail-order shoes and encyclopedias for a living.

Around three o'clock in the afternoon the bus pulled into the parking lot next to the town hall in Duston Heights. When Johnny got out, he had his pack and his sleeping bag strapped on his back and his cardboard suitcase in his hand. He looked this way and that, and then he saw the professor and Grampa standing next to the professor's old mud-spattered Ford. Although Grampa was wearing his usual gray shirt and gray wash pants, the professor was all done up in his blue pinstripe suit, with the vest and the Phi Beta Kappa key that dangled from his gold watch chain. They were both smiling and waving at Johnny, but as he waved back it suddenly struck him that their smiles were forced. There was something in their eyes that said *Johnny, we have bad news for you*. With fear clutching at his heart, Johnny wondered if the bad news had something to do with Gramma.

CHAPTER NINE

Johnny shook hands with the professor and Grampa. He introduced Fergie, who plunged into the milling crowd of relatives and Scouts and came back dragging his dad. Mr. Ferguson turned out to be a mild little man with glasses and thinning hair. He said hello and then headed off with Fergie in the direction of their car. There was an awkward silence until the professor coughed and said brusquely that it was time to be heading back.

Johnny stowed his luggage in the trunk of the car. He climbed into the front with the professor, Grampa climbed into the back, and off they went. Except for the hum of the motor there was absolute silence. To Johnny this was maddening. He wanted to yell, *What is it? What's the matter?*, but his fear and his usual timidity forced him to keep his mouth shut. Finally they arrived at 28 Fillmore Street.

The professor pulled up with a jolt and a sudden screech of the brakes. There, standing on the steps with a big smile on her face, was Gramma! Johnny was amazed, and he felt very relieved. The way Grampa and the professor had been acting, he had expected to find a wreath with a black ribbon on the door and Gramma laid out in a coffin in the living room. But, no, there she was, leaning on a cane with a funny white stocking cap on her head. Her eyes were bright, and she seemed very cheerful. Johnny let out a wild shriek of delight, ran up the walk, and threw his arms around her.

"Gramma!" he yelled. "You're okay! Hooray!"

"Well, I'm sorta okay," said Gramma, frowning. "Your grandfather is gonna scold me for comin' out here. But I didn't wanta be lollin' around in the parlor like some kinda *invalid*."

Soon Grampa and the professor were at Gramma's side. They were clucking like a couple of elderly hens, telling her that she was supposed to be inside lying down. Somehow, with a lot of door-slamming and shuffling around, everybody got back inside the house. Grampa helped Gramma into the parlor and got her seated in the big bristly brown easy chair. Then the professor went out to the kitchen and started fixing Sunday dinner. The professor could cook, which was a

good thing—Johnny didn't know if he could take another of Grampa's ghastly meals. Every now and then
Johnny would glance at Grampa and see the same secretive look he had noticed before. What were they hiding
from him?

Eventually dinner was served in the dining room. With
Grampa's help Gramma hobbled out to join them. It was
a good meal—shepherd's pie, a dish the professor had
learned to make when he was in England, and ice cream
sundaes for dessert. But halfway through dinner Gramma
got drowsy and started to complain of a headache. So
Grampa helped her into the back bedroom, made her
comfortable, and came back to finish his meal.

After dinner the professor asked Johnny to join him
and Grampa in the parlor. *Uh oh*, thought Johnny, *here
comes the bad news.*

The professor sat down on the sofa. He rubbed his
hands nervously and looked solemn. "John," he began, in
a tight, strained voice, "there is a passage in Shakespeare
that goes, *When troubles come, they come not single
spies, but in battalions.* And that has certainly been the
case lately around here. Your grandmother's trouble is
over with—at least, we hope it is. But on Thursday your
grandfather got a telegram from the Department of Defense. And it was bad news. Your father's plane was shot
down over North Korea, in enemy territory."

There was a heavy silence in the room. Johnny felt a

tightening in his chest. With an effort he forced himself to speak. "Is . . . is he . . ."

The professor sighed wearily. "We don't know. There's no word one way or the other. He was a good pilot, with good reflexes. I think there's reason to believe that he could have parachuted to safety, in which case he is probably a prisoner now, or will be soon. But as bad as that is, it's better, far better than . . . the alternative."

"It sure is," said Grampa, nodding. He patted Johnny on the back and smiled sadly at him. "Don't you worry, John. Your dad'll be okay. I read in the paper the other day about how a pilot who got shot down stole a rowboat an' rowed all the way to Japan an' got rescued. Don't you worry—he'll be back soon."

Yeah, thought Johnny gloomily. *He will if he's still alive.* He thought about Chad Glomus, who either was or was not alive. And then he thought about all the stories he had ever read about missing persons. There was the famous Judge Crater, who had gone out to dinner one evening and had never come back. There was Amelia Earhart, the aviator who had disappeared in her plane. Would his dad become a missing person like that? Would Johnny be waiting twenty or thirty years from now for some news of the great Korean War pilot who had vanished without a trace? Black despair filled his heart. He had been so happy about coming home. He had planned to tell Grampa and the professor about his mysterious midnight meeting with Chad Glomus and about the secret passage and everything. But now he didn't want to talk about anything.

The late-afternoon sunlight fell slanting through the parlor windows. It was a nice day outside—for some people.

Finally the professor spoke. He was not much good at comforting other people because he was such a prickly, snappish person, but he tried. "Well, John," he said, "all we can do is hope and pray. There's no reason to despair until there are definite *reasons* for despair."

The professor was being logical, but logic wasn't going to help Johnny much right now. It took a real effort to shove himself to his feet and go upstairs to work on the Latin homework assignment that Sister Mary Anthony had given the class to do during the week's vacation. He opened his Latin book, heaved a great sigh, and soon he was busy with *fruor* and *ulciscor* and *fungor* and lots of other lovely deponent verbs. But over and over as he turned the pages of his book he saw in his mind's eye his father's jet plane bursting into a bright bloom of fire.

October passed. The loud winds of autumn stripped the leaves from the trees on Fillmore Street. Johnny helped his grandfather rake the leaves into a pile in the driveway, and then they had a bonfire, and Johnny threw chestnuts into the fire to make them pop. Gramma got steadily better every day, and soon she was up and about—against the doctor's advice. On school days Johnny went back and forth between his home and St. Michael's School. Some days after school he would go down to Peter's Sweet Shop, a soda fountain on Merrimack Street, and talk with Fergie, and gobble various gooey concoctions. And often in the evening Fergie would come over to Johnny's house to play chess or have weird-fact contests or just sit around and blab. At six P.M. every day Johnny would turn on the television set and listen to the *CBS Evening News*. He kept hoping that he would hear some news about a jet pilot named Harrison Dixon or see a picture of his dad being turned loose by the North Koreans. But the Korean War raged on, and the newscasters said nothing about any prisoners being released. "No news is good news," said the professor, meaning that at least they hadn't heard that Johnny's dad was dead. But this bit of "comfort" did not help Johnny, and day by day, bit by bit, his gloom and pessimism deepened.

Ever since his mother had died of cancer, Johnny had been gnawed by the fear that he would be abandoned, that he would be left alone. To Johnny this now seemed like more than a possibility—it seemed terribly likely. His mother was dead, and his dad was missing in action; his grandmother had been terribly ill, and her illness might return. And then, if Gramma died, Grampa might get so gloomy that he wouldn't want to go on living. Then he would die, and Johnny would be left alone. There was the professor, of course, but Johnny was sure he wouldn't want to adopt him. Hadn't he heard the professor say, many times, that he enjoyed living alone? No. There would be no help there. If everybody close to him died, Johnny would be alone.

Johnny let this fear of abandonment grow. He worried about his father a lot, and he was always glancing anxiously at his gramma to see if she was all right. And now, strangely enough, Johnny's brooding about his grandmother's health brought him back to the lost Glomus will. His reasoning was that if Gramma got sick again, it would take a great brain surgeon to save her. They'd need money to pay one, but now that they had cashed in their savings bonds to pay for her first operation, they were next door to broke. All they had left was a small nest egg, something in a savings account, and something more in that tin can in their kitchen. Johnny didn't know how much great brain surgeons charged for their services, but he figured that it must be a lot. If only he could get the ten thousand dollar reward for finding the Glomus will, he would hire the best surgeon there was to operate on Gramma if her sickness came back.

This "reasoning" of Johnny's was a daydream, but it helped him handle his deep, dark fears. The Glomus will would save him when all else failed, and soon Johnny became obsessed with it. He thought about it all the time, and he became strangely secretive. He never did tell Grampa or the professor about his strange midnight meeting with Chad Glomus. Nor did he tell Grampa about his "Staunton Harold" theory, his guess about where the will was hidden. He wanted very much to discuss his theory with Fergie, but something made him hold back. He was afraid that Fergie might accidentally tell the professor or Grampa and that the two of them would get worried and try to stop him from going after the will. If he was going to save Gramma, he would have to be allowed to work out the puzzle and then do whatever was necessary after that. Until he was ready to make his move, Johnny figured that he'd better stay clammed up.

Often in the evening Johnny went to the public library to find out what he could about the Glomus family and their estate up in the White Mountains. He didn't find much, except for a little about Chad's disappearance in the back issues of *The Boston Globe*. He also managed to locate an article about the Staunton Harold estate in an old picture book called *Stately Homes of New England*. There were a few murky engravings, and there was the surprising information that Mr. Glomus was buried in a mausoleum on the grounds of the estate. All this was very interesting, but it did not throw any light on what the YE OLDE TEA SHOPPE sign meant. Sadly Johnny had to admit that he was up against a blank wall. He had tracked the will as far as the estate, but unless he were Superman, with X-ray vision, he didn't see how he was ever going to discover where it was hidden.

One cold, dark day early in November Johnny came home from school to find that nobody was there. Under the sugar bowl on the dining room table was a note, and it said,

> *Dear Johnny,*
> *Have gone to take your grandmother to the*
> *hospital. Nothing to worry about. Just a checkup.*
> *We'll be back by dinnertime.*
>
> *Grampa*

As he read this Johnny felt his blood run cold. If he had been in a more reasonable frame of mind, he would have known that there was nothing strange about Gramma's going back to the hospital for a checkup. But now he was convinced that Gramma was dying. What on earth could he do?

Johnny sat very still on one of the dining room chairs. Some people yell and scream when they are upset, but Johnny always got very quiet, cold, and withdrawn. He stared at the picture of the Last Supper that hung over the sideboard. But the picture was just a blur to him. Instead, he saw Mount Chocorua and the crumbling stone arch that said Staunton Harold. He saw a train chugging northward up into the White Mountains. And now, slowly, as the Sessions clock ticked on the sideboard, a plan began to form in Johnny's fevered brain. He would go up to New Hampshire, to the estate called Staunton Harold. He would get a room at the hotel that the fussy old lady ran. What was its name? Oh, well, it didn't matter. He had some stationery with the hotel's name and phone number on it—it had been passed out to the Scouts so they could write letters home. Then he'd go out to the estate, and somehow, by hook or by crook, he would find the lost Glomus will, claim the reward, and use the money to get a brain surgeon for Gramma.

This was a crazy plan, and in one corner of his brain Johnny knew it. It was also dangerous, but, strangely enough, the danger attracted him. Even though Johnny was timid, the kind of kid who always looks six ways before crossing the street, every now and then he got the urge to do wild, untimid things. He was always longing to break free from his nervous, scaredy-cat side. *All right, then. He would go.* He wouldn't tell the professor and he wouldn't tell Fergie, either. Johnny wanted this to be his triumph, his alone. *Okay. Let's get organized.* What did he need?

The quiet, reasonable Sessions clock ticked on. The shadows in the dining room grew longer. Johnny sat like somebody who is under a spell. His eyes shone, and his mind was racing like a runaway steam engine, churning out a plan, a wonderful, improbable plan.

CHAPTER TEN

⋙ ● ⋘

Later that same day, when Gramma and Grampa got back from the hospital, they told Johnny that the checkup had gone okay—everything was all right. Johnny did not believe them for a minute. He was convinced they were faking. And so, quietly and secretly, as the November days passed, Johnny got ready to put his plan into action. He went down to the railroad station and asked the station master about trains that ran up into the White Mountains. He found there was a Boston & Maine train that stopped in Kancamagus Center twice a day, early in the morning and then again late at night. The late train, which left Duston Heights at five P.M. was the one Johnny wanted. He could duck out of the house around four thirty, catch the train, and be far away before anyone knew that he was missing.

Then there was the matter of money. He would need to pay for the train ticket and for his hotel room. Although Johnny didn't have any money stashed away, he knew that his grandparents did. They'd lived through the Depression of the 1930's, when the banks had failed, and they'd never gotten over their distrust of banks. So they kept most of their savings on the top kitchen cupboard shelf, inside a red Prince Albert tobacco can. It wasn't much—about a hundred dollars in small bills. Johnny felt very bad about taking it, but he told himself that it was the only way. To keep Grampa from getting suspicious he decided to leave the money where it was until the day came when, suddenly, he would leave.

Johnny also replaced the batteries in his old beat-up flashlight and started picking out the clothes he would need. He'd want all his warm winter things, that was for sure—his parka, his stocking cap, his leather gloves, and his woolen muffler. New Hampshire could turn into a real icebox, and according to the weather reports, there had already been snow up in the northern counties. He wondered what the chapel and the old gloomy mansion would look like in the winter. With a little thrill and a little nervousness, he realized that he would soon be finding out.

And when was he leaving? For a while he himself wasn't sure, but then he decided on November 15 for no special reason. Since it was coming up soon, he stepped up his preparations. And through it all he hugged his secret tightly to him, like a miser with a bag of gold, terribly afraid that somebody would find out what he was up to and try to stop him.

On the morning of November 14 Johnny woke up and found that he had a cold. He felt feverish and achy, and his head was all stuffed up.

Johnny groaned. He wanted to be in top shape for the expedition. Should he postpone it, then? Wouldn't it be better to wait till he was really ready? He wavered and fussed all through breakfast, on his way to school, and during school too. The more he thought, the more convinced he became that he should wait till he was feeling better. But, on the other hand, Gramma could be dying. Time was important. At three thirty, when school let out, he had still not reached a decision.

On his way home Johnny stopped by the library. He wanted to look at that book that contained the article about the Glomus estate. He headed straight into the stacks, took the book down, went to a table, and opened it up. The first time Johnny had read it, the article hadn't really sunk in. But this time it made an unforgettable impression. Once again he read that the mansion was adorned with statues of the Nine Worthies, whoever they were. The chapel was a replica of a seventeenth-century English chapel built by an English nobleman named Sir Robert Shirley. His estate was called Staunton Harold, which was where Glomus got the name from. And then Johnny noticed something new: an inscription over the doorway of Glomus's chapel in honor of Sir Robert Shirley, just as there was over the doorway of the original chapel. At the bottom of the page there was an enlarged version of this inscription so it could be easily read. Johnny had studied it before, but he had only half-understood it. Now he read it again.

Suddenly it was as if a light had gone on in his brain. Another part of the puzzle was, maybe, solved.

"Wow!" Johnny exclaimed. He slammed the book shut and got a loud "Shhh!" from the librarian. Normally he would have been embarrassed, but right now nothing mattered except the lost will. He was closer to it than ever. Well, that settled it. He would go tomorrow evening as he had planned, and he would find it.

That evening went by quickly, with dinner, dishes, and homework. After everybody had gone to bed, Johnny got up and started packing his battered cardboard suitcase. He threw in clothes and the big screwdriver from the tool chest in the basement. Then he went downstairs to the kitchen, climbed up on a chair, took down the Prince Albert can, and counted out the money. Johnny still felt very bad about doing this, but he believed it was the only way he could save Gramma's life. With a heavy heart he went back upstairs to finish his packing.

The next morning when Johnny looked out the window, he saw that it was going to be a bright, sunny day. In the sky was a flock of those little gray clouds that have dark bottoms. They always reminded Johnny of boats and made him think of travel.

Downstairs at breakfast he heard on the radio that the first big snowstorm of the winter was sweeping down out of Canada. It would be snowing hard in the White Mountains area by that night. That might put a crimp in things. . . . But, then, weather reports were often wrong —the professor was always saying that. Johnny went hastily over his plans in his mind: He would have to sneak out of the house with his suitcase about half an hour before the train came. Then he would have to hike across town to the railroad station. Should he leave a note of some kind? He'd better, or Gramma and Grampa would think that he had thrown himself into the Merrimack River.

"So, what's on your mind besides hair? Huh?" This was Gramma, who was sitting across from Johnny, munching toast and drinking coffee.

Johnny looked up, alarmed. "Oh, nothin', Gramma," he said quickly. "I was just . . . worryin' about my Latin test."

Gramma snorted. "You can thank your stars that's all you got to worry about," she grumbled. "I hafta go back to the hospital again for more o' them crazy tests. This time it's that hospital over in Amesbury. What's its name, now, Henry?"

"Bon Sekoors," he said, after thinking a second. "French name—dunno what it means, though. We won't be back till after dinnertime, Johnny. Gramma made some sandwiches and put 'em in the icebox for ya."

Johnny looked at Gramma and Grampa. He felt like crying. They were so nice to him, so kind, and here he was running out on them! And with the money out of the can, on top of everything else! They would feel awful when they found out he was gone. How could he tell them that he was doing it all for Gramma?

Johnny went off to school, and the day passed like some sort of strange dream. He felt that everybody was looking at him, that Sister Mary Anthony and all the kids knew what he was up to. Finally, when he walked down the stone steps and out into the sunlight at a quarter past three, Johnny found that he was getting cold feet. He really didn't want to go. It would be so easy just to head home, unpack his suitcase, and relax. Johnny sighed wearily. Yes, that was what he would do, call the whole stupid thing off.

As he walked home Johnny felt better. A great weight had been lifted from his shoulders. He ran quickly up the steps of his house and across the porch and opened the front door. On the kitchen floor lay the day's mail. It must have arrived after Gramma and Grampa had left. As Johnny bent over to pick up the letters, he stiffened. He could see the return address on the businesslike envelope that was lying at the top of the heap:

DIGBY AND COUGHLAN / UNDERTAKERS

Johnny's heart began to pound. He knew what this meant. Gramma was getting ready for her own funeral. She was a very practical, no-nonsense sort of person. And it was just like her to plan the whole business beforehand. A choking sob rose up in Johnny's throat. He couldn't stand by and let something like this happen! The best brain surgeon in the world would be at her side soon if John Michael Dixon had anything to say about it!

Up the stairs he galloped. He tore open the door of his room and then, panting, forced himself to calm down. It was only twenty minutes to four. He had lots of time. First he opened the top drawer of his bureau. Inside lay the wad of bills from the Prince Albert can with a rubber band around it. Next to it was a brass waterproof matchbox with an enameled inset of an Indian's head against the background of a large white star on the lid. This was the lucky matchbox Professor Childermass had given to Johnny. The professor had carried it all through World War One and had come out with only one small injury. *If I ever needed luck, I need it now*, thought Johnny, and he stuck the matchbox in his pocket. He put thirty dollars in his wallet and stuffed the rest into his suitcase, which he dragged out, all packed, from under his bed. He checked its contents once more, then ran downstairs to the basement and came back with an old rusty iron crowbar. After that was packed too, he ran back downstairs to eat the sandwiches they had left for him. Mmmm—roast beef with mustard and mayonnaise! Normally this would have been a real treat, but Johnny's nose was stuffed up, and everything tasted funny. Oh, well—it was food, and he was hungry. He wolfed them down, drank a glass of milk, and then headed upstairs again. He sat down at his desk and wrote the following note:

Dear Gramma and Grampa,
I have to do something very important. It is a life or death matter, and it can't wait. I'll be back in a few days, so don't worry. Don't be angry, please. I'll explain everything later.

Sincerely yours,
John

PS: I'm sorry I can't tell you where I'm going. It must remain a secret.

Sadly Johnny took the note downstairs and left it under the sugar bowl. For the last time he tramped back upstairs to his room. With his suitcase in hand and a lump in his throat he wondered when he would see it again. Then quickly he turned, marched out the door and down the stairs. His suitcase banged against the banister as he went. Though Johnny's face was pale and drawn, he looked incredibly determined. He also looked scared.

Professor Childermass had not seen Johnny for a while. And for a good reason—he had been out in Springfield, in the western part of the state, attending his brother's funeral. Having arrived back in Duston Heights on the evening of the fourteenth, dead tired and in a foul mood, he had not wanted to see anyone. But now, twenty-four hours after his return, he was anxious to play a few tough, hard-fought games of chess with Johnny. After fixing an early dinner, he drove up to a candy shop in New Hampshire, bought a pound of dark chocolate creams (they were for Gramma, who loved them), and roared back down Route 125 toward Duston Heights. He pulled up in front of the Dixons' house at just about the time that Johnny was buying his ticket at the railroad station.

The professor jumped out of the car, whistling a jaunty tune. With the candy box in his hand he trotted up the front walk, mounted the steps, threw open the screen door, and marched quickly across the porch. There was a bell, but he preferred to bang on the door with his fist. No answer. He hammered some more and finally in desperation pushed the bell button. Still no answer. "Bah! Phooey!" he said, and started back across the porch. But just then he heard the sound of a motor, saw the flash of headlights, and turned toward the Dixons' car coming into the driveway.

"Ah!" said the professor, grinning, as he ran down the steps to meet his friends. Grampa rolled down his window and peered out.

"That you, Rod?" he called.

"It is, indeed!" intoned the professor. "Who did you think it'd be, the Grand Master of the Knights of St.

John? And I was just about to give up on you folks and go home. By the way, where's John?"

Grampa looked puzzled. "Huh? You mean he's not in the house?"

The professor scowled. "Well, he may be in the bathroom or hiding in the coal cellar. But I am not in the habit of barging into my friends' houses when no one answers the door. Now, then! As soon as you folks can pry yourselves out of your car, let's go in and see if he's anywhere on the premises."

A few minutes later Gramma, Grampa, and the professor were huddled around the dining room table. Gramma was shaking her head, and she was starting to cry. Grampa looked stunned. The flesh of his face sagged, and he seemed very old. The professor, who was standing across the table from Grampa, was holding the note in his trembling hand. The muscle in the corner of his mouth had begun to twitch. Suddenly he threw the note out onto the middle of the table.

"We . . . have . . . got . . . to . . . stay . . . *calm*! LET'S STAY CALM, FOR GOD'S SAKE!" he roared. And to show how calm he was, the professor pounded both fists on the table. The sugar bowl jumped and came down on its side, spilling sugar everywhere. "*Where* on *earth* can he have gone? This is not like him—not like him at all. Oh, John, John, I thought you were so levelheaded and reasonable! Judgment, thou art fled to brutish beasts, and men have lost their reason! Oh, God, God, God!"

Ranting and raving in this way, the professor paced up and down the dining room. Grampa kept staring vacantly into space while Gramma cried silently. Finally the professor stopped and planted himself next to Grampa.

"Henry, you must have *some* idea where he has gone!" he cried out in exasperation.

Grampa turned slowly to face the professor, his cheeks wet with tears. As soon as he saw Grampa's face the professor's attitude changed. He winced, sank down into a chair, and put his head in his hands.

"I'm a cranky old man," he said quietly, through his fingers. "Please forgive me. Now, we must keep our heads and try to figure out where he is." He drew a shuddering breath and wiped his hands over his face. "All right, he can't have gone to Korea to look for his dad, so we can eliminate *that* possibility. I assume he hasn't got enough money to go far. Henry, how much allowance do you give him?"

"A dollar a week," said Grampa wearily. "I wish we could give him more'n that, but . . ." His voice trailed away. A thought had just struck him. "Oh, dear!" he exclaimed, clapping his hand to his forehead. "You don't think . . ."

While the professor stood watching, Grampa went out to the kitchen. There was a sound of scuffling and bumping, and then he came back with the Prince Albert can. He dumped it, upside down, on the table; it was empty.

"A hundred dollars!" he gasped. "He took the hull darned thing! I don't believe it!"

Gramma blew her nose loudly and looked up. "I bet I know what happened," she said in a voice thick with crying. "Some burglar probably broke in an' made Johnny give him the money. Then he held a gun to Johnny's head an' made him write that note. An' then he kidnaped Johnny."

The professor gazed skeptically at Gramma. "Madam," he said solemnly, "not to insult you, but your house is not the sort that would be selected by a burglar, unless that burglar was a nitwit." The professor scratched his nose and gazed abstractedly out the window. Then he snatched up the note and read it again.

"Life-or-death matter . . ." he muttered. "What in blue blazes does *that* mean?" He turned to Grampa. "Henry, would you mind terribly if I went up to Johnny's room and poked around a bit? I might find something that would indicate what he was up to. I mean . . ."

Suddenly the professor's mouth grew wide with alarm. "Great Caesar! You don't suppose . . . but no. He wouldn't! But even so. . . . Look, you two must excuse me for a minute."

And with that the professor ran out into the front hall and dashed up the stairs. Gramma and Grampa watched him through the wide arch that separated the front hall from the dining room. And then they turned and looked at each other in utter astonishment.

CHAPTER ELEVEN

❦

The train whistle blew. It was a long, lonely, mournful sound. Johnny heard it and smiled faintly. He was sitting in a seat near a window, and he felt groggy. Because of his cold and fever, he kept drifting in and out of sleep. He wondered what Gramma and Grampa and the professor were doing. Were they ranting and raving and tearing their hair? Had they called the police? Or were they crying? Johnny felt guilty. *But it's the only way*, he said silently. *It'll all work out—I promise. You'll see, you'll see. . . .*

Johnny looked around. There was only one other passenger in the car, an old lady in a brown winter coat and a flowered babushka. Apparently not many people wanted to travel up to the White Mountains at this time of year. Now a frightening thought struck him: What if the Squam House was closed for the winter? Well, then, he would find some other place to stay.

The door at the end of the car slammed open. A fat man in a blue uniform stepped in.

"Kancamagus Center!" he called out. "This way out!"

It was a little after nine o'clock at night. Johnny dragged himself to his feet, pulled his suitcase down from the overhead rack, and moved toward the door. Steam hissed and billowed around him as he walked down the iron steps. Blearily he looked around. A light was on in the little old-fashioned station, and next to it was a car with an illuminated sign on top that said TAXI. Johnny started to walk faster. Now, if only the cab would take him where he wanted to go!

A few minutes later Johnny's cab pulled up in front of the Squam House. The old inn looked pretty much the way it had when he had seen it last, and the downstairs windows were lit up, which was a hopeful sign. Johnny got out, dragging his suitcase out after him. As he was paying the driver, another wave of fear and loneliness swept over him.

"Is . . . is this place open in the winter?" he asked falteringly.

The driver laughed. "Well, if it ain't, kid, you're gonna hafta sleep under them bushes over there!" Then, when he saw Johnny's scared look, he added, "Old Mrs. Wood-ley keeps this place open all winter for the rich types who come up here to ski." He looked at Johnny. "By the way, you're kinda young to be ridin' the rails alone, aintcha? What're you up here for?"

Johnny thought quickly. "I'm here to meet my grampa," he said, glancing toward the hotel. "He's coming over from Center Sandwich to get me."

The driver peered at Johnny closely. He seemed to be on the verge of saying something. But he changed his mind, and without another word he rolled up his window and drove off.

Again Johnny felt afraid. But with an effort he pulled himself together, grabbed his suitcase, and walked toward the hotel.

At first there was no answer when he rang the bell. Then Johnny saw a shape moving behind the pleated curtain in the window on his right. The door rattled open, and there stood Mrs. Woodley, looking just as grim and forbidding as Johnny had remembered her being back in October. When she saw who was on her porch, she seemed startled. But then her whole attitude changed. The scowl vanished, and Mrs. Woodley smiled a warm, welcoming smile.

"Why, my goodness!" she exclaimed. "It's the young man from the camp who came to use my phone! What on earth are *you* doing up here? Come in, come in! You'll catch your death of cold out there!"

Johnny was startled by the woman's sudden change in attitude. But he was glad that Mrs. Woodley wasn't throwing him out. Incredibly tired, feverish, and sniffly, he lugged his suitcase in and set it down by the reception desk. Mrs. Woodley told him to wait there, that she'd be back in a minute. She disappeared into a back room, and Johnny stood by the desk. He dug his hand into his parka pocket, and it closed over something cold and hard—the lucky matchbox. Johnny pulled the matchbox out and fiddled with it. Rubbing the smooth surface comforted him somehow.

When Mrs. Woodley returned, she was holding a guest book bound in green leather and a fountain pen. She set the book down in front of Johnny and handed him the pen. Johnny paused before signing. Should he use a fake name? No, it was possible that Mrs. Woodley remembered his real name. Bending over the book, he signed *Johnny Dixon* slowly and carefully.

Mrs. Woodley went on chattering while he signed the book. "Well, it certainly is nice to have guests this time of year!" she said cheerfully. "This is the in-between season, you know. The leaves are off the trees, and the snow hasn't fallen yet. What are you up here for, by the way? If you don't mind my asking, that is?"

Johnny laid down the pen and glanced distrustfully at Mrs. Woodley. He did not like this incredible cheeriness. *Was she putting on an act or what?* As for the question about what he was doing, Johnny had figured it was coming, sooner or later. And he had an answer ready—the same one that he had given the taxi driver.

"I uh, I'm gonna meet my grampa. He lives near here, over in Center Sandwich. He's gonna come over and get me tomorrow, soon's he can. He, uh, he might be late on account of his . . . his cow is sick." Rather unnecessarily Johnny added, "He, uh, he lives on a farm."

Johnny paused and waited for Mrs. Woodley's reaction. He had pored over a road map on the way up, and he had picked Center Sandwich because it didn't look like it was on any railway line. Would Mrs. Woodley fall for this little fib?

Apparently she would. Closing the guest book, she gazed placidly at Johnny. "Well, young man, you're welcome to stay here as long as you need to. You're my only guest at present, and I'll show you all the hospitality that I can. Have you had dinner?"

Johnny had eaten before he left home. But that didn't matter—he still felt hungry. "Uh, no, I . . . I haven't," he muttered, looking around stupidly. "Can I get something to eat?"

Once again Mrs. Woodley was all grandmotherly kindness. "Why, of course you can! Good heavens, and you've got a cold too! You're supposed to eat well when you have a cold—it builds up your resistance. Come on, now, let's go out to the kitchen and see what we can find."

And, clucking and crooning like the Queen of All Grandmothers, Mrs. Woodley led Johnny out of the lobby and down a short hall that smelled of wood smoke and into a big, old-fashioned kitchen.

Later, after Johnny had finished his meal, Mrs. Woodley took him upstairs to his room. It was a comfortable room with white woodwork and a high walnut bed. Over the bureau hung a little picture that seemed odd to Johnny. It showed an eye shining out of a pyramid, and on top of the pyramid was a motto:

Thou God seest ME

After Mrs. Woodley had explained to Johnny where the bathroom was and told him to sleep well, she left, closing the door softly behind her. Johnny was alone. He looked around the room. Except for the weird picture, it seemed very homey and friendly. He ought to be worn out and ready for bed, but for some reason he wasn't. Something inside him was humming like a dynamo, keeping him keyed up and wide awake. He threw his suitcase on the bed and started taking things out of it and putting them in the drawers of the bureau. When the suitcase was empty—except for the crowbar, the screwdriver, and the flashlight—Johnny snapped it shut and stood it in a corner. He folded down the bed covers and fluffed up the pillow. Still there was this humming in his ears. Still there was a voice inside him saying, *Watch out. There's something wrong.*

Johnny felt frustrated and puzzled. Unless he got some sleep tonight, he would be a total wreck tomorrow when he was supposed to go out to the estate and hunt for the will. He went to the bureau and got out his pajamas. He laid them on the bed, and he was just starting to unbutton his shirt when he had a silly, ungovernable urge to play with his flashlight. Johnny laughed.

Ever since he was a small kid, he had loved flashlights. He'd owned a wonderful old-fashioned one once, with a long, nickel-plated handle that he would shine out his bedroom window at night for fun. This flashlight had had a blinker button on it, and Johnny had used it to send pretend Morse code messages from imaginary spies or people on sinking ships. Maybe playing with the flashlight now would help him relax. Johnny went to the suitcase and snapped it open. With the flashlight in his hand he moved to the window.

It was a small, slightly crooked sash window, but with some shoving Johnny got it to slide up. Cold air flowed in, and Johnny shivered. He snapped on the flashlight and shone it out into a mass of pine trees in the distance. The circle of light moved over banks of dark green needles. *Flash-flash-flash.* Johnny pushed the button— this flashlight had one too—and imaginary messages leaped out into the night. *Ship sinking. Send Help.* What Johnny was really sending with his flasher was just *dah-dit, dah-dit, dit-dit-dit-dah.* This was Morse for CV, the initials of Champagne Velvet, the champagne of bottled beer. He had gotten it from the radio commercials, and he sent it over and over again. But this little routine soon got boring. Now Johnny wanted to see how far the flashlight's beam would carry. He could just barely make out, in the open space beyond the pines, the side of a white clapboard house. Would the beam reach it? He held his arm out the window, stretching as far as he could. Despite his efforts, the shaft of light died before it could reach the house. Sighing, Johnny snapped the flashlight off and jerked his arm back. But as he did this, the tip of his elbow struck the sill. His arm went numb, his hand opened, and the flashlight fell.

"Darn!" Johnny yelled. Annoyed, he peered down at the ground, where there were several little bushes. Maybe they had broken the fall. If the flashlight was smashed . . . well, Johnny didn't want to think about that. Hastily he ducked his head back inside the window and slid the sash down. He went to the closet, got out his coat, and put it on. Then, moving slowly and cautiously, he opened the door and stepped out into the hall. It was true that he was the only guest in the hotel, but he certainly didn't want Mrs. Woodley to hear him. He tiptoed down the hall and down the narrow back staircase. The steps complained loudly, but there was not much that Johnny could do about that. At the bottom of the stairs there was a door with a bolt on the inside. Johnny drew back the bolt, opened the door, and moved out into the chilly, dark yard. Suddenly he had a thought. He went back, found a brick, and stuck it in the door.

Twigs and gravel crunched under his feet as he picked his way around the corner of the building. Now he was on the side of the inn where his window was. Stooped over, he sidled along, rubbing his rear against the foundation stones. It was pitch black. With his hand Johnny combed the top of a low juniper bush. Nothing there. Well, on to the next one. . . . Ah! There it was, lying on a soft, springy bush, as neat as could be! Johnny reached out and picked the flashlight up. He clicked it on and off. It worked. He heaved a deep sigh of relief and was about to start back toward the door he had come out of when suddenly he froze.

A voice was speaking, somewhere above him. It was Mrs. Woodley's voice, drifting out through a partly opened window. Johnny held his breath and listened. At first it just sounded like a wordless muttering, but as he listened more intently Johnny could make out what the old woman was saying. And the words made the hairs on the back of his neck stand on end.

CHAPTER TWELVE

"Chad? Chad? Is that you?" said the cracked, querulous voice. "You've come to stare at me again, have you? Well, my fine young nephew—my *former* nephew, I suppose I should say—I've put up with worse things in my time than your homely face peering down at me. When I learned to control the Guardian, I did some things that you would have run screaming away from when you were alive. Go ahead, shake your head, see if I care! I know, I'm supposed to feel guilty because I put you out of the way. Well, I don't. I have some rights in this life. I've worked hard, and I deserve to have some comforts in my old age. If I had let you find my dear brother's will—and you were just the one who might have done it—what would have happened to me? Answer me that! What if the will had said that dear Herbert had cut me off without a cent? At least, without the will I get *something*! And that, dear boy, is why you had to leave us. I don't know if you were close to finding it. But I wasn't going to take any chances—no sirree!"

Mrs. Woodley had stopped talking. Johnny heard the faint sound of perhaps a bed or chair creaking, a coughing noise, and then the old woman's voice again. "Don't look at me like that, please. I know you feel bad, but there's nothing I can do about it, is there? You were a reckless and irresponsible young man, and well, what's done is done. And I'll tell you something else. There's somebody who's going to be joining you soon. It's that little snot, that boy who was up here last month. You remember—the one I sent that little greeting card to, to try and warn him off? Yes, he's here right now, staying at my hotel!"

Mrs. Woodley laughed, a nasty, sneering laugh. "Yes, and he's after the will. How do I know? Well, when he was here in October, he made a phone call at my hotel, and it so happens that I can read lips. Of course he had no idea that I understood every word he was saying. Yes, he's figured out a great deal, and I'm sure he'd find the will, if I were to let him continue. But just between you and me let me tell you something: He's not going to get anywhere near it, because tomorrow morning he's going to meet with a little accident, and then he'll be where you are. Just think! You'll have some company! Won't that be nice?"

Silence. Johnny crouched under the windowsill. Sweat was pouring down his face, and his body felt goose-pimply all over. So Mrs. Woodley was Mr. Glomus's sister! She knew the will was up there on the estate, and she had killed Chad—or had she? Maybe she was just crazy. She was just talking to herself, or . . .

At that moment Johnny saw something—saw it and felt it too. It was like a gray luminous fog, a hovering cloud shaped like a human being. It drifted out of Mrs. Woodley's bedroom window, and as it moved away Johnny felt icy cold. His scalp tingled, his heart beat faster, and he found it hard to breathe. The shape moved off into the darkness, hovered by the pines, and then faded into nothing.

Johnny closed his eyes and shuddered convulsively. He wished with all his heart that he had never come up here. He wanted to be home safe in his bed. But he wasn't at home. He was up here in New Hampshire, out in the cold and dark, staying in a hotel run by a woman who was planning to kill him. What should he do? He wanted to run off suddenly into the night and hide down by the railroad station till a train came. But his money was up in the dresser drawer in his room. Everything was up there, including the tools he was going to use during his search for the will. Was he going to have to give up on his search, then, to escape from this wicked old woman who seemed to have some kind of super-natural powers?

But Johnny was a pretty strong person, in spite of his timidity. He was panicked, scared half out of his mind, but as he huddled there against the wall he fought it down. Once again his old determination came back.

Johnny thought hard. Many times in chess games he had tried to figure out what his opponent would do next so that he could outwit him. Now he tried to figure out what Mrs. Woodley was going to do. Nothing, probably, for the time being. Tomorrow morning, when he was getting ready to go out to the Glomus estate to poke around—that was when she said she would try to stop him. All right, then, he would mess up her plans. He would escape tonight. He'd just have to go back upstairs and get a few things—the crowbar, the screwdriver, his money, and the map of the roads around Lake Chocorua. Could he summon up enough courage to go back up there? Johnny bit his lip. He closed his eyes, took a deep breath and let it out slowly. Yes, he was ready now. He had to go back.

Cautiously Johnny moved down the wall, scuttling sideways like a crab and gripping the precious flashlight tight in his hand. Around the corner he went and then straightened up to open the door. He set the doorstop aside. Soundlessly he let the door close, and then up the stairs he tiptoed. More creaking—he couldn't stop that. Then down the hall to his room. Johnny slipped inside, closed the door, and let out a deep sigh of relief. Quickly, darting this way and that, he moved about the little room, gathering up the things he needed. Crowbar. Screwdriver. Map. Money. Wallet. Finally he was ready to go again.

It wasn't far to Mount Chocorua and the Glomus estate. Johnny had a fairly good sense of direction, and once he got out onto Route 16, he thought he would remember which way to go. Fearfully he eyed the door of his room. What might be waiting for him outside? With an effort he jerked it open. Nothing but the musty carpeted hallway. Johnny made the sign of the cross, awkwardly, because he was still holding the flashlight, then out into the hall he went.

For hours the professor's car had been speeding along on New Hampshire State Route 16. The professor was behind the wheel, hunched over, gripping it tightly. In his mouth was an unlit Sobranie cigarette, and on his face was a look of crabby determination. A scrubby old deerstalker's cap was on his head, and the fur-lined flaps were tied down over his ears. Sitting next to the professor was Fergie Ferguson. The professor had persuaded him to come along because he was convinced that Fergie could help him find Johnny. After dashing madly from the Dixons' house with some "clues" crammed into his pocket, the professor had driven with lightning speed across town to the Fergusons'. He had barged in on them in the middle of their dinner and, after frightening poor Mrs. Ferguson half to death, had managed to convince the family that he badly needed Fergie's help. The professor was a good guesser. He had found some stationery from the Squam House in Johnny's bureau and was sure that Johnny was after the Glomus will. Then, guessing wildly this time, the professor had decided that maybe Johnny and Fergie knew something about it that they weren't telling him. So after taking Fergie into a back room of the Ferguson home, he gave him the good old-fashioned third degree. At first Fergie had refused to tell him anything. But then, when he realized that Johnny's life might be in danger, he changed his mind and told him about the strange midnight meeting with Chad Glomus and Chad's terrifying disappearance. That was all the professor needed. He persuaded the puzzled Fergusons that their son ought to go with him. They were reluctant to give their permission at first, but the professor pleaded and wheedled. He also added that there was no danger involved—this was not true, but the professor was not above lying to get something he wanted. Finally the Fergusons had insisted that the police be contacted. And the professor had said blandly that of course he intended to do so immediately. This was another lie—for reasons of his own the professor had no intention of bringing the police into this strange and desperate manhunt.

On roared the professor's car. He was a terror on wheels, even when he wasn't on a life-or-death mission. He jammed the accelerator down, and the needle flicked past ninety. Fergie sat rigidly, gripping the edge of the seat with his hands. Once he had ridden with Father Higgins, the parish priest at St. Michael's. He had been bad, but he hadn't been anything like this.

"Professor?" said Fergie in a tight, strained voice. "How . . . how far do we have to go?"

"Oh, not so far now. That town we just passed through is Center Ossipee. It's only about twelve miles to Kancamagus Center. We'll get there soon—don't worry."

Now the tires squeeched loudly as the car rounded a difficult S-curve. Fergie was thrown first against the door, then back the other way.

"Where do you think he'd go?" the professor barked out suddenly without taking his eyes off the road.

Fergie thought hard. "Gee. I dunno. Did you say he bought a ticket at the train station?"

"Yes. I checked there because it was the only possible way for Johnny to get up to that idiotic estate. The ticket was to Kancamagus Center. Could he walk out to the Glomus place from there?"

Fergie thought some more. "Maybe, only I don't think he would want to, unless he's *really* flipped his lid. I bet he'll just sack out somewhere for the night, and then bomb on out to the old estate in the morning."

The professor considered Fergie's suggestion. He grimaced, as he often did when he was thinking, and the cigarette bobbed up and down in his mouth. "Hmm. I think, Byron, that you are most probably right. After all, John doesn't know that anyone is following him, and he can certainly afford to pay for a room. Did I tell you that he swiped about a hundred dollars from his grandparents before he lit out?"

"Yeah, you did. That's not so great."

The professor opened his mouth to sigh, but as he did the cigarette fell out. "Blast!" he snapped. Then he shook his head, and his face tensed up. "I certainly hope he's all right," he said softly, and he pushed the accelerator pedal down harder.

CHAPTER THIRTEEN

A short time later the professor's car came rolling into Kancamagus Center, where houses, trees, steeples, the wide grassy common, all were still and dreamlike on this frosty November night. The sky was clear, and you would never have guessed that a snowstorm was on its way. But snow was what the weatherman on the radio had said. The professor had heard the report more than once today, and it had filled his mind with fear for Johnny's safety. Now he pulled over to the curb next to the deserted common, turned the motor off, and heaved a small sigh. After some fumbling in the glove compartment, he found his pack of Balkan Sobranie cigarettes and lit one.

"So, Byron," he said, turning to Fergie. "I wonder what our next move ought to be. If we are right, Johnny is holed up somewhere here in town. This Squam House —the one whose letter paper Johnny had—is probably our best bet, don't you agree?"

Fergie nodded. "Yeah, I guess so. We could ask the lady that runs the place if he's there. Only it's really late, an' Johnny told me that she's an unbelievable witch. I think she'd raise hell if we was just to go up an' hammer on her door now."

The professor turned on the dome light in his car. He peered at his watch, which said ten after twelve, and then flipped the light off. "Ye-es," he said slowly, considering, "I imagine she would get into a bit of a snit if we woke her up now. Unfortunately, however, I am a very impatient sort, and I am not going to sit here smoking cigarettes and fidgeting until the dawn's early light. So Mrs. Whosis will just have to get herself into a Grade-A snit. We are going over there *now*!"

And with that the professor turned the ignition key. The car sprang to life. But then, abruptly, the professor turned the motor off.

"What's wrong?" Fergie asked anxiously.

"Nothing much. I just realized I don't know where that idiotic inn is." Suddenly an idea struck him. He turned the dome light on, again reached over and dug into the glove compartment, and came out with a wrinkled piece of letter paper. He uncrumpled it, and Fergie saw that it was a piece of the Squam House's stationery. At the top was a picture of the inn in green ink, and down below was the motto *The friendly white inn on the common.*

The professor's mouth curled into a sarcastic grin. "Friendly, eh? Well, we shall see."

The professor started up his car again. Slowly the battered old Ford crawled along the dark street, which was getting darker by the minute as black clouds rushed in to cover the moon. The professor peered out the car window owlishly as he examined one blank staring house front, then crept on to the next one and the next one. Finally, with a look of triumph on his face, he put on the brakes. There was the inn, identical to its picture on the letterhead. Although a carriage lamp on a post was shining out in front, the windows were dark.

The professor turned off the motor and sat with arms folded. Looking out at the inn, he shook his head slowly. "She's going to be in a rare mood when we wake her up," he said. "But I'm afraid there's no help for it. Come on, Byron—unless, of course, you'd rather stay in the car."

"Naw, I'll come," said Fergie, grinning maliciously. He thought it might be fun to see a nasty old woman after she had been awakened out of a sound sleep.

Two car doors slammed. Walking side by side, Fergie and the professor strode up the walk, up the steps, and onto the wide porch. The professor harrumphed in a nervous way and jabbed at the bell with his index finger. It was a loud bell, and they could hear it ringing deep inside the inn. At first nothing happened. Fergie rubbed his mittened hands and the professor puffed his cigarette and sang "*Cadet Roussel,*" a French nonsense song that he liked. But soon lights began to come on. There was the sound of chains rattling, and then the door swung open. Mrs. Woodley stood before them, wearing a blue quilted dressing gown with a little ruffled collar and holding a small black flashlight. Cold cream covered her face, and she looked very, very angry.

"Well?" she said. Her voice trembled with indignation as she eyed the two of them. "You've gotten me up in the middle of the night—I congratulate you. What do you want?"

Normally the professor was able to hold his own against even the crankiest and most forbidding people. But there was a strange aura about Mrs. Woodley that suggested . . . well, something more than ordinary nastiness. The professor took a step backward, and there was genuine fear in his eyes. But then he pulled himself together and put on his most brusque and businesslike manner.

"Madam," he said crisply, "I deeply apologize for waking you out of a sound sleep on such a cold night and at such a late hour. But the fact is, this is somewhat of an emergency. We are looking for a young man named John Dixon. He's about twelve, and he's pale, blond, and wears glasses. We have reason to believe that he came up here by train and intended to spend the night at your, uh, establishment. Is he here?"

Mrs. Woodley's mind was racing. If she told this man

that the boy was here, then he'd take the boy away, and she'd be rid of him, wouldn't she? But he might come back. No, it would be better to be rid of him once and for all.

"There's nobody staying here tonight but me," she said in her grimmest, most final tone. "I don't get much business at this time of year. Now, if that is all you have to say to me . . ."

Mrs. Woodley stepped back and took hold of the edge of the door, getting ready to shut the two intruders out. But the professor had been watching her like a hawk, and he thought he saw something in her eyes that suggested she might be lying. With a sudden spring he leapt forward and planted both feet on the doorsill.

Mrs. Woodley's mouth dropped open. "I beg your *pardon!*" she began, her voice rising an octave or two.

"Thank you, I accept your invitation," snapped the professor, and with that he shoved rudely past Mrs. Woodley and dashed into the lighted lobby of the inn. This was a desperate gamble on the professor's part. He wanted to get inside to see if he could find something, anything that would prove that Johnny had been there. Wildly the professor looked this way and that. He took in the couches, the easy chairs, the fussy mahogany tables with oil lamps and bric-a-brac on them. But meanwhile Mrs. Woodley was advancing on him, bubbling over with rage.

"*Now, see here, you!*" she yelled. "*What do you think gives you the right to come barging in here and—*"

"Ah-*hah*!" screeched the professor. He leaped toward the reception desk and swept up something in his right hand. He held it up triumphantly between his thumb and index finger. It was Johnny's waterproof matchbox. "So he *was* here after all! And you were lying to me, you foul-tempered old bat! *Lying!*"

The professor waved his accusing finger in Mrs. Woodley's face. But now she had grown dangerously calm. She folded her arms and glowered at him. "That matchbox is mine," she said grimly. "And you are trespassing. I'll thank you to give it back to me, take that ugly little snot over there, and leave *right now*, before I call the police!"

As Fergie watched the professor and Mrs. Woodley facing each other down in the middle of the room, the air between them seemed to shimmer with tension. The professor held the matchbox up and waved it back and forth before Mrs. Woodley's eyes.

"You deny that this is Johnny's?" he shouted, in a voice that was rising in pitch with every instant. "You actually *deny it*?"

Mrs. Woodley glared stonily, saying nothing. A sudden evil inspiration darted into the professor's head. He turned on his heel and strode to the long polished table that stood between the two rows of armchairs. On it was a group of carefully arranged objects: Staffordshire china dogs and cats, glass paperweights, a blue glass medicine bottle, and a Dresden figurine of a minstrel playing a mandolin. The professor remembered now the story Johnny had told him about the fussy old lady who was afraid he would break the vase on her phone table. With a sudden swoop he reached out and picked up a small china dog, wheeled around, and threw it into the fireplace. The dog shattered into thousands of tiny white pieces.

"There!" said the professor with a snort of satisfaction. He turned back to Mrs. Woodley. "Now, then! If you don't want something like that to happen again, you malignant old hag, I suggest that you tell me what you have done with Johnny!"

Mrs. Woodley's face was a mask of cold hatred, and a vein in her neck was throbbing. Suddenly she flicked out her left hand, and as she did this the professor felt a sharp stab of numbing pain. His right hand—which he had used to throw the dog—felt as if an enormous bee had stung it. Clutching the throbbing hand to his chest, the professor reeled back. His eyes were wide with fear.

"That's what you get," crooned the old woman maliciously, "for willfully destroying private property!" Now her tone became harder, angrier. She advanced on the professor, and he retreated, still clutching his wounded hand. "Get out of here!" she snarled. "Get out of here, and don't come back!"

The professor and Fergie did not need any more encouragement. Fergie went first, and the professor dashed after him, slamming the door as he went. Together they stumbled down the stairs, and they were halfway down the walk before Mrs. Woodley emerged on the porch. Her face was purple with rage, and little white flecks of foam appeared at the corners of her mouth.

"*If you ever find him, you may not like what you see!*" she screeched in a voice that was scarcely human. "*And if you try to meddle in things that don't concern you, you'll wish you hadn't!*" With that she stepped back and slammed the door loudly. The thunderous sound seemed to reverberate in the still, frosty night air. Then there was silence, and the lights inside the inn went out.

The professor and Fergie stood by the car, staring in wide-eyed horror at the darkened building. Neither of them said anything for a long while.

Finally the professor spoke. "My God! I never imagined . . . I mean, who could possibly have guessed . . . ?"

Fergie glanced nervously back at the inn. He tugged at the professor's arm. "Come on. Let's get outa here before she comes back and really takes care of us."

The professor nodded. They ran around the car and jumped in.

"I'm going to have to do this one-handed for a bit," said the professor, gasping with pain. "It'll be awkward, but I'll manage." He turned the key and the motor started. Then, bracing his left arm against the wheel and shifting gears with his right, he got the car going. It moved in a wobbly, uncertain way, and he nosed it around to the other side of the common. Then he pulled over to the curb, turned off the motor, and just sat staring blankly at the windshield.

Fergie was worried. Maybe the professor was sick, or dying. "Are . . . are you okay, sir?" he asked falteringly.

"No," intoned the professor. Then he laughed and smiled reassuringly. "In my mind I am blowing up the Squam House with sticks of dynamite. But except for that, I am as well as can be expected, as my sickly aunt Sally always used to say. But what do we do now? *That* is what I want to know!"

Fergie also tried hard to think. "Is she a witch?" he asked at last.

The professor groaned. "Oh, God! Let's not go into that! She's a . . . a *something*, that's for bloody sure!" And with his good hand he pounded on the steering wheel.

"Do you suppose she's holdin' Johnny prisoner?" Fergie asked. "I mean, bound and gagged in a cellar or . . . or somethin' like that?"

The professor shook his head. "No. No, I don't think so. That last thing she shrieked, about 'if you ever find him' . . . that says to me that he's out there in the dark somewhere. No, he must have escaped from her—for now, anyway. That may be why she's so incredibly angry. We can't be sure of anything, of course. But first of all I guess we'd better head out to that awful estate . . . Tooting Stanton, or whatever its name is. If Johnny is anywhere, he's out there. And I hope, I very much hope that we can get in by way of that secret passage that you told me about. Do you think you can direct me to the estate?" Fergie nodded. "I . . . I guess so, Professor Childermass. It's dark, but once we get to the road that goes out to the camp, I think it'll look kinda familiar."

The professor flipped on the headlights and started the motor. "I hope so," he said. Then he put the car in gear and roared away in a cloud of exhaust smoke.

Meanwhile, up in her bedroom, Mrs. Woodley was dragging a strange, bulky object from her closet. It was like a small square chest covered with cracked, goose-pimply leather. Muttering unpleasantly to herself, the old woman folded the top back and part of the front down. Now the box resembled a small stage on which miniature actors might move about. It was dark inside but . . . No! Mrs. Woodley said a word, and it started to glow with a quivering blue light. Strange signs and a picture of a comet with a long flaring tail slowly became visible on the wood. In a row on the tiny stage stood several glass bottles. One was tall and thin, one was pear-shaped, one was very small, and another was all bulbs with a long spout projecting from it. A hissing blue flame shot from the spout, making all the bottles glow. Twisted strands and loops of fire burned inside each one—purple, red, orange, yellow. From a drawer in the front of the box Mrs. Woodley took a small metal holy-water sprinkler. She shook drops over the glowing bottles, and they began to shiver and send up a high-pitched wailing music, like the sound of a glass harmonica. Suddenly a formless patch of golden light appeared on the wall behind the box. In the center of the patch of light was a pyramid with an eye in its center. And over the pyramid were some Hebrew letters glowing with red fire. The mingled colored lights flitted about Mrs. Woodley's face as she stared at them intently. Her lips formed strange phrases, and an incantation rose to mingle with the bottles' eerie wail.

Johnny walked quickly along a dark, gravelly road that cut through great masses of trees. It led from Camp Chocorua to the old estate, and it was a road that he remembered well. Passing through the deserted picnic grounds by dark, still Lake Chocorua had been strange. Although he had not been able to see the mountain itself, he had felt its looming presence. Johnny was surprised to find out what a good hiker he was. Maybe the week in October had done him some good. Whatever the reason, he had covered the three miles in a relatively short time.

His head cold was still a problem, of course. Every now and then he had to set down his crowbar and fish his handkerchief out of his pocket so he could blow his nose. But he wasn't collapsing or anything. He felt strong and brave and purposeful, even though the fear of Mrs. Woodley hovered in the back of his mind.

Johnny slowed down. He played the flashlight's pale beam along the left-hand side of the road as he searched for the little stone that marked the path to the lodge.

Had he come too far? No! There it was, half-buried in leaves. He felt a triumphant surge in his chest. He was doing it! He was on his way!

Johnny turned onto the path and walked on, peering into the darkness as he went. It was easier to see through the trees now that they were bare. In the distance he could make out the quaint steep-gabled cottage with its gothic doodads and carvings. Rushing toward it now, Johnny felt something cold hit his cheek. Snow! Oh, well, it wasn't coming down very hard. As Johnny tramped on, swinging the crowbar jauntily, the lodge drew closer and closer until finally he was standing before it.

Johnny laughed. He felt like Hansel and Gretel at the old witch's cottage. The lodge was like that, a weird fairy-tale house that an old witch might live in. What if he opened the door and found Mrs. Woodley standing there, grinning evilly at him? Johnny shuddered. He really did not like thoughts like that.

After a quick nervous look around, Johnny set the crowbar down next to the doorway. He played the flashlight beam along the row of carved stone ballflowers that ran along the lintel over the door. *Which one had it been?* Ah . . . that one, with the hole in it! Standing on tiptoe, Johnny reached in and pulled out the small, old-fashioned key, fit it into the lock, and heaved open the door. Then he picked up the crowbar and stepped inside.

The room was as musty and dismal and empty as it had been before. Mr. Glomus leered down at him from his frame over the mantel, and for the thousandth time Johnny thought about what a very strange old coot he must have been. However, he had not come here to think about Mr. Glomus. He was here on business.

Johnny examined the front of the fireplace. The smiling children with their cereal bowls gazed blandly down at him. One of those heads was the knob. One, two, three . . . the third one up from the right looked slightly worn. Cautiously Johnny reached up and tried to twist the head. It moved. To his great delight Johnny heard the grumbling of machinery, of hidden chains and counterweights. Slowly, inch by inch, the massive stone slab at the back of the hearth rose up. But then, quite suddenly, the noise stopped. The slab was stuck! By the light of the flashlight Johnny could see a dark opening that was only about a foot high.

Johnny sighed. He knelt down and shuffled on his knees into the mouth of the fireplace to inspect the narrow opening. Could he fit through it? Well, he would have to. First he slid the all-important crowbar into the opening as far as it would go. Then, with his flashlight in his hand, he flattened himself on the floor, wriggled forward over the sooty hearthstone, and squeezed himself through.

On the other side Johnny pulled himself to his feet. For a moment he thought about searching for the lever that would make the slab go back down. But it occurred to him that he might want to come back this way, and if he closed the door, he might—for all he knew—be closing it for good. So Johnny brushed the soot off the front of his parka and picked up the crowbar once more. With the flashlight beam playing before him, he advanced into the dank, foul-smelling tunnel.

Johnny moved forward through the dark. Suddenly, for no reason at all, he remembered his matchbox. He felt in his pockets. Oh, no! It was gone! He had probably left it back at the inn. No time to go back now, though. He pressed on. And now the fear of the Guardian began to creep over him. Inside his head he heard Chad Glomus's horrible screams and remembered what he had said: "The Guardian might be anything: It might be a pool of moonlight on the floor, or a chair, or smoke drifting in the air. It will come for you if you get too close to the will...."

Johnny tried to laugh his fear off. He tried to believe what Fergie believed, and he told himself stubbornly that Chad's disappearance had been faked. He was rich and screwy, and right now he was probably drinking a gin and tonic in a bar in Bermuda. Anything was possible if you were rich, Johnny told himself. But then he thought of the things he had seen and heard when he was crouching under Mrs. Woodley's window, and the fear crept back, chilling him to the bone.

Johnny kept walking. He went up two broad shallow steps to the second level of the tunnel, till he finally saw, far ahead, the stout nail-studded door that led to the crypt beneath the chapel. He stopped, listening for sounds. Nothing. The silence was complete and abso-

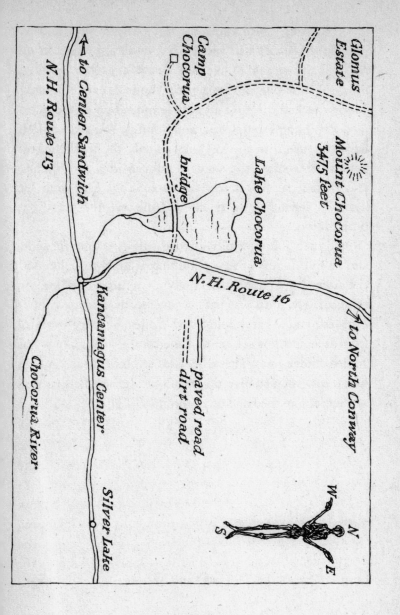

Glomus
Estate

Camp
Chocorua

Mount Chocorua
3475 feet

Lake Chocorua

bridge

to Center Sandwich

N.H. Route 113

N. H. Route 16

to North Conway

Kancamagus Center.

paved road
dirt road

Chocorua River.

Silver Lake

N
W
E
S

lute. Nervously he flashed the light to one side, and he jumped a foot. It had picked out a carved skeleton on the wall. A streak of ice ran down over the carving, blocking out one of the figure's hollow eyes. Quickly Johnny jerked the light away. He moved up to the door. The key hung from a nail, and Johnny had to use both hands to turn it in the keyhole. Finally the lock clicked. Johnny shoved at the door. It moved in a few inches, and then it stuck—it had hit something. He stuck his head in through the crack and played the flashlight beam down.

And then Johnny's blood froze. His eyes opened wide, and he felt fingers of fear clutching at his throat. Beyond the door lay a body, the body of a man in a yellow raincoat. His head was partly covered by a black rubber rain hat, and what Johnny saw made him very grateful that he could not see more. One of the man's arms was folded under him. The other was stretched out, and his hand was splayed flat on the floor. It was brown and withered, like the hand of a mummy.

CHAPTER FOURTEEN

Johnny closed his eyes. A wave of sick terror swept over him. He was afraid that he would faint, or die. But his resolve was strong, and he summoned up all the courage that was in him.

When he opened his eyes, the horrible shape was still there, sprawled on the cold stones. In the midst of his panic Johnny felt terribly sorry for Chad. He had been peculiar, but he had tried to be nice to Johnny and Fergie. He hadn't been particularly likable, but he hadn't been evil. Johnny swallowed hard, and another sick, convulsive shudder ran through his body. This cleared his head, somehow. He had no time to get upset, not now. He had to press on, and if the Guardian caught up with him . . . well, at least he would go down fighting. Johnny got a good tight grip on the crowbar and the flashlight. Then, turning his eyes away, he edged around the slumped body and flashed his light this way and that. The crypt was a low, gloomy chamber, a sort of basement under the chapel. Rows of stone arches stretched away into the distance. *Was there a door that led upstairs?* There had to be. Johnny crept forward cautiously, past heavy round pillars. Ahead, at the top of a low flight of stone steps, he saw what he was looking for. Up the steps he went. The door opened easily, and he found that he was peering into a narrow stairwell. More steps corkscrewed upward. He followed them, and at the top was yet another door. He opened it and found that he was in the chapel.

Because it was dark, Johnny had only a dim idea of what the place looked like. He played the flashlight beam about and saw high wooden pews, a stone altar with a bronze crucifix on it, and a series of gothic arches that marched down the side aisles. Johnny loved strange old buildings, and at another time he might have stopped to explore. But he was in a hurry. So, putting on a look of the grimmest determination, he tramped purposefully down the aisle. At the back of the chapel, under the organ loft, was a big, pointed wooden door with two leaves that were held together by a bolt in the middle. There were spring bolts at the top and the bottom. Johnny slid them back. He pulled the handle and the door swung outward. Cold air rushed in, and snowflakes stung Johnny's face. He was out in the open air again at last.

Johnny felt grateful and extremely relieved. He just stood there a moment, eyes closed, and let the tiny frigid white dots hit his face. He had not been cooped up in the tunnel and the crypt for very long, but it had seemed like ages. Greedily he gulped cold air into his lungs. Johnny wanted to stand there forever, but he knew he couldn't. Doggedly he dragged his mind back to the job that was at hand.

Johnny picked his way down the short flight of steps that led to the open space in front of the chapel. He turned and glanced to his right. Beyond the swirling snow he could just barely see the vast black shadow of the mansion. Before him rose the chapel's tower, a stubby structure with battlements on top. Although the church was gothic, the doorway was classical. It was flanked by fluted pillars with scrolled capitals, and there was a fancy stone cornice over the door. Above the cornice was a triangular stone slab called a pediment. Set in its center was a square tablet made of white marble, and on the tablet was the inscription that had excited Johnny so much when he'd read it for the second time in the book he had found in the library. He had copied the inscription out of the book and had pored over it on the train ride up to New Hampshire. In the dark Johnny could not make out the inscription. Nevertheless he could have recited it by heart:

In the yeare 1653 when
all thinges Sacred were throughout ye nation
Either demolisht or profaned
Sir Robert Shirley, Barronet,
Founded this church;
Whose singular praise it is,
to haue done the best things in ye worst times,
and
hoped them in the most callamitous.
The righteous shall be had
in everlasting remembrance.

Johnny loved the inscription. It sounded grand and thrilling, even though he didn't know anything about Sir Robert Shirley or the calamitous times that he had lived in. He was also filled with smug self-satisfaction, because he had figured out that the *ye* in YE OLDE TEA SHOPPE referred to the two *ye*'s in the inscription. He even knew, thanks to the professor, that *ye* in the old days was sometimes just a funny way of writing *the*. But Johnny didn't have time to pat himself on the back. He had to find some way of getting up to the place where the inscription was so he could examine it more closely.

With a sinking heart Johnny realized that this was not a part of the treasure hunt that he had planned very carefully. Were there any ladders around? He hadn't seen any, and ladders were not the kinds of things that people left lying about on a deserted estate in the wintertime. Then suddenly Johnny grinned. He had been staring at the solution all the time. A mass of ivy vines grew up one side of the carved doorway, twisting about the columns till they spread their hundreds of spidery tendrils across the inscribed stone tablet at the top. And there was even a little ledge under the tablet. If he ever got up that high, Johnny was sure he could stand on it.

Johnny took off his gloves and put them into a pocket of his parka. Then he reached out, took hold of the vines, and started to climb. It turned out to be surprisingly easy. The vines were spread out all across the face of the doorway, and Johnny found handholds and footholds everywhere. And so, before long, Johnny was stepping out onto the narrow ledge that stood atop the doorway. He was still clinging to the vines for dear life, terribly afraid he might slip. But when he finally had a firm footing on the ledge, he let go. Now he was standing over the doorway of the church. It was not a terribly long way down, but even so, if he had taken a step backward, he would have had a pretty nasty fall. Johnny tried not to think about that. Instead he slowly lowered himself to his knees until the inscription was at eye level. From the left-hand pocket of his parka he took out the flashlight. He examined the first ye, but there was nothing odd about it. The letters were no more deeply cut than the others around them. Johnny tried the other ye, and this time his heart jumped. Around the word was a faint ragged line—a crack in the stonework. It looked as if the crack had been smeared over with plaster at one time, but wind and weather had eaten most of the plaster away. Johnny dug his hand into the pocket on the right side of his parka and pulled out the screwdriver. Holding the flashlight steady with his left hand, he poked at the crack. Immediately more plaster flaked away. The crack got wider, the tip of the screwdriver sank in deeper, and Johnny wiggled it around to widen the crack. All around the wandering circle he went, poking and prying and loosening. Tiny gray flakes fluttered down onto the ledge. Excitedly Johnny pulled back his right hand, and he stabbed as hard as he could. The tip of the screwdriver sank in an inch or more. Johnny pried, and the slab started to move. But the work would take two hands, and so he laid down the flashlight. Now he heaved with all his strength, and the thick slab of stone fell out onto the ledge with a *chunk*. Excited, Johnny snatched up his flashlight and peered into the ragged hole. He expected to see a legal-looking bundle tied with red ribbon, or a metal strongbox with a padlock on it.

But what he saw was neither of these. It was a small square can. The label said Herb-Ox Bouillon Cubes.

Johnny could have cried. Was this it then? Was this what he had come up here for, in the snow, in the dark, in the cold? One last flickering hope remained. Maybe the can contained microfilm, and the will was printed on it. Impatiently Johnny pried the lid off. Inside were little cubes wrapped in gold-colored foil. He unwrapped the first one. And the second and the third and all the rest. Chicken bouillon cubes.

With a violent heave, Johnny hurled the can off the ledge and listened as it clattered on the pavement below. He felt like the biggest fool who ever walked on two legs. By now the professor and his grandparents would be frantic with worry. The police were probably out beating the bushes around Duston Heights. Police dogs were sniffing for him in the woods outside town. And when he came back to them, what could he bring? Bouillon cubes.

Johnny knelt there, facing the wall. He wanted to cry, but the tears would not come. His mind was racing through all the possibilities. If Mrs. Woodley really was a witch, maybe she had changed the will into a can of Herb-Ox Bouillon Cubes. It was an idiotic thought, but right now the idea seemed about as reasonable as any-thing else that he could come up with. He shook his head and heaved a deep, shuddering sigh. The game was over. He would just have to go home. Glumly Johnny picked up the flashlight, stuffed the screwdriver into his pocket, and carefully pulled himself to his feet. Edging to the right, he reached out in the dark and felt for handholds and footholds among the tangled vines. Now he was making his way down, and he found, strangely enough, that he was thinking of hot cereal. He wanted to be in a nice warm room, in his pajamas and bathrobe, eating a steaming bowl of Gramma's oatmeal, with maple syrup and brown sugar and cream.

But when his foot touched the ground Johnny turned around. It seemed to be snowing harder. He wanted to get away, far from this awful place as quickly as he could. With a sinking heart, he realized that he would probably have to go back down through the crypt. There was a high, spike-topped iron fence around the estate, and he didn't feel up to scaling it. But as he turned back toward the dark doorway of the chapel, he saw something. Someone was coming down the steps toward him with arms outstretched. A figure in a yellow raincoat. A figure with hollow mummy eyes and a withered mummy face and clawlike mummy hands. Moving with an awful, tottering, unsteady gait, it came toward him.

CHAPTER FIFTEEN

Johnny screamed. He dropped the flashlight and ran blindly into the night as the snow swirled around him. Now he saw the vast shadow of the old mansion looming up before him. He could make out its blank, forbidding wall of stone towering up into the night. Madly Johnny raced along the wall, looking for a door. He wished he could see where he was going! It was pitch black out, and if a pit suddenly opened up before his feet, he would fall right in. Now the wall was turning. Johnny turned too. He had seen a couple of tall windows in heavy stone frames. But no doors, none at all. . . .

Then he saw it. A low door, half-sunk in the ground. He could hide till morning, and maybe the awful thing would go away. Johnny was filled with terror. He didn't want to die. He didn't want to end up like Chad. No, not like that. . . .

He was at the door. He shook the knob, but it held tight. Johnny shut his eyes and screeched: "*Let me in!* LET ME IN!" He pounded on the door. Horribly he felt something clawing weakly at his back. Was Chad trying to stop him from entering the building? Was he trying to help him? The thought raced madly through Johnny's brain. *Oh, God, oh, God, please* . . . Johnny gasped, and then, incredibly, the door opened. He did not stop to wonder why but plunged in and slammed it shut behind him.

He had escaped. But what had he escaped into? There had been a little light outside, but there was none at all here. Groping like a blind man, Johnny found a stair railing. Up he went, shuffling, one step at a time. At the top he found another door and opened it. A musty, shut-up smell rushed out to meet him. While Johnny was wondering what kind of room he was in, thunder rumbled overhead, and lightning flashed. For a brief instant he saw a huge kitchen with a long counter running down the middle, and copper kettles hanging from a rack overhead. At the far end of the kitchen was another door. He felt like a rat caught in a maze, or the pinball in a pinball machine. Lightning flashed again, and this time Johnny made a dash for it.

The heavy door boomed behind him. Now he was in the dark again. But as he felt his way along, his hand rubbed the top of something smooth—a table, probably.

Again there was a sudden flash of lightning in the three tall windows, and Johnny had a brief glimpse of an enormous paneled dining room. A table as long as a bowling alley ran down the middle, and rows of high-backed chairs flanked it. He was standing by a low side table, and on the table were . . . candles! Just what he needed! Now, if only he could find some matches! Blindly he groped across the dusty surface of the table. He heard things fall, and something rolled off the table and smashed on the floor. Then his hand closed over a small box. He pushed at the end, and it slid in. A matchbox! Johnny's fumbling fingers found small stick matches. He felt the side of the box and *br-rr-rip!* went the match. A pinpoint of sulfurous light flared, and with a trembling hand Johnny lit the candle. Ah, blessed light! Johnny tottered forward across the dusty floor. The candlelight glimmered in a row of tall mirrors to his right. His shadowy reflection made Johnny jump. He stumbled this way and that, holding the candle up and straining his eyes till his head ached. There had to be a way out—a main entrance, or another side entrance . . . something, anything! Johnny gritted his teeth. He would get out if it killed him. Ghosts or no ghosts, mummies or no . . .

A silvery voice began to sing, high-pitched and mocking:

> A tisket, a tasket,
> A will in a wicker basket!

and then:

I found it, I found it,
I green and yellow found it!

The voice died away. Then Johnny glanced at his candle. The flame was burning blue! The Guardian was here! For a second he went numb with terror, but he summoned up all his willpower and forced himself to stumble ahead across the dusty floor. He pushed open a set of tall French doors and crossed another room. He paused and looked this way and that in utter bewilderment. And then the walls of the room began to shake. A cobwebbed chandelier trembled overhead, and its thousands of glass pendants set up a loud, alarmed clattering. Panicked, Johnny rushed off to the right. He had seen another set of French doors there. The walls and the floor continued to pitch and heave, like the deck of a ship in a storm. Johnny slipped to his knees. The flame of the candle wavered but did not go out. Staggering to his feet, he made it to the doors, shoved them open, and stepped out onto a curved stone balcony. In the distance, beyond the chapel and the iron fence, he saw headlights. A car! But whose car, and what were they doing? Then he turned and looked up. A row of ornamental stone doodads ran along the top of the mansion —vases, balls, obelisks with carved swags and lions' heads on them. And they were all lit with a ghostly green fire that flickered and made haloes in the air.

A sudden gust of wind blew snow at Johnny, and his candle went out. But then lightning flashed, and Johnny saw that he was standing next to something—a huge statue of a warrior in chain mail. The warrior wore over his suit of mail a surcoat with a Maltese cross on it. The warrior's face was grim, and he had a long drooping mustache. His enormous arm clutched the hilt of his sword, and he seemed to be just about to draw it from the scabbard. On the base of the statue a name was carved. Johnny had seen it only for a tenth of a second, but he had been able to make it out. It was a name he knew from history books: *Godfrey de Bouillon*.

Godfrey de Bouillon
Herb-Ox Bouillon Cubes

Johnny's brain turned somersaults. It spun like a merry-go-round gone crazy. What if? What if he had found the will? Had he thrown away the greatest clue of all? Could he still . . .

As if in answer, the building rocked. It shook as if the walls were made of cardboard, and pieces of stone, roof tiles, and bricks from the chimney stack came raining down. The room that Johnny had just left was already on fire. Huge jagged cracks had opened in the floor, and red flames were shooting up through them. Again the mansion shook. The enormous statue tottered on its base and then went crashing through the railing of the balcony. Johnny clung to a carved pilaster and prayed: *Jesus, Mary, and Joseph, hear our prayers and grant our petitions, Jesus, Mary, and—*

Something hit him in the head, and he blacked out.

CHAPTER SIXTEEN

When Johnny woke up he found that he was lying in a hospital bed. It was daytime, and cold winter light was streaming in through large windows. Next to him, sitting in an armchair by the bed, was the professor. He was wearing an egg-stained brown sweater, and he was smoking one of his eternal black-and-gold cigarettes as he grinned broadly at Johnny.

"So!" he exclaimed in a pretend-gruff voice. "You've decided to favor us with your presence at last! And about time too! How do you feel?"

Johnny was still dazed and uncertain. He didn't know quite how he felt. But now he realized that there was something on his head. He reached up and touched the stiff white cloth of a bandage. Then he remembered being out on the balcony and getting hit on the head.

"Have I been . . . ?" he began, but he found he was having trouble putting words together. He felt vaguely dizzy, and when he moved, a throbbing headache started, just above his left eye.

"Yes, you have been *indeed!*" said the professor, smiling gently. "You have been totally unconscious for about two days. It's a concussion—no, don't worry, it's not fatal. I had one myself once, when I was hit in the head with a shell casing at the Battle of the Argonne Forest. You'll be up and around in a few days. In case you're wondering, you're in a hospital in North Conway, New Hampshire. It's the nearest one we could find. North Conway is a rich little town where people come to ski and drink and sit around and be bored. You should see the overpriced dump that *I'm* staying in. It's a fake Swiss chalet, with cuckoo clocks and everything. Fortunately it isn't the skiing season yet, or the room would cost me half my year's salary at the college. And the bed is lumpy too—would you believe it?"

The professor crabbed on. Johnny grinned and listened appreciatively. He knew that this was cheerful crabbing, a sign the professor was in a good mood. And as the professor talked Johnny found that the cobwebs in his head were clearing away. He remembered why he had come up here—the will, the reward, and everything. He thought about Mrs. Woodley, and Chad, and Godfrey de Bouillon. There were a million questions that he wanted to ask.

"Is . . . is the mansion all burned down?"

The professor nodded. "It is indeed. Burned to a nice crunchy crisp. It's just a heap of rubble now. But it was still going strong when Fergie and I arrived on the scene. We—"

"*Fergie?*" exclaimed Johnny, interrupting. "What was he doing up here?"

The professor eyed Johnny sardonically. "He came up here with me to rescue you. And you will have to admit, my friend, that you needed some rescuing. You were lying in the bushes near the mansion when we found you. The mansion was going like . . . well, it was going like a house afire. Flames shooting out of all the windows, walls crashing down all over the place. Well, Fergie—or Byron, as I prefer to call him—Byron and I fought our way in, and it was hot, let me tell you. But we got to you and pulled you free just before the whole bloody wall came down—blooey, crash, bam!—right where you'd been not a moment before. How about that, eh?"

Johnny was silent. So he had missed death by just that much.

"Mrs. Woodley probably started that fire," the professor went on as he lit another cigarette. "And she started the earthquake and the lightning and all the other fireworks that helped to wreck the mansion. She did it by remote control, with the aid of a very strange witchcraftical box that she found when she was nosing around out at the estate, looking for the will. And how do I know all this? Because of a diary that was found in the bedroom of the dear sweet departed old—"

"*Departed?* You mean she's—"

The professor nodded solemnly. "Yes, I'm afraid so. Kindly old Mrs. Woodley, the proprietor of the friendly Squam House, has gone to glory . . . or she has gone to someplace, at any rate. They found her in her bedroom, slumped over that witch box I told you about. Heart attack, I'm told. If she were alive, she'd have a lot to answer for. According to her diary, she did in Chad Glomus and three other people she found poking around the estate. She was obsessed with her brother's will—terrified somebody would find it and it would turn out that she had been cut off without a nickel. Mrs. Woodley was a clever old bat, I'll give her that. Like you, she figured out the "Staunton Harold" part of the puzzle. But she couldn't get any further. Did you manage to figure it all out? The tea shop sign and everything?"

Johnny frowned. "Sort of. Only I didn't know it. When I got to the last clue, I didn't realize what it was. I thought I'd got rooked. Do you wanta hear about it?"

The professor nodded. And as he smoked, Johnny told him about the inscription over the chapel door. He explained about the two *ye*'s and the can of bouillon cubes and the statue of Godfrey de Bouillon. ". . . and so I think the will has got to be inside of the statue," Johnny concluded. "I mean, it stands to reason that that's where it'd be. Do . . . do you think you could have the police go and find out if it really is there?"

The professor considered this. "Hmm. Well, I guess we'd better have them investigate the matter. The mansion is just a ruin now, as I said before. But the statue is probably there somewhere in the rubble. Godfrey de Bouillon. Huh! Well, you know, while I was waiting for you to recover, I read the little guidebook that you had in your coat pocket. And I did notice the part about the Nine Worthies."

"Yeah," said Johnny. "Who were they, anyway?"

The professor smiled smugly, as he always did when he knew something that somebody else didn't know. "They were sort of a Hit Parade of warriors and heroes of the ancient world," he said. "Let's see, there's Joshua, David, Judas Maccabeus, Hector, Alexander . . . um, don't rush me. . . . Ah, yes! And there's Julius Caesar, and King Arthur, good old Charlemagne, and of course our soupy old friend, Godfrey de Bouillon, the noted knight and leader of the Crusaders. That's nine, isn't it? And in case you're interested, I also know all about the inscription over the chapel door and what it means. But I'll bore you with that some other time. We have more important things to discuss now."

The professor's jaunty, kidding manner disappeared. He grew serious and solemn. "Did you know that Fergie and I were arrested?" he asked.

Johnny was stunned. "You *were*? What for?"

"For arson, trespassing, and attempted burglary . . . those are all the charges, I think, though there may be more. You see, as soon as we had dragged you away from the burning building, we heard this incredible racket. It was the firemen and policemen bashing open the gate in the fence to get in! Yes, indeedy! There must've been about eight fire trucks and I don't know how many police cars, and, luckily, there was also an ambulance. But when the cops found us, they figured we had set the fire. Can you imagine! I mean, what a bunch of ninnies!"

Johnny was worried. "Are . . . are you gonna hafta go to jail?"

The professor chuckled and shook his head. "No, we aren't going to jail. You see, in a case of this sort the owners of the property would have to prefer charges. As you know, the owners are the surviving members of the Glomus family. And when they found out about Mrs. Woodley—Mr. Glomus's sister that was—and the *thing* that was discovered in the ruins of the mansion, and all the other *things* that were scattered all over the grounds of the estate . . . well, they were in no mood to prefer charges against *anybody*!"

Johnny's mouth dropped open. "Things? What things?"

The professor smiled wryly and flicked the ash off the end of his cigarette. "Oh, not much. Just a few hard-to-explain items. First, the police found a mummified body in the ruins of the house. From the clothes, and from the ring and the wallet and the other personal belongings, they have concluded, reluctantly, that it is the body of Chad Glomus. They're going to have to consult dental records to be sure, but for myself I have no doubt that it's the young man who disappeared early in October. Nobody can figure out how the body came to be—"

"I didn't tell you everything," said Johnny, interrupting. "I mean, Fergie and me, we were with Chad just before he died. We . . . we kind of wanted to keep it a secret."

"Yes," said the professor quietly. "I know. Fergie has already spilled the beans. And I must say, it is quite an amazing tale. There's more too. The police decided to do a thorough search of all the buildings on the estate. And what do you suppose they found in Mr. Glomus's mausoleum? The bodies of three other people who disappeared up here during the last few years. They were mummies too, and they were standing up, stiff as boards, against a wall. They were all local characters— two old derelicts and a woman who lived in a tar-paper shack near Mount Chocorua. And they all must've made the mistake of breaking into the estate and nosing around. Mrs. Woodley found out, and that was the end of *them*!"

The professor paused for breath. He heaved a deep sigh and folded his arms. "Well, now, would you like to see what the newspapers have been making of all this?"

Without waiting for an answer, the professor reached

down beside his armchair, picked up a thick sheaf of newspapers, and threw them onto Johnny's bed. They were all copies of the Manchester *Union-Leader*, the most popular paper in New Hampshire. Johnny looked at the headline that was lying on top. HORROR MUMMIES IN CEREAL MAGNATE'S TOMB. He flipped to the next one and read THE WITCH OF KANCAMAGUS CENTER? Another said WAS CHAD MURDERED? MYSTERY DEEPENS.

Johnny flipped quickly through the stack. "Oh, my gosh," he said. It was not much of a comment, but it was the only one he could come up with.

"You see?" said the professor, cocking his head to one side and grinning in that know-it-all way that he had. "This whole shindig has given the Glomus family some very undesirable publicity. And as far as I can tell, they would like to have it all hushed up as quickly as possible. So unless I miss my guess, they're not going to charge the three of us with anything. There will, however, be an inquest. There *has* to be when four bodies are discovered. And you know something? I would *love* to know what those crime-lab clowns are going to say about those mummies! I wonder what sort of silly, trashy, pseudoscientific flummery they will—"

"Hey!" said Johnny, interrupting again. He sat up suddenly, and then, as a sharp searing pain slashed through his head, he sank back onto the pillow. "I . . . we . . . we have to do something! Right now! We have to get the cops to go out to the mansion an' look inside of that statue to see if the will's there! I mean . . . I mean,

Gramma's sick, an' if I don't get the reward money right away, she might *die*! Please, professor! Can you get 'em to do something, right now? Can you?"

The professor put his hand over his face. "For Pete's sake!" he said through his fingers. "Is *that* why you went after the will? John, as Jimmy Durante would say, you been laborin' under a misprehamprehension! Your grandmother isn't dying! The operation was a success, a complete and unqualified success! Of course, she's no spring chicken, but still . . . good grief, why didn't you *ask* somebody?"

A tear trickled down Johnny's cheek. "I was scared. I mean . . . I mean, I got all this bad news, about Dad and all, and I thought the world was comin' to an end! And then I found that letter from the undertakers, so I thought . . ."

The professor nodded somberly. "I see it all now. What a comedy of errors! John, my lad, do you know what that letter was probably about?"

Johnny sniffled. He took a tissue from a box on the table and blew his nose. "Nope. What was it about?"

The professor grinned. "A few years ago your grandfather's brother Willie died. He was next door to being a bum, and after the funeral Willie's wife wrote a check to the funeral parlor, and the check bounced. Well, the undertakers had a fit, and they got after Willie's widow, and she went to your grampa for help. There was a big fight in your grampa's family about who would foot the bill, and, well, your grampa finally persuaded his other

) 160 (

brother, Vic, to pay it. Vic is a filthy rich farmer up in Menominee, Wisconsin, and he could afford it. So I suspect—though I'm not absolutely sure—that the letter you saw was just a note from somebody at the funeral parlor thanking your grampa because he had managed to pry the money out of his tight-fisted brother. I'd be willing to bet that that's all there was to that ridiculous letter. And next time if you have any doubts about a letter's contents, steam the bloody thing open and peek inside, for heaven's sake!" With an exasperated "Hmph!" the professor ground out his cigarette in the ashtray. He dug another one out of his pocket and lit it.

Johnny's lower lip began to tremble. Tears were rolling down his cheeks. "I . . . I'm sorry," he stammered. "I didn't know, I . . ."

The professor was shocked—he hadn't meant to make Johnny cry. With an agonized look on his face he jumped out of his chair and rushed over to Johnny's bed. He took the cigarette from his mouth and, after looking about distractedly, he dunked it in a glass of water that stood on the bedside table. When he turned back to Johnny, the professor's eyes were filled with tears.

"Oh, John!" he cried as he seized the bedsheet in his hands and began to twist it. "*Please* don't cry! I'm just a cranky old man, and I can't help sounding grumpy sometimes! It's one of my many faults."

Johnny smiled and dried his eyes with a tissue. "It's okay, Professor," he said, sniffling. "I just feel . . . kinda weird right now, and it's easy to cry. And I'm happy I'm not gonna be alone in the world. That makes me wanta cry too."

"Well, you mustn't!" said the professor, and he smiled a weak, wan, half-joking smile. Still twisting the bed-sheet, he stared hard at Johnny. "Look," he said in a grave but gentle voice. "I . . . I think I understand why you did what you did. And in connection with that I have something to tell you. I was going to save this for later, but . . . your dad has been found." Johnny's eyes opened wide and he exclaimed, "When—" But the pro-fessor replied quickly, "I'll give you the details later; I just wanted you to know he's all right. But even if he hadn't been found, and even if both your grandfather and your grandmother were to die, I'd still be there to take care of you. I've never had any children of my own, but if they'd let me, I'd adopt you. I'm only seventy, you know. My father made it to a hundred and three, and his father was ninety-eight when the horse he was riding threw him. You don't need to worry about ever being an orphan."

Johnny was going to say something in answer to the professor, but the old man turned away quickly and walked to the window. As he stood glaring out at the snow-covered hillside he harrumphed loudly several times and clicked his false teeth in and out. The profes-sor hated it when he got emotional in front of other people. Then he sat down and talked with Johnny about his father.

Johnny stayed at the hospital in North Conway for a week. During that time the professor went on living at the expensive hotel, and Fergie stayed with him for a day or two. Together they visited Johnny at the hospital every day. Finally Fergie gave a statement to the local police, and then he went home on the train to Duston Heights. After the police got statements from Johnny and the professor, an inquest was held. The coroner's jury decided that Chad and the other three had died "of unexplained causes."

Acting on information from Johnny, the police went out to the Glomus estate, poked around in the ruins, and found the broken, charred statue of Godfrey de Bouillon. By tapping with hammers they discovered that the base of the statue was hollow. A sliding panel of stone could be pulled back, and inside the base of the statue they found . . . a small heap of ashes. The statue had fallen into the basement of the burning building, and the heat there had been so intense that it had been like a brick oven. The will of Mr. H. Bagwell Glomus was gone forever.

Johnny was unhappy when he heard this, but now that he knew his grandmother wasn't dying, the will had become far less important to him. The professor merely repeated what he had said when he heard that Mrs. Woodley had died—*Good riddance to bad rubbish!*

After a week the professor drove Johnny home to Duston Heights. When he arrived, he got lots of hugs and kisses from his grandmother, who was bustling around like her old self now. And Grampa shook the professor's hand so many times that the professor finally had to tell him to stop.

That evening Fergie came to visit Johnny. Despite their chats at the hospital, they had not had a chance to have a really private conversation. So, the first chance Johnny got, he took Fergie up to his room, and they had a long and excited gabfest. Later, while they played chess, it occurred to Johnny that he had at least gotten one good thing out of this whole mess: He had found a new friend.

The next day Johnny went back to school. He tried to pretend that nothing had happened, but everyone had read about Johnny's adventure in the newspapers. They all wanted to ask him questions, and some kids even wanted his autograph. So, by the time he left school at three fifteen, his nerves were thoroughly frazzled. As he turned onto Fillmore Street and started walking toward his house, he found that he had yet another jolt in store for him on this busy, trying day. There was a car parked in front of his house, a sleek black limousine with a chauffeur at the wheel. A wild thought leaped into Johnny's mind: Could it be his dad?

But it wasn't his dad. Johnny's grandmother met him at the door. She was clearly quite upset and nervous as she explained that there was a lady waiting for him in the parlor. Johnny felt let down, but he was still curious. Who could it be? When he walked in, he saw, seated on the couch, a tall, haughty-looking old woman. She wore an expensive flowered silk dress and a pearl necklace. Rings glittered on her fingers, and her iron-gray hair was arranged in a ripply permanent wave. When she saw Johnny, the woman smiled. Surprisingly it was not merely a polite smile but one of genuine warmth and friendliness.

"How are you!" she said, rising and holding out her hand. "My name is Annabelle Glomus. My husband was H. Bagwell Glomus. You've heard of him, I believe?" Mrs. Glomus's eyes gleamed with amusement. And to Johnny's amazement she winked at him!

"I, uh . . . I, uh . . ." Johnny began, but he couldn't get any further than that. He was really tongue-tied.

Still smiling, Mrs. Glomus sat down again. Johnny sank into a seat next to her. What on earth did she want?

Then Mrs. Glomus picked up her large patent-leather purse. She opened it up and took out a checkbook and a gold-plated fountain pen. As Johnny watched she began to write out a check.

"I have heard about your exploits up in New Hampshire," she said with a faint tinge of amusement in her voice. "And I must say that I'm sorry, profoundly sorry, that the famous Glomus puzzle led you on a wild-goose chase and almost turned out very badly indeed. For myself I never thought there was a will at all. I believed the puzzle was merely something dreamed up by my late husband to drive us all mad. But now that it seems there was a will, I must say that I am *extremely* glad it was destroyed. At my age I have no stomach for bickering. It was those greedy sons of mine who advertised in the paper and hounded me into putting up the reward money. They both thought that the will would make them richer—though I could never figure out why. I mean, my dear sweet late husband was capable of doing a lot of strange things. He *might* have left my sons a bundle. On the other hand, he might have left his money to the Ku Klux Klan or to a cat hospital in New South Wales. So, on the whole, I think we're much better off with no will at all. But since you did find the will— that is, you found out where it was hidden—and fair is fair, I want you to have this."

When she had gotten out this last sentence, Mrs. Glomus tore the check out of her checkbook and handed it to Johnny. It was made out to him, for ten thousand dollars.

Johnny was stunned. He tried to say something, but once again words failed him. While he was stammering, Mrs. Glomus stood up and started to leave. At the door she paused and turned back to him once more.

"Good day to you, young man. I hope you do something enjoyable with the money. And I hope you will realize that not all of the members of the Glomus family are like my late husband's sister. Some of us are quite sane and reasonable . . . and nice people too." And with that, Mrs. Glomus turned and swept grandly out of the room, leaving Johnny alone with the check in his hands.

As soon as Johnny had recovered from the shock he ran out into the kitchen to tell his grandmother and grandfather.

"Well, my Lord!" exclaimed Gramma, holding the check up and peering at it in astonishment. "Who woulda thought it? I mean, heavens to Betsy, *who*?" She handed it back to Johnny and shook her head solemnly. "Well, my boy," she said, putting her hand on Johnny's arm, "this has really been a time for s'prises for us all lately! Do you think the s'prises are all over with? For now, I mean?"

Johnny said that he figured they were. But he was wrong. In fact, he had just barely finished speaking when there was a loud squeal of brakes outside. His first thought was that it was Mrs. Glomus coming to take the check back. But when he rushed out to the bay window in the parlor, he saw that the car that had just pulled up was khaki-colored. On its door words were stenciled in white paint: U.S. ARMY. Then Johnny saw the door on the passenger side open. Somebody got out. With a joyful whoop Johnny rushed to the front door and tore it open. He galloped across the porch and down the front steps. Standing next to the car was a man in a gray U.S. Air Force uniform. Battle ribbons and medals covered the left side of the man's uniform jacket, and on his cap and shoulders were the insignia of a captain. His face was craggy, seamed with wrinkles, and deeply tanned. But in spite of the tan, the man's face looked pinched and worn, as if he had just been through a bad time. Nonetheless he was smiling broadly and holding out his arms to Johnny. Rushing forward with happy yells and yips and whoops, Johnny threw himself against the man and hugged him tight. The man hugged him back, and now he was crying. The two of them just stood there, holding each other for a long time.

ABOUT THE AUTHOR

John Bellairs was the critically acclaimed, best-selling author of many Gothic novels, including *The Lamp from the Warlock's Tomb*; *The Spell of the Sorcerer's Skull*; *The Revenge of the Wizard's Ghost*; and the novels starring Lewis Barnavelt, Rose Rita Pottinger, and Mrs. Zimmermann: *The House with a Clock in Its Walls*; *The Figure in the Shadows*; *The Letter, the Witch and the Ring*; *The Ghost in the Mirror*; and *The Vengeance of the Witch-Finder*.

John Bellairs died in 1991.